CONSUMPTION TAX POLICY AND THE TAXATION OF CAPITAL INCOME

The art of taxation consists of plucking the goose so as to obtain the most feathers with the least hissing.

Jean Baptiste Colbert (1619–1683)

Consumption Tax Policy and the Taxation of Capital Income

Raymond G. Batina
and
Toshihiro Ihori

OXFORD
UNIVERSITY PRESS

OXFORD
UNIVERSITY PRESS

Great Clarendon Street, Oxford OX2 6DP
Oxford University Press is a department of the University of Oxford.
It furthers the University's objective of excellence in research, scholarship,
and education by publishing worldwide in

Oxford New York

Athens Auckland Bangkok Bogotá Buenos Aires Calcutta
Cape Town Chennai Dar es Salaam Delhi Florence Hong Kong Istanbul
Karachi Kuala Lumpur Madrid Melbourne Mexico City Mumbai
Nairobi Paris São Paulo Singapore Taipei Tokyo Toronto Warsaw

with associated companies in Berlin Ibadan

Oxford is a registered trade mark of Oxford University Press
in the UK and certain other countries

Published in the United States
by Oxford University Press Inc., New York

British Library Cataloguing in Publication Data

Data available

Library of Congress Cataloging in Publication Data

Batina, Raymond G.
Consumption tax policy and the taxation of capital income / Raymond G. Batina and Toshihiro Ihori.
p. cm.
Includes bibliographical references and index.
1. Taxation of articles of consumption—Mathematical models.
2. Capital levy—Mathematical models. I. Ihori, Toshihiro, 1952– II. Title.
HJ5711 .B38 2000   336.2'71—dc21   00–029667

ISBN 0-19-829790-4

1 3 5 7 9 10 8 6 4 2

Typeset in 10.5 on 12.5pt Garamond by
Kolam Information Services Pvt Ltd, Pondicherry, India
Printed in Great Britain
on acid-free paper by
Biddles Ltd
Guildford and King's Lynn

Preface

There is clearly much dissatisfaction with the taxation of income in a number of countries and many countries have tried reforming their tax system over the years, with limited success. In particular, many have become disenchanted with the income tax as source of revenue and have turned to the taxation of consumption as an alternative. This is somewhat ironic, since many countries began with retail sales taxes early in their fiscal history and gradually introduced the taxation of income much later when they came to "reform" their sales tax systems.

The literature on consumption taxation has grown dramatically in the last few years and much of the recent work has focused its attention on the taxation of capital income. Yet, there is no single book to guide the interested reader through the literature. We have written our book with this in mind. Thus, the main purpose of this book is to guide the reader through the technical literature on consumption taxation and the taxation of capital.

Our book summarizes the literature on the consumption tax and the taxation of capital, the early literature on optimal tax theory in dynamic overlapping generations models, the more recent literature on optimal taxation in the Ramsey growth model and models of endogenous growth, and the literature on taxation in open economies. We also extend the literature in a variety of ways by complicating the models used to study tax issues. For example, we study the effects of income and consumption taxation on bequeathing behavior. Other extensions included in our study are the time consistency problem and the so-called capital levy, charity and privately produced public goods, environmental externalities and renewable resources, durable goods and land, and money used in exchange and as an asset.

The summaries included in the book will be of value to people doing research in these various areas. We hope the extensions contained in the book, mainly in Chapters 6–11, will also attract their attention. The research described will also be useful to economists who are generally interested in tax policy. Graduate students, who might come to do research in these areas, will also find the book attractive since many of the mathematical derivations are included. This will facilitate their understanding of how to manipulate a dynamic general equilibrium model, how to interpret results, and basically how to conduct research on tax policy. Advanced undergraduates can also learn quite a bit about how research in economics is carried out. Finally, a well–informed individual can read the text, skip most of the mathematics, and still learn quite a bit about the consumption tax and the taxation of capital income.

Each chapter is reasonably self-contained. We use a variety of models in each chapter, rather than just one model, to study the issue at hand. In many cases different models make different predictions, and this is the source of some controversy and much interesting research. For example, in Chapter 10 we study several models of a monetary economy and point out how the different models yield different predictions about the effects of the consumption tax and the capital income tax. A reasonably complete description of each model used in each chapter is provided. There is some unavoidable overlap and repetition across the different chapters. However, the interested reader can open the book to any chapter and find a self-contained discussion of the subject matter without having to go to earlier chapters to find a description of the notation, definition of terms, and so on. We should also stress that much of the material in the book is not covered in the usual textbooks in public finance. Thus, our book is complementary to these other textbooks.

We are indebted to numerous students and colleagues for useful comments in preparing the book. We wish to thank especially Tatsuo Hatta, Junichi Itaya, Hirofumi Shibata, Jeff Krautkraemer, and Steve Perez.

A book of this magnitude and scope could not have been written without the tremendous support of our families. We dedicate our efforts to Lori and Julia, and Nami and Kumi. Without their help, love, wisdom, and laughter, we could not have written the book.

Contents

Figures

Tables

1

Setting the Stage for the Debate

1.1. Introduction

It is probably fair to say that people generally do not like to pay taxes. Yet at the same time they benefit from publicly provided goods, services, subsidies, insurance, and transfer programs. Some way must be found to pay for these programs, and hence the need for a tax system arises. However, different tax systems will have different properties and will affect the economy in a variety of different ways.[1]

The purpose of this book is to study the consumption tax policy and the taxation of capital in detail. We will introduce and summarize the substantial literature on the consumption tax policy and related topics such as taxing capital income. The main arguments for and against the consumption tax will be presented and discussed. We will also present the main theoretical and empirical results appearing in the technical literature. Finally, we will extend the literature in a number of useful ways.

The literature on the consumption tax policy is of interest for a variety of reasons. First, the consumption tax is a viable alternative to the income tax for any country considering a reform of its income tax system. It has the potential of generating a significant amount of revenue that can be used to supplement an income tax, or it can generate the same amount of revenue as an income tax.

Second, this literature is a good point of departure for someone who wishes to learn more about the structure of the arguments that can be brought to bear on any given issue in choosing policy. For example, a debate about the interest elasticity of saving erupted in the late 1970s. At the time, many regarded the outcome of that debate as of critical importance for deciding the magnitude of the welfare cost of taxing capital income and for deciding whether or not capital should be taxed. However, early results from the literature on optimal tax theory in dynamic models indicate that it may actually be certain labor supply elasticities that are more important in determining whether or not capital income should be taxed, rather than the interest elasticity of saving. And more recent results tend to indicate that the optimal tax on interest income in the long run is zero, regardless of these empirical elasticities. More recently still, analysts have shown that the general income tax on capital income can permanently lower the growth rate of the economy. Thus, the structure of the argument that can be made criticizing the taxation of capital has changed over time as more powerful models and techniques have been developed.

Third, we will study certain technical results that may involve models and techniques of which the reader may not be aware. For example, we will study the Ramsey growth model of a decisionmaker with an infinite planning horizon in the context of a competitive economy that is growing endogenously and will describe how tax policy affects the economy's growth rate. Public finance specialists may be unaware of the literature on endogenous growth models, since this area has typically been under the purview of macroeconomists. As another example, we will also study the time consistency problem as it relates to the so-called capital levy. It is optimal for the government to promise not to tax capital income at the beginning of its planning horizon. Later, however, when the capital has already been accumulated and the stock is fixed, the government will realize it is optimal to tax capital income at a very high rate since it is a fixed factor. This problem has typically been studied by macroeconomists and game theorists. However, it will also be of interest to anyone who is curious about policymaking in a dynamic environment.

Fourth, the work on the consumption tax policy provides a good example of the way in which economics as a science evolves and, more specifically, of how policy debates evolve. A problem arises. A potential solution is proposed. Debate takes place. Evidence is brought to bear. Alternative arguments are made and the various arguments are refined and improved. Eventually, a consensus on certain key issues emerges, while debate continues on certain other questions. And new issues occasionally emerge as the debate continues.

For example, in the 1970s evidence began to mount that the growth rate in North America and Europe was slowing down. Later, it appeared that the growth rate was slowing down in other parts of the world as well. A variety of culprits were mentioned as possible causes of the slowdown in growth, including a possible shortage of capital investment. The various faults of the general income tax were pointed out and the consumption tax was proposed as an alternative. The main selling point (among others) of the consumption tax at the time was that it did not cause the sort of welfare cost associated with the taxation of capital income. It was also argued that it would probably promote capital formation, although the effect of a shift from the income tax to the consumption tax on capital accumulation was regarded by many as ambiguous. Skeptics emerged and joined in the debate on a number of key points. Finally, a new model of endogenous growth developed by macroeconomists was applied to the tax problem and a strong case was made for not taxing capital income because it might permanently lower the growth rate. However, as we show, there are many cases where taxing capital income is desirable in a growing economy. The debate has lasted for over twenty years and does not appear to be dying out.

As we describe the literature along the way, we will continually refer to "the consumption tax," which will make this term seem as if it uniquely captures a single policy. The reader should keep in mind, however, that there are different versions of the tax.[2] One is the value added tax, or VAT, which is quite popular in Europe. A version of this tax was introduced by Japan in 1989 and the tax rate was recently increased. Under a general VAT, a tax is imposed on the value added at each stage of production. Another version of the consumption tax is the national sales tax, which taxes the sale of final goods and services. Still another version, the cashflow version of the tax, which is similar in spirit to the income tax, would have the taxpayer add all sources of income on a cashflow basis and subtract any net additions to wealth. This leaves consumption as the tax base.

The single feature that distinguishes these taxes from the main alternative, the income tax, is their favorable treatment of saving. Indeed, it is this single feature that defines the collection of tax policies that are typically referred to as "the consumption tax." We will focus attention on the cashflow version of the personal consumption tax for analytical convenience. This is what we will mean when we use the term "the consumption tax," unless otherwise indicated.

We will also focus attention on how the various tax policies affect the consumer, omitting study of the effects of taxation on the corporation. Indeed, under what Bradford (1986) refers to as "a full-fledged personal cashflow" consumption tax, corporations would not be taxed at all. Instead, an individual investor would subtract the purchase of equities from her cash receipts and add any dividend income and realized capital gains from the sale of equities to her receipts in calculating her tax liability. This is not to say that the taxation of corporations is an unimportant topic, but simply to say that it is beyond the scope of the present study. Many of the tools and techniques we use could also be applied to models including a corporation as an agent in the model. Unfortunately, inclusion of such material would have made this book too long.

Finally, we believe the material contained in the book is especially useful for students who wish to learn some of the tools and techniques used by public finance economists and macroeconomists interested in public finance issues, and some of the traditional literature on taxation. We make use of some of the standard techniques such as differential incidence analysis in general equilibrium models. We also present several examples of state-of-the-art technique, for example the primal problem in a dynamic optimal tax model. We cover some of the traditional areas in public finance and areas currently receiving attention, including international tax issues, bequest models, land taxation, environmental externalities, and privately produced public goods, as well as several less traditional areas, for example taxation in monetary economies. The derivations of the main results are included in the text to facilitate learning the technique.

In the next section we present general definitions of the income tax base and the cashflow consumption tax base. The income tax base is founded on a notion of "comprehensive" or "accrual" income that is difficult to measure. Most of the problems with this concept involve measuring capital income for tax purposes. In Section 1.3 we discuss two general principles of taxation, the benefits-received principle and the ability-to-pay principle. In particular, the ability-to-pay principle has been used to justify income taxation with a progressive rate structure. Both principles are somewhat difficult to put into practice, and as a result compromises have to be made in implementing them. We will briefly introduce the concepts of static and dynamic efficiency, in Section 1.4. We will also briefly introduce the overlapping generations model and the Ramsey growth model, the two most popular models in the literature in this area. Equity concerns will be discussed in Section 1.5. Section 1.6 contains a comparison of the cashflow version of the consumption tax with the prepayment approach to calculating the consumption tax base. Finally, Section 1.7 concludes the chapter by describing the plan for the rest of the book.

1.2. Defining the tax base

Most advanced countries rely heavily on the taxation of personal and corporate income for generating tax revenue. However, a number of countries have instituted versions of a consumption tax in order to raise revenue. Many European countries have introduced the value added tax (VAT) since World War Two.[3] In the United States retail sales taxes are still used extensively at the state and local level. And a version of the VAT was introduced in Japan in 1989 to help raise revenue and reduce the budget deficit; indeed, the tax rate was recently raised in order to generate more revenue from this source.

Table 1.1 lists the major tax sources for the world's largest economies, Canada, France, Germany, Italy, Japan, the United Kingdom, and the United States. Consumption based taxes play a major role in most of these seven countries, although less so in the United States.[4]

Interestingly enough, the consumption tax has also been rejected in a number of instances. In 1942 the Treasury Department in the United States proposed introducing a consumption tax to reduce consumer demand, which officials thought was causing inflationary pressure to build up. The Senate Finance Committee rejected the proposal in less than a week. The tax was introduced in both India and Sri Lanka but was later repealed because of its unpopularity. Sri Lanka even tried to impose the tax a second time, only to have it rejected a second time.[5]

Table 1.1.   International comparison of tax revenues

	Canada	France	Germany	Italy	Japan	UK	USA
Corporate income taxes	9.7	6.7	6.4	12.4	23.8	12.8	12.7
Individual income taxes	45.1	24.9	41.5	36.9	33.7	31.6	50.0
Consumption taxes	30.9	48.0	47.0	38.6	23.8	42.6	22.8
Property-based taxes	14.2	20.5	5.1	12.1	18.8	12.9	14.5

Source: *OECD Revenue Statistics 1965–1997*. Each entry is the ratio of each source of tax revenue to total tax revenues for 1996. This includes national taxes plus local taxes.

Tax experts have focused attention on what has become known as "comprehensive" income in order to define a base for taxation. A number of different definitions have been put forth for this concept. However, eventually the definitions coalesced to one similar in spirit to that given by Simons (1938): "[comprehensive income] may be defined as the algebraic sum of the market value of rights exercised in consumption and the change in the value of the store of property rights between the beginning and end of the period in question."

This became known as the Haig–Simons definition of comprehensive income.[6] Bradford (1980a, b, 1986) refers to this concept of income as "accrual income."

Let C represent consumption, E represent current earned income plus any transfers received, W represent wealth, and r represent the return on wealth, for example the interest rate on a savings account. Under the Haig–Simons definition, comprehensive income is equal to $C + \Delta W$. However, as a simple matter of accounting, this is also equal to $E + rW$. Thus, $E + rW = C + \Delta W$ is taken as the tax base under an income tax. It is useful to think of ΔW as saving that can be negative if the individual is borrowing. So the base under a comprehensive income tax could also be described as consumption plus saving under a uses definition of income. On the other hand, the tax base under a consumption tax would simply be C or $E + rW - \Delta W$ instead. Thus, the consumption base will be lower (higher) than the income base for a net saver (borrower). The consumption base in the aggregate will be smaller than the income base if society is accumulating capital $(\Delta W > 0)$.

The basic notion behind the definition of comprehensive or accrual income is that it measures an individual's command over resources. A change in accrual income would signal a change in the individual's command over resources. If, for example, an individual experiences an unexpected capital gain on an investment, her power to consume has increased and presumably she should pay more in income tax as a result. Note that this is true even if the gain has not actually been realized, but has only accrued, as in the case of an increase in the value of one's home.

The prevailing view among tax theorists until only very recently was that individuals should pay tax on the basis of their comprehensive income and that the driving force in tax policy should be to carefully define and measure comprehensive income. Unfortunately, measuring comprehensive or accrual income can be difficult, if not impossible, to accomplish for several reasons, as pointed out by Bradford (1986), and Kay and King (1986), among others. First, it requires placing a value on wealth, and this, in turn, requires that accrued value be included. For example, unrealized capital gains on a variety of assets would have to be calculated. However, placing a value on infrequently traded assets may be difficult to do. In addition, some assets like human capital or future pension rights cannot be easily valued. Indeed, the marketplace will not generally allow people to borrow against their most important asset, future human capital, because its value is so difficult to determine.

Second, one would have to impute a service flow for durable goods since this represents a command over resources now and in the future. When consuming the services of a durable good, the household can be thought of as a producer. It combines capital, in the form of the durable good, with its own labor to produce services from which it benefits. Alternatively, the household can be thought of as "buying" the service directly from an outside firm. In either case, the value of the flow of services should be included in comprehensive income. However, imputing a value for these services for tax purposes in even the most obvious cases of a house or a car, not to mention the less obvious cases of a stereo, cooking utensils, or a wristwatch, is a difficult task. Furthermore, most consumption is made up of durable goods. This method would require a service flow be computed for each of these commodities. Clearly, this would not be possible.

In addition to this, the service flow from a durable good is endogenous and will respond to the tax rules chosen by the government. A homeowner, for example, must make maintenance expenditures over time in order to maintain the ability of her house to generate a service flow. The rule the tax authority chooses to calculate the service flow from the house will generally affect the maintenance expenditures chosen by the homeowner and hence the service flow from the house. This further complicates the calculation of the flow and its value. Any practical rule will be somewhat arbitrary.

Third, inflation, even mild inflation, can create serious measurement problems for valuing the depreciation of assets, capital gains on investments, the real interest rate, and so on. An inflation adjustment should be made, otherwise the taxpayer can experience a large nominal gain on an asset, and hence incur a large tax liability, when in fact the real capital gain may be much smaller or even negative. The issue arises under an income tax because the purchase price of the asset in one year must be subtracted from the sale price of the asset in another year to obtain the increase in value, yet the purchasing power of the currency may have changed in the intervening years. The capital gain should be adjusted for this.[7]

Consider the following simple example. Suppose the real interest rate is 2 per cent and the taxpayer is in the 25 per cent tax bracket. Her real after-tax return is 1.5 per cent in the absence of inflation. However, if the nominal interest rate jumps to 8 per cent because of an inflation rate of 6 per cent, the real after-tax rate of return is zero: $(1 - 0.25) \times 0.08 - 0.06 = 0.0$. If the inflation rate is higher than 6 per cent, or if the taxpayer is in a higher tax bracket, her real after-tax return is negative. As another example, consider a stock that doubles in price after ten years. If the general price level also doubles during the same time period no real gain has occurred, yet the agent may incur a large tax liability if the tax is based on nominal magnitudes. Indeed, even low rates of inflation artificially alter tax liabilities. This provides individuals and businesses with a strong incentive to hire tax lawyers and accountants in order to minimize their tax burden. This can be very costly to society.

In addition to this, some price indices that one might use in adjusting for inflation may be biased themselves. For example, the Consumer Price Index (CPI) typically used in the United States to adjust some labor contracts and social security benefits is thought to overstate inflation. This would lead to understating real magnitudes and, thus, understating the adjusted tax liability. This would impart further bias in a tax based on comprehensive income.

The upshot of this discussion is that objectively measuring "comprehensive" or "accrual" income is very difficult to do. This leaves us with imposing the income tax on a very imperfect measure of comprehensive income, or seeking another tax base like consumption. A consumption tax imposed on a cashflow basis can avoid all of these thorny measurement problems.

For quite a long time, analysts regarded the consumption tax as the preferred method of raising tax revenue but also thought it impossible to administer. Indeed, Hobbes, John Stuart Mill, Alfred Marshall, Irving Fisher, John Maynard Keynes, and A. C. Pigou were all in favor of the tax but thought it could not be put into practice. However, first Fisher (1937), and later Andrews (1974), convincingly showed how the tax could be imposed on a cashflow basis. Simply sum all receipts in the current tax period, such as wages, salaries, transfers, realized capital gains, interest, and so on, and subtract any net additions to wealth in the form of new saving in the current tax period to obtain the consumption base. Unrealized capital gains, future pension rights, the future value of one's own stock of human capital, depreciation allowances, imputed service flows from durable goods, and so on do not have to be calculated under the cashflow version of the consumption tax. Indeed, Bradford (1980b) argues that the cashflow consumption tax requires the same information that an annual income tax does yet omits the features of the income tax that involve the most difficult measurement problems such as placing a value on accruing capital gains.

And inflation does not pose a problem for the cashflow consumption tax. Why? Because the cashflow version of the tax requires information only on current-year transactions. The taxpayer's tax liability is always calculated on a consistent basis as a result. In contrast, adjustments have to be made in order to calculate depreciation allowances, capital gains, and the real interest rate under an income tax since a tax on accrual income typically involves transactions that take place in different years. This cannot be done in a completely objective manner.

Of course, some experts prefer the income tax to the consumption tax. In fact, Goode (1980) provides a spirited defense of the income tax. First, he argues that a wealthy miser who saves most of his income will escape taxation under the consumption tax but will pay tax under an income tax. This is viewed as inequitable.

Second, Goode disputes the use of lifetime comparisons. He argues that a cross-sectional view is more appropriate in choosing the relative tax burden to impose across different groups of taxpayers at a moment in time.

Third, he argues that the tax base under the consumption tax will be smaller than the general income tax if there is net saving in the aggregate. As a result, the consumption tax rate will have to be higher than the corresponding income tax rate to raise the same revenue. It follows that the labor supply decision will be more distorted under the consumption tax than under the general income tax. Thus, the consumption tax distorts the labor supply decision more but does not distort the intertemporal consumption decision the way the income tax does. Goode argues that it is not immediately obvious that a comparison of these relative distortions favors the consumption tax.

He also notes there are significant transition problems in switching to a consumption tax. People will have an incentive to hide assets during the transition period. Also, some asset owners are locked into their investment decisions and will bear an unfair amount of the burden of the switch to the consumption tax. Furthermore, many older taxpayers will already have paid the bulk of their lifetime taxes under the income tax and would get hit with a large tax increase when the switch is made.

Lastly, Goode argues that a consumption tax will be subject to the same political pressures that produced the imperfect income tax. The result would probably be a very imperfect consumption tax that would not necessarily dominate the imperfect income tax. As evidence, he cites the cases of India and Sri Lanka, where the consumption tax introduced in both countries contained numerous exemptions. This was also the case in Japan.[8]

Of course, there are counter-arguments to these particular points and, like many arguments, the outcome of the debate is still in question.[9] First, the miser will eventually leave an estate to his heirs and they will pay the consumption tax when the estate is consumed. In addition, some have recommended that the consumption tax be supplemented with a wealth transfer tax for equity reasons.[10]

Second, taking a lifetime perspective rather than a cross-sectional view can alter one's thinking about a variety of public policy issues and so would appear to have some value. For example, a student may be poor precisely because she is a student; yet later in life her college degree will significantly raise her earnings. Should she be considered poor by a welfare agency and thus eligible for welfare benefits when her income is low—say, when she is a student—even though later in life she will experience a much higher income? Perhaps not. The point is that a lifetime perspective informs the debate and thus is important to consider. And consumption may be a better indicator of a lifetime perspective than income. This may be especially true if consumers are forward looking and choose their current consumption taking into account their future income.

Third, the efficiency aspects of the different tax systems will be discussed at great length in Chapters 3–6. There are two extreme cases to consider: a pure consumption tax, where capital is exempt from taxation, and a pure income tax, where capital and labor are taxed at the same rate. Neither extreme case is generally optimal. If capital is imperfectly mobile and private agents experience a finite planning horizon, some taxation of capital income will probably be appropriate. However, the optimal tax structure must balance a number of competing influences, such as equity, static and dynamic efficiency, economic growth effects, potential capital flight, and other concerns involving environmental externalities.

Fourth, there are several basic transition problems that we will discuss in greater detail in Chapter 3. These problems can be mitigated by phasing in the consumption tax and cross-checking financial records under the income tax with those of the consumption tax in the transition period.

Goode's last point is an important one, however. The consumption tax will be subject to the same political pressures as the income tax has been in any country where the tax is introduced. We would expect special interest groups to lobby for deductions, exclusions, and exemptions under the consumption base just as they did under the income base. Indeed, there were numerous exemptions to the consumption tax when it was introduced in India, Sri Lanka, and Japan. To make a consumption tax politically palatable, exemptions seem almost inevitable wherever the tax is introduced. The definition of "consumption for tax purposes" is critical. Will medical expenses, housing, and school tuition be considered "consumption for tax purposes"? If not, then these economic decisions will be distorted by the consumption tax, and the resulting loss in efficiency diminishes the case for switching to the consumption tax.

It is difficult to make comparisons between two imperfect tax policies without being explicit about the features of each system, and it would seem that there is an almost endless supply of comparisons that could be made. Is a consumption tax preferred to an income tax when both allow housing expenditures to be deductible? Is a consumption tax preferred to an income tax if tax rates are equally progressive in their impact on the income distribution? Is a consumption tax preferred to an income tax when child allowances or educational expenses for, say, tuition, can be written off? Under some of these comparisons the consumption tax may achieve a higher level of utility on average, whereas under others the income tax may dominate. This is the material of future research.

1.3. General principles of taxation

It is probably safe to say that most taxpayers do not like paying taxes. Yet, they also appear to have a strong demand for the goods and services that their tax revenue finances.[11] Thus, a need exists for some sort of taxation. To proceed in an orderly fashion in designing the most appropriate tax system, a general guiding principle for choosing one tax base over another is useful. Traditionally, two general principles have been applied to direct taxation: the *benefits-received* principle and the *ability-to-pay* concept.

Under the benefits-received principle, those who specifically benefit from the public provision of a particular good or service should pay for the good or service through a particular tax or fee. For example, under the benefits-received principle boat owners who benefit from a lighthouse and a good harbor with reliable docking facilities should pay for the operation of the lighthouse, the construction of the dock, and the dredging of the harbor. Owners of homes near a lake should pay for mosquito control since they obviously will benefit from it. Drivers who use a road or highway should pay for the building and maintenance of the road or highway. And campers in a national forest should pay for the use of a campsite in the forest. In a sense, the benefits-received principle relies on mimicking a market transaction.

There are several problems with the application of the benefits-received principle to the choice of a tax system, however. First, in some cases it is not practical to charge those who benefit from use of the good. For example, it would be difficult, if not impossible, to charge users of city sidewalks for use of the sidewalk.

Second, if the good being provided is a pure public good, say an uncongested highway, the government must determine each individual's willingness to pay for the marginal unit of the good in order to charge the individual her appropriate Lindahl price.[12] Unfortunately, it may be difficult to determine the marginal benefit for each individual. In many cases where the benefits-received principle is used to charge a fee, only one price is charged, the "average" price.[13] For example, everyone is charged the same entrance fee to a museum, a zoo, or a national forest. In that case, people with a low marginal willingness to pay will be subsidizing those who have a high willingness to pay. For a private good it is the opposite; everyone pays the same price but is free to consume different quantities.

Third, there might be additional spillover effects that are difficult to capture or even measure. For example, maintaining the lighthouse and harbor facilities might reduce the cost of fishing and eventually lead to lower prices for fish in the grocery store. Should consumers of fish pay taxes that go toward covering the costs of the lighthouse? The answer might very well be yes if there are large "spillover" benefits. Unfortunately, it might be impossible to determine everyone who receives these "spillover" benefits. In addition, it might be difficult to impose a tax on those who do. For example, some consumers might end up consuming the fish outside the taxing jurisdiction of the government that provided the harbor and the lighthouse.

Fourth, there may be some people who would benefit from the provision of a particular public good but would be unable to pay for it. So it may be appropriate to take equity into account when applying the principle. For example, people living in poverty might not be able to afford to pay for use of a highway to get to work every day.

Lastly, there are expenditure programs specifically designed to alleviate poverty. How should they be financed? For example, who should pay for housing allowances and health care subsidies for the poor or the elderly? Who should pay for school lunch programs for needy children? It will be difficult to apply the benefits-received principle for these programs.

An example where the benefits-received principle can be used is a flat-rate social security program financed on a pay-as-you-go basis. Young workers pay into the program while retirees receive a benefit, and the young workers expect to receive a benefit in the future when they retire. If the benefit is actuarially fair, then those who benefit from the program are also those who finance it. However, some social security programs include additional benefits that are not funded by those who specifically gain from the extra benefit. For example, the social security program in many countries includes a spouse benefit provision whereby a benefit paid to non-working spouses is not financed by the spouse's own contributions to the program. As another example, some social security programs include an element of progressivity, either in the funding of the program or in the manner in which the monthly benefit is calculated. Thus, workers with a high level of lifetime earnings subsidize those with a lower level of lifetime earnings. It is difficult to justify these additional benefits on the basis of the benefits-received principle.

The difficulty of applying the benefits-received principle leads to a second basic principle of taxation, the ability-to-pay principle. Under this principle those taxpayers with greater ability to pay should pay more for the goods and services provided by the government than those who are perceived as having lower ability to pay. Sometimes this has been interpreted as the equal-sacrifice principle; people should make an equal sacrifice toward financing the goods and services from which all benefit. This does not necessarily mean that they should pay the same amount in tax, however. If a poor man and a wealthy man are to make an equal sacrifice and diminishing marginal utility for income holds, then the wealthy man will pay more income tax under this principle for a given marginal sacrifice.[14]

The two main issues involved in applying this principle are measuring an individual's ability to pay and choosing the progressivity of the tax system. We will not pursue the progessivity issue further except to note that many proponents of the consumption base support a progressive consumption tax. However, this will mean higher tax rates on average than under the income tax because the consumption base is smaller. It follows that labor supply decisions will be more distorted under the consumption tax than under the income tax, as we will see in the next section. Second, it will also mean that the intertemporal consumption decision will be distorted by the consumption tax. Ironically, the fact that the consumption tax with a flat-rate structure does not distort this decision was a major selling point of the consumption tax, especially during the 1970s.

In terms of the first issue, income and wealth have been taken as measures of an individual's ability to pay taxes. Unfortunately, both are subject to measurement problems as discussed in Section 1.2. Alternatively, consumption could be taken as a measure of ability to pay. Wealthy people tend to consume more than poor people and would, therefore, have a greater ability to pay than the poor would. "Conspicuous consumption", defined to include estates that pass on to the next generation at death, could form the basis of a comparison across individuals. And, if one believes the permanent income hypothesis, consumption is more smooth than income, and thus might serve as a better proxy for the individual's own expectations about his future income than his current income does.

1.4. Efficiency

1.4.1. Two-period life cycle model

The concept of economic efficiency has been used to supplement the benefits-received and ability-to-pay principles. The simplest dynamic framework to study efficiency in is a two-period life cycle model. Suppose the taxpayer supplies L_j units of labor in period $j = 1, 2$, earning a wage w_j in exchange, consumes c_j in period j, saves s in the first period, and receives rs in interest income plus principal s, where r is the interest rate. The taxpayer's budget constraints in the presence of the different taxes are given by

$$w_1(1 - t_{w1})L_1 - s - (1 + \theta_1)c_1 = 0, \tag{1.1}$$

$$w_2(1 - t_{w2})L_2 + [1 + r(1 - t_r)]s - (1 + \theta_2)c_2 = 0, \tag{1.2}$$

where t_{wj} is the tax rate imposed on labor earnings under the income tax in period j, t_r is the interest income tax imposed on capital income under the income tax, and θ_j is the consumption tax rate imposed under a consumption tax in period j.

The preferences of the consumer are represented by a well defined utility function given by[15]

$$U(c_1, h_1, c_2, h_2), \tag{1.3}$$

where $h_j = 1 - L_j$ is leisure in period j. We might expect the agent to take more leisure in the second period than in the first since it is the last period of the life cycle. In the extreme case, the agent is completely retired in the second period and $h_2 = 1$. This is typically assumed by analysts working with the overlapping generations model. In the special case where preferences are time-separable, we have instead

$$U(c_1, 1 - L_1) + \beta U(c_2, 1 - L_2), \tag{1.3'}$$

where $\beta = 1/(1 + \rho)$ is the discount factor and ρ is the discount rate.

Several remarks are in order. First, notice that there is no reason for the consumption tax rate to be constant over the life cycle. If the tax is progressive, the taxpayer could easily find herself in different tax brackets over the course of her life cycle and thus would pay different tax rates in those periods. Second, under a general income tax, $t_{w1} = \tau_1$ in the first period, $t_{w2} = t_r = \tau_2$ in the second period, and $\tau_1 = \tau_2 = \tau$ if the tax is a flat-rate general income tax. On the other hand, if the tax is progressive, $\tau_i > \tau_j$ when her income is higher in period i than in period j.

The consumer chooses consumption, labor supply, and life cycle saving to maximize (1.3) subject to (1.1), (1.2), and the constraints $c_j \geq 0$, and $1 \geq Lj \geq 0$. Assuming that preferences are time-separable, the first-order conditions can be written as

$$U_1(c_1, 1 - L_1)/\beta U_1(c_2, 1 - L_2) = (1 + \theta_1)[1 + r(1 - t_r)]/(1 + \theta_2), \quad (1.4)$$

$$U_2(c_1, 1 - L_1)/U_1(c_1, 1 - L_1) = w_1(1 - t_{w1})/(1 + \theta_1), \quad (1.5)$$

$$U_2(c_2, 1 - L_2)/U_1(c_2, 1 - L_2) = w_2(1 - t_{w2})/(1 + \theta_2), \quad (1.6)$$

where a subscript associated with the utility function denotes a partial derivative; for example, $U_1(c_1, 1 - L_1) = \partial U(c_1, 1 - L_1)/\partial c_1$, $U_1(c_2, 1 - L_2) = \partial U(c_2, 1 - L_2)/\partial c_2$, and so on. Equation (1.4) governs the optimal intertemporal consumption decision. Equation (1.5) governs the optimal leisure–consumption tradeoff in the first period, while (1.6) governs the same decision in the second period. The lefthand side of each equation is the marginal rate of substitution (MRS) while the righthand side is the marginal rate of transformation (MRT). In general, we would expect consumption and labor supply to differ over the life cycle.

A tax system is said to be *distorting*, or to cause a *distortion*, and thus an excess burden or deadweight loss in welfare, if one or more of the tax rates enters one or more of the MRTs in the first-order conditions of an agent's decision problem. Otherwise, the tax is said to be *non-distorting*; if none of the tax parameters enter any of the MRTs, the tax is non-distorting. A distorting tax system will tend to misallocate resources.

Under the income tax, the MRTs are given by, respectively,

$$[1 + r(1 - t_r)], w_1(1 - t_{w1}), \text{ and } w_2(1 - t_{w2}).$$

From this it follows that the general income tax distorts all three decisions. A wage tax distorts the leisure–consumption tradeoff since t_{w1} enters (1.5) and t_{w2} enters (1.6). The interest income tax distorts the intertemporal consumption decision since t_r enters the MRT in (1.4).

On the other hand, under a consumption tax the MRTs are given by, respectively,

$$(1 + \theta_1)(1 + r)/(1 + \theta_2), w_1/(1 + \theta_1), \text{ and } w_2/(1 + \theta_2).$$

It is immediate from this that a progressive consumption tax, where the taxpayer is in different tax brackets over her life cycle, will also distort all three economic decisions. In the special case of a constant, proportional consumption tax, typically the case considered in the literature, $\theta_j = \theta$ for all j, and the MRTs are given by

$$(1+r), \quad w_1/(1+\theta_1), \quad \text{and} \quad w_2/(1+\theta_2).$$

The flat-rate consumption tax does not distort the intertemporal consumption decision since the consumption tax rate does not enter the MRT in (1.4). However, the consumption tax will distort both labor supply decisions. In addition, the tax rate will have to be larger under the consumption tax in order to generate the same revenue as the income tax since the consumption tax base will generally be smaller than the income tax base if there is net saving in the aggregate. To see this, consider a flat-rate consumption tax and notice that the wealth constraint is

$$w_1 L_1 + R w_2 L_2 = (1+\theta)(c_1 + R c_2),$$

where $R = 1/(1+r)$. Under a flat-rate labor income tax, we have instead

$$(1 - t_L)(w_1 L_1 + R w_2 L_2) = (c_1 + R c_2),$$

where t_L is the labor income tax rate. The two taxes are equivalent in the distortions they cause if $(1 - t_L) = 1/(1 + \theta)$. However, under a general income tax, we have instead

$$(1 - t_y)(w_1 L_1 + R_n w_2 L_2) = c_1 + R_n c_2,$$

where $R_n = 1/[1 + r(1 - t_y)]$ and t_y is the general income tax rate. If the tax is symmetric, savers pay a tax, $t_y rs > 0$, where $s > 0$ is saving, while borrowers receive a credit, $t_y rs < 0$, where $s < 0$ is borrowing. However, if there is net saving in the aggregate, $t_y rs$ is collected from that saving under the general income tax, where $s > 0$ is aggregate saving, and less revenue needs to be collected by taxing labor income. Thus, $t_y < t_L$, and the distortion of the labor supply decisions will be greater under the consumption tax.

It follows that the excess burden of the two taxes cannot be ranked without careful empirical research even in this simplest of comparisons. Of course, if the consumption tax is progressive, then $\theta_1 \neq \theta_2$, in general, and the intertemporal consumption decision will also be distorted by the tax as well, which clearly weakens the efficiency case for the consumption tax.

As we will see in later chapters, versions of the two taxes will distort a variety of economic decisions including bequests, charitable contributions, durable goods, and liquidity, under certain conditions. In addition, the pattern of distortions will differ between the two taxes, making a simple comparison of the excess burden difficult to undertake. Unfortunately, even careful empirical research may not decide this issue. In general, what must we know in order to pose and answer the question of the effect of a tax reform on welfare? First, we must know how agents respond to each tax policy separately. Second, we must know the general equilibrium response to the change in policy. How do relative prices respond? Finally, we must know the specific tax experiment being studied.

1.4.2. *The overlapping generations (OG) model*

To make this more concrete, consider a closed-economy, overlapping genera-tions model, with a representative agent, who lives for two periods but works only in the first period of life. (See Section 2.4 for a full description of the OG model.[16]) Set $L_1 = L = 1, L_2 = 0$, and assume that utility is given by $U(c_1, c_2)$ so labor supply is fixed. The first-order condition of the consumer's decision problem is a version of equation (1.4),

$$U_1(c_1, c_2)/U_2(c_1, c_2) = (1 + \theta_1)[1 + r(1 - t_r)]/(1 + \theta_2),$$

where $c_1 = [w(1 - t_w) - s]/(1 + \theta_1)$ and $c_2 = [1 + r(1 - t_r)]s/(1 + \theta_2)$. We can solve the first-order condition to obtain the saving function $S[w(1 - t_w), q_1, q_2]$, where $q_1 = (1 + \theta_1)$ and $q_2 = (1 + \theta_2)/[1 + r(1 - t_r)]$ are the prices of first- and second-period consumption, respectively.

To close the model, N_t identical young agents are born at time t and popula-tion evolves according to $N_t = (1 + n)N_{t-1}$. There is one consumption good produced via a neoclassical, constant-returns-to-scale technology. Output per worker is given by $f(k_t)$, where k is capital per worker. Identical firms maximize profit and thus, the marginal product of capital will equal the real interest rate according to $df/dk = f_k(k) = r$. In addition, profits are zero in equilibrium, so $w = f(k) - rk$. Solving the marginal productivity condition, we have $k(r)$, where $k_r = dk/dr < 0$. And we can write the wage as a function of r according to $w(r) = f(k(r)) - k(r)r$, where $w_r = dw/dr = -k$. In a steady state, the excess demand for capital is given by

$$E(r, t_w, t_r, \theta_1, \theta_2, n) = k(r)(1 + n) - S(w(r)(1 - t_w), q_1, q_2). \quad (1.7)$$

In a steady state equilibrium, $E(r^*, t_w, t_r, \theta_1, \theta_2, n) = 0$, where r^* is the steady state equilibrium interest rate.[17]

Finally, we need to know the government's budget constraint and the exact tax policy experiment to be studied. Specifying the policy experiment entails choos-ing one policy variable as the exogenous control variable and at least one policy variable that will respond endogenously so the government's budget constraint holds with equality. In general, we can represent the government budget con-straint in the following general way: $G(r^*, t_w, t_r, \theta_1, \theta_2, n, g) = 0$, where g is a per capita expenditure on a public good that does not directly affect utility or the technology. For example, under a wage tax the government's budget constraint is $w(r^*)t_w = g$; under a flat-rate consumption tax, we have instead $\theta[c_1 + c_2/(1 + n)] = g$.[18]

One policy experiment that has received some attention in the literature is the following: $t_w = t_r = t, \theta_1 = \theta_2 = \theta$, and $d\theta > 0$, where θ is the control variable and the income tax rate t responds endogenously so the government's budget constraint holds with equality. We then have a two-equation system $E(\ ) = 0$ and $G(\ ) = 0$, in two endogenous variables, r and t, and one control variable, θ. Let (r^*, t^*) satisfy the two equations with equality. The purpose of the experiment is to calculate the derivatives $dr^*/d\theta$ and $dt^*/d\theta$. Unfortunately, the results even in this simple model are likely to be ambiguous since the derivatives will depend in a complicated way on the form of the saving function, the technology, and the way in which the two interact.

One important purpose of studying such an experiment is that it can elucidate the various effects that may occur and this can inform the policy debate. Theory can suggest the existence of a particular effect. It is then up to empirical researchers to uncover evidence on the significance of the effect.

We can also calculate the effect of the tax reform on steady state welfare by using the indirect utility function, which is defined by substituting the budget constraints, the saving function, and $w(r^*)$ into (1.3) to obtain

$$V(r^*, t_w, t_r, \theta_1, \theta_2) = U[w(r^*)(1 - t_w) - s]/(1 + \theta_1),$$
$$[1 + r^*(1 - t_r)]s/(1 + \theta_2)], \tag{1.8}$$

The effect of the reform will depend on two elements, as indicated by the arguments of the indirect utility function. First, the tax parameters will generally have a direct impact on welfare. Second, the response of the economy's relative prices, as measured by the real interest rate, will affect welfare as well. The first effect involves a change in pre-existing tax distortions when the tax system is reformed and is a static efficiency effect. The second effect involves dynamic efficiency and a comparison of the position of the competitive economy relative to the optimal growth path.

Following the classic discussion by Diamond (1965) consider a social planner who chooses consumption and capital per worker to maximize steady state welfare $U(c_1, c_2)$ subject to the steady state resource constraint, $f(k) = c_1 + c_2/(1 + n) + nk$. The first-order conditions are $U_1/U_2 = 1 + n$ and $df/dk = f_k = n$. The latter condition is known as the "golden rule" and describes the optimal stationary path for the economy in the sense that consumption is maximized in a steady state on the golden rule path. Diamond showed that either $r > n$, or $n > r$ can occur under competition. Thus, the competitive economy may not be efficient in a dynamic sense. If, for example, $r > n$, the competitive economy is undercapitalized relative to the golden rule level of capital, and vice versa if $n > r$. A change in policy that moves the economy closer to the golden rule may improve welfare in the steady state.

It is possible for a tax reform to reduce the excess burden associated with distorting taxation but to move the economy further away from the golden rule growth path, making the representative agent worse off as a result. Indeed, in our example the consumption tax is a non-distorting tax when labor supply is fixed in the simple model, so greater reliance on it will reduce the excess burden of taxation and improve welfare. However, people might respond to the experiment by saving and investing less. If the economy is undercapitalized to begin with, the reform will move the economy further away from the golden rule path. The dynamic efficiency effect might easily outweigh the so-called "Harberger triangle" calculation of the static excess burden, implying the reform is undesirable.

One can also calculate the transition path the economy will follow after the reform is instituted. This would involve the time dated two-equation system. The welfare calculation can also be made describing how the reform will affect utility on the transition path. It is possible for a reform to have one effect on steady state welfare and the opposite effect on the transition path.[19] For example, the generations alive when the reform is instituted may be made worse off, while the agents living in the new steady state, and thus in the infinite future, are made better off. Unfortunately, the people currently alive would have little incentive to pass the necessary reform unless they feel altruistically about future generations.[20]

One additional problem should be mentioned. The example of a tax reform we just gave is very simple and unrealistic. However, complicating the model will most likely make the analytical results not less ambiguous, but more so. Labor supply can be made endogenous, human capital accumulation can be included, bequests can be allowed, environmental externalities may exist, durable goods can be added, people can use money for transactions, and so on. All of these extensions are worthwhile and some will be studied in this book. Unfortunately, the results that emerge from these extensions in many cases will not typically favor one tax over the other on efficiency grounds.

1.4.3. The Ramsey growth model

Another popular model used extensively in the literature is the Ramsey growth model. The main difference between this model and the OG model is that the representative agent in the model experiences an infinite planning horizon. The agent obtains utility from consumption and leisure each period. Her preferences are given by

$$\sum_{t=0}^{\infty} \beta^t U(c_1, 1 - L_t),\tag{1.9}$$

where the period utility function, $U(c_t, 1 - L_t)$, is well behaved, and where $\beta = 1/(1 + \rho)$ is the discount factor and ρ is the rate of time preference.

There is a neoclassical technology that governs production of the one consumption good available, $y_t = f(k_t)$, that is also well behaved. Identical firms produce the one good using capital and labor. Profit maximization implies $r = f_k(k)$, where r is the real interest rate. With constant returns to scale the wage is given by $w = f - rk$.

The agent is endowed with one unit of labor each period and chooses how much to work, consume, and save. Her budget constraint for time period t is given by

$$w_t L_t + (1 + r_t)k_t - k_{t+1} - c_t = 0 \quad \text{for } t = 0, 1, 2, \ldots \tag{1.10}$$

She chooses infinite sequences of consumption, capital, and labor supply to maximize (1.9) subject to the sequence of constraints given by (1.10), taking k_0 as given.

One important conclusion of this model is that on an equilibrium path the economy will be efficient in a dynamic sense. This is not necessarily true in the OG model. In that model, it is possible for agents to overaccumulate capital and drive the real interest rate below the optimal level. This cannot happen in the Ramsey growth model because the agent experiences an infinite planning horizon. Let λ be the Lagrange multiplier for the constraint and set up the following Lagrangean:

$$\sum \beta^t \{ U(c_t, 1 - L_t) + \lambda_t [w_t L_t + (1 + r_t) k_t - k_{t+1} - c_t] \}.$$

Differentiate with respect to k_{t+1} to obtain

$$-\lambda_t \beta^t + (1 + r_{t+1}) \lambda_{t+1} \beta^{t+1} = 0.$$

In a steady state this implies $r = \rho$. Since $r = f_k(k)$, it follows that $\rho = f_k(k)$, which is the optimal level for capital per worker.

In the simplest version of the model, growth eventually slows down and stops because of diminishing returns in capital per worker. However, one can extend the model in order to make the growth rate of the economy endogenous, following Romer (1986) and Lucas (1988). In particular, Lucas (1990) incorporated human capital accumulation into the model and studied the properties of the balanced growth path where the growth rate of the economy was constant but endogenous. He showed that the growth rate will generally respond to tax policy. Indeed, he argued that the capital income tax will permanently reduce the economy's steady state growth rate and thus will permanently reduce welfare. This also needs to be taken into account when evaluating the desirability of a particular tax reform. For recent empirical evidence that supports the endogenous growth model using data from the OECD see Kneller, Bleaney, and Gemmell (1999).

1.5. Equity

In terms of the equity of the tax system, horizontal equity (HE) refers to treating people in an "equal position" in the same way and vertical equity (VE) refers to treating people who are in a different position differently. The early literature cited by Musgrave (1976), Edgeworth for example, focused on income as a measure of "equal position." In that case, two people with the same income should be treated in the same way under horizontal equity and two people with different incomes should be treated differently under vertical equity. Later, writers working in the tradition of Schanz, Haig, and Simons focused their attention on the definition of income and sought to make it as comprehensive as possible.[21] As previously mentioned, this meant including accrued capital gains, imputations of services from durable goods like a house, and inflation adjustments. Two people with the same "comprehensive" income should be treated in the same way by the tax system under HE while two people with different "comprehensive" income should be treated differently. Under the equal sacrifice principle and diminishing marginal utility of comprehensive income, under VE a wealthy person should pay more in tax than a relatively poorer person. Of course, the problems associated with the notion of comprehensive income we have already discussed make exact comparisons between people somewhat subjective.

As noted by both Musgrave (1976), and Feldstein (1976) it is more appropriate to use utility rather than income as a measure of "equal position." Two people who experience the same level of utility should be treated in the same way by the tax system, and the ranking of people by utility level should be maintained after imposition of the tax system. However, both Musgrave and Feldstein recognized that there were problems with implementing these definitions. For example, if tastes, as represented by a well defined cardinal utility function, differ across people, then no tax system will satisfy these two notions of equity.

To see this, consider two people A and B. If tastes and budget sets are the same, any tax system will satisfy HE and VE. If A and B are literally the same, they will choose the same consumption bundle. The income tax and the consumption tax will impose the same tax burden on the two people. Next, suppose that tastes differ. Following Feldstein, suppose A is a "consumption lover," with preferences $U = C^2(1 - L)$, where C is consumption, $1 - L$ is leisure, and L is labor, and B is a "leisure lover," with preferences $U = C(1 - L)^2$. Suppose the wage is $w = 1$ for both so the feasible budget set is the same for both. Utility maximization implies $C = 2/3$ and $L = 2/3$ for the consumption lover, $C = 1/3$ and $L = 1/3$ for the leisure lover, and $U = 4/27$ for both. HE implies that both should receive the same treatment from the tax system. However, it is straightforward to show the consumption lover's utility is reduced more than the leisure lover's utility under both taxes. Therefore, neither tax satisfies HE when tastes differ. According to Feldstein, this strongly suggests that HE is a separate criterion that needs to be balanced against efficiency in choosing the parameters of the optimal tax system.

Next, following Feldstein, suppose that tastes are the same, people are endowed with ability, there are two dimensions of ability—wit and strength—and people differ in their respective endowments of wit and strength. A and B may have different endowments of wit and strength, yet receive the same income and thus achieve a different level of utility because of differences in the work they do. Imposing the same tax on A and B would violate HE if comprehensive income is used as a measure of "equal position."

Furthermore, it is useful to take a lifetime perspective since utility depends on consumption and leisure over the entire lifetime. Only a consumption tax maintains HE in general. Suppose A and B have the same lifetime tastes and labor supply is fixed. Then the present value of the individual's lifetime income is an appropriate tax base. A constant proportional wage tax and a constant proportional consumption tax will be equivalent since consumption and wage income will have the same present value. However, if the tax must be progressive, only the consumption tax will satisfy HE. If A and B experience the same level of lifetime utility and tastes are constant, they must experience the same consumption path and thus pay the same consumption tax, regardless of whether or not the tax is progressive. However, it is possible for the present value of their respective wage income paths to be the same even though the time path of their earnings might differ. But if the time path of their earnings differs, they might very easily incur a different tax burden under a progressive income tax. This would violate HE.

Unfortunately, neither tax will achieve HE if tastes can differ, as shown before. If A and B have different tastes, they can experience different consumption paths but the same level of lifetime utility. HE would require that they pay the same tax. However, their respective tax burden will differ under the consumption tax since they will experience different consumption paths, and similarly for the income tax.

The general conclusion appears to be that it is not immediately obvious that one tax clearly dominates the other on either efficiency or equity grounds, even in the simple setting considered so far in this chapter. This is even more true when the comparison is between imperfect tax systems, where realistic economic behavior is much more complicated than in our models and where tastes and budgets can differ across taxpayers. The importance of this literature, however, is that it can lead to additional work in the future that may make some of these issues a bit more clear than they are today. It can also provide a solid theoretical background that can be used to judge whether or not an argument supporting one tax over another is sound.

1.6. The cashflow consumption tax versus the prepayment method

There are different versions of the consumption tax that vary in some of their details. In this section we wish to examine two popular versions of the tax, the cashflow version and the prepayment version.

Let us return to the two-period model where the agent supplies L_j units of labor in period of life j. Her budget constraints are given by the following two equations in the absence of taxation:

$$w_1 L_1 - s - c_1 = 0,$$
$$w_2 L_2 + (1 + r)s - c_2 = 0.$$

Under the cashflow version of the consumption tax, we can take the tax base to be receipts minus assets acquired in this simple setup. The tax base under this definition in the first period is $w_1 L_1 - s$, which is equal to c_1, and in the second period is $w_2 L_2 + (1 + r)s$, which is equal to c_2. The budget constraints become

$$(1 - \tau_1)(w_1 L_1 - s) = c_1,$$
$$(1 - \tau_2)[w_2 L_2 + (1 + r)s] = c_2,$$

or

$$w_1 L_1 - s = [1/(1 - \tau_1)]c_1,$$
$$[w_2 L_2 + (1 + r)s] = [1/(1 - \tau_2)]c_2.$$

If we let $1/(1 - \tau_j) = 1 + \theta_j$, then imposing a consumption tax rate of τ on the lefthand side of the budget constraints presented above will yield exactly the same first-order conditions as if we had imposed θ on the righthand side of the constraints. Indeed, the cashflow version of the consumption tax can be interpreted as an income tax with a deduction for saving. It is straightforward to show, by examining the first-order conditions of the consumer's decision problem, that the labor supply decision in both periods, as well as the intertemporal consumption decision, will be distorted by the tax as long as the tax rate is not constant over time.

Under the prepayment version of the tax, no deduction is allowed for saving, nor is the income generated by saving included in the base. The tax base under this definition in the first period is $w_1 L_1$, which is equal to $s + c_1$, and is in the second period $w_2 L_2$, which is equal to $c_2 - (1 + r)s$. The budget constraints become

$$(1 - \delta_1)w_1 L_1 = s + c_1,$$
$$(1 - \delta_2)w_2 L_2 = c_2 - (1 + r)s,$$

or

$$w_1 L_1 = [1/(1 - \delta_1)](s + c_1),$$
$$w_2 L_2 = [1/(1 - \delta_2)][c_2 - (1 + r)s],$$

where δ_1 and δ_2 are the tax rates. Once again, the labor income tax can be interpreted as a consumption tax where $1/(1 - \delta_j) = 1 + \psi_j$ and ψ_j is the consumption tax rate.

It appears that tax is paid on saving in the first period but that saving income is deducted in the second period. Thus, the tax is said to be "prepaid." More generally, the consumer's tax liability is shifted toward periods when assets such as house, car, equity shares, and so on are accumulated. Under the life cycle saving hypothesis, for example, an agent borrows early in life to acquire a house and car and repay student loans, saves during the middle years, and finally draws down her assets when retired. Since she is acquiring the bulk of her assets when young and middle-aged, her tax liability will shift to those periods from other periods, namely retirement. Finally, the agent will pay no tax when retired if consumption is financed entirely out of previous saving income under the prepayment approach.

The first-order conditions from the consumer's decision problem under prepayment are given by

$$U_1(c_1, 1 - L_1)/\beta U_1(c_2, 1 - L_2) = 1 + r, \tag{1.4'}$$

$$U_2(c_1, 1 - L_1)/U_1(c_1, 1 - L_1) = w_1(1 - \delta_1), \tag{1.5'}$$

$$U_2(c_2, 1 - L_2)/U_1(c_2, 1 - L_2) = w_2(1 - \delta_2). \tag{1.6'}$$

The intertemporal consumption decision is not distorted by this version of the tax even when the tax rate varies. However, both labor supply decisions will be distorted by the tax. It follows from this that the two versions of the tax are not generally identical in their effects on behavior. However, under a flat-rate tax these two versions of the consumption tax would affect the first-order conditions in the same manner, given our assumptions.

Next, suppose there is a second asset treated under the prepayment method while saving is not. The tax base in the first period is $w_1 L_1 - s$ or $c_1 + pA$, where p is the price of the asset. The tax base in the second period is $w_2 L_2 + (1 + r)s$, which is equal to $c_2 - p'A$, where p' is the new price of the asset. Thus, $p' > p$ implies there has been a capital gain. It is straightforward to show that the intertemporal consumption decision will be distorted by the tax. To see this, note that the first-order condition for intertemporal consumption is given by

$$U_1(c_1, 1 - L_1)/\beta U_1(c_2, 1 - L_2) = (1 + r)(1 + \theta_1)/(1 + \theta_2).$$

If the tax is progressive and the taxpayer is in different brackets over her life cycle, then her intertemporal decision will be distorted by the tax.

1.7. Plan for the book

In Chapter 2 we begin by presenting a discussion of the early literature on the consumption tax proposal. Early writers were concerned that people pay tax on what they take out of society in consumption rather than on what they put into society in labor and capital investment. The main argument against a general income tax was that such a tax "double taxes" saving and that consumption is preferred as a tax base. Indeed, the consumption tax has had some illustrious proponents, including Mill, Marshall, and, later, Pigou, Keynes, Irving Fisher, and Kaldor.

The key paper in sparking renewed interest in the consumption tax in the 1970s, if one could be so chosen, was Feldstein's (1978a) "Welfare Cost" paper. Feldstein addressed four mistaken propositions in vogue at the time about taxing capital and he calculated an enormous welfare cost associated with the taxation of capital income using data from the United States. Boskin (1978) provided further ammunition in the debate by econometrically estimating a large interest elasticity of saving for the United States, although this was viewed with a fair degree of skepticism. In a more realistic model, where agents experience a longer horizon, Summers (1981) simulated an interest elasticity an order of magnitude larger than Boskin's empirical estimate. This dramatically increased the deadweight loss associated with taxing capital and provided further support for the consumption tax policy. Evans (1983) pointed out that Summers's result was sensitive to his assumptions about certain key parameters, for example the rate of time preference and the growth rate of the economy. Under a variety of alternative assumptions, he calculated elasticities much smaller in magnitude. This means that the gain in switching to the consumption tax is much smaller than calculated by either Feldstein or Summers.

In Chapter 3 we derive the optimal tax formulae in a two-period overlapping generations model, where the government behaves as a Stackelberg leader in the so-called open loop policy game played between the government and the private sector, following Atkinson and Sandmo (1980) and King (1980). As it turns out, it is actually the wage elasticities that are most important in determining whether a zero tax rate on capital income is optimal, not the interest elasticity of saving. Moreover, the position of the economy relative to the optimal expansion path is also of critical importance in determining the structure of the optimal tax system. There is no presumption that capital should be exempt from taxation in this early literature.

We briefly summarize some of the empirical work on tax incentives and saving, consumption, and labor supply behavior. Unfortunately, the evidence is somewhat inconclusive and does not strongly support one tax system over the other. In addition, we study the computer simulation results of Seidman (1983, 1984), Auerbach and Kotlikoff (1987), and Lord and Rangazas (1992). The advantage of using such models is that they can provide quantitative answers to difficult and important policy questions. However, simulation models are obviously dependent on the functional forms and the parameters chosen for the simulation. Some of the results are sensitive to these choices and some are not. The main conclusion of this work is that a move toward the consumption tax from the general income tax has the potential to improve welfare. This is tempered by the problems associated with the transition period when the reform is carried out. It is also tempered by the fact that only simple tax policies have been considered. It is an open question whether a move from the imperfect and complicated income tax actually in place toward an imperfect and complicated consumption tax would improve welfare on average.

In Chapter 4 we discuss the more recent literature on optimal taxation which relies on versions of the Ramsey growth model. Arrow and Kurz (1970), Judd (1985), Chamley (1986), and later Lucas (1990) showed that it is actually suboptimal to tax capital income in the long run. This is especially true in the endogenous growth model studied by Lucas because a tax on interest income will permanently lower the growth rate of the economy and hence welfare.

However, there are a number of caveats to this result. It may be suboptimal to exempt capital from taxation if any of the following conditions hold: government spending is strictly proportional to output; precautionary saving arising from incomplete insurance markets exists; there is productive public spending that enhances private investment; there are liquidity constraints; and negative externalities associated with production exist. The general case for the consumption tax is very weak in the presence of any of these phenomena. And, as discussed by Krusell, Quadrini, and Rios-Rull (1996), voters in a democracy may prefer a general income tax system over a consumption tax as well, since it tends to reduce the level of redistributive taxation.

In Chapter 5 we study the effects of opening up the economy to international capital flows. We briefly describe the different principles of international taxation, the residence principle, and the source principle. Under the residence principle the government taxes the income of its residents regardless of source. Under the source principle the government taxes income generated within the country. We also discuss the problems associated with taxing capital income when capital is somewhat mobile.

In particular, Razin and Sadka (1991a) and Gordon (1992) have argued that it may be difficult, if not impossible, for a small open economy to tax capital because of capital flight. If capital is perfectly mobile, and thus cannot be taxed, then a wage tax or consumption tax may be the only alternative. Source taxation is ruled out since it violates the production efficiency result due to Diamond and Mirrlees (1971a). Thus, residence-based taxation is preferred by a small open economy. However, if the government cannot monitor the foreign source income of its residents, it will have to rely on taxation of domestic capital income, labor, or consumption. This will, in turn, lead to domestic investors shifting their capital abroad or investing in foreign companies that reinvest locally, thus avoiding domestic capital income taxes altogether. Unfortunately, production efficiency may not hold if pure profits are untaxed and transfers between countries are not forthcoming. As suggested by Keen and Piekkola (1997), for example, it may be optimal to employ source-based taxes when production efficiency does not hold. Taxing capital flows serves as a substitute for profit taxation and transfers.

The general problem of taxing mobile capital has led to countries signing so-called tax treaties whereby information is shared and harmonization of tax treatment is undertaken so that investors do not face perverse incentives to move their capital to another country simply because of adverse tax treatment. This may also have a downside, however; Kehoe (1989) has shown that harmonization may not improve welfare because of the so-called capital levy problem. There is an incentive for the government to promise not to tax capital income generated in the future when it applies the famous Ramsey optimal taxation rule because saving behavior may be highly elastic. However, when the future arrives, the capital stock is fixed by past saving decisions and the government should tax capital at a very high rate if it is able to reapply the Ramsey rule. This is the so-called capital levy problem. If several governments sign a tax treaty, and there is no safe haven for an investor to avoid capital income taxes, the governments as a group may try to exploit the capital levy.

In Chapter 6 we study the time consistency problem as it pertains to tax policy. The famous capital levy is an example of this phenomenon. Unfortunately, this problem is usually ignored in the optimal tax literature.[22] However, in most countries the government in power cannot bind future governments to its policy, and history is replete with examples of governments changing tax policy. The existence of the time consistency problem in this context would tend to favor the income tax over a consumption tax because of the temptation to tax fixed factors like capital at a high rate. However, we show that if tax evasion is taken into account this may be reversed. If it is easier to evade taxes on capital income than taxes imposed on labor income, we show that it may be optimal to tax labor income at a higher rate than capital income in the time-consistent equilibrium. Thus, illegal evasion plays the same role as capital flight in tempering the behavior of the government.

In Chapter 7 we study the interaction between taxation and a variety of privately produced public goods. Charity and private contributions to public goods are important features of most economies for a large portion of the population. This is typically modeled as a "subscription game," where donors make contributions to a public good, charity. However, there are different motives for donating to charity. We examine two motives, one where the donor cares about the actual amount donated and another where the donor cares about the ultimate recipient's consumption. As it turns out, the incidence of tax policy will differ dramatically depending on the motive for donating.

We extend the basic model in several ways. First, we include labor supply and study the interaction between supplying labor and donating cash transfers to a public good. We also extend the model by including donated labor. This raises the interesting possibility that wealthy individuals may donate cash while poor individuals may donate their labor instead if donated labor is decreasing in the wage. Second, we incorporate contributions to a privately produced public good into the Ramsey growth model and study the incidence of the interest income tax and the consumption tax. The interest income tax reduces capital accumulation, consumption, and contributions to privately produced public goods in the long-run equilibrium. The consumption tax that does not tax contributions has no effect at the margin on capital accumulation, reduces consumption, and increases cash contributions to the public good.

Finally, many governments are attempting to reconstruct their budgets by reducing their fiscal deficits. Indeed, many small developing countries have experienced problems involving large foreign debt and need to reconstruct their budgets by reducing their spending and foreign debt levels. This process can be modeled as special interest groups each contributing to a public good, namely the reconstruction of the government's budget. It is shown that the consumption tax may make it more difficult to solve the budget crisis and that reducing spending targets may be a preferred way of solving the budgetary problem.

In Chapter 8 we study the interaction between taxation and two major issues in the economics of the environment, renewable resources and harmful stock externalities. It is known that in an OG model it is possible for agents under competition to acquire too large a stock of an asset relative to the optimal level. This includes any asset including a resource stock. Self-interested decisionmakers will acquire assets to smooth their own consumption, and certain arbitrage conditions must hold across assets. However, there is nothing that keeps agents from saving too much in the aggregate, thus driving down returns below their socially optimal level. This important point was made by Diamond (1965). A general income tax, which includes a tax on capital income, will lower the return to acquiring an asset and may improve welfare if it moves the competitive economy closer to the optimal expansion path. In contrast, the consumption tax will not distort the decision to hold an asset at the margin. The exception to this is when the resource asset has an additional amenity value that provides the agent with utility. In that case the consumption tax favors "amenity consumption" of the asset over general consumption if the amenity cannot be taxed.

We also consider harmful stock externalities. The acts of consumption and production may cause damage to the environment that needs to be addressed by government policy. We show that it is optimal for the government to tax capital in the long run in the presence of a production externality. Labor should also be taxed and the labor tax rate will depend on both the consumption and production externalities. We also consider the case where private agents themselves can make contributions to cleaning up pollution. A consumption externality will not be internalized if private agents behave atomistically. A consumption tax imposed on general consumption but not on contributions to cleaning up the environment can allow the competitive economy to support the optimal allocation.

In Chapter 9 we study the interaction between durable goods and tax policy in a variety of models. If the durable good is merely an asset, then taxation of the interest income of other assets causes the durable good to be favored. The consumption tax will have no impact on the durable good in this case. If the durable good also provides utility which is not taxed, then the consumption tax will generally distort the durable good decision by favoring the durable. Finally, if the durable good can depreciate over time but can be maintained by an expenditure made by the consumer, the implications of the consumption tax become more complicated. The consumption tax will generally distort either the decision to buy the durable good, the decision to maintain it, or both, depending on how the tax is imposed.

We also consider the important case where the service flow from the durable is taxed under the extended consumption tax. If the services of the durable are taxed at the consumption tax rate, the consumption tax will generally distort the decision to buy the durable good and the maintenance decision. There will be less of an incentive to invest in durable goods as a result of the consumption tax on the services of the durable, and we would expect the demand for the durable good to fall as a result.

In Chapter 10 we study the interaction between money and taxation. Different models of money generate different results regarding the pattern of distortions of the different tax systems. The income tax will generally distort the intertemporal consumption decision. If a separate demand for liquidity exists, as it does in the money in the utility function (MUF) model, then both the income tax and the consumption tax will distort the decision to hold cash balances. Under the strictest form of a consumption tax where cash balances are not taxed, the consumption tax favors liquidity relative to consumption and the imposition of such a tax will induce agents to seek greater liquidity. On the other hand, if cash balances are taxed under the consumption tax, then the accumulation of capital is favored as an asset relative to cash balances and agents will hold less cash in their portfolios when the tax is imposed. It is difficult to introduce the consumption tax so as to be perfectly neutral. This occurs because money serves two roles: as liquidity and as a store of value.

In the Lucas–Stokey cash-in-advance model it is assumed cash must be used to purchase some consumption while credit can be used to finance the rest. Consumption of both the cash good and the credit good decreases with either the income or the consumption tax. However, the demand for money to buy the cash good will decrease with the income tax but may increase with the consumption tax in order to pay the consumption tax imposed on the cash good. Another important model of money, due to Wallace (1983, 1984), generates a demand for money by imposing a legal restriction on the private sector's ability to intermediate. A reserve requirement is an example. The interest income tax will still distort decisions in the credit market. However, the consumption tax will not distort the decision to hold cash balances. This is because the decision to hold cash in a "constrained reserve" equilibrium is exogenous and money is a perfect substitute for capital in the "excess reserve" equilibrium and hence must pay the same rate of return as capital.

We also consider the case where cash reserves are taxed under the consumption tax. All three models predict that the cash balances decision will be distorted by the consumption tax. Furthermore, the MUF model and the legal restrictions model predict that the demand for money will fall while the LS model's prediction is ambiguous. Thus, the impact of either tax system on the economy will depend on the model of money one uses. In general, both taxes are distorting.

In Chapter 11 we incorporate bequests into the simple life cycle model and study the incidence of taxing bequests under the consumption tax. There are different models of bequeathing, and the results of any policy analysis depend critically on the motive for bequeathing. In the model where the parent cares about the size of the bequest per se, the bequest is like parental consumption and should be taxed under the consumption tax policy to maintain neutrality. On the other hand, if the parent cares about the full income or welfare of the offspring, then the bequest is more like an asset and should not be taxed under the consumption tax in order to maintain neutrality. If the population is made up of heterogeneous people with different motives for bequeathing, it will be impossible to impose the consumption tax in a neutral fashion that does not distort someone's bequest decision. Thus, the proportional consumption tax will not be completely neutral with respect to intertemporal decisionmaking in the presence of bequests, even when labor supply is exogenous. These results are similar to those of Chapter 7.

Chapter 12 concludes the book with a brief summary of results and conclusions about research on the consumption tax. We eschew strong policy conclusions, since this is an area of ongoing and thriving research activity—although, it is probably fair to say that we can rule out the extreme cases of taxing capital at a high rate and not taxing capital at all, for a variety of reasons discussed throughout the book.

NOTES TO CHAPTER 1

1. Indeed, tax issues appear to have galactic significance. In the new *Star Wars* prequel movie, *The Phantom Menace*, taxes on trade have disrupted the delicate balance in the universe. From the opening credits of the movie: "Turmoil has engulfed the Galactic Republic. The taxation of trade routes to outlying star systems is in dispute." See Menand (1999).

2. Bradford (1986) describes six different versions of the "consumption tax": a VAT, a national sales tax, and four versions of an income style consumption tax (a two-tiered cashflow tax proposed by Hall and Rabushka, a pure cashflow tax proposed by Aaron and Galper, the Treasury Department's Blueprints cashflow tax, and a phase-in of the cashflow tax in the presence of an income tax). More recently, the term "consumed income tax" (CIT) has become popular for describing the cashflow consumption tax.

3. According to data from the OECD, only Austria, France, Greece, and Portugal collected more in taxes on goods and services than on income (personal and corporate) in 1994. In the United Kingdom about the same percentage of revenue was collected under the personal and corporate income tax as was collected under taxes on goods and services in 1994. See Revenue Statistics of OECD Member Countries, 1995.

4. Several new proposals for reforming the income tax code have been put forth recently in the United States. Each tends to favor greater taxation of consumption rather than income, the primary focus being the reduction, or even elimination, of taxes on capital income. Under the Armey–Shelby proposal, the tax base would include wages and pension receipts but exclude interest, capital gains, and social security benefits. The base would be taxed at a flat 17 per cent after allowing certain standard exemptions.

The tax base for businesses would equal revenue minus labor costs and the cost of purchases from other businesses. Under the Nunn–Dominici proposal, individuals could deduct net saving from income to obtain the tax base, which effectively converts the income tax to a consumption based tax. Businesses would pay a VAT instead of the current corporate income tax. Both proposals would eliminate many of the itemized deductions that exist in the current tax law. As of the fall of 1999, however, neither had been adopted. See the paper by Toder (1996) for a good analysis of these proposals.

5. See the discussion in Goode (1969, 1980).

6. Goode (1980) pointed out that it is perhaps more appropriate to call this the "Schanz–Haig–Simons" definition of income. Chapter 2 in Bradford's (1986) book contains a good discussion of the definition of comprehensive income and accrual accounting.

7. See the excellent discussion on this in Chapters 2 and 3 of Bradford (1986).

8. For a good discussion of Japan's experience with the consumption tax, see Ishi (1993).

9. See Mieszkowski (1980).

10. The Meade Commission (Meade 1978) made this recommendation, for example.

11. One rather popular method for raising revenue that is politically expedient involves issuing government debt. The weekly newsmagazine *The Economist* recently reported that the debt–GDP ratio for most OECD countries, including Japan, had increased between 1992 and 1996. In fact, for two OECD countries, Belgium and Italy, net public debt was larger than GDP. Only Norway and Finland have net public sector assets, and only Norway's financial position had improved since 1992.

12. Under Lindahl pricing everyone consumes the same amount of the public good but is charged a different price for it, the marginal willingness-to-pay. See Atkinson and Stiglitz (1980) on Lindahl pricing.

13. In some cases children and senior citizens are charged a lower price for the good even though they may have a greater willingness-to-pay for the good. For example, children probably have a greater demand for visiting a zoo yet are typically charged a lower admission fee. This may be justified by a concern for equity.

14. The optimal income tax literature strongly suggests, however, that it is not generally optimal to have a high degree of progressivity built into the income tax. Both Mirrlees (1971) and Atkinson (1973) surprisingly found rather low tax rates to be optimal. In addition to this, Sadka (1976) and others have shown that it is optimal to set the top tax rate equal to zero to provide an incentive to supply more labor at the margin. See the discussion of these results in Atkinson and Stiglitz (1980). There is also some experimental evidence that supports the incentive effect associated with a zero top tax rate: see Sillamaa (1999).

15. We will assume that the utility function is a member of the class of C2 functions and hence is smooth enough for differentiation at least twice, is monotonically increasing in each argument, and is quasi-concave.

16. For a useful exposition of public finance issues studied within the context of the OG model, see Auerbach and Kotlikoff (1987) or, more recently, Ihori (1996a).

17. The equilibrium may not be unique. Following much of the literature, we will assume that it is.

18. A popular technique is to include a non-distorting tax in the model and adjust a distorting tax rate and the non-distorting tax to maintain the government's budget constraint. In that case, we are comparing the equilibrium under the distorting tax with the equilibrium under the non-distorting tax. For example, under a wage tax with a rebate of the revenue $g = 0$ and the government's budget constraint is $T + w(r)t_wL = 0$, where $T < 0$ is a non-distorting transfer and L is labor supply. As it turns out, t_w is a non-distorting tax when labor supply is fixed.

19. To quote Auerbach and Kotlikoff (1987), "The short-run response to certain announced future changes in the tax base can be exactly opposite to those motivating the switch in tax bases."

20. Most federal governments among the OECD countries are running large budget deficits which have gotten larger in recent years as a percentage of GDP. This would tend to suggest that people alive today care less for the future than they once did.

21. See Simons (1938).

22. For example, it is essentially assumed away in the classic papers on optimal taxation in dynamic models; see e.g. Atkinson and Sandmo (1980), Chamley (1986), and Lucas (1990).

2

The Early Literature

2.1. Early advocates

Early proponents of the consumption tax include John Stuart Mill, Alfred Marshall, and, later, A. C. Pigou, John Maynard Keynes, and Irving Fisher. Indeed, most of the early analysts believed strongly that an income tax that exempts saving from taxation, which is similar to a consumption based tax, was the preferred method of raising revenue. Both efficiency and equity arguments were made in favor of the consumption tax. In terms of efficiency, for example, Mill (1967) noted the disincentive effects on "thrift and enterprise" of a general income tax that included a tax on capital income. Even Ramsey (1927), in a little-cited passage from his famous paper on optimal taxation, argued that "income tax should be partially but not wholly remitted on savings," under the assumption that the demand for saving was perfectly elastic while the supply elasticity was positive but finite.

Most of the early advocates of the consumption tax focused their primary attention on equity considerations, however. In testimony before the Committee on Income and Property Tax in 1861, Mill (1967) stated: "if you could exempt from taxation what any person does save, you would have done him full justice." Early proponents thought it best to tax someone on the basis of what they took out of society in the form of consumption rather than on what they put into it in the form of their labor which produced income. Kaldor (1955) quotes Hobbes as the originator of this philosophical position:

the Equality of Imposition consisteth rather in the Equality of that which is consumed, than of the riches of the persons who consume the same. For what reason is there, that he which laboureth much, and sparing the fruits of his labour, consumeth little, should be more charged, than he that living idlely, getteth little and spendith all he gets ... But when the Impositions are layd upon those things which men consume, every man payeth Equally for what he useth ... (Kaldor 1955: Chapter 1)[1]

Furthermore, since wealthy people consume more than the poor, it was also thought at the time that taxing consumption, especially the consumption of luxury goods, would impose a heavier tax on the wealthy than on the poor and thus serve to redistribute wealth.

However, the main theoretical argument in favor of taxing consumption rather than income was that an income tax imposed on capital income double-taxes saving. It was thought that this was not only inefficient, and would lead to less saving and a subsequent shortage of capital, but also inequitable. It was thought unfair to tax a person twice on the same income, once when it was initially saved and a second time when the saving generated new income. In particular, Mill (1888) noted the double taxation argument:

the proper mode of assessing an income-tax would be to tax only the part of income devoted to expenditure, exempting that which is saved...unless, therefore, savings are exempted from income-tax, the contributors are twice taxed on what they save, and only once on what they spend. (Mill 1888: 545)

Unfortunately, almost all of the early proponents of the consumption tax thought the tax would be too difficult to administer. Mill (1967) stated that the "only perfectly unexceptionable and just principle of income tax" is to "exempt all savings" (p. 551). However, he recognized that "the amount of saving cannot be got at in an individual case" (p. 552). Both Marshall and Keynes thought the tax superior to the general income tax but also thought it impossible to administer. Marshall also believed the consumption tax unattainable:

If it were possible to exempt from income-tax that part of income which is saved, to become the source of future capital... then an income-tax graduated with reference to its amount...would become a graduated tax on all personal income...The way to this ideal perfection is difficult; but it is more closely marked than in regard to other Utopian goals. (Marshall 1925: 350–351)

Keynes simply stated that, although the tax was "perhaps theoretically sound, it is practically impossible."[2]

At the time, the main problem with introducing the consumption tax was the perception that the tax had to be imposed on consumption expenditures per se. It was thought that a record of each transaction would have to be maintained until tax time. Enforcing compliance with such a law would be next to impossible since people could easily evade their tax liability, as suggested earlier by Mill.

It was Fisher (1937, 1939) who solved this problem. He pointed out that a simple accounting identity exists between income, saving, and consumption. Capital or investment income plus labor earnings are equal to consumption plus the change in wealth. One did not need to force taxpayers to save all of their receipts when they consumed their income: all they had to do was keep track of their income and their net saving over the course of the tax year. Subtracting the latter from the former would yield the consumption tax base under one version of the consumption tax. To quote Irving Fisher and Herbert Fisher,

How do we figure what we spend in a day? We need only two data:

1. The amount we had to spend; that is, what we had or received during the day.
2. The amount we did not spend; that is, the amount left over as determined by counting at the end of the day. (Fisher and Fisher 1942: 4)

Of course, even this might have been too difficult to accomplish earlier in this century because it would have forced savings institutions to maintain detailed records of transactions involving saving accounts, stock funds, and so on, and report the results to the taxpayer and the government for tax purposes.

After discussing the equity and efficiency aspects of both the income and consumption taxes, A. C. Pigou (1947) concluded: "A general expenditure tax, therefore, is *prima facie* preferable to a general income tax" (p. 122). However, "dishonest citizens might make a practice of saving in one year, thus escaping taxation, and secretly selling out and spending their savings in the next year" (p. 123). Interest in the consumption tax died out in the 1930s and 1940s because of the presumed difficulties in implementing the tax.

Renewed interest was sparked in the 1950s, however, with the publication of Kaldor's (1955) important book on the consumption tax. Kaldor strongly advocated the consumption tax on the basis of a concern for equity. He argued that income was not a good measure of what he called a person's "taxable capacity." For example, a wealthy person who receives income from capital investments has a larger "taxable capacity" than a person who receives the same amount of income from labor, presumably because the wealthy person can also work. So income is not a good measure of "taxable capacity." He also provided a practical way of administering the consumption tax as well.

However, the consumption tax per se did not generate much excitement among tax specialists in the 1950s and 1960s. The main intellectual principle used at the time to study taxation by tax theorists and practitioners alike involved equity, and the focus of attention was directed at finding ways to make the income tax more equitable by making the tax progressive. As a practical matter, only India and Sri Lanka attempted to introduce an expenditure-based tax during this period. In both cases the tax was supposed to supplement the income tax in generating revenue, not replace it, and in both cases many exemptions were allowed. Unfortunately for advocates of the consumption tax, both countries rescinded the tax shortly after it was introduced because of political opposition. Sri Lanka tried valiantly to introduce the tax a second time, but with little success.

Interest in the consumption tax re-emerged in the 1970s because of the slowdown in economic growth that began in many countries in the early part of the decade and because of the high inflation rates experienced by many countries at the time. A number of economists began advocating the consumption tax as an alternative to the income tax. It was pointed out that a general income tax might reduce the incentive to save and thus reduce the amount of saving available for investment. The difficulties of measuring capital income for tax purposes, especially in the presence of inflation, were discussed. It was also pointed out that savings portfolios might be distorted as a result of the differential tax treatment of various assets under the income tax.[3]

In addition to this, work on optimal tax structures revealed that a progressive income tax might not be desirable from an equity viewpoint. Mirrlees (1971) studied the optimal nonlinear income tax in a static model and concluded that the optimal tax was not very progressive under a utilitarian welfare criterion. Later, Atkinson (1973) used the Rawlsian social welfare criterion and showed that the optimal income tax rates were not much higher than what Mirrlees found and were still surprisingly low. One would think that the income tax would be highly progressive if the welfare of the least well off person were used as the social welfare indicator, as under the Rawlsian criterion.

A number of countries issued studies on tax reform in the 1970s, including Canada, Sweden, the United States, and the United Kingdom. In particular, the Meade Commission in the UK strongly urged that a switch be made to the consumption tax coupled with a tax on wealth distributions (Meade 1978).

In the next section we will describe Feldstein's influential 1978 paper on the welfare cost of capital income taxation which set the tone for the debate in the 1970s. A formal analysis appears in Section 2.3. Section 2.4 presents Diamond's incidence analysis of the interest income tax. Section 2.5 discusses the saving elasticity controversy that was the subject of great debate during this period, and Section 2.6 concludes the chapter.

2.2. Feldstein's "Welfare Cost" paper

Feldstein's (1978a) paper was designed to clear up several misconceptions that existed at the time regarding the taxation of capital income. Feldstein made four key points and provided a measure of the welfare cost of taxing capital income. First, many advocates of reducing taxes on capital income argued at the time that a reduction in the capital income tax rate coupled with a revenue-neutral increase in the tax on labor would necessarily increase saving. Feldstein pointed out that saving is equivalent to an expenditure on future consumption: when a person saves, she is really "buying" future consumption. An increase in the net return on saving is tantamount to a reduction in the "price" of future consumption. It is certainly theoretically possible for one to purchase more future consumption without saving more if the "price" of future consumption has fallen, as would be the case with a reduction in the tax on capital income.

In addition to this, Feldstein argued that even a revenue-neutral shift from a general income tax to a wage tax might not cause saving to increase. Under such a tax reform, the timing of a person's tax liability shifts from the end of the life cycle to the beginning. It is possible in such a case for the individual to consume more in the future while saving less if the individual's tax liability in the future falls enough.

Feldstein's second point was a response to the notion, widely held at the time, that efficiency required taxing labor earnings or consumption but not capital income. As was evident in Chapter 1, a tax on capital income alters the marginal rate of transforming current consumption into future consumption, which is the source of an excess burden. Imposing a tax on labor income alone, or taxing current and future consumption at the same rate, does not distort the intertemporal consumption choice. However, as Feldstein pointed out, this ignores the distortion of the labor–leisure choice by the wage or consumption taxes. The theory of the second best instructs us in this case that it is generally optimal to distort both the intertemporal consumption decision and the labor–leisure choice when imposing the optimal set of taxes.

Feldstein applied the Ramsey rule of optimal tax theory, which was derived in a static model, to the intertemporal context of a two-period life cycle model. In the simplest version of the static model there are three commodities, X_1, X_2, and X_3, and one of them, say X_3, cannot be taxed. X_1 can be interpreted as first-period consumption in a life cycle of two periods, X_2 can be interpreted as second-period consumption, and X_3 can be interpreted as leisure, the untaxed commodity. He shows that exempting capital income from taxation may not necessarily be optimal. However, if utility is separable in leisure, then a wage tax alone is optimal. Even though he recognizes that this condition is unlikely to hold in a real economy, Feldstein concluded that "it may be desirable to move in the direction of a consumption tax from the current US tax structure that actually taxes capital more heavily than labor income" (see p. S34).

A formula for the welfare gain of a tax reform that shifts the tax burden from general income to labor earnings alone was also derived. Assuming that both labor supply and saving are perfectly inelastic, Feldstein calculated the welfare gain to be approximately 1.87 per cent of the initial labor earnings per year when saving is 10 per cent of net income, and 3.6 per cent of initial labor earnings when saving is 20 per cent of net income. This estimate would increase if saving were somewhat elastic but would fall if labor supply were somewhat elastic. These results provided some support for switching from the general income tax to a consumption tax.

Third, many economists believed that a tax on capital income would create a distortion and thus a loss in welfare only if the utility-constant supply of saving responded to the net of tax return on saving. However, Feldstein showed that this too was not true; it is possible for the capital income tax to impose a large welfare loss even if the effect of the tax on net savings is negligible. This is because it is the effect of the tax on the intertemporal consumption decision that is important, not the effect of the tax on saving. For example, in a stationary economy there is no net saving in the aggregate. However, the capital income tax will still distort each individual's intertemporal consumption decision. He essentially adapted a formula due to Harberger (1964) to the life cycle context in showing there could be a large welfare loss in taxing capital income even if saving does not respond to the tax.

Finally, Feldstein also discussed the horizontal equity aspects of the consumption tax. Under the conventional wisdom at the time, it was claimed that taxing capital income contributed to horizontal equity. Under the Haig–Simons definition of income, two people with the same "income" should pay the same tax regardless of the source. Excluding capital income from taxation would be inequitable by this definition. However, Feldstein argued that the Haig–Simons definition is at odds with a definition of horizontal equity that ranks people according to their utility level over the life cycle. Consider two people with the same tastes and present value of lifetime income. They will experience the same present value of consumption and hence the same level of lifetime utility. A proportional tax on the present value of income leaves the two people ranked in the same way. A proportional tax on consumption is equivalent to a wage tax in present-value terms and both are equivalent to the proportional tax on the present value of lifetime income; either tax will leave the ranking of the two people unchanged. However, a tax on capital income obviously will not. There-fore, to maintain the utility ranking of the two taxpayers, only a consumption or wage tax is appropriate on equity grounds.

2.3. A formal analysis

To capture the spirit of the analysis, consider a simple, two-period model of a life cycle consumer. This will allow us to focus attention on the intertemporal consumption decision.

The consumer works in the first period for a wage and is retired in the second period. Her lifetime preferences for the one consumption good available are represented by

$$U(c_1, c_2), \tag{2.1}$$

where c_j is consumption in period of life j, and $U()$ satisfies the usual assump-tions.[4] We can interpret c_1 as current consumption and c_2 as future consumption. We will assume that the agent has perfect foresight throughout the book to simplify the analysis.

The agent's budget constraints for the two periods are:

$$w(1 - t_w) = (1 + \theta_1)c_1 + s, \tag{2.2a}$$
$$[1 + r(1 - t_r)]s = (1 + \theta_2)c_2, \tag{2.2b}$$

where s is saving, w is labor earnings, t_w is a tax on earned income, r is the return to saving, t_r is the tax rate on the return, a proxy for capital income taxation, and θ_j is a tax on consumption in period j. As long as $s > 0$, we can collapse the constraints to obtain the present-value wealth constraint of the consumer:

$$w(1 - t_w) = (1 + \theta_1)c_1 + (1 + \theta_2)c_2/[1 + r(1 - t_r)] \tag{2.3}$$

Following Feldstein, we can define the "price" of current consumption to be

$$q_1 = 1 + \theta_1,$$

and the "price" of future consumption to be

$$q_2 = (1 + \theta_2)/[1 + r(1 - t_r)].$$

This allows us to write the lifetime wealth constraint as

$$w_n = q_1 c_1 + q_2 c_2, \tag{2.3'}$$

where $w_n = w(1 - t_w)$ is the after-tax wage rate.

It is imagined that the consumer will choose his lifetime consumption profile (c_1, c_2) so as to maximize (2.1) subject to (2.3) or (2.3'). Solve (2.3) for c_2, substitute into (2.1), and differentiate with respect to c_1 to obtain the first-order condition

$$U_1/U_2 = (1 + \theta_1)[1 + r(1 - t_r)]/(1 + \theta_2) = q_1/q_2, \tag{2.4}$$

where subscripts associated with $U(\ )$ are partial derivatives. The lefthand side of (2.4) is the marginal rate of substitution of c_2 for c_1 (MRS) and the righthand side is the marginal rate of transformation (MRT). This is similar in spirit to equation (1.4) in Chapter 1.

First, notice that the wage tax does not enter the MRT. It follows that the wage tax is a non-distorting tax. It will cause only income or wealth effects in this model. Later we will relax the assumption that labor supply is exogenous. In that case, the wage tax will distort the labor supply decision.

Second, notice that, if the consumption tax rate is constant over time, the MRT is given by $[1 + r(1 - t_r)]$. Clearly, the capital income tax distorts the intertemporal consumption decision. However, the consumption tax will not distort this decision as long as the consumption tax rate is constant over the taxpayer's life cycle. Therefore, it follows that even mild progressivity in the consumption tax rate structure will possibly lead to a distortion of the taxpayer's intertemporal consumption profile unless the taxpayer is in the same tax bracket for her entire life cycle.

We can solve (2.4) for c_1 using the implicit function theorem to obtain the consumption function

$$c_1 = C(w_n, q_1, q_2) \tag{2.5}$$

From (2.4) it follows that the after-tax wage causes only an income or wealth effect, while $1 + r(1 - t_r), \theta_1$, and θ_2 also cause substitution effects in addition to the wealth effect because each enters the MRT of the intertemporal consumption decision. For example, an increase in the price of first-period consumption sets up a substitution effect from first-period consumption toward second-period consumption. It also lowers wealth. If first-period consumption is a normal good, the wealth effect will also reduce first-period consumption. In this case, c_1 is decreasing in q_1. Of course, if first-period consumption is an inferior good, the wealth and substitution effects work in opposite directions and the uncompensated price effect is ambiguous.

The comparative statics of the consumer's decision problem are derived in Appendix 2A. Under rather weak conditions, first-period consumption is increasing in the net wage and it is decreasing in its own price if first-period consumption is a normal good. Furthermore, the response of first-period consumption to the price of second-period consumption is ambiguous. In the two-period model the substitution effect is positive: an increase in the price of future consumption induces substitution toward current consumption. However, an increase in the price of future consumption also reduces wealth. If the substitution effect dominates, then first-period consumption will be increasing in the price of second-period consumption and the two goods will be gross substitutes. On the other hand, they are gross complements if the wealth effect dominates. Thus, $C_w = \partial c_1/\partial w_n > 0$, $C_1 = \partial c_1/\partial q_1 < 0$, and $C_2 = \partial c_1/\partial q_2 > (<) 0$ if current and future consumption are gross substitutes (complements).

Under these assumptions, the consumption tax paid in the first period reduces current consumption. The consumption tax paid in the future increases (decreases) current consumption if current and future consumption are gross substitutes (complements). The wage tax lowers wealth and reduces current consumption as a result, while the interest income tax increases (decreases) current consumption by raising the price of future consumption if current and future consumption are gross substitutes (complements).

The saving function can be defined in the following way:

$$S(w_n q_1, q_2) = w_n - C(w_n, q_1, q_2). \tag{2.6}$$

Its derivative properties are derived from those of the consumption function according to the definition in (2.6) and are also presented in Appendix 2A. The uncompensated responses to the net wage and the prices are given by

$$\partial s/\partial w_n = S_w(\ ) = 1 - C_w(\ ), \tag{2.7}$$

$$\partial s/\partial q_j = S_j(\ ) = -C_j(\ ). \tag{2.8}$$

From this and the definition of q_2, it follows that

$$\partial s/\partial t_r = -rq_2^2 C_2(\ ). \tag{2.9}$$

The first point to consider is whether or not a reduction in the tax rate on capital income will necessarily lower first-period consumption and increase saving. A decrease in the interest income tax rate lowers the "price" of future consumption, q_2, which sets up a substitution effect from current consumption to future consumption, possibly causing saving to increase. However, a decrease in the interest income tax rate also increases wealth, which could cause first-period consumption to increase and saving to fall since first-period consumption is a normal good. In other words, the derivative C_2 is ambiguous in (2.9). It is possible for $C_2 < 0$, causing saving to fall in response to a decrease in the interest income tax rate, if the wealth effect is large enough in magnitude.

For example, suppose $U = [(c_1)^{1-\sigma} + \beta(c_2)^{1-\sigma}]^{1/(1-\sigma)}$. Then it is straightforward to show that $c_1 = w_n/[q_1 + (\beta q_1)^{1/\sigma} q_2^{(\sigma-1)/\sigma}]$ by solving the first-order condition of the consumer's decision problem. First-period consumption is increasing in the net wage and decreasing in its own price. However, the sign of dc_1/dq_2 depends on the magnitude of σ. First-period consumption increases (decreases) with the price of second-period consumption if $\sigma < (>) 1$. Thus, saving decreases (increases) with the price of second-period consumption if $\sigma < (>) 1$. Therefore, an increase in the net interest rate can reduce saving in this example if $\sigma < 1$.

One might take this argument a step further and argue that saving decreases with the interest income tax rate when compensated, that is when utility is held constant. In Appendix 2A we show that saving increases with the return to saving when utility is held constant. However, this may be an artifact of the special two-period model presented in this section. The compensated response of saving to the real return may be ambiguous in a more general model that includes other dimensions of economic decision making, such as human capital accumulation. For example, suppose agents acquire human capital when young. A compensated increase in the real interest rate might induce the agent to reduce current saving to acquire more human capital in order to increase his productivity and hence income in the future.

A more sophisticated argument is that a tax revenue-neutral decrease in the interest income tax rate coupled with an increase in the tax rate, imposed on labor income to maintain the present value of tax revenue, would raise saving. However, Feldstein pointed out that saving need not increase in response to this sort of reform. If the wage tax rate increases and the capital income tax rate falls, the timing of the taxpayer's tax liability will shift toward the beginning of the life cycle when the agent is working. Saving can fall as a result of this tax reform because the timing of the taxpayer's tax liability has shifted; it is easier to finance future consumption after the tax reform, so less saving may be needed.

To see this, recall that the uncompensated saving function is given by $s = S\{w(1 - t_w), 1, 1/[1 + r(1 - t_r)]\}$. The response to the proposed tax reform is

$$ds/dt_r = rq_2^2 S_2 - wS_w(dt_w/dt_r). \qquad (2.10)$$

If we can rule out the "Laffer curve" effect, $dt_w/dt_r < 0$ and a decrease in the interest income tax is coupled with an increase in the wage tax rate.[5] However, if $S_2 < 0$, then it is possible for saving to fall in response to the proposed tax reform. Furthermore, this is consistent with the present-value constraint. The present value of the tax revenue collected from the taxpayer is

$$PV = wt_w + rRt_r s,$$

where $R = 1/(1 + r)$. Under the proposed reform, we have

$$0 = dPV/dt_r = w(dt_w/dt_r) + rRs + rRt_r(ds/dt_r). \qquad (2.11)$$

It follows from this that we cannot rule out the case where $dt_w/dt_r < 0$ and saving falls with the reform.

To further analyze this question, we can treat the interest income tax rate as a control variable and the wage tax rate as an endogenous variable that responds to maintain the present value of tax revenue collected from the taxpayer. In that case we can solve (2.9) and (2.10) to obtain the following responses to the proposed tax reform:

$$ds/dt_r = rs(q_2^2 S_2 + sRS_w)/(1 - rt_r RS_w),$$ (2.12)

$$dt_w/dt_r = -rsR(1 + rt_r q_2^2 S_2)/w(1 - rt_r RS_w).$$ (2.13)

The denominator in (2.12) and (2.13) will be positive if $(1 + r)/rt_r > S_w$, which seems empirically reasonable since $1 + r > 1$, $1/rt_r > 1$, and $S_w < 1$. If the response of saving to the price of future consumption is positive, or negative but small in magnitude, it follows immediately that saving will fall under a tax reform that reduces the interest income tax rate. In addition, the Laffer curve phenomenon will not occur under these assumptions. Saving will only increase with a fall in the interest income tax rate only if $S_2 < 0$ and large in magnitude from (2.12). However, this may also cause the Laffer curve phenomenon to occur, from (2.13), which is empirically difficult to justify.

As discussed in Chapter 1, the welfare effects of the tax reform can be studied by use of the indirect utility function. The indirect utility function is given by

$$V = U(w(1 - t_w) - s, (1 + r(1 - t_r))s),$$

where s solves the first-order condition of the consumer's decision problem, and where we have substituted the budget constraints (2.2) into the utility function (2.1). Totally differentiating, while assuming that factor prices are fixed, we obtain

$$dV/dt_r = -wU_1(dt_w/dt_r) - rsU_2.$$ (2.14)

First, notice that if the Laffer curve effect occurs both terms are negative. In that case a reform that lowers both tax rates will improve welfare. However, if we can rule out the Laffer curve phenomenon, the first term is positive while the second term is negative, and the net response is ambiguous.

We can rewrite this last formula in different ways in order to interpret the effect of the reform on welfare. For example, substitute from (2.11), use the first-order condition from the consumer's decision problem, and simplify to obtain

$$dV/U_1 dt_r = rRt_r(ds/dt_r) - r^2 t_r sRq_2.$$

Suppose that saving does not respond to the tax reform, i.e., that $ds/dt_r = 0$. A welfare effect still exists, and the reform works in the direction of improving welfare since the second term is negative: $dt_r < 0$ under the reform so $dV > 0$ if saving is fixed. The intuition is that the distorting interest income tax is being replaced at the margin by the non-distorting wage tax.

Next, for a different interpretation, use the first-order condition from the consumer's problem in (2.14), substitute (2.12) into (2.14), and simplify to obtain the following equation instead:

$$dV/U_1 dt_r = -r^2 t_r R q_2 s (q_2 C_2 + C_w)/(1 - r t_r R S_w), \qquad (2.15)$$

where we have also used $S_2 = -C_2$ and $S_w = 1 - C_w$. Once again, the denominator will most likely be positive. Therefore, the impact of the reform on welfare depends on the numerator. The first term captures the response to the interest income tax, while the second term captures the response to the wage tax. If first-period consumption and second-period consumption are uncompensated substitutes, then $dV/dt_r < 0$ and the reform of reducing the interest income tax improves welfare. Welfare improves because a non-distorting wage tax is replacing a distorting interest income tax.

We can also see Feldstein's point about there being a welfare cost associated with taxing capital income even if saving does not respond to the tax when utility is held constant. According to the Slutsky equation, $S_2 = S_{2u} - c_2 S_w$, where S_{2u} is the utility-constant response of saving to the price of second-period consumption. Suppose compensated saving is unresponsive to the price of second-period consumption, $S_{2u} = 0$; then, the parenthetical expression in the numerator of (2.15) is given by

$$q_2 C_2 + C_w = C_w - q_2 S_2 = C_w + q_2 c_2 S_w = C_w + s S_w,$$

when $S_{2u} = 0$. In general, this will be positive, implying that $dV/dt_r < 0$.

There are several extensions of this analysis that are useful. For example, the present-value constraint presented above is not the government's budget constraint. If the timing of tax payments changes at the aggregate level, the government may very well have to respond by issuing debt or saving itself by retiring debt, which Feldstein recognized but did not analyze in detail in his "Welfare Cost" paper.

Second, factor prices were held constant throughout the above analysis. In the next section we will examine the results obtained by Diamond (1970) on the incidence of the interest income tax in a general equilibrium setting, the overlapping generations model. The incidence and welfare effects of a tax policy may be dramatically affected by this extension.[6]

Third, the welfare cost calculations and the discussion involving the optimal structure of taxation by Feldstein were carried out using formulae derived in static models. We will study the optimal tax problem in a dynamic context in the next three chapters. As it turns out, the static results do not necessarily carry through in a straightforward way to a dynamic model. This is because the position of the economy relative to the optimal growth path is important but is not taken into account in a static model. This involves the dynamic efficiency of the economy. A tax reform may improve welfare in a static sense, yet move the economy away from the optimal expansion path. It is entirely possible for the latter effect to dominate the static welfare effects. The point is that the advice taken from a static model may be incorrect since it ignores the dynamic efficiency effect.

Finally, there are other features of economic behavior that may be critically important in determining whether or not a tax reform improves welfare. For example, it would be useful to include labor supply, human capital accumulation, the accumulation of other assets and durable goods, intergenerational transfers, capital flight, and so on. This could significantly affect the conclusions of the model. Feldstein certainly recognized this in his discussion of optimal taxation, where he also mentioned the distortion of the labor–leisure decision by taxation.

To underscore this point, consider extending the simple model to include a labor–leisure tradeoff. Assume the agent is endowed with one unit of labor in the first period and none in the second, and that the agent has a preference for leisure according to $U(c_1, c_2, 1 - L)$, where L is labor supply and $1 - L$ is leisure. The wealth constraint becomes

$$w(1 - t_w)L - c_1 - c_2/[1 + r(1 - t_r)] = 0.$$

In addition to the first-order condition governing the agent's choice of intertemporal consumption, there is also a first-order condition governing the labor–leisure tradeoff,

$$U_3/U_1 = w(1 - t_w),$$

where U_3 is the marginal utility of leisure. The wage tax distorts the labor–leisure decision. It is also easy to show that the consumption tax will also distort the labor–leisure decision, even if $\theta = \theta_2$.

Feldstein's conclusions about the welfare cost of taxing capital income are strengthened, ceteris paribus, if the taxpayer's saving behavior is more responsive to the after-tax real interest rate than not. The more responsive the intertemporal consumption decision is to the return, the larger is the welfare loss associated with capital income taxes. We will examine this issue in section 2.5.

2.4. Tax incidence in an overlapping generations model

Diamond (1970) studied the incidence of an interest income tax in his classic paper in the context of a dynamic general equilibrium model of a closed economy. He assumes that the government introduces an interest income tax into the economy coupled with a rebate of the revenue. The purpose was to study the effect of the tax experiment on the steady state equilibrium of the economy, the expansion path of the economy, and welfare within the context of a neoclassical overlapping generations economy.

Output is produced via a constant-returns-to-scale technology according to $y_t = f(k_t)$, where y is output per worker and k is capital per worker. It is assumed that $f(k)$ is concave, twice continuously differentiable, montone-increasing, and satisfies the Inada conditions. Population grows at rate n. N_t identical agents are born at time t and live for two periods, young and old, and supply labor only when young. Labor is supplied in a perfectly inelastic fashion. Markets for capital, labor, and output are perfectly competitive in the sense that individuals take aggregate variables, prices, and government policy parameters as beyond their control.

The representative consumer's preferences are represented by a utility function of the form of (2.1) and her budget constraints are given by a version of (2.2):

$$w_t - c_{1t} - s_t = 0,$$

$$T_{t+1} + [1 + r_{t+1}(1 - t_{rt+1})]s_t - c_{2t} = 0,$$

where T is a lumpsum rebate of the tax revenue. The agent chooses consumption and saving to maximize lifetime utility subject to the budget constraints as before. The resulting saving function can be written as $S[w_t, T_{t+1}, r_{t+1}(1 - t_{rt+1})]$.

Profit maximizing firms choose capital per worker so that $r_t = f_k(k_t)$. Solving, we obtain the demand for capital per worker at time t, $k_t = K(r_t)$, where $dk_t/dr_t = K_r < 0$. The wage rate is given by $w_t = f(K(r_t)) - r_t f(K(r_t)) = W(r_t)$ in equilibrium, where $dw_t/dr_t = W_r = -k < 0$.

The equilibrium condition in the capital market is

$$S[W(r_t), T_{t+1}, r_{t+1}(1 - t_{rt+1})] = (1 + n)K(r_{t+1}); \tag{2.16}$$

that is, the supply of new capital per worker must equal the demand for it. Alternatively, since the total amount of the good available at time t is $k_t + y_t$ per young person and the total demand for it is $c_{1t} + c_{2t-1}/(1 + n) + (1 + n)k_{t+1}$ per young person, the resource constraint at time t is

$$k_t + y_t = c_{1t} + c_{2t-1}/(1 + n) + (1 + n)k_{t+1}.$$

If the government collects net revenue from the private sector and spends it, we would have to include government spending on the righthand side of the constraint. In a steady state we have

$$y = c_1 + c_2/(1 + n) + nk,$$

where nk is net investment.

The government collects revenue from the taxation of interest income and rebates it to the taxpayer in a non-distorting fashion in the same period. This eliminates any timing effects that might exist by holding the consumer's disposable income in each period constant. The government's budget constraint is

$$T_{t+1} = r_{t+1}t_{rt+1}S[W(r_t), T_{t+1}, r_{t+1}(1 - t_{rt+1})]. \tag{2.17}$$

The steady state conditions are

$$S[W(r), T, r(1 - t_r)] = (1 + n)K(r), \tag{2.18}$$

and

$$T = rt_r S[W(r), T, r(1 - t_r)]. \tag{2.19}$$

An equilibrium in the absence of tax policy is a sequence for the real interest rate, $\{r_t\}_{t=1}^{\infty}$, such that (2.16) holds when $T_t = t_{rt} = 0$ for all t. A steady state equilibrium in the absence of tax policy is a real interest rate r that satisfies (2.18) when $T = t_r = 0$. More generally, an equilibrium is an interest rate sequence $\{r_t\}_{t=1}^{\infty}$ and a sequence for tax policy, $\{t_{rt}, T_t\}_{t=1}^{\infty}$, such that (2.16) and (2.17) hold with equality, where the sequence $\{t_{rt}\}_{t=1}^{\infty}$ is treated as exogenous. A steady state equilibrium in the presence of tax policy is an interest rate and a tax policy that satisfy (2.18) and (2.19) where t_r is an exogenous variable.

In equilibrium, consumers choose their consumption and saving to maximize utility subject to their budget constraints, firms maximize profit in choosing how much capital per worker to use, the capital market clears, and the government's budget constraint is satisfied. It is imagined that the economy is in equilibrium and the government introduces the interest income tax with a rebate. The transfer or rebate is an endogenous variable that adjusts so the government's budget constraint holds with equality in equilibrium.

It is shown in the Appendix 2B that, if $S_r > 0$ and $(1 - t_r)S_r - kS_w - (1 + n)K_r > 0$, then the steady state equilibrium in the absence of the tax policy is locally stable. Furthermore, if c_1 and c_2 are both normal goods and gross substitutes, the equilibrium will be unique (see Appendix 2C).

In terms of the tax experiment, first consider the introduction of an interest income tax into an otherwise undistorted equilibrium according to $dt_r > 0$. Differentiate the government's budget constraint and evaluate at the initial no-tax equilibrium, $rsdt_r = dT$. Next, differentiate (2.18) and use $rsdt_r = dT$ from the government's budget constraint to obtain the following result:

$$dr/dt_r = (rS_r - rsS_T)/D = rS_{ru}/D, \qquad (2.20)$$

where $D = (1 - t_r)S_r - kS_w - (1 + n)K_r > 0$ and $S_{ru} > 0$ is the utility-constant response of saving to the interest rate. The second equality follows from use of the Slutsky equation, $S_r = S_{ru} + sS_T$.

Under our assumptions, it follows that the real interest rate is increasing in the interest income tax rate since saving is increasing in the interest rate when compensated. This is one of Diamond's main results. The intuition is that the interest income tax provides a disincentive to save and invest at the margin. As a result of this disincentive effect, the supply of savings decreases with the tax and the reduction in savings raises the real interest rate.

Also notice that the response of the capital stock and the wage are given by

$$dk/dt_r = K_r(dr/dt_r),$$
$$dw/dt_r = w_r(dr/dt_r).$$

It follows that both the capital stock per worker and the wage fall with the tax. This provides some theoretical support for the argument that cutting taxes on capital income may boost capital per worker and raise the real wage rate.

More generally, suppose the initial equilibrium is distorted by the interest income tax and consider a marginal increase in the tax rate coupled with a rebate of the revenue. Differentiate the steady state conditions:

$$Ddr + S_T dT = rS_r dt_r, \qquad (2.21)$$

$$\{t_r s + rt_r[(1 - t_r)S_r - kS_w]\}dr - (1 - rt_r S_T)dT = -(rs - r^2 t_r S_r)dt_r. \qquad (2.22)$$

Solving, we obtain the following responses:

$$dr/dt_r = rS_{ru}/\Delta, \qquad (2.23)$$

$$dT/dt_r = rs[D + t_r S_r(1 + rK_r/k)]/\Delta = rs[1 + t_r S_{ru}(1 + rK_r/k)/\Delta], \qquad (2.24)$$

where we have used the Slutsky equation in both equations to simplify and where $\Delta = D + t_r(1 + n)S_T(rK_r + k)$. We need to sign the term $rK_r + k$. Formally, its sign is ambiguous. However, if the first term dominates, it will be negative. For example, consider the Cobb–Douglas technology, $y = k^\alpha$, where $\alpha < 1$. Then $r = \alpha k^{\alpha-1}$, $K(r) = (r/\alpha)^{1/(\alpha-1)}$, $K_r(r) = [1/\alpha(\alpha - 1)](r/\alpha)^{(2-\alpha)/(\alpha-1)}$, and $rK_r + k = \alpha k/(\alpha - 1) < 0$.

First, notice that (2.23) and (2.24) collapse to our earlier result in (2.20), where (2.24) is given by $dT = rsdt_r$, when we evaluate (2.23) and (2.24) at $t_r = 0$. The additional terms appear in the denominators, $t_r(1 + n)S_T(rK_r + k)$, and as the second term in the numerator of (2.24), $t_r S_{ru}(1 + rK_r/k)$. Second, if $(rK_r + k) < 0$, then each denominator is positive since saving is decreasing in the tax rebate.

It follows from this that the real interest rate is once again increasing in the interest income tax rate. Furthermore, we can rule out the Laffer curve effect if

$$t_r S_{ru} > -\Delta/(1 + rK_r/k),$$

from (2.24), which can also be written as

$$(t_r/r_n)(r_n S_{ru}/s) = (t_r/r_n)\varepsilon_{ru} = -(1 + n)\Delta/(k + rK_r),$$

where $\varepsilon_{ru} = (r_n S_{ru}/s)$ is the compensated saving elasticity, and $r_n = r(1 - t_r)$ is the after-tax interest rate. If the lower bound condition on the response of saving to the interest rate multiplied by the net tax rate, t_r/r_n, holds, then the transfer is increasing in the tax rate.

Finally, we can ask how the policy affects utility. The indirect utility function in this model is

$$V = U(W(r) - s, T + [1 + r(1 - t_r)]s),$$

where s solves the consumer's decision problem. Differentiate,

$$dV/dt_r = U_2(dT/dt_r - rs + s(1 - t_r)dr/dt_r) + W_r U_1 dr/dt_r,$$

or

$$dV/U_2 dt_r = dT/dt_r - rs - [t_r + (r - n)(1 - t_r)]k dr/dt_r,$$

evaluated at the new equilibrium, where we have used the fact that $W_r = -k$ and the equilibrium condition, $s = (1 + n)k$. After substituting from (2.23) and (2.24), this becomes

$$dV/U_2 dt_r = (rkS_{ru}/\Delta)\{t_r[n(1 + rK_r/k) + rK_r/k] - (r - n)(1 - t_r)\}. \quad (2.25)$$

This derivative takes the sign of the expression in braces, and there are two terms in this expression. The first term, $t_r(n(1 + rK_r/k) + rK_r/k)$, captures the static efficiency effects of imposing a distorting tax on capital. Since $(1 + rK_r/k) < 0$ and $rK_r/k < 0$, it is negative. Increasing the distorting tax on capital at the margin reduces welfare, ceteris paribus.

The second term captures the dynamic efficiency effect. This involves a comparison between the expansion path of the competitive economy and the optimal expansion path. Consider a version of the steady state planning problem studied by Diamond. The social planner in a steady state chooses consumption and capital per worker to maximize $U(c_1, c_2)$ subject to the resource constraint $f(k) = c_1 + c_2/(1 + n) + nk$. It can be shown that the first-order conditions of this problem are $U_1/U_2 = 1 + n$ and $f_k(k^g) = n$. The first condition is Samuelson's (1958) "biological interest rate," while the second condition is the so-called "golden rule" of growth theory, where k^g is the golden rule capital per worker.

Diamond showed that the competitive economy need not be on the golden rule expansion path. Atomistic private agents may not save the right amount that allows the competitive economy to achieve the golden rule level of capital, k^g. They may under or over-accumulate capital. Indeed, it would be almost by accident if they accumulated just the right amount of capital in the aggregate. In particular, if private agents underaccumulate capital, $k^c < k^g$, then $f_k(k^c) = r > n = f_k(k^g)$ by the concavity of the technology, where k^c is capital per worker under competition. If the government introduces a capital income tax into such an economy, as studied above, then the economy will move further away from the golden rule and this will reduce welfare.

2.5. The savings elasticity controversy

In the mid to late 1970s, there was increasing evidence that the growth rate in the United States and other western European countries was slowing down, especially the growth rate of labor productivity. A number of industries in the United States, for example steel and autos, were threatened by foreign competition, and massive layoffs in those industries had begun. This was cause for great concern. Other countries like the United Kingdom and Italy experienced similar problems of declining industries and high unemployment in the 1970s. Later, in the 1980s, the savings rate in the United States fell dramatically and this exacerbated the problem of a slowing growth rate. The savings rate fell in most other European countries as well; however, it rebounded in the UK and the Scandinavian countries later in the decade.[7]

Many policy analysts in the 1970s and early 1980s advocated policies designed to increase savings and investment in the belief that this would increase productivity, raise the growth rate, and reduce inflationary pressures. Even though Feldstein's theoretical work provided several counterexamples to this policy prescription, such as the fact that a cut in the interest income tax might not raise savings, it is probably fair to say that reducing taxes on capital in order to boost productivity had become part of the conventional wisdom by the late 1970s. The focus of attention then shifted toward empirical work and, more specifically, toward work on the interest elasticity of saving. Early work tended to produce rather low estimates for this elasticity, typically in the neighborhood of 0.10–0.20, meaning that a decrease in the interest rate from 10 to 5 per cent would reduce savings by approximately 13 per cent if the elasticity were 0.20.[8] However, there were some estimates of the savings elasticity that were insignificantly different from zero.[9]

Typically, in this early literature aggregate consumption or saving was regressed on several variables including income or wealth, unemployment, and the interest rate. The time series data were transformed by taking natural logs and so the estimated coefficients in the resulting linear regression equation were interpreted as elasticities. In particular, if aggregate saving is regressed on the interest rate, among other variables, the resulting estimated coefficient on the interest rate variable is taken to be the elasticity of savings.

Boskin (1978), however, estimated an elasticity nearly twice the magnitude of earlier estimates. His result was quite controversial and started a debate over the magnitude of the elasticity of saving which is summarized in Table 2.1. He estimated an ad hoc consumption function and used an instrumental variables technique to control for the possible endogeneity of some of the regressors, such as income. The data used were annual time series observations for the United States for the period 1929–1969 omitting the war years. Boskin's estimated range for the savings elasticity was between 0.30 and 0.60, with the preferred estimate being 0.40, which was twice the magnitude anyone else had found using similar data. Furthermore, his preferred estimate of the savings elasticity implied that the taxation of capital income causes an *annual* excess burden of approximately $60 billion—an astonishing result, to say the least.[10]

The key to this large estimate is the interest rate variable used in the estimated regression equation. The theoretically preferred variable is the real, net-of-tax, interest rate. Unfortunately, this variable is not directly observed: it must be constructed, and a number of thorny measurement issues arise. First, which interest rate should be used? Clearly, the applied econometrician would like to use the rate people actually use in their own calculations because this is what generated the data in the first place. However, it is far from obvious which rate or rates people do actually use in a complicated economy with a proliferation of rates and potential market imperfections.

Second, the interest rate must be adjusted for taxes. Again, it is not immediately obvious how to do this when there is more than one tax rate and more

Table 2.1.   Results on the saving elasticity controversy

Analyst	Type of study	Result
Early work	Econometric	0.1–0.2
Boskin (1978)	Econometric	0.4
Howry and Hymans (1978)	Econometric	Close to 0.0
Summers (1981)	Simulation	3.0 or more
Evans (1983)	Simulation	0.3 or less

than one government, for example federal and local, imposing taxes on capital income.

Third, the interest rate must be adjusted for inflation; it is the real rate that is of importance for intertemporal decisionmaking. Which price index should be used to calculate the inflation rate? The recent controversy over the use of the Consumer Price Index for indexing government transfer payments in the United States makes this problem perhaps more important now than it was in the late 1970s.

Fourth, it is the *expected*, real, net-of-tax interest rate that belongs in the consumption or savings function equation. Calculating the expectations of the taxpayer and aggregating up to the economy level is a difficult task. To accomplish this, Boskin estimated the expected real interest rate using an autoregressive process, but he was not explicit about the actual details of his technique. Clearly, any technique used will be somewhat arbitrary and difficult to defend.

There are several other problems with the empirical analyses in the early literature. No adjustment was made for the demographics of the population. The age structure of the population and the rate at which it is growing will be important elements in determining the response of aggregate saving to a tax reform. Finally, the consumption function estimated is somewhat ad hoc; it was not derived from first principles. This makes it somewhat difficult to interpret the specific results because it is unclear what the parameters mean. This is an application of the so-called Lucas critique.[11]

Howry and Hymans (1978) put forth a loanable funds theory of saving and undertook a broad sensitivity analysis of Boskin's work. They could not replicate Boskin's main result. Dropping the observation for 1934, which appeared to be an outlier, dropping the years of the Great Depression, using the actual interest rate adjusted for inflation instead of Boskin's expected net interest rate series, and adding lagged unemployment typically led to an insignificant coefficient for the interest rate variable. This implies that the interest rate did not appear to affect consumption. More generally, they concluded that the interest rate has little or no discernible effect on consumption and hence on savings behavior. Furthermore, they argued that this might explain why savings in the United States has been relatively constant, at least from the late 1940s to the late 1970s, even though the interest rate has varied considerably during this era.

Of course, Howry and Hymans's work is subject to some of the same criticism that Boskin's work is subject to. For example, an adjustment for taxes imposed on capital should be made, but it is unclear how to do this correctly given the proliferation of tax rates. The upshot of their work, however, is that Boskin's result appears to be very sensitive to his assumptions; it is apparently not a very general result. Their own work tends to confirm the earlier results of a small interest elasticity.

In an important paper, Summers (1981) argued that wealth is related to the interest rate: the higher the interest rate, the lower the present value of future labor earnings and the lower the level of wealth will be. Using a two-period model where the agent works in the first period alone to study the capital income tax issue does not fully capture the influence of the interest rate on wealth. Furthermore, including wealth in a consumption function along with an interest rate variable, as Boskin did, would also tend to confound the different effects, according to Summers. The interest elasticity of savings, which takes into account the effect of the interest rate on wealth, could be much higher than previously thought. Using a calibrated computer simulation model, Summers simulates the model and calculates an interest elasticity an order of magnitude larger than Boskin's empirical estimates. If true, the welfare costs of taxing capital income would be much larger than anyone had previously thought.

Consider the two-period life cycle model studied earlier, but suppose that the consumer also receives labor income in the second period. Her two budget constraints are

$$w_1 - c_1 - s = 0$$

and

$$w_2 + (1 + r)s - c_2 = 0,$$

where w_j is labor earnings in period j. If $U = \ln(c_1) + \beta \ln(c_2)$, where $\beta = 1/(1 + \rho)$ and ρ is the rate of time preference, then it is straightforward to show that the consumption function is given by

$$c_1 = [1/(1 + \beta)]W, \tag{2.26}$$

where $W = (w_1 + Rw_2)$ is wealth, and savings is given by

$$s = w_1 - W/(1 + \beta). \tag{2.27}$$

If wealth is held constant, savings does not respond to the interest rate at all and the savings elasticity with respect to the interest rate is zero. However, it follows from the savings function that savings responds to the interest rate when wealth is not held constant, according to

$$ds/dr = (ds/dW)(dW/dr) = w_2 R^2/(1 + \beta) > 0. \tag{2.28}$$

Not only would the savings elasticity be positive in this case, it is also possible for it to be greater than 1 in magnitude! And it will also vary with income. In this example the savings elasticity is

$$\varepsilon = rR^2 w_2 / (\beta w_1 - Rw_2).$$

The denominator must be positive for savings to be positive. If the following condition holds, the elasticity is greater than one in magnitude:

$$w_2 / w_1 > (1 + r)(1 + rR) / (1 + \rho).$$

For example, interpreting the formula on an annual basis, suppose $r = 0.02, \rho = 0.01$; then this requires that $w_2 / w_1 > 1.029$. On the other hand, if $r = 0.025$ and $\rho = 0.01$, then $w_2 / w_1 > 1.039$. This requires the wage profile to increase by at least 3.9 per cent, which might be empirically unlikely if we interpret the inequality as involving an annual comparison. On the other hand, if we interpret the two-period example as one in which each period is twenty-five to thirty years long, a generation, then an annual interest rate of 2.5 per cent would have a doubling time of about one generation, or twenty-eight years. So if we set $r = 1$ in the two-period example and $\rho = 0.5$, then $w_2 / w_1 > 2$. Wages would have to at least double over a single generation in order for the condition to be satisfied. This seems empirically reasonable.

Summers used the CES utility function and derived a savings rate out of labor income that depends in a complicated fashion on the parameters of the model. He assumes that the consumer experiences a planning horizon of T years, where retirement occurs after $T' < T$ years, that capital markets function perfectly, and that labor supply is fixed. The population grows at rate 1.5 per cent per year and productivity grows at 2 per cent per year. The simulations of the partial equilibrium model strongly suggest that the savings elasticity is much larger than 1 in magnitude. In some of the simulations it is well over 3, an order of magnitude larger than the empirical estimates.

Next, Summers adds a Cobb–Douglas technology to the model and simulates the effects of several tax reforms on the steady state equilibrium assuming a log utility function. He also uses a value for the elasticity of substitution that yields a large savings elasticity when he simulates the general equilibrium model. His main result is that it is beneficial to switch to the wage tax or the consumption tax from a capital income tax and that the consumption tax is preferred to the wage tax in the sense that it yields a larger gain in welfare than switching to the wage tax. For example, a switch from a capital income tax to the consumption tax raises steady state welfare by 11.7 per cent of the consumer's initial lifetime income. In terms of US data, this would increase welfare by approximately $200 billion in 1980.

There are two reasons why the consumption tax dominates the wage tax in improving welfare under the simulated reform in Summers's model. First, the capital intensity of production is higher under the consumption tax reform. This raises the wage and hence consumption above the increase resulting from the wage tax reform because the economy moves closer to the golden rule level of capital under the consumption tax reform than under the wage tax reform. This is due mainly to the fact that under a wage tax the taxpayer pays the bulk of her taxes when she is working, whereas under a consumption tax the tax liability is more evenly spread out over the life cycle. Thus, under a consumption tax the taxpayer has to save more when working in order to pay her future tax than she does under the wage tax, so saving and the capital intensity of production is higher, as noted by Feldstein.

Second, the present value of the taxpayer's tax liability is lower under the consumption tax reform than under the wage tax reform. This occurs because those who are alive at the time of the transition will experience a heavier tax burden than those who are living in the new, post-reform steady state. Steady state welfare calculations may be a poor indicator of the true costs and benefits of a tax reform, however, as noted by Summers, although, in an earlier paper he showed the transition to be very rapid, meaning that only a few generations might be worse off under the proposed reform.

Evans (1983) criticized Summers's work on several grounds. In the first place, he argued that simulation models are useful tools for providing guidance but are not the same as doing careful empirical work; a key parameter like the interest elasticity of savings can be uncovered only through careful empirical analysis. Furthermore, Evans showed that the large interest elasticity that Summers calculated is not robust to small changes in the assumed parameters of the simulation model. For example, Evans showed that the larger the rate of time preference is, the lower the interest elasticity of savings will be. And the lower the population growth rate and the growth rate of the economy are, both empirically relevant for the 1970s and 1980s, the smaller the interest elasticity will be. For example, if both growth rates are 1 per cent rather than 1.5 and 2 per cent, respectively, and the intertemporal elasticity of substitution is $1/3$, then the interest elasticity of savings calculated by Evans is only 0.35 when the time preference rate is zero. This cannot be ruled out, given the range of empirical estimates cited by Evans. These savings elasticities are much closer to the empirical literature on the subject and are also slightly lower than Boskin's preferred estimate of 0.40, but they are an order of magnitude lower than Summers's result.

Third, Summers's calculation of the interest elasticity is partial equilibrium in nature: it does not include the feedback effect of greater savings on the interest rate. In a partial equilibrium, the capital stock and hence the wage rate and the gross interest rate may be taken as exogenous. This might be justified under a small country assumption where capital flows are beyond the local government's control. In that case it makes sense to calculate the interest elasticity of savings since the interest rate is exogenous. However, in a general equilibrium model an exogenous increase in the net interest rate—say, because the presumed exogenous interest income tax rate has fallen—will induce more savings. But the greater flow of savings this period will raise the capital stock next period and thus will reduce the interest rate next period. This will tend to reduce savings next period and thus to moderate the total increase in savings in response to the initial increase in the net interest rate. As a result, the general equilibrium elasticity will be smaller than the partial equilibrium elasticity. In defense of Summers, however, whether the general equilibrium calculation of Evans is more appropriate depends entirely on whether or not the economy is open to capital flows, and this is an empirical question. If the small economy assumption is appropriate, the interest rate and wage are fixed by exogenous influences and it is hard to see how increasing saving can improve welfare.

Fourth, Evans connects generations by cash bequests arising from altruism, thus making the consumer's horizon infinite. It is well known that the *partial* equilibrium elasticity of savings is infinite in this case. However, Evans shows that the *general* equilibrium elasticity for the parameters used by Summers yields an interest elasticity of only 1.33 when generations are connected by bequests.[12] Since this is an upper bound, Summers's assertion that the elasticity is greater than 2.00 is "out of the question."[13] Indeed, in general, Evans shows that the larger the bequest, the larger the saving rate and the wealth–income ratio, but the smaller the interest elasticity of savings. Under one plausible case, the interest elasticity is only 0.2 and in some cases it is even negative, for example -0.01.[14]

Of course, these extensions will substantially alter the calculation of the welfare gain to be had from the tax reforms considered by Summers. Evans simulates the tax reforms under two sets of assumptions: first, where there is a large elasticity of substitution in consumption and no bequests, and, second, where there is a small elasticity with significant bequests. In the former case the results are much as Summers had obtained; however, under the second set of assumptions the gain in consumption is much smaller. Under the first set of assumptions there is a gain of 67 per cent in consumption under a switch from capital income taxation to the consumption tax; under the second set of assumptions there is only a 2 per cent increase in consumption. And under the switch to a wage tax, consumption, wealth, and income fall under the second set of assumptions.

There are several other criticisms that may be relevant. First, it is not surprising that the switch to a consumption tax from a capital income tax yields such large gains in welfare in Summers's model because the consumption tax is non-distorting. In fact, if labor supply were endogenous, the consumption and wage tax alternatives would also distort the labor supply decision. It is not immediately obvious in that case whether the consumption tax would necessarily be superior to the capital income tax. In addition, there are other endogenous elements of "labor supply" that have not been incorporated into the model, for example human capital accumulation and retirement, both of which may respond to tax policy. Finally, in most countries social security is financed through a wage tax. Therefore, when Summers and Evans assume that the tax on the wage is only 20 per cent, this might significantly underestimate the total tax rate actually imposed on labor.

Whether or not a particular tax policy is superior to another tax policy is a difficult question to answer. We will probably never be able to calculate "the" optimal tax rates. What is of greater importance is the structure of the argument one can make in favor of one tax policy over another. For example, if after a tremendous amount of empirical research we could confidently conclude that labor supply, human capital accumulation, and retirement behavior are all exogenous, but that savings behavior is highly elastic, then we would be able to argue for the superiority of the consumption tax relative to the general income tax which includes a tax on savings income. The value of theoretical work is to point us in the right empirical direction in determining which parameters are important and which are not. In the next chapter we will study a class of overlapping generations models which strongly suggest that it is not the interest elasticity of saving that is of critical importance in determining whether or not we should tax capital income, but certain *labor supply elasticities*.

2.6. Conclusion

In this chapter we have studied the early literature on the taxation of capital and the consumption tax proposal. Early writers were concerned that people pay taxes on what they take out of society in consumption rather than on what they put into society in labor and capital investment. The main argument against a general income tax, though, was that such a tax taxes saving twice, once when the income is earned and a second time when the saving generates income.

Later analysts focused their attention on the efficiency aspects of taxing capital income. Feldstein's (1978a) paper on the welfare cost of capital income taxation was especially influential. He cleared up several misconceptions regarding the taxation of capital income that were prevalent at the time and calculated the welfare cost associated with capital income taxation. Applying a static formula, he calculated a significant gain in welfare from a shift away from a capital income tax toward a wage tax (see also Feldstein 1978b).

We also studied the incidence of the interest income tax in the overlapping generations framework due to Diamond. Diamond very carefully derived the result that an increase in the interest income tax rate induces a decrease in saving and capital accumulation and tends to raise the real rate of interest. He also calculated the welfare loss associated with the policy. A key element in the analysis is the possibility that the tax may move the competitive economy away from the optimal expansion path, further reducing welfare, in addition to the loss in static efficiency noted by Feldstein.

Feldstein's work led to a controversy over the interest elasticity of savings. The more responsive saving is to the net return, the larger the welfare cost associated with taxing capital. In particular, Boskin's empirical estimate was twice as large in magnitude as earlier estimates, implying an extraordinary welfare cost of taxing capital income. However, Howry and Hymans called into question the generality of his result in undertaking a sensitivity analysis of his work.

Summers provided further theoretical support for the notion that taxing capital income created a large excess burden. He argued that wealth depended on the present value of future earnings. A higher return on capital lowered this present value and hence wealth, thus creating a wealth effect on saving in addition to the direct effect involving the net return. This additional wealth effect is obscured in a two-period life cycle model where labor occurs only in the first period. His computer simulations in a more general T-period model implied an interest elasticity an order of magnitude larger than Boskin's empirical estimates. This significantly raised the welfare cost of taxing capital income.

However, Evans (1983) challenged that conclusion. He argued that Summers's result was sensitive to his assumptions about certain key parameters, such as the rate of time preference, the growth rate of the economy, and the growth rate of the population. Under a variety of alternative assumptions, the partial equilibrium elasticity is typically much smaller than that calculated by Summers. Evans also pointed out that in a general equilibrium the interest rate is endogenous. Strictly speaking, the *interest* elasticity of *savings* does not make sense in a general equilibrium model since both variables are endogenous. Evans calculated a long-run general equilibrium elasticity where the interest rate is endogenous of only 1.33 under Summers's assumptions in an infinite horizon model where the partial equilibrium elasticity is *infinite*. For other choices of the parameters, the general equilibrium elasticity is usually much smaller than this and much closer to the empirical estimates. This means that the gain to switching to the consumption tax may be much smaller than that calculated by either Boskin or Summers. However, this did not deter Feldstein (1989) from reaffirming his view that a switch to the consumption tax would improve matters for the US economy significantly.

APPENDIX 2A: COMPARATIVE STATICS

First consider the first-order condition when c_1 is chosen:

$$U_1[c_1, (w_n - q_1c_1)/q_2] - U_2[c_1, (w_n - q_1c_1)/q_2]q_1/q_2 = 0.$$

Totally differentiate the first-order condition to obtain

$$[U_{11} - 2(q_1/q_2)U_{12} + (q_1/q_2)^2 U_{22}]dc_1 + [U_{12} - (q_1/q_2)U_{22}](dw_n/q_2$$
$$-c_1 dq_1/q_2 - c_2 dq_2/q_2) - (U_2/q_2)dq_1 + (q_1/q_2)U_2 dq_2/q_2 = 0.$$

Solving we obtain the income effect:

$$dc_1/dw_n = -[U_{12} - (q_1/q_2)U_{22}](1/q_2)/[U_{11} - 2(q_1/q_2)U_{12} + (q_1/q_2)^2 U_{22}],$$

and the price effects:

$$dc_1/dq_1 = (dc_1/dq_1)_u - c_1(dc_1/dw_n),$$
$$dc_1/dq_2 = (dc_1/dq_2)_u - c_2(dc_1/dw_n),$$

where $[U_{11} - 2(q_1/q_2)U_{12} + (q_1/q_2)^2 U_{22}] < 0$. The compensated own price effect is

$$(dc_1/dq_1)_u = (U_2/q_2)/[U_{11} - 2(q_1/q_2)U_{12} + (q_1/q_2)^2 U_{22}] < 0,$$

and the compensated cross price effect is

$$(dc_1/dq_2)_u = -(q_1/q_2^2)U_2/[U_{11} - 2(q_1/q_2)U_{12} + (q_1/q_2)^2 U_{22}] > 0.$$

Next, consider the alternative of choosing savings instead of first-period consumption. The first-order condition of the consumer's decision problem can also be written in the following way when savings is chosen:

$$-U_1[w - s, T + (1 + r_n)s] + (1 + r_n)U_2[w - s, T + (1 + r_n)s] = 0,$$

when the consumer chooses saving, where we have substituted the budget constraints into the utility function.

Totally differentiate the above first-order condition and solve to obtain the uncompensated price effect,

$$S_r = ds/dr = -[U_2 - (U_{12} - (q_1/q_2)U_{22})]/[U_{11} - 2(q_1/q_2)U_{12} + (q_1/q_2)^2 U_{22}],$$

the compensated price effect,

$$S_{ru} = (ds/dr)_u = -U_2/[(U_{11} - 2(q_1/q_2)U_{12} + (q_1/q_2)^2 U_{22}] > 0,$$

and the income effect,

$$S_T = ds/dT = [U_{12} - (q_1/q_2)U_{22}]/[U_{11} - 2(q_1/q_2)U_{12} + (q_1/q_2)^2 U_{22}].$$

It follows that $S_r = S_{ru} + sS_T$ is a version of the Slutsky equation.

APPENDIX 2B: STABILITY

To investigate the stability of the equilibrium, notice that the real interest rate is the only dynamic variable in the model. Totally differentiate equation (2.16), holding tax policy constant:

$$dr_{t+1}/dr_t = -kS_w/[(1 - t_r)S_r - (1 + n)K_r],$$

where $S_r = -q_2 S_2$ and where we have used $w_r = -k$. We require $|dr_{t+1}/dr_t| \leq 1$ in the neighborhood of a steady state equilibrium for stability. If $S_r > 0$, a sufficient condition for stability is that $D = (1 - t_r)S_r - kS_w - (1 + n)K_r > 0$.

APPENDIX 2C: UNIQUENESS

Write the equilibrium condition in the absence of tax policy as

$$(1 + n)k_{t+1} = S[f(k_t) - k_t f_k(k_t), f_k(k_{t+1})],$$

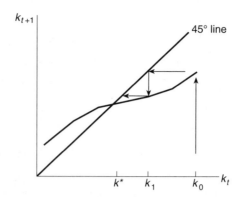

Figure 2.1.   Steady state equilibrium

where we have substituted $w_t = f(k_t) - k_t f_k(k_t)$ and $r_{t+1} = f_k(k_{t+1})$, and solve the equilibrium condition $k_{t+1} = A(k_t)$. Clearly, $k_{t+1} = 0$ when $k_t = 0$, so the trivial equilibrium exists, $0 = A(0)$. Differentiate the equilibrium condition, $dk_{t+1}/dk_t = A_k$, where $A_k = -kf_{kk}S_w/(1 + n - S_r f_{kk})$. If S_r, $S_w > 0$ and $f_{kk} < 0$ on the domain, then $0 < dk_{t+1}/dk_t$. If $A_k > 1$ for $k < \underline{z}$ and $A_k < 1$ for $k > \underline{z}$, an equilibrium will exist by the continuity of A. Furthermore, if A is monotone, $A_k(0) > 1$, and $A_k < 1$ at a steady state equilibrium $k > 0$, then the steady state equilibrium will be asymptotically stable and unique (see Azariadis 1993).

   An example of a unique, stable equilibrium is depicted in Figure 2.1. Suppose the initial capital stock is greater than the steady state level of capital, $k_0 > k^*$. The economy will follow a path such as the one depicted until the steady state is reached asymptotically.

NOTES TO CHAPTER 2

1. See also Hobbes, *Leviathan* (1985, chapter 30). This particular statement appears to confuse two issues. The first issue has to do with imposing taxation on what someone puts into society (labor) as opposed to what someone takes out (consumption). The second issue has to do with the labor–leisure tradeoff in comparing one worker who "laboureth much" with another worker who lives "idely." Certainly, it is possible for one who lives "idely" to spare "the fruits of his labour," and for one who "laboureth much" to "spendith all he gets."
2. See Kaldor (1955, page 12).
3. For example, housing services are not taxed under most income taxes even though homeowners receive implicit rents. It follows that people will hold more of their portfolio in housing than would otherwise be the case, and this may have a detrimental effect on the economy's growth rate.
4. The utility function is a member of the class of C2 functions so it is twice continuously differentiable, quasi-concave, and monotonically increasing in both its arguments.
5. Legend has it that in the late 1970s Arthur Laffer drew an inverted U-shaped curve that purportedly related tax revenue (on the vertical axis) to the tax rate (on the

horizontal axis) on a cocktail napkin in a restaurant at lunch with several congressmen. Laffer was trying to convince the congressmen that the same amount of tax revenue could be generated with a lower tax rate. The argument was that a lower tax rate would spur greater work effort, saving, and investment; this would increase output and income as a result, and income tax revenue would increase. This argument formed the basis of the "supply side theory" of tax cuts, although the argument was not original to Laffer. The inverted U-shaped curve has since become known as the "Laffer curve." There is little empirical support for it; tax rate cuts usually lead to a loss of revenue, as occurred in the United States after the massive tax cut of 1981. See Feldstein (1986) for a critique of supply side economic theory and evidence.

6. For early work in this regard, see Feldstein (1974a, b).
7. See the survey paper on the consumption function by Muellbauer and Lattimore (1995).
8. See the table in Atkinson and Stiglitz (1980, page 93).
9. See Blinder (1975).
10. See Boskin (1978, page S19).
11. There are a variety of other problems associated with the estimation technique used by Boskin that were not known at the time. These mainly have to do with the time series properties of the data. For example, it is now known that most of the data used by Boskin contain unit roots. This could mean that Boskin's results are entirely spurious.
12. In calculating the general equilibrium elasticity, Evans assumes the interest income tax is endogenous and that there is a surprising change in the tax rate. He then calculates the interest elasticity in the long run to this exogenous change in the net interest rate. Of course, the gross interest rate is equal to the marginal product of capital in a competitive general equilibrium and is, therefore, fully endogenous. It would not make sense to ask what the savings response is to the gross interest rate in a general equilibrium, since both variables are endogenous at the aggregate level in equilibrium, even though the individual agent takes the gross interest rate as exogenous to her decisions.
13. See Evans (1983, page 404).
14. This is somewhat ironic because, in another paper with Kotlikoff published the same year, Kotlikoff and Summers (1981) argued that most wealth in the United States was generated by bequests. According to Evans, this would dramatically reduce the interest elasticity of savings. Of course, whether bequests are chosen optimally or occur because of the uncertainty associated with the length of life is still an open empirical question.

3

At First Look at the Optimal Taxation of Labor and Capital

3.1. Introduction

We will begin this chapter by studying the optimal taxation of labor and capital income in a representative agent overlapping generations model, following the work of Atkinson and Sandmo (1980), King (1980), and Park (1992). As mentioned in the last chapter, the interest elasticity of savings will not be the key parameter in determining whether or not capital income should be taxed. Instead, it will be several labor supply parameters that are of greater importance in this regard when equity is ignored and certain covariances between the taste for consumption and the agent's lifetime endowment of disposable income when heterogeneity and equity are taken into account. In general, it will be suboptimal to exempt capital income from taxation. However, under some settings of the key parameters it may actually be optimal to subsidize capital accumulation.

Second, we will present further evidence of the deadweight loss associated with capital income, as derived by Chamley (1981) in a dynamic Ramsey model with an infinite horizon. He calculates a consumption equivalent excess burden of capital income taxation that is about 3.2 per cent of consumption and approximately 26 per cent of the revenue collected. Interestingly enough, it is not the intertemporal elasticity of substitution in consumption that is important in determining this result, but the elasticity of substitution between labor and capital in the technology. We also discuss the important paper by Judd (1987). Using a model similar to Chamley but extended to include wage taxation and an investment tax credit, Judd derived a much larger welfare cost associated with the taxation of capital income. He also showed that a move toward greater wage taxation coupled with an investment tax credit is welfare improving.

Next, we will discuss the empirical work on savings and labor supply. This is of some importance since the optimal tax rates will be very sensitive to the behavioral parameters of the model. First, there is some controversy over the responsiveness of savings to the important variables in the theoretical model, such as the interest rate. Second, labor supply tends to be highly inelastic. It was once thought that female labor supply was more wage elastic than male labor supply. However, more recent work by Mroz (1987) indicated that the difference in results across studies of female labor supply is due mainly to variations in the data sets and statistical techniques used. When these variations are held constant, Mroz finds that female labor supply is just as inelastic as male labor supply.

Finally, we also discuss the computer simulation models that have been used to study tax policy. Analytical models can become difficult to manipulate. The literature might tend to focus attention on rather simple models as a result. However, computers can be programmed to run countless simulations that can usefully point out important parameters and behavior for further study. Functional forms and certain key behavioral parameters must be chosen and then the resulting model can be simulated. Much of the work done in the 1980s provided strong support for the reform of switching to the consumption tax on efficiency grounds.

The chapter is organized in the following way. We will first look at a simple static model of optimal taxation that is standard in the literature to see what tools are employed and to gain some intuition behind the results in the next section. This leads to the famous Ramsey rule of optimal tax theory. The deadweight loss of the tax system under this rule is carefully balanced across markets so that when the optimal commodity tax system is introduced the proportionate reduction in demand is constant across markets. In some cases the results of the static literature carry over directly to a dynamic model. However, in other cases the interpretation does not carry over. We study the optimal taxation of capital and labor in an overlapping generations model in Section 3.3. Section 3.4 describes Chamley and Judd's welfare cost calculations. Section 3.5 discusses the empirical work on savings and labor supply. Section 3.6 describes the computer simulation literature, and Section 3.7 concludes the chapter.

3.2. Basic principles of optimal tax theory

Consider a static model where there are n private goods produced by labor according to a linear technology. The linearity assumption serves to fix the producer prices of the outputs, $p = (p_1, p_2, \ldots p_n)'$. This assumption is innocuous; it can be replaced by assuming constant returns to scale without affecting the results.

There is one consumer who chooses labor supply and demand for the n goods to maximize a well defined utility function $U(x, 1 - L)$, where $x = (x_1, x_2, \ldots, x_n)'$ is the demand vector, $1 - L$ is leisure, and L is labor supply, subject to a budget constraint. The utility function is twice continuously differentiable, quasi-concave, and monotone increasing. The budget constraint is $wL = q \cdot x = \sum_j q_j x_j$, where $q_j = p_j + \tau_j$ is the consumer price, τ_j is the tax rate, and $w = 1$ is the wage rate. The solution to the decision problem is a labor supply function and the demand vector, $L(w, q)$ and $x(w, q)$, respectively. The indirect utility function is defined as

$$v(w, q) = U(x(w, q), 1 - L(w, q)).$$

It has the following derivative properties: $\partial v/\partial w = v_w = \lambda L$ and $\partial_v/\partial q_i = -\lambda x_i$, where $\partial_v/\partial I = \lambda$ is the marginal utility of income evaluated at $I = 0$. The Slutsky equation is $x_{ij} = \partial x_i/\partial q_j = s_{ij} - x_j x_{iI}$, where $s_{ij} = (\partial x_i/\partial q_j)_u$ is the compensated, or utility constant, price effect, and $x_{iI} = \partial x_i/\partial I$ is an income effect evaluated at $I = 0$.

The government wishes to raise Re in revenue and confronts the following government budget constraint:

$$\sum_j \tau_j x_j \geq Re, \tag{3.1}$$

which will hold with equality in equilibrium. It chooses tax rates to maximize a social welfare function, represented by the consumer's utility function, subject to (3.1) at equality. The government is constrained to choosing commodity tax rates in the classic optimal tax exercise and cannot tax leisure or labor income. In the representative agent economy, the social welfare function is the utility function of the representative consumer.

The first-order condition of the government's decision problem is

$$-\lambda x_i + \alpha x_i + \alpha \sum_j \tau_j x_{ji} = 0, \tag{3.2}$$

where α is the Lagrange multiplier for (3.1). Following Diamond (1975), we can define the social marginal utility of income as

$$\mu = \lambda + \alpha \sum_j \tau_j x_{jI}. \tag{3.3}$$

Imagine the consumer receives an extra unit of income. The value the consumer places on the extra unit of income is λ. However, the receipt of the income will alter the demand for taxed commodities and hence tax revenue according to $\sum_j \tau_j x_{jI}$, and $\alpha \sum_j \tau_j x_{jI}$ is the social value of the change in tax revenue. Thus, μ is the social marginal utility of lumpsum income. Using (3.3) in (3.2), we obtain, upon rearranging,

$$\left(\sum_j \tau_j s_{ij}\right)/x_i = (\mu - \alpha)/\alpha, \tag{3.4}$$

where we have used the symmetry of the Slutsky matrix. This is the *Ramsey rule* of static optimal tax theory.

Following Samuelson (1986), we can interpret this formula in the following way. The compensated demand function is $x_i(w, q, u)$. Take a Taylor's series expansion of the compensated demand function to obtain

$$\Delta x_i = x_i(w, q, u) - x_i(w, p, u) \cong \sum_j \tau_j s_{ij}, \tag{3.5}$$

where higher order terms have been omitted. Combining (3.4) and (3.5),

$$\Delta x_i/x_i \cong (\mu - \alpha)/\alpha. \tag{3.6}$$

It is approximately true for small taxes that the proportionate decrease in demand should be constant across taxed goods since the righthand side of (3.6) does not depend on i.

There are several special cases of interest that help in interpreting the Ramsey rule.[1] For example, suppose $x_{ij} = 0$ for $i \neq j$. Then (3.4) becomes

$$\tau_i = \phi x_i / x_{ii},$$

where $\phi = (\lambda - \alpha)/\alpha$. This is the famous inverse elasticity rule. Thus, the greater the price elasticity of demand for a good, ceteris paribus, the lower the optimal tax rate should be. It also follows from this that

$$\theta_i / \theta_j = \zeta_j / \zeta_i,$$

where $\theta_k = \tau_k / q_k$ is the tax rate expressed as a percentage of the consumer price and $\zeta_k = -x_k / q_k x_{kk}$ is the uncompensated own price elasticity of demand. The tax rate expressed as a percentage of the consumer price for good i is higher than the tax rate for good j expressed the same way if the uncompensated own price elasticity of demand for good j is greater than for good i.

Finally, notice that when there are two taxed goods (3.4) can be written as

$$\sum_j \theta_j \sigma_{1j} = (\mu - \alpha)/\alpha,$$
$$\sum_j \theta_j \sigma_{2j} = (\mu - \alpha)/\alpha,$$

where $\sigma_{ij} = (q_i / x_j)(dx_i / dq_j)_u$ the compensated elasticity. Collapsing the last two equations, we obtain the following formula:[2]

$$\theta_1 / \theta_2 = (\sigma_{11} + \sigma_{22} + \sigma_{1L})/(\sigma_{11} + \sigma_{22} + \sigma_{2L}).$$

Thus, $\theta_1 > \theta_2$ if $\sigma_{2L} > \sigma_{1L}$. From this it follows that we should tax goods that are more complementary to leisure at a higher rate than goods that are not. Taxing goods that are complementary to leisure is an indirect way of taxing leisure.

Following Atkinson and Stiglitz (1972), we can apply these results to a life cycle consumer. Suppose the individual consumes x_t in period t, experiences an n-period horizon and so consumes n "commodities," works only in the first period, and confronts a perfect capital market. They showed that, if the utility function is additively separable and homothetic, that is if income elasticities are unity, then the optimal tax is a flat-rate consumption tax; it is suboptimal to tax capital income. More generally, the tax on consumption at later dates may not optimally be the same as the tax on consumption at earlier dates, thus implying that a subsidy or tax on capital income may be part of the optimal tax structure.

The static optimal tax problem can be altered and extended in numerous ways. For example, heterogeneity and a concern for equity, untaxed commodities, and pre-existing distortions such as externalities have been included. In the next section we will apply these methods to the optimal tax problem in a dynamic setting where capital is being accumulated over time and the economy need not evolve along the optimal growth path.

3.3. Optimal taxation in the overlapping generations model

We will follow the important work of Atkinson and Sandmo (1980) and King (1980) on optimal taxation in an overlapping generations economy in this section. Consider an overlapping generations economy that lasts forever. N_t identical agents are born at time t and population grows at rate n. Each agent lives for two periods, supplying labor (L_t) in the first period and being exogenously retired in the second period. The representative agent's preferences in the tth generation depend on consumption in both periods, c_{1t} and c_{2t}, and leisure in the first period, $h_t = 1 - L_t$, according to

$$U(c_{1t}, h_t, c_{2t}).$$

A special case of this is where the utility function is time-separable. In that case utility is represented by $U(c_{1t}, 1 - L_t) + \beta U(c_{2t})$, where $\beta = 1/(1 + \rho)$ is the discount factor and ρ is the rate of time preference. We will assume that the utility function satisfies the usual assumptions. The agent's wealth constraint is

$$w_{nt} L_t = c_{1t} + R_{nt+1} c_{2t},$$

where $w_n = w(1 - t_w)$ is the net wage and $R_n = 1/[1 + r(1 - t_r)]$ is the net "price" of second-period consumption, as in the last chapter.

The agent's decision problem is to choose consumption and labor supply to maximize lifetime utility subject to the wealth constraint. The first-order conditions are

$$U_1(c_1, h, c_2)/U_2(c_1, h, c_2) = 1 + r(1 - t_r),$$

$$U_h(c_1, h, c_2)/U_2(c_1, h, c_2) = w(1 - t_w),$$

which are similar in spirit to the conditions presented in Section 1.4, where $U_1 = \partial U/\partial c_1$, $U_2 = \partial U/\partial c_2$, and $U_h = \partial U/\partial h$ is the marginal utility of leisure, and where we have left the time subscripts off for simplicity.

In the special case where the utility function is additively separable, the first-order condition governing the intertemporal consumption decision is

$$U_1(c_1)/U_2(c_2) = \beta[1 + r(1 - t_r)].$$

It follows immediately from this that the consumption profile is flat; that is, $c_1 = c_2$, if $\beta[1 + r(1 - t_r)] = 1$ or $r(1 - t_r) = \rho$. In this case the competitive economy will be undercapitalized relative to the optimal growth path if the real interest rate reflects the marginal product of capital per worker and the capital income tax rate is positive; that is, $r > \rho$ if $t_r > 0$. However, we tend to notice that consumption profiles increase over the life cycle. A rising consumption profile is consistent with $r(1 - t_r) > \rho$ and the competitive economy will still be undercapitalized relative to the optimal growth path if the tax on capital income is non-negative. Indeed, this is overly strong, since $r > \rho$ can be true even if $t_r < 0$ and small enough in magnitude so that $r(1 - t_r) > \rho$. So a flat or rising consumption profile is consistent with the competitive economy being undercapitalized relative to the optimal growth path in the special case of an additively separable utility function.

The solution to the consumer's decision problem is a consumption function and a labor supply function that depend on the net prices w_n and R_n,

$$c_{1t} = C^1(w_{nt}, R_{nt+1}) \quad \text{and} \quad L_t = L(w_{nt}, R_{nt+1}). \tag{3.7}$$

It follows that life cycle saving can be defined as

$$S(w_{nt}, R_{nt+1}) = w_n L(w_{nt}, R_{nt+1}) - C^1(w_{nt}, R_{nt+1}). \tag{3.8}$$

Let S_w and S_R denote the derivatives with respect to the two arguments, respectively. The response of savings to the net prices is generally ambiguous. However, it is most likely the case that $S_w > 0$ and $S_R < 0$. (see Section 2.3). Similarly, second-period consumption is given by

$$C^2(w_{nt}, R_{nt+1}) = [w_{nt} L(w_{nt}, R_{nt+1}) - C^1(w_{nt}, R_{nt+1})]/R_{nt+1}. \tag{3.9}$$

Let C_w^2 and C_R^2 denote its derivatives. Again, the derivatives are ambiguous. However, $C_w^2 > 0$ and $C_R^2 < 0$ seem reasonable. An increase in the wage will most likely cause labor supply and hence labor earnings to increase, and most likely some of this will be saved.

We can define the indirect utility function for the representative consumer in several equivalent ways. One convenient way is as follows:

$$V(w_n, R_n) = U(C^1(w_n, R_n), 1 - L(w_n, R_n)) + \beta U((w_n L(w_n, R_n) - C^1(w_n, R_n))/R_n).$$

Its derivative properties are given by the following results:

$$V_w = \partial V/\partial w_n = \beta U_2 L/R_n = U_1 L = \lambda L, \tag{3.10a}$$
$$V_R = \partial V/\partial R_n = -\beta U_2(R_n)^{-2}s = -\beta U_2(R_n)^{-1}c_2 = -\lambda c_2, \tag{3.10b}$$

where λ is the marginal utility of wealth.

The government lives for ever and is entirely benevolent. The classic problem for the government is to choose its stock of debt and tax policy for each period of its horizon at the beginning of its planning horizon. As time proceeds the government is absolutely committed to its optimal policy; it does not reoptimize once the horizon has begun, but simply implements the rule it knew was optimal at the beginning of its planning horizon. This is known as the *open loop* decision problem. We will discuss the closed loop policy game at length in Chapter 6.

Following Arrow and Kurz (1970), we can adjust the social welfare function to take a growing population into account. The government's objective function for this problem is

$$\sum_{t=1}^{\infty} \beta^{*t-1} V(w_{nt}, R_{nt+1}), \qquad (3.11)$$

where we have normalized on the first young generation by setting $N_1 = 1$ and where $\beta^* = (1+n)/(1+\rho) = (1+n)\beta$ is the social discount factor, $\beta = 1/(1+\rho)$, and ρ is the representative agent's rate of time preference.[3] We will assume $\rho > n$. As it turns out, any constant discount factor that is less than one in magnitude is admissible since it yields an objective function that is bounded.

The government chooses a tax policy for each generation, and hence a sequence for tax rates, and issues debt that matures in one period. The use of debt will allow us to set a benchmark that is useful for comparative purposes. Let B_t be the stock of debt that comes due at time t. Debt pays the competitive interest rate. The government's budget constraint is

$$w_t t_{wt} L_t N_t + r_t t_{rt} s_t N_{t-1} + B_{t+1} = G_t + (1+r_t)B_t, \qquad (3.12)$$

where G_t is government spending at time t. It is typically assumed in the optimal tax literature that government spending does not directly affect the technology or preferences of the agents in the model. We can assume, for example, that the government finances a pure public good that enters either the technology or the utility function of the representative agents in a separable manner. In that case government spending will not enter the consumption or saving functions, or the demand for capital per worker as a separate argument.

The aggregate resource constraint for the economy at time t is given by

$$F(K_t, Z_t) + K_t - K_{t+1} - N_t c_{1t} - N_{t-1} c_{2t-1} - G_t \geq 0,$$

where $Z_t = N_t L_t$ is aggregate labor supply, and K_t is capital available at time t. In per capita terms, we can write this as

$$F(k_t, L_t) + k_t - (1+n)k_{t+1} - c_{1t} - c_{2t-1}/(1+n) - g_t \geq 0, \qquad (3.13)$$

where g is per capita government spending. The equilibrium condition in the capital market for the economy is $B_{t+1} + K_{t+1} = N_t s_t$ or

$$(1+n)(b_{t+1} + k_{t+1}) = s_t = w_{nt} L_t - c_{1t}. \qquad (3.14)$$

It is convenient to rewrite the government's control problem so that it chooses (w_{nt}, R_{nt+1}) instead of the tax rates directly. To this end, substitute the capital market equilibrium condition (3.14) into the taxpayer's first-period budget constraint for s_t and substitute the resulting equation into the resource constraint (3.13) to obtain

$$F(k_t, L(w_{nt}, R_{nt+1})) + k_t - w_{nt} L(w_{nt}, R_{nt+1})$$
$$- C^2(w_{nt-1}, R_{nt})/(1+n) - g_t + (1+n)b_{t+1} = 0. \qquad (3.15)$$

Next, substitute the taxpayer's wealth constraint into (3.13) to obtain

$$F(k_t, L(w_{nt}, R_{nt+1})) + k_t - (1+n)k_{t+1} - w_{nt}L(w_{nt}, R_{nt+1})$$
$$+ R_{nt+1}C^2(w_{nt}, R_{nt+1}) - C^2(w_{nt-1}, R_{nt})/(1+n) - g_t = 0. \qquad (3.16)$$

Equations (3.15) and (3.16) represent the resource constraint and the government's budget constraint, respectively.

The government chooses the sequence $\{w_{nt}, R_{nt+1}\}$ to maximize (3.11) subject to (3.15) and (3.16), taking k_1 and b_1 as given. First, consider the condition governing the optimal choice of government debt and the equation governing the state variable, capital, respectively,

$$[\beta(1+n)]^{t-1}\alpha_t(1+n) \geq 0, \qquad (3.17)$$
$$-[(\beta(1+n)]^{t-1}(1+n)\gamma_t + [\beta(1+n)]^t(\alpha_{t+1} + \gamma_{t+1})(1+r_{t+1}) = 0, \quad (3.18)$$

where α is the multiplier for (3.15) and γ is the multiplier for (3.16). If the government can choose the stock of debt optimally, then (3.17) implies $\alpha_t = 0$ for all $t \geq 1$. In a steady state, (3.18) becomes

$$\gamma = \beta(1+r)(\alpha + \gamma). \qquad (3.18')$$

Since $\alpha = 0$ when debt can be chosen optimally, it follows immediately from (3.18') that in a steady state

$$r = F_k = \rho, \qquad (3.19)$$

when debt policy is chosen optimally. Equation (3.19) characterizes the optimal growth path in this model.

Next, consider the government's choice of w_{nt} and R_{nt+1}. The first-order conditions in a steady state are given by

$$(\lambda - \pi)L + \pi w t_w L_w + (\gamma R_n - \beta\pi)C_w^2 = 0, \qquad (3.20)$$
$$-(\lambda - \pi)c_2 + \pi w t_w L_R + (\gamma R_n - \beta\pi)C_R^2 - \alpha c_2 = 0, \qquad (3.21)$$

where we have used the definition $\pi = \alpha + \gamma$. Using the Slutsky equation for the price derivatives in (3.20) and (3.21), symmetry in the Slutsky matrix, equation (3.18'), and the collapsing the resulting two equations to one, we obtain the following formula that necessarily must hold at the optimum,

$$\phi_w(\sigma_{ww} - \sigma_{Rw}) + (F_k - \rho)R = \phi_r(\sigma_{wR} - \sigma_{RR}), \qquad (3.22)$$

where $\phi_w = t_w/(1 - t_w)$, $\phi_r = r\,t_r\beta$, and where σ_{ij} are the compensated elasticities, e.g., $\sigma_{RR} = (R_n/c_2)(dc_2/dR_n)_u < 0$, $\sigma_{ww} = (w_n/L)(dL/dw_n)_u > 0$, $\sigma_{Rw} = (w_n/c_2)(dc_2/dw_n)_u$, and so on. Equation (3.22) provides us with information regarding the relative tax rates.

The method used to derive (3.22) is a direct application of the technique studied in the last section. However, there is an additional term not accounted for in the static model used in the last section: the term $(F_k - \rho)R$ involves a comparison of the position of the economy under competition to that on the optimal growth path. This term captures a *dynamic efficiency effect* that does not exist in a static model. Thus, the interpretation of the relative taxes embodied in (3.22) can differ from the interpretation of the relative tax rates in the classic static model.

First, consider the case where the stock of government debt can be chosen optimally. Then $\alpha = 0$ in the steady state and we obtain a version of the classic Ramsey rule:

$$\phi_w(\sigma_{ww} - \sigma_{Rw}) = \phi_r(\sigma_{wR} - \sigma_{RR}). \qquad (3.22')$$

It follows that, if either $\sigma_{wR} = \sigma_{RR}$, or $\sigma_{wR} = \sigma_{RR} = 0$, it is optimal to tax interest income and not wage income. On the other hand, a wage tax alone is optimal if either $\sigma_{Rw} = \sigma_{ww} = 0$, or if $\sigma_{Rw} = \sigma_{ww}$.[4] In general, neither special case will hold and it will be optimal to tax both wage and interest income at different rates. Clearly, the actual optimal tax rates will be highly sensitive to the estimated compensated elasticities.

It is interesting to note that the optimality of the capital income tax depends on the compensated *wage* elasticities and not on the interest elasticity of saving. This is one of the more interesting results obtained by Atkinson and Sandmo (1980) and King (1980). For this question the interest elasticity of savings controversy is not relevant, at least not in the context of this particular model. Indeed, in a formal sense, the saving elasticity does not even enter the optimal tax formula at all: it is the elasticity of second-period consumption with respect to the price of second-period consumption that enters the formula, as suggested by Feldstein (1978a, b).

However, Batina (1990a) has argued that it is unrealistic to assume that the government can perfectly control the economy by choosing the stock of debt to maintain the economy on the optimal growth path. Therefore, we should not rule out the case where debt policy cannot be chosen optimally. In that case, the real interest rate will generally differ from the social rate of time preference in this model and this will affect the choice of the optimal tax policy.

If debt policy cannot be chosen optimally, then $r > \rho$ implies that the tax on capital income will be higher than would otherwise have been the case, ceteris paribus, from (3.22). A higher tax on capital causes the taxpayer to increase her savings to pay her future tax liability. This raises the capital intensity of production and shifts the economy closer to the optimal expansion path. Of course, the opposite will be true if $\rho > r$. When the economy is overcapitalized relative to the optimal growth path, it is optimal to tax capital at a lower rate than would otherwise have been the case. The intuition is that a lower tax rate on capital income reduces the consumer's future tax burden and induces the consumer to save less. It is even possible for a subsidy on capital to be optimal when $\rho > r$ since this would reduce capital accumulation and move the economy closer to the optimal growth path. This is a *tax timing effect*: receiving a subsidy tied to capital accumulation later in life reduces the incentive to save when young.[5]

Consider the following Cobb–Douglas example due to Atkinson and Sandmo (1980). Suppose preferences are given by

$$U = a_1 \ln (c_1) + a_2 \ln (c_2) + a_3 \ln (1 - L),$$

where $0 < a_j < 1$ and $\sum a_j = 1$ for simplicity. It is straightforward to show that the uncompensated demand and supply functions are given by

$$c_1 = a_1 w (1 - t_w), \quad c_2 = a_2 w (1 - t_w)[1 + r(1 - t_r)], \quad L = 1 - a_3.$$

It can also be shown that the compensated elasticities are given by $\sigma_{ww} = a_3 = \sigma_{Rw}$ and $\sigma_{RR} = a_2(1 - a_2)$. It follows that the tax on capital is zero according to (3.22) if the economy is on the optimal growth path. It also follows that life cycle saving is given by $s = a_2 w(1 - t_w)$. Hence, $ds/dr_n = 0$ and the uncompensated interest elasticity of savings is zero! So, even though the uncompensated saving elasticity, about which there was so much controversy, is zero, it is still suboptimal to tax capital income in this case.

Of course, if the economy is undercapitalized relative to the optimal growth path, then (3.22) will still imply that capital income should be taxed. The reason is again due to a timing effect; a tax on interest income induces the taxpayer to save more to pay her future tax liability, and capital accumulation increases as a result. So, ironically, it is still optimal to tax capital income even when saving is unresponsive to the after-tax real interest rate, since people will save more now to pay their future tax liability.

Another comment is in order. King (1980) pointed out explicitly that an empirical researcher who estimates a Cobb–Douglas model of life cycle saving behavior will be unable to shed light on the optimal tax structure. One cannot estimate the elasticities using the Cobb–Douglas functional form, substitute into the model, and "discover" which tax system is optimal. This is so because the Cobb–Douglas form implies that the consumption tax is optimal before the estimation is even undertaken.

There does not seem to be a general presumption that the best tax system is one that exempts capital income. Indeed, suppose $\sigma_{ww} = \sigma_{Rw}$ and $\sigma_{wR} - \sigma_{RR} = 1$, a reasonable estimate, as noted by King. Equation (3.22) becomes

$$t_r = (1 - \rho/r)(1 + \rho)/(1 + r),$$

in the absence of an optimal debt policy. For example, if $r = 1$ and $\rho = 0.9$, the optimal relative tax rate on capital income is only 9.5 per cent. If $r = 1$ and $\rho = 0.5$, the optimal relative tax on capital is 37.5 per cent. If $\rho = 0.25$ instead, then the optimal relative tax rate on capital is about 47 per cent.

How can we reconcile these results with the ostensibly large gain in welfare to be had if the capital income tax were to be eliminated? For example, Boskin

(1978) calculated the annual welfare cost of taxing capital at $60 billion with a present value of over $1 trillion. This is consistent with the calculations made by Feldstein and Summers, as we have seen in earlier chapters. The answer lies in how these studies treat labor supply. Boskin, for example, calculated the welfare gain from replacing the capital income tax in the United States with a lumpsum tax. Summers assumed labor supply was fixed. Both analysts thus ignore the welfare cost associated with other taxes, like the wage tax, or the consumption tax, which would have to be increased to maintain the total amount of revenue collected if the capital income tax were reduced. Feldstein (1978) assumed that the uncompensated elasticities were zero. Unfortunately, this implies that the consumption tax is optimal when the economy is on the optimal growth path. King (1980) showed that under this assumption $\sigma_{ww} = \sigma_{Rw}$ and the aforementioned conclusion follows. Thus, the gain to eliminating taxes on capital calculated by Feldstein is the gain to be had if the consumption tax is optimal, but this is not necessarily assured.

We should also note that the foregoing results involve a government introducing a tax system into a pristine economic environment that was essentially undistorted. However, this is not the way tax systems typically evolve over time. Instead, tax systems are introduced and then appear to undergo continual adjustments that are usually undertaken in a piecemeal fashion over time.

Ihori (1984) argued that in a second-best environment, where the initial equilibrium is distorted, it may not be optimal to reform the tax system by lowering the capital income tax rate even if the capital income tax rate is already high in the initial equilibrium. He essentially uses the same model employed by Atkinson and Sandmo (discussed above) but assumes that the initial equilibrium is distorted by the wage and capital income taxes. It is also assumed that the government will reform the tax system while maintaining the level of tax revenue. Ihori is able to show that, if the economy is undercapitalized relative to the optimal growth path to begin with, it is actually optimal to increase the capital income tax rate at the margin. The reason is due to the tax timing effect: increasing the tax burden imposed later in life causes rational taxpayers to save more at the margin when they are young than would otherwise have been the case. And this particular result is very robust to a wide range of parameter values when Ihori simulates the model.

King (1980) discovered that the capital income tax rate is very sensitive to the empirical elasticities used in the optimal tax formulae and thus is very fragile if the initial equilibrium is undistorted. Plausible cases where capital is taxed at a low rate are easy to find. However, Ihori showed that the optimality of raising the capital income tax rate under a so-called piecemeal tax reform is extremely robust; it is optimal to reform the initially distorting income tax system by raising the capital income tax rate under a broad range of the empirical parameters.

We can extend these results by incorporating into the model heterogeneity and a concern for equity. Ordover (1976) studied the optimal taxation of labor and interest income with limited heterogeneity in an overlapping generations economy. He found cases where high taxation of capital income was justified. Ordover and Phelps (1979) presented results on the optimal nonlinear taxes on labor and second-period wealth in a similar model. And Svensson and Weibull (1987) studied a similar optimal tax problem while incorporating limited lumpsum taxation.

More recently, Park (1992) extended this work by including a consumption tax and heterogeneity in tastes as well as in labor productivity. Detailed solutions are presented for the Cobb–Douglas case where the government again chooses taxes generation by generation. Park assumes that debt policy is chosen optimally and derives necessary conditions for tax rates that hold in a steady state equilibrium. He derives the following formula for the interest income tax rate:

$$t_r = [(1 + n)/(1 + n - \beta)](\text{cov}_2 - \text{cov}_1)/(1 + \text{cov}_2),$$

where cov_1 is the normalized covariance between the agent's taste for first-period consumption and lifetime disposable income, and similarly for cov_2.

If labor supply and saving are both strictly increasing in the agent's ability, then the more able individual will have greater labor and interest income than a less able individual, ceteris paribus. In that case, the ability distribution will match up with the income distribution in a one-for-one manner. Furthermore, if more able individuals have a greater taste for second-period consumption than for first-period consumption than less able individuals, then $\text{cov}_2 > \text{cov}_1$ and the optimal interest income tax is positive. The intuition is that the interest income tax is a way of imposing a greater tax burden on more able agents who have a particularly strong taste for future consumption and thus accumulate more capital than less able individuals. Of course, if agents have identical tastes, the optimal interest income tax rate is zero, even when the government has a concern for equity, as long as the economy is on the optimal growth path.

The general conclusion of this literature is that the theoretical case for the pure consumption tax, where capital is not taxed, is somewhat fragile at best. The tax on capital income in the overlapping generations model can be positive if the economy is undercapitalized relative to the optimal growth path, ceteris paribus. It can be positive if the compensated wage elasticity of labor supply is greater than the compensated interest elasticity of labor supply. And it can be positive if the government has a concern for equity, if there is heterogeneity in tastes and labor productivity, and if more able individuals have a greater taste for future consumption than current consumption than less able individuals. It can even be optimal to increase the capital income tax rate under a reform of the income tax if the initial equilibrium is distorted by the income tax even if the capital income tax rate is already greater than the labor income tax rate.

A comment is in order on the way the policy game is played between the government and the private sector. Formally, this version of the government's decision problem is known as the open loop decision problem mentioned above;

the government solves its infinite planning horizon problem at the beginning of its horizon by choosing a rule, like the Ramsey rule for setting its tax parameters as embodied in (3.20) and (3.21). As time proceeds, the government simply implements the optimal tax policy rule chosen at the very beginning of its planning horizon. We can label this version of the game played between the government and the private sector the *open loop policy game*. This definition follows naturally, since the government solves an open loop decision problem while the private agents play the game passively by taking the government's tax policy rule as beyond their individual control when they solve their own decision problems.

It is important to note that the government chooses a tax policy for each generation in this framework: it does not choose the policy that is optimal at a moment in time. At time t, for example, the policy rule instructs the government on how to choose the wage tax and this is implemented in the same period. The rule also instructs the government how to choose the interest income tax and this is implemented at time $t + 1$. The wage tax for the tth generation is implemented immediately because that is when members of that generation are working, while the interest income tax is not implemented until the next period when the young are retired and thus are earning their interest income. Implicitly, Atkinson and Sandmo assume there is *one-period commitment*. We can generalize this in the following way. If each generation lives for H periods, then the government would be committing itself to its tax policy for H periods in the open loop policy game when it chooses taxes for each generation. We can label this sort of commitment *generational commitment*.

The effect of this assumption is to make the recursive solution to the government's decision problem equivalent to the solution to the open loop problem. The recursive solution is obtained by utilizing Bellman's principle of optimality, as discussed for example by Atkinson and Sandmo. Because the government is assumed to be choosing a tax policy for a generation in each period, the solution to the recursive problem is the same as that of the open loop problem. To see this, suppose the government chooses its policy at time t for time $t + j$ for $j > 0$. This yields the first-order conditions (3.20) and (3.21) for $t + j$. Next, note that, if the government reoptimizes at time $t + j$, the same first-order conditions hold when it chooses the tax policy for the $(t + j)th$ generation. Therefore, the solution will be the same.

This is not so when the government can simply choose the best tax policy to implement at a moment in time. At time t, for example, capital is fixed, and therefore the tax on interest income becomes a lumpsum tax. Under the Ramsey rule it becomes optimal to impose a high tax rate on any fixed factor, in this case capital. However, this generally violates the open loop policy rule since the rule was chosen when the supply of capital was responsive to the taxes and not fixed. This is known as the capital levy problem. Thus, without commitment the government's tax policy in the open loop game will be time-inconsistent in the sense that the government will generally find it optimal to deviate from its initially optimal policy rule if it can reoptimize when the future arrives. We will discuss the time consistency of tax policy as it pertains to the consumption tax debate in Chapter 6.

3.4. Further results on the welfare cost of capital taxation

The two-period overlapping generations model, or its extension by Summers (1981), for example, to a longer life cycle horizon of $T > 2$ periods, is a useful model for a variety of reasons. The fact that many people will experience a period of retirement at the end of their life provides them with a strong motive for saving and the OG model is useful for characterizing a general equilibrium involving this sort of behavior in a tractable way. Other motives for saving exist, however. One motive we will examine in greater detail later in Chapter 11 is to save in order to leave a bequest to one's heirs. This can dramatically expand the decisionmaker's planning horizon and may alter certain policy conclusions derived in models where people either do not save, as in a static model, or save only for life cycle reasons, as in the classic OG model.

Consider the simplest case, where the individual lives for only one period, accumulates capital in order to leave a bequest under pure altruism toward her offspring, and where tastes are constant across generations. Suppose the utility of the parent is given by

$$U^t = u(c_t) + \beta^+ U^{t+1},$$

where c_t is the parent's consumption, $\beta^+ = 1/(1+\rho) < 1$ is the generational discount factor. The offspring's preferences are given by

$$U^{t+1} = u(c_{t+1}) + \beta^+ U^{t+2},$$

and similarly for all future generations. We can solve this difference equation using the forward expansion method to obtain the following utility function:[6]

$$U^t = \sum_{j=0} \beta^{+j} u(c_{t+j}). \qquad (3.23)$$

The existence of the bequest connecting generations creates an infinite horizon for the parent at time t. The parent's decision problem is to choose her own consumption and the bequest to leave to the next generation so as to maximize (3.23) subject to her budget constraint,

$$w_t + (1 + r_t)b_t - b_{t+1} - c_t = 0, \qquad (3.24)$$

where b_t is the inheritance received and b_{t+1} is the bequest given to the next generation (and her offspring's budget constraint). To close the model, note that in equilibrium $k_t = b_t$. This model of finitely lived agents who leave bequests has been used to justify the Ramsey growth model where the decision maker experiences an infinite horizon.[7]

Chamley (1981) used the infinite horizon Ramsey growth model to calculate the excess burden of taxing capital income. Under his experiment the government completely eliminates the interest income tax and replaces it with a lump-sum tax. Chamley calculates a quadratic approximation of the welfare gain to undertaking this sort of tax reform and uses this as a measure of the welfare loss associated with taxing interest income. For a reasonable set of parameter values for the technology and preferences, and a capital income tax rate equal to 50 per cent, he calculates a welfare cost equal to 26 per cent of the tax revenue collected. The gain to eliminating the tax on capital is significantly smaller if labor supply is endogenous. When the capital income tax rate is 30 per cent, the welfare cost is only 11 per cent of the revenue obtained. Surprisingly, the welfare cost does not appear to be much affected by the intertemporal elasticity of substitution in consumption but rather is affected by the elasticity of substitution between capital and labor in the technology—the greater this latter elasticity, the larger the welfare cost of the tax.[8]

Judd (1987) studied a model similar in spirit to Chamley's but extended to include wage taxation and an investment tax credit. He also studied permanent as well as temporary changes in tax policy, and a number of interesting conclusions emerged from his study. First, quantitative results were extremely sensitive to the choice of parameters. This strongly suggests that specific quantitative conclusions on the welfare cost of a given tax system in the form of a point estimate may not be forthcoming. Second, wage taxes typically induced less of an excess burden than capital income taxes. Third, the welfare cost associated with capital income taxes was typically larger than the cost calculated by Chamley. And, fourth, the investment tax credit was self-financing. It follows from this that a move toward wage taxation coupled with an investment tax credit would be welfare improving. Finally, the anticipated timing and duration of a change in tax policy can be as important to the final result as the taste and technology parameters are.

The main problem with these models is that they take a very simple view of the labor market. Numerous dimensions of labor supply are not modeled. Labor force participation, education and training that generates human capital, work effort per hour, nonlinear budget constraints, and non-convex constraints resulting from taxes or social security are not included, yet these dimensions may be as important as the hours decision. Indeed, some have suggested that the hours decision is really under the purview of the employer and not the employee.[9]

We should point out that a tax on wages is not identically equivalent to a tax on consumption even if both collect the same amount of revenue in a present-value sense. A tax on wages will be paid when the taxpayer is young and working but not when she is retired. A tax on general consumption, on the other hand, will be paid throughout the taxpayer's lifetime. Relative to the wage tax, a tax on expenditures shifts some of the taxpayer's liability into the future. The main effect this will have is to induce the rational, forward looking taxpayer to save more to pay her future tax liability under an expenditure tax. So we should expect capital accumulation to be higher under the consumption tax than under a wage tax even if the present value of the two taxes is the same.

A second way the two taxes may differ is in their pattern of distortions. Decisions made after retirement may be distorted by the consumption tax but will not be distorted by the wage tax. For example, suppose the parent lives two periods, works only in the first period, chooses labor supply in the first period optimally, and makes a bequest to his offspring on the basis of altruism in the second period. The wage tax will distort only the parent's labor supply decision, not the intertemporal consumption decision, or the bequest decision relative to the parent's own retirement consumption. However, a flat rate consumption tax that taxes the bequest will not only distort the parent's labor supply decision, it will also distort the decision between the parent's retirement consumption and the bequest. As we will see in Chapter 11, this is because the parent will take into account the fact that the offspring will pay the consumption tax when the bequest is consumed, and thus taxing the bequest when it is made double-taxes the bequest. The point is that this pattern of distortions is different from that induced by the wage tax.

The pattern of distortions will also differ between the two taxes if there are different expenditures that can be written off under the two taxes. If the expenditure items that are exempt from taxation, for example medical expenses, are the same under the two taxes, the pattern of distortions will be the same. If, however, the exemptions differ between the two taxes, then the pattern of distortions will differ as well. For example, under a wage tax out-of-pocket expenditures on human capital might be made exempt since such expenditures could be interpreted as an "investment." However, under a consumption tax a case can be made for interpreting such expenditures as "consumption." In that case they would be included in the tax base.

3.5. Empirical results on savings, consumption, and labor supply

The optimal tax formulae and the welfare cost of taxation inevitably rely on the responsiveness of various dimensions of economic behavior to relative prices and hence on the tax policies that affect those prices. For example, to implement the optimal tax formula (3.22), we require information on the labor supply and consumption elasticities with respect to the wage and the interest rate. In this section we will briefly survey some of the empirical work on saving and labor supply since this is most directly related to the theoretical models discussed earlier in this chapter and in the next chapter. First we will consider several studies that explicitly concern the response of savings behavior to tax policy. Then we will discuss the empirical work on consumption and labor supply in turn.

There are several problems when results from the empirical literature are used in the optimal tax formulae, however. In the first place, the best we can expect of the empirical literature in measuring the responsiveness of economic behavior to tax policy is a point estimate of an elasticity with a tight confidence interval. Unfortunately, the optimal tax formulae are extremely sensitive to the range of empirical estimates appearing in the literature even when the estimated parameter is highly statistically significant.

Second, sometimes contradictory assumptions are made between the empirical literature and the optimal tax literature, or assumptions are made in the empirical literature that have implications for the optimal tax system. In that case the empirical results cannot be used to make inferences about the optimal tax system. For example, if preferences are weakly separable between leisure and goods in a static setting, the optimal tax system will involve only the taxation of labor earnings or, equivalently, a uniform commodity tax. Unfortunately, an empirical researcher may assume separability in deriving a labor supply equation to estimate. The empirical results from such a study cannot be used to settle the issue as to whether or not the optimal commodity tax system is uniform, since an assumption has been made by the empirical researcher that implies the optimal commodity tax system is uniform.

Third, the position of the economy relative to the optimal growth path may be more important in determining the optimal tax system than the behavioral elasticities. If the government cannot effectively use its monetary or debt policy to maintain the economy on the optimal long-run expansion path, the tax system can be used to move the economy closer to that path. This would obviously tend to make the empirical work on consumption and labor much less important than would otherwise be the case. And there is some empirical evidence which tends to suggest that the United States is undercapitalized, as we will see later in this section.

Finally, in many cases the optimal tax formulae require information on compensated responses. However, in some cases empirical researchers estimate responses that are uncompensated. To obtain the compensated response, the empirical researcher must be able to estimate the wealth or income effects. This is a challenging task that may not always be successful.

3.5.1. Saving incentives

With these difficulties in mind, we turn to the important book edited by Slemrod (1990), *Do Taxes Matter? The Economic Impact of the Tax Reform Act of 1986,* an extensive study of the impact of the tax reform introduced in the United States in 1986. Tax rates were reduced at the margin and the base was broadened as many exemptions were eliminated. The main conclusion of the book is that there is a hierarchy of response to taxation relative to the specific tax reform of 1986 in the United States. First, and foremost, taxation tends to affect the timing of transactions. Second, and next in importance, it would appear to be the case that taxation tends to affect allocation decisions. Finally, and least of all, taxation tends to affect decisions about levels. This suggests that we might expect the behavioral elasticities appearing in optimal tax formulae like (3.22) to be small in magnitude.

The tax treatment of savings is an excellent starting point in any discussion of how policy might affect behavior. Concern over lagging growth in productivity in the United States, possibly resulting from a capital shortage, led to a dramatic expansion of the tax subsidy for saving in the early 1980s.[10] Expanded coverage of the so-called IRA (Individual Retirement Accounts) and 401(k) plans led to a dramatic increase in savings, or so it seemed. For example, IRA eligibility was expanded in 1981 and contributions to IRAs soared from $5 billion in 1981 to over $30 billion in 1982; from 1982 to 1986 contributions to IRAs increased by about $170 billion. On the surface, this would seem to indicate that aggregate savings responded very strongly to the tax incentive. However, during the same period the savings rate fell from approximately 6 per cent of GDP to less than 4 per cent by 1987 and to as low as 3 per cent in 1994.[11] This suggests that the tax incentive may possibly have affected the *allocation* of savings between tax pre-ferred and non-preferred assets but not necessarily the *level* of savings, since there was no stipulation in the law that only new savings would receive the tax advantage. This conclusion would tend to coincide with that of the aforemen-tioned study, *Do Taxes Matter?*

This led to a controversy about whether the increase in contributions to IRAs and 401(k) plans was new saving, a reallocation of existing savings, or both. A reduction of the income tax on one form of savings, say, an IRA, would certainly create a substitution effect toward the preferred method of saving. However, such a policy change would also cause a wealth effect and a capitaliza-tion effect. Measuring these various effects is complicated by the data that are available. For example, if aggregate data are studied, the composition of the population might have as much to do with the ultimate effect of policy as the various income and substitution effects associated with the policy have. If the population is made up of mostly young people, for example, who are saving to buy a house, a car, education for their children, or their own retirement, then aggregate savings may respond significantly to a tax incentive; if the population is made up of mostly elderly people who are dissaving, the opposite may be true. Capturing all of these effects in a single empirical model of savings is difficult to achieve.

Poterba, Venti, and Wise (1996) surveyed the positive side of the debate on the effect of taxation on savings in IRAs and 401(k) plans. They concluded that the subsidy programs for savings significantly increased savings; while Engen, Gale, and Scholz (1996) provided a survey of the literature that came to the opposite conclusion. Poterba, Venti, and Wise examined panel data on individuals, cross-sectional evidence, and a synthetic cohort and concluded that most of the money flowing into IRAs and 401(k) plans in the 1980s was new saving. Their primary argument is that taxable asset accumulation other than IRAs and 401(k) plans does not appear to have been much affected by the availability of these tax preferred forms of saving. So the money flowing into tax preferred savings vehicles must have been new saving.

On the other hand, Engen, Gale, and Scholz (1996) examined similar data and concluded just the opposite: there was no net increase in savings during this period. People were either shuffling their assets toward tax preferred forms of saving, such as 401(k) plans, or were increasing home equity loans at the same time, so there was no *net* increase in saving when balanced against the extra debt that households took on in the 1980s. Furthermore, they argue that other changes in the economic environment that are difficult to control for could also have induced people to save more and this is what Poterba *et al.* are picking up. Examples include the dramatic increase in the real interest rate during the 1980s, and social security reform in 1983 which dramatically lowered lifetime benefits; in addition, pension coverage fell as fewer employers offered pensions to their workers, and marginal tax rates were reduced. People could have saved more because of any or all of these factors. The results of Engen, Gale, and Scholz tend to coincide with the evidence cited in *Do Taxes Matter?* namely that taxes might affect allocation decisions but tend not to affect level decisions much.

Hubbard and Skinner (1996) and Poterba, Venti, and Wise point out that some of Engen, Gale, and Scholz's results are highly sensitive. So perhaps a "middle ground" position is safe; saving incentives in the United States appear to have a small but possibly significant effect.[12] Hubbard and Skinner also point out that one must take into account the cost side of the policy, in other words tax revenue forgone. According to their calculations, even a small increase in savings resulting from favorable tax treatment can pass the benefit–cost test; the benefits of the increased saving appear to outweigh the cost in tax revenue forgone. Hubbard and Skinner provide three reasons to subsidize savings: to increase capital accumulation in order to raise productivity, to reduce the welfare cost of taxation, and to provide people with an incentive to plan for their own retirement. This last reason ensures that fewer of the elderly are living in poverty and requiring future assistance from anti-poverty programs. They concluded that the first two effects are somewhat small in magnitude but that the third may be of some importance.

3.5.2. Consumption

Next, we turn to the empirical literature on consumption and labor supply. The more technical literature on consumption behavior has not been quite so concerned with the impact of tax policy as with developing estimation techniques and models of consumer behavior. The empirical work on saving and consumption has evolved quite significantly, from the early emphasis on the Keynesian consumption function to more sophisticated work using an infinite horizon model like the Ramsey growth model employing rational expectations and estimating the Euler equations that stem from dynamic optimization.

The general conclusion of this literature is that the strictest and simplest hypothesis of savings, the so-called rational expectations permanent income life cycle hypothesis, does not withstand careful empirical scrutiny, although there is some recent evidence that supports the life cycle model. It must be extended in order to explain the data and a number of extensions have been undertaken in recent years. These include incorporating uncertainty coupled with a precautionary motive for savings, liquidity constraints confronting some house-holds, habit formation and costs of adjusting consumption behavior quickly, studying finite horizons, uncertainty about the length of the retirement period, including durable goods, and paying attention to aggregation issues. Unfortu-nately, few if any of these extensions have been included in the theoretical literature on optimal taxation. Thus, one criticism of the optimal tax literature is that it assumes a model of behavior that empirical researchers suggest may not be an appropriate description of actual behavior.

Hall (1978) modeled a consumer who will maximize an intertemporal utility function that is time-separable, $\sum \beta^t U(c_t)$, subject to the wealth constraint, $\sum R^t(w_t - c_t) + A_0 = 0$, where A_0 is the initial level of assets, which is taken as given, $\beta = 1/(1 + \rho)$ is the discount factor, and $R = 1/(1 + r), r$ is the real interest rate, and where it is assumed that the real interest rate is constant. It is straightforward to show that the Euler equation of this decision problem is given by

$$U_c(c_t) = E_t[\beta(1 + r)U_c(c_{t+1})],$$

where E is an expectations operator and the expectation is conditioned on the information available when the decision is made at time t. If it is also assumed that $r = \rho$, it follows that $\beta(1 + r) = 1$. Finally, if it is assumed that instantaneous utility is quadratic, we obtain the approximation

$$c_{t+1} = c_t + \varepsilon_t,$$

where ε_t is a white noise random variable; that is, $E(\varepsilon_t) = 0$, $E(\varepsilon_t \varepsilon_t) = \sigma^2$, and $E(\varepsilon_t \varepsilon_{t-j}) = 0$. Consumption follows a martingale. Essentially, this equation states that current consumption embodies all the relevant systematic information required for forecasting future consumption one period ahead. No other infor-mation is needed once current consumption is known. Hall (1978) tested this hypothesis by including other variables, such as lagged income, in the regression equation and found that he could not reject this theory for time series data on the United States. Although stock prices did help forecast consumption, the effect was very small in magnitude.

Later researchers, however, found that lagged income could help explain consumption using data sets covering different time periods and countries. This led to the notion that consumption was excessively sensitive to income; lagged income had an effect on current consumption independent of the infor-mation already embodied in past consumption. In addition to this, Deaton (1987, 1992) discovered that consumption appeared to be excessively smooth. Suppose that consumption is linearly related to permanent income and permanent income is highly positively correlated with current income. In that case an innovation in income will feed through permanent income to cause a response in consumption. Indeed, the variance of consumption ought to be very close in magnitude to the variance of income if the theory is correct. However, Deaton found that the variance of consumption is much lower than income using US data and concluded that consumption is "too smooth" as a result.[13]

This led to work that relaxed Hall's restrictive assumptions. Indeed, habit formation and costs of quickly adjusting consumption behavior, credit restrictions on borrowing, and precautionary motives for saving can explain the apparent excess sensitivity and smoothness of aggregate consumption. Muellbauer and Lattimore (1995) argue that these extensions can be used to justify an error correction model of consumption.[14] Hall (1989) also notes that habit formation, durable goods consumption, and some form of a liquidity constraint are useful for explaining consumption behavior. Unfortunately, habit formation, adjustment costs, and so on have not been incorporated into studies of optimal taxation for a variety of reasons, including tractability, and so it is difficult to relate the empirical results that stem from models incorporating these extensions to results in optimal tax theory. However, if habit persistence exists (for example), this would tend to suggest that saving and consumption behavior may be less elastic at the margin than would otherwise have been the case. This might tend to favor income taxation over the consumption tax on efficiency grounds.

Hall (1989) also summarizes the evidence on the interest elasticity of savings. The basic equation derived in the literature can be written as

$$\Delta \ln \left(c_t \right) = a + \sigma^* r_t + e_t,$$

where a is a constant related to the covariance of r and $\Delta \ln \left(c \right)$, the variances of the two variables and the rate of time preference, and σ^* is the intertemporal elasticity of substitution in consumption. If the expected real interest rate net of tax increases by 1 per cent, the consumer will substitute σ^* per cent of her consumption at t for consumption at $t + 1$. Most researchers working in the more recent literature have estimated an elasticity approximately equal to one, although Hall himself estimated it as being close to zero.[15] This is much lower than either Boskin or Summers thought and tends to favor the income tax over the consumption tax (see Section 2.5 above).

More recently, DeJuan and Seater (1999) use data from the US Consumer Expenditure Survey to estimate the Euler equation of the consumer's decision problem. This particular data set contains a rich amount of information about expenditures on durables and nondurables and assets at the micro level. Their main result is that they find support for the permanent income life cycle hypothesis. Second, consumption appears to be very interest insensitive. However, this could be due to the fact that the panel in the CES is very short and there might not be enough cross-sectional variation in the data to yield a large interest rate effect.

3.5.3. Static labor supply

Interestingly enough, the situation with respect to labor supply is similar to that involving consumption. Empirical researchers have discovered that the simple models of labor supply behavior do not hold up to empirical scrutiny and that extensions are required in order to explain behavior.[16] In the static models of labor supply it is imagined that a worker has utility for leisure and goods and can exchange some of his labor endowment for a wage which is used to buy consumption. Almost all prime age adult males in Europe, Japan, Canada, and the United States work and thus are at an interior solution with respect to their labor supply decision. The main empirical result of this large literature that has developed over the last thirty years is that male labor supply tends to be very wage-inelastic. The mean value of the compensated prime age male labor supply elasticity with respect to the wage for the studies surveyed by Pencavel (1986) for US data is 0.11 and that for British data is approximately 0.20.[17] Similar results were obtained for Japan.[18] A small compensated wage elasticity of labor supply biases the optimal tax system in favor of the consumption tax or wage tax.

The labor force participation of women has increased in many industrial economies over the last thirty or forty years, and many women are choosing to work full time and are pursuing careers rather than simply working to supplement the family's income. Clearly, female labor will also be affected by tax policy, and the husband's labor supply decisions may be affected by the policies confronting the wife and vice versa. Careful empirical research in the 1970s and early 1980s led to a wide range of estimates for the labor supply elasticities for women. Indeed, the range of estimates was somewhat bewildering.[19] Researchers at the time concluded that female labor supply was more elastic than male labor supply with respect to the wage rate. However, more recent work tends to conclude that female labor supply is almost as inelastic with respect to the contemporaneous wage as male labor supply. Mroz (1987) undertook a broad based sensitivity analysis of female labor supply controlling for selectivity bias and the possible endogeneity of work experience. His compensated wage elasticity estimates are surprisingly close to zero.[20] Again, a low wage elasticity supports the optimality of the consumption tax or the wage tax over the general income tax that includes a tax on capital.

3.5.4. Dynamic labor supply

Finally, we can turn to studies of dynamic life cycle labor supply. Consider an individual who lives T periods and will supply labor from time $t = 0$ to time $t = R^*$ when he retires. His retirement period is $T - R^*$ in length. Preferences are given by

$$\sum_{t=0}^{T} \beta^t U(c_t, 1 - L_t),$$

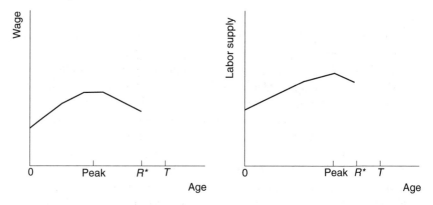

Figure 3.1.   Wage and labor supply profiles

where L is labor supply and $1 - L$ is leisure. The wealth constraint is

$$\sum_{t=0}^{R^*}[1/(1+r)]^t w_t L_t + A_0 = \sum_{t=0}^{T}[1/(1+r)]^t c_t.$$

Given the profile of wage rates $\{w_t\}_{t=0}^{R^*}$ over the life cycle, the worker chooses labor supply and consumption profiles, $\{L_t\}_{t=0}^{R^*}$ and $\{c_t\}_{t=0}^{T}$, to maximize lifetime utility subject to his wealth constraint. An example of the wage and labor supply profiles is depicted in Figure 3.1, where the labor supply profile peaks before the wage profile does.

There are two types of qualitative response in a dynamic model such as this. First, labor supply and consumption evolve along a certain path contingent on the profile for the wage. Thus, for example, labor supply will appear to change over the life cycle as it evolves along its optimal path, as long as the wage path is not constant. This is known as an evolutionary change in behavior. Second, a shift of the entire net wage profile, say because tax policy has unexpectedly changed, will cause the entire time path of labor supply to shift. The latter response is depicted in Figure 3.2.

MaCurdy (1981) first estimated the dynamic life cycle labor supply model using an addilog utility function that is separable over time with US data, the Michigan PSID, a panel data set that tracks the same individuals over time. The intertemporal labor supply elasticity he estimated exhibited a central tendency of 0.20. Thus, a 10 per cent increase of the wage along the fixed wage profile as depicted in Figure 3.1 induces a 2 per cent increase in hours worked. However, the standard errors for his point estimates were very large. Thus, the null hypothesis that evolutionary changes in the wage (along the wage profile) cause no increase in labor supply cannot be rejected. This provides mild support for the contention that labor supply is relatively unresponsive to the wage.[21]

In addition to this, MaCurdy's estimates tend to indicate that the marginal product of capital exceeds the rate of time preference by 2 to 4 points. This

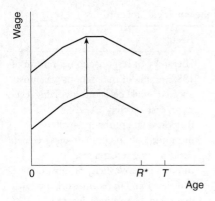
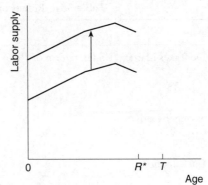

Figure 3.2.   Shifts in the profiles

strongly suggests that the US economy is undercapitalized relative to the optimal expansion path. If agents are identical, as in the optimal tax models studied earlier in this chapter, it is natural to equate the social discount rate with the representative agent's rate of time preference. In that case, MaCurdy's result would tend to indicate that the marginal product of capital is greater than the social discount rate. Thus, the term $\gamma(F_k - \rho)R$ in (3.22) would be positive and would serve to make the interest income tax rate higher than would otherwise have been the case had the economy been on the optimal expansion path.

There is also some indirect evidence regarding the comparison between the social discount rate and the marginal product of capital for the US economy in the postwar period. Apparently, the Michigan panel data used extensively by labor supply researchers indicate that the labor supply profile for full time male labor supply, as measured by hours worked, tends to increase and peaks before the wage profile peaks. This is depicted in the Figure 3.1, where the wage profile peaks before the labor supply profile, indicating that the real interest rate is greater than the worker's rate of time preference, $r > \rho$.

The intuition for this is as follows. The higher the interest rate, the greater the incentive to work more now and less later in order to save more now and earn a higher rate of return on the extra savings, ceteris paribus. On the other hand, a higher rate of time preference makes working in the future less onerous than working today and would encourage the individual to shift labor supply into the future, ceteris paribus. Suppose the worker confronts a lifetime wage profile that is rising but peaks and then eventually turns down near the end of his lifetime. If the interest rate is greater than the rate of time preference, the individual worker will choose a rising labor supply profile that peaks before the wage profile does. If the rate of time preference were higher than the interest rate, labor supply would be shifted into the future and would peak after the wage profile peaks, not before. Thus, we can conclude that $r > \rho$ given the evidence on male labor supply and wage profiles. Of course, this argument is predicated on the assumption that

Table 3.1. Results of the empirical literature

Area	Result
Do Taxes Matter? (US tax reform of 1986)	Hierarchy of response to tax reform of 1986: timing of transactions was most affected, while decisions involving levels were least affected.
Saving incentives	Response was probably small in magnitude, although sharp disagreement exists among researchers.
Consumption	Intertemporal elasticity of substitution is between 1 and 0; recent work indicates that saving is relatively interest insensitive.
Static labor supply	Male and female labor supply is wage-inelastic.
Dynamic labor supply	Life cycle labor supply appears wage-inelastic; some evidence suggests $r > \rho$.

agents are choosing their labor supply behavior according to the life cycle model of labor supply.

Finally, we should note that to our knowledge the relationship between labor supply and the interest rate has not been documented at the micro level. Thus, the compensated elasticity of labor supply with respect to the interest rate is as yet unknown. While tremendous progress has been made and much has been learned about labor supply and consumption behavior, we cannot use the empirical results uncovered to date to state definitively that one tax system is preferred over another. About all that can be said is that the low wage elasticity of labor supply tends to favor the consumption tax over the income tax, on the one hand. However, on the other hand, evidence on the expansion path of the economy for the United States tends to suggest that the real interest rate is greater than the rate of time preference. This tends to support higher taxation of capital. The results are summarized in Table 3.1.

3.6. Simulation models

One of the difficulties of doing purely analytical work is that theoretical models can become intractable very quickly, especially dynamic models. A number of researchers have turned to the computer simulation model in order to undertake more complicated analyses than can be done analytically. For example, Summers (1981) simulated a one-sector model without labor supply in order to make the case that the interest elasticity of savings was much larger than previously thought. His results were challenged by Evans (1983), as discussed in Chapter 2. Seidman (1983, 1984) incorporated bequests into a life cycle simulation model and simulated various tax policies with emphasis on the transition phase of the reform. He assumed that the parent/donor cares about the bequest directly but not about the consumption or welfare of the offspring/recipient. In Chapter 11 we will label this model the bequest as consumption model and study its theoretical properties at length.

In Seidman's basic model there is a representative consumer who cares about her own lifetime consumption and the terminal stock of capital left at the end of her life cycle as a bequest to her offspring. In discrete time, the parent's utility is given by

$$U = (1 - 1/\sigma)\left[\sum_{t=0}^{T} \beta^t u(c_t)^{1-1/\sigma} + b\beta^T (K_{T+1})^{1-1/\sigma}\right],$$

where c_t is the agent's own consumption, k_{T+1} is the terminal stock of capital left as a bequest to the next generation, and b is a parameter that weights the bequest relative to the parent's own consumption. Lifetime wealth is given by

$$\sum_{t=0}^{T} R^t (w_t - c_t) + H - R^T k_{T+1} = 0,$$

where w is the wage rate or labor earnings, since labor supply is fixed at unity, H is the inheritance received, $R = 1/(1 + r)$, and r is the market interest rate. A neoclassical technology is appended to the model, $y = Ak^\alpha$, where k is capital per worker. Firms maximize profits, and in a steady state this implies that $k = (\alpha/r)^{1/(1-\alpha)}$.

Seidman (1983) simulates the effects of different tax policies on the steady state equilibrium while maintaining the level of tax revenue. His main conclusion is that a bequest motive may imply that the consumption tax is no longer neutral with respect to capital accumulation. In this particular model, the bequest enters the model in the same way as parental consumption, once in the utility function and once in the wealth constraint. As explained in Chapter 11, if the bequest is treated differently from parental consumption under the consumption tax, the bequest decision will be distorted. In this case, if the bequest is not taxed at the same rate as consumption, it is a *favored* activity in this model and the agent will undertake more of it at the margin when the consumption tax system is introduced. If bequests are not taxed as the consumption of the parent in the bequest as consumption model, the distorting consumption tax is preferred to the general income tax because it yields a higher capital–labor ratio.

However, there is a caveat to this result. Other models of bequeathing have been studied and some of them will have different implications for the pattern of distortions generated by the tax system. For example, in Chapter 11 we will also study the altruism model, where the parent cares about the consumption or welfare of the offspring rather than the bequest itself. In the altruism model the parent will take into account the possibility that the offspring will pay the consumption tax when he consumes the bequest. The parent in the bequest as consumption model will ignore the use of the bequest by the offspring and thus will ignore the possibility that the offspring will incur the tax when the bequest is consumed. The consumption tax in the altruism model will be neutral only when the bequest is not taxed, the opposite conclusion of the model where the parent cares about the bequest itself.

Seidman (1984) noted that earlier researchers had discovered that the generations alive when the consumption tax is first introduced may be made worse off by conversion from the income tax to the consumption tax. This is one of the most important transition problems associated with the consumption tax. Some of these generations may involve people who are retired and thus have already paid the bulk of their tax liability under the income tax. Upon conversion to the consumption tax, they will experience a marked increase in their lifetime tax liability. Seidman shows that if generations are connected by bequests, however, the discount rate is higher and the resulting optimal consumption path is less steep. This tends to moderate the transitional losses when the consumption tax is imposed. He also considers an age phasing policy, whereby generations adversely affected by the consumption tax are taxed at a lower rate when the consumption tax is introduced. This too will reduce the transitional losses.

His four main results are as follows. First, a consumption tax will generally lower the welfare of existing cohorts even if steady state welfare improves unambiguously. Therefore, ignoring the transition phase of the reform could be seriously misleading. Second, the greater the bequest motive and the higher the discount rate generating a given capital stock, the smaller the transitional losses will be because consumption will grow more slowly and thus more in line with income. Third, age phasing can reduce the transitional losses. Finally, it is typically assumed in life cycle models that consumption grows at the same rate in retirement that it grew at when the individual was younger. If consumption grows less rapidly in retirement, transitional losses will again be smaller as well.

It should be noted that these results are predicated on labor supply being fixed and bequests not being taxed under the consumption tax. If bequests are taxed when the consumption tax is imposed, say, for equity reasons, then saving for bequests will surely fall and this may adversely affect capital accumulation. The welfare gain to be had from switching to the consumption tax will be reduced as a result. The gain may also be reduced if the consumption tax is not flat but graduated since the intertemporal consumption decision will generally be distorted under a progressive consumption tax.

Auerbach and Kotlikoff (1987) incorporate endogenous labor supply and a realistic life cycle wage profile and simulate a general version of the OG model where each person lives for 55 economic years so that there are 55 overlapping generations coexisting in their model. The preferences of the representative agent of the tth generation are given by

$$U = [1/(1 - 1/\sigma)] \sum_{t=1}^{55} \beta^{t-1} u(c_t, 1 - L_t),$$

where $u(\ ) = [c_t^{(1-1/\eta)} + a(1 - L_t)^{(1-1/\eta)}]^{(1-1/\eta)}$. The constant elasticity of substitution between consumption and leisure is given by η, which measures the response of the ratio $(1 - L)/c$ to the wage rate. The constant intertemporal elasticity of substitution is given by σ, which measures the response of the ratio c_{t+1}/c_t to the interest rate. And the discount factor is $\beta = 1/(1 + \rho)$, where ρ is the discount rate. The agent's budget constraint is

$$\sum_{t=1}^{55} R^{t-1}(w_t e_t L_t - c_t) = 0,$$

where e represents a stock of human capital, which is taken as exogenous. The consumer chooses a sequence of consumption and labor supply to maximize lifetime utility subject to her wealth constraint.

Firms confront a technology that is also isoelastic:

$$Y_t = A[\varepsilon K_t^{(1-1/\zeta)} + (1 - \varepsilon)L_t^{(1-1/\zeta)}]^{(1-1/\zeta)},$$

where ζ is the constant elasticity of substitution between capital and labor and measures the response of the ratio K/L to the ratio w/r, and ε is a parameter measuring the intensity of the firm's use of capital. Firms choose inputs to maximize profit and this yields the demand for labor and investment in private capital.

The model is closed by assuming that a tax policy is imposed by the government and that markets clear. It is assumed the government can issue debt and so its budget need not balance each period, but must balance over time. The parameters of the equilibrium are chosen whenever possible from the empirical literature, much of which we surveyed earlier in this chapter.[22] To simulate the model, the initial steady state equilibrium is calculated, the new steady state equilibrium after the policy reform is introduced is calculated, and then the transition between the two equilibria is calculated. It is assumed the transition will take less than 150 years.

Auerbach and Kotlikoff's main findings are as follows. First, a switch from a tax system that taxes general income to the consumption tax generates greater capital accumulation than a switch to either a wage tax or a capital income tax. Second, proportional consumption taxation is more efficient than the proportional general income tax. Third, some tax reforms that increase the capital available per worker may actually lower welfare in the new steady state, for example a switch from the general income tax to the wage tax. Fourth, the short-run response on the transition path may differ dramatically from the long-run response and may even be of the opposite sign. For example, while the capital–labor ratio, the wage, the savings rate, and welfare are all higher under the consumption tax, they fall in the initial part of the transition.

Several comments are in order. The initial generations alive when the switch to the consumption tax occurs are made worse off under the reform, especially retirees, as noted by Seidman and others. This is because the consumption tax is essentially equivalent to a lumpsum tax on the elderly who have retired coupled with a tax on the labor of the young. If the welfare of the agents living in the transition period is not held constant via lumpsum taxes, the gain from switching to the consumption tax is much smaller. These results are also contingent on human capital being exogenous. It is certainly possible that the consumption tax may reduce the incentive to accumulate human capital. This would also serve to reduce the gain to switching to the consumption tax.

Finally, Lord and Rangazas (1992) simulate a dynamic model where the representative parent in the model acquires human capital and makes a bequest to her offspring. Generations are connected via altruistic cash bequests where the parent cares about the welfare of the offspring. The inclusion of bequests and human capital tends to raise the compensated interest elasticity of saving in their model. Their main conclusion is that a reform of the tax system that replaces the income tax with a pure consumption tax excluding bequests from taxation is hardly affected at all by the inclusion of bequests and human capital in the model. Tax reforms typically involve a variety of effects including the usual substitution and income effects. In addition, there may be tax timing effects.[23] The combination of effects may be offsetting and may reduce the importance of bequests in determining the final outcome of the tax reform.

In the pure life cycle model, Lord and Rangazas show that the tax reform increases saving by about 34 per cent when all of the effects are included and increases the capital–labor ratio by about 32.3 per cent. In the presence of bequests and human capital, the reform increases savings by about 36 per cent and increases the capital–labor ratio by about 34 per cent. Thus, including cash and human capital bequests does not seem to affect the effect of the reform on the economy much. This is somewhat surprising because it was thought, especially by early advocates of the consumption tax, that including intergenerational transfers would dramatically increase the saving elasticity, and that a switch to the consumption tax would therefore dramatically raise savings and capital accumulation.

One possible conclusion to draw from the simulation models is that it might be optimal to switch to the consumption tax, but not for the reasons cited by early advocates. It is possible that the tax timing effects, which induce greater savings because of a shift in the timing of tax payments within the life cycle, might dominate the substitution effects in inducing greater savings at the margin. However, the loss in welfare on the transition path cannot be ignored. Special "age phasing" policies such as lumpsum transfers may be required during the transition period.

3.7. Conclusion

In this chapter we have studied the early literature on the optimal taxation of labor and capital income. The optimal tax formulae were derived in a two-period, OG model where the government behaves as a Stackelberg leader in the open loop policy game. It was seen that it is actually the labor supply elasticities that are most important in determining whether a wage tax or consumption tax is optimal per se, and not the interest elasticity of saving. Second, the position of the economy relative to the optimal expansion path is also of critical importance in determining the structure of the optimal tax system. As long as the government cannot perfectly control the position of the economy relative to the optimal path, capital income taxation may very well be optimal. Paradoxically, this is especially so if the economy is undercapitalized to begin with, because taxpayers will save more now if they know they will face a capital income tax liability in the future.

The more recent work on the welfare cost of capital income taxation carried out in the 1980s by Chamley (1981) and Judd (1987) tended to indicate that the welfare cost of capital income taxation was significant. This later work used the Ramsey model, which relies on market clearing and optimizing agents who experience an infinite horizon. Judd's results are of special interest. He shows how fragile the quantitative estimates of the excess burden can be. However, several general results emerge from his study which tend to indicate that a move toward a wage tax coupled with an investment tax credit could improve welfare substantially.

We have briefly summarized some of the empirical work on tax incentives and savings, consumption, and labor supply behavior. Unfortunately, the evidence is somewhat inconclusive and does not strongly support one tax system over the other. On the one hand, labor supply for both prime age men and women tends to be very unresponsive to the wage in both static and dynamic models of labor supply behavior. This tends to favor the consumption tax over the income tax. On the other hand, there is some evidence which suggests that the US economy is undercapitalized relative to the optimal expansion path. This tends to favor taxation of capital and hence the income tax over the consumption tax because of tax timing effects. Finally, the evidence also tends to indicate that the interest elasticity of savings may be much smaller than thought by Boskin or Summers.

We also briefly discussed the computer simulation models used to study tax reform. Most of the work in the 1980s on these models used versions of the neoclassical growth model with overlapping generations. Functional forms are chosen for the tastes and the technology of the representative agents, and parameters involving labor supply and consumption behavior are chosen from the empirical literature. The main result is that welfare improves when a switch is made from the income tax to the consumption tax. However, some agents alive during the transition period may be made worse off. Therefore, some sort of age phased policy, such as transfer to retirees, whereby the utility of these generations is maintained in the transition period, may have to be added to the tax reform in order for the reform to generally improve welfare.

NOTES TO CHAPTER 3

1. See the survey paper by Sandmo (1976) or the discussion in Atkinson and Stiglitz (1980).

2. We can define the expenditure function as

$$e(q, w, u) = \min\{q_1 x_1 + q_2 x_2 + w(1 - L) : U(x, 1 - L) \geq u\},$$

where $e(q, w, u) = w$. By the homogeneity properties of the expenditure function, $\sum_j q_j S_{ij} + w S_{iw} = 0$. Write this last equation in elasticity form and use when collapsing the system.

3. We have equated the social rate of time preference to the representative agent's rate of time preference. This seems natural in a setting where private agents are identical. However, in general, the social rate of time preference may differ from the private rate.

4. To quote King (1980), "An expenditure tax (which corresponds to $t_r = 0$) will be the optimal tax system if, and only if, $\sigma_{ww} = \sigma_{Rw}$ [our notation]" (page 9).

5. There is a presumption that private agents will save too little, thus implying that the competitive economy will be undercapitalized relative to the optimal growth path. See the discussion in King (1980), e.g. section 1.3, where he argues that the economy will be undercapitalized "because of the failure of each generation to take into account the welfare of future generations." If the current generation saves more, the capital stock will be larger than would otherwise have been the case and the wage paid to the next generation will also be larger as a result. Even if the individual agent cares about the welfare of her offspring, she cannot affect her offspring's wage through her own saving since it is simply too small relative to the aggregate level of saving.

6. Alternatively, rearrange, $U^{t+1} - (1/\beta)U^t = u(c_t)/\beta$, use the lag operator L, $(1 - 1/L\beta)U^{t+1} = -u(c_t)/\beta$, where the lag operator L is defined as $LX_t = X_{t-1}$ and hence $L^{-1}X_t = X_{t+1}$. Solve the difference equation forward to obtain (3.23).

7. Under this interpretation, the capital stock is generated by bequests. As we will see in Chapter 11, this is counterfactual. Other motives for saving also appear to be empirically relevant.

8. Chamley also studied the misallocation of capital that can occur if capital in different sectors of the economy is taxed at different rates, as is the case under the corporate income tax used in many countries. He assumes there are two sectors producing the same good but that capital in only one sector is taxed under the corporate income tax. He then studies the same policy experiment, i.e. elimination of the capital income

tax. Interestingly enough, he finds that the welfare cost associated with the misalloca-tion of capital arising from the corporate income tax is 4.4 times larger than the distortion of the intertemporal consumption decision for his chosen parameter values. It is interesting to note that this has not been more ardently pursued in the literature to date.

9. See the survey by Pencavel (1986).

10. An IRA (Individual Retirement Account) allows an individual to save up to a certain amount tax free, and interest earned is not taxed until the income is drawn on at retirement. However, interest plus principal cannot be drawn on penalty-free until the age of 59 years 6 months. 401(k) plans operate in a similar fashion except that the program must be offered by the employer and deductions are made regularly by the employer, whereas under an IRA the individual can decide when to make a contribution.

11. See Engen, Gale, and Scholz (1996).

12. The same small effect is probably also true for Japan; see Tachibanaki (1996).

13. Another way of stating this is to note that most empirical researchers working in this area believe that income follows a random walk, possibly with drift and is non-stationary as a result; i.e., the stochastic process for income contains a unit root. (See Hamilton (1994) on unit roots and stationarity.) If income and consumption are linearly related, consumption will also follow a random walk, possibly with drift. In that case, an innovation to income ought to cause a permanent response in con-sumption and the variance in consumption ought to be close to the variance in income. However, Deaton (1887, 1992) found that the variance in consumption was much smaller.

14. Consider a model according to $x_t = A_1 x_{t-1} + A_2 x_{t-1} + E_t$, where x is an n-vector of variables, A_j is an $n \times n$ matrix of coefficients, and E is a vector of white noise error terms. Subtract x_{t-1} from both sides to obtain $\Delta x_t = (A_1 - I)x_{t-1} + A_2 x_{t-2} + E_t$, where I is the identity matrix and $\Delta x_t = x_t - x_{t-1}$. Finally, notice that this can be written as

$$\Delta x_t = (A_1 + A_2 - I)x_{t-1} - A_2 \Delta x_{t-1} + E_t.$$

The last version of the system is known as the error correction model. Applying this idea to consumption behavior, Muellbauer and Lattimore (1995) present the error correction model for consumption,

$$\Delta c_t = \beta_0 + \beta_1 \Delta y_t + \beta_2 (y_{t-1} - c_{t-1}) + \varepsilon_t,$$

where y is a measure of income.

15. See Hall (1989, page 170).

16. Pencavel (1986) surveys the empirical literature on male labor supply, while Killings-worth and Heckman (1986) provide a survey of the literature on female labor supply.

17. See tables 1.19 and 1.20 in Pencavel (1986, pages 69 and 73, respectively).

18. See Tachibanaki (1996).

19. See Killingsworth and Heckman (1986, table 2.26), which includes the results of over 40 studies.

20. See tables 2.27 and 2.28 in Killingsworth and Heckman (1986, pages 194 and 197, respectively).

21. These results were confirmed by later work. See the surveys by Pencavel (1986) and Killingsworth and Heckman (1986).
22. See Auerbach and Kotlikoff (1987, chapter 4, page 50) for a discussion of their parameter choices.
23. See Ihori (1987) on tax timing effects.

4

Taxation and Economic Growth

4.1. Introduction

In this chapter we will review the more recent literature on optimal taxation in dynamic models. One response to the possible ambiguity of the results in the two-period overlapping generations model, or extensions of it, is to generalize the model in terms of the type of behavior allowed and then to choose specific functional forms and parameters and simulate various policies via the computer. One can examine the transition path of a tax reform, for example, and choose one reform over another on the basis of their respective welfare implications. As discussed in the last chapter, Seidman (1983, 1984), Auerbach and Kotlikoff (1987), and Lord and Rangazas (1992) undertake this sort of exercise and show there are large gains in welfare to be had from switching from an income tax system to a consumption tax.

An alternative theoretical model may be used that is perhaps more tractable than the OG model in certain respects. Many analysts have recently studied the optimal tax issue in the context of a version of the so-called Ramsey growth model. The prototypical model in this literature assumes that there is one good produced via a neoclassical, constant-returns-to scale technology, and a set of consumers each of whom experience an *infinite* planning horizon. The length of the planning horizon is critical to the model and can lead to some interesting, albeit model-specific, results. The individual consumer in the model chooses an infinite sequence of consumption and labor supply in order to maximize lifetime utility subject to a sequence of budget constraints and non-negativity conditions. Competitive firms produce the one good available and markets clear each period. The government imposes taxes on labor and capital in order to finance its own spending.

Using this sort of model, Arrow and Kurz (1970), Judd (1985), and Chamley (1985a, b, 1986) showed that in the long run it is optimal not to tax capital income; the capital income tax rate is zero in the long-run steady state equilibrium. Thus, the general income tax is suboptimal in the long run; only labor or consumption should be taxed in the long-run steady state, not capital.

This zero tax result stands in marked contrast to the results in the early literature which relied mainly on the overlapping generations model populated with finitely lived agents as in the last chapter. In particular, Chamley argues that there is a tradeoff when agents have a long horizon between taxing capital at the beginning of the horizon and taxing future capital income. A tax on "old" capital already in place is essentially a lumpsum tax, while a tax on "new" capital can distort the capital accumulation decision. At the beginning of the planning horizon, the lumpsum nature of a tax on "old" capital dominates, causing "old" capital to be taxed at a high rate. However, eventually, this effect is dominated by the distortions caused by taxing "new" capital. In the steady state, capital should not be taxed at all.

In the two-period OG model this will not necessarily be true when agents have a finite horizon, as we showed in the last chapter. However, there is one special case of interest where it will be true. This is the case where generations are connected by cash bequests via altruism where the parent cares about the welfare of the offspring. Such altruism connects generations in an infinite chain, and Chamley shows that his main result will also go through in such a model. Indeed, the model with finitely lived agents and altruism across generations within the family is one way of motivating the Ramsey model where the representative agent is assumed to experience an infinite horizon.

In a more recent contribution, Chamley (1998) argues that the long-run result depends on the horizon and the completeness of markets. He provides an example of a model of precautionary savings where labor income fluctuates but capital markets are imperfect. He derives the result that the long-run tax on capital is positive (negative) if the correlation between savings and the marginal utility of consumption is negative (positive).

As it turns out, the "primal" problem becomes important as a method for studying optimal taxation in the Ramsey model, as opposed to the more familiar "dual" problem studied in the last chapter. Atkinson and Stiglitz (1972) posed the optimal tax problem in a novel way by having the government solve the primal problem of choosing quantities rather than tax rates directly, as is the case in the dual approach popularized by Samuelson (1986) and Diamond and Mirrlees (1971a). Indeed, Ramsey's original formulation of the optimal tax problem was in quantity space. One of the applications studied by Atkinson and Stiglitz involved an additively separable intertemporal utility function. They showed that if the agent has a finite horizon it is generally optimal to tax interest income under certain conditions on preferences. This result, coupled with the results from the OG model of the last chapter, strongly suggests that the important distinction across these different models involves the length of the individual taxpayer's planning horizon and the motive for saving.

Most recently, analysts have begun studying optimal taxation in the context of endogenous growth models. In the neoclassical Ramsey growth model, either growth is exogenous, if there is exogenous technical change occurring, or the economy grows on a transition path but approaches a steady state where growth stops. This means that either the government cannot affect the growth rate, or the economy eventually stops growing and there is little anyone including the government can do about it. The various endogenous growth models imply that the growth rate of the economy is fully endogenous and thus can respond to policy. It is a straightforward matter to show that the capital income tax rate will permanently lower the economy's growth rate. Indeed, this was the main message of Lucas (1990). Thus, the government should not tax capital in Lucas's model when the economy is on the long-run balanced growth path. It follows that the consumption tax is optimal in this case. Jones, Manuelli, and Rossi (1993) extend this result to a model with physical and human capital and show that taxes should not be imposed in the long run on labor, either, if human capital accumulation takes place since this will also adversely affect the economy. In their model it is optimal for the government to impose high tax rates on both types of capital early in its horizon, build up a budget surplus, and then reduce all distortionary tax rates asymptotically to zero.

However, there are several important caveats to this long-run result. First, it need not hold in the short run, either when agents are finitely lived and not connected by altruistic cash transfers, or when the economy is on the transition path to the long-run balanced growth path. The tax policy that is optimal in the long run may be a poor approximation to the optimal tax structure in the short run. Second, Judd, Chamley, and Lucas, among others, assume that the government solves its decision problem only once, at the very beginning of its planning horizon. This is absolutely critical. The government is not allowed to reoptimize when the future arrives. Both Chamley and Lucas recognized that the time consistency problem can occur in this model, but chose to ignore it. It is always optimal for the government to reoptimize and tax the existing capital at a very high rate because that capital is now in fixed supply and thus is "old" capital. This is an application of the famous Ramsey rule of optimal tax theory. A corollary of the rule states that factors in fixed supply should be taxed at very high rates. Unfortunately, private investors can come to expect this and will accumulate less capital as a result. We will study this problem further in Chapter 6.

Third, Correia (1996) showed that the Judd–Chamley result would not necessarily go through if there were a third factor in the model that could not be taxed optimally. Any restrictions on the government's ability to impose taxes on the private sector leads to additional constraints on the government's decision problem, and this may mean that taxing capital becomes optimal once again. Correia showed that, if the third untaxed factor and physical capital are complements, a tax on capital income is optimal. The intuition is that taxing capital income is a way of indirectly taxing the factor that cannot be taxed directly. Of course, if capital and the third factor are substitutes, a subsidy for capital is appropriate instead.

Fourth, Jones, Manuelli, and Rossi (1993) show that it is optimal to impose taxes on capital if government spending affects the investment of the private good positively within the context of an endogenous growth model. Productive public capital that increases the impact of investment at the margin can induce profits in the private sector that can be taxed under a capital income tax.

Fifth, Aiyagari (1995) argued that, in the presence of shocks and incomplete insurance markets, "precautionary" savings may occur but are inefficient because they are due to the incompleteness of the insurance markets. In Aiyagari's model, agents will be constrained in periods when they experience a large negative income shock and cannot borrow enough to smooth their consumption, so they build up a stock of precautionary savings against the future possibility of experiencing such a shock. The precautionary savings occur in the absence of complete insurance markets. Aggregate saving, and hence capital accumulation, is too high as a result of such "precautionary" savings, and a capital income tax can be used to reduce savings and improve welfare.

Hubbard and Judd (1986) and Browning and Burbidge (1990) also point out that some consumers may be liquidity-constrained. It is shown that use of an interest income tax can improve welfare in the face of a liquidity constraint. This is especially true if young people cannot borrow to finance their human capital accumulation. The intuition is that taxation of capital income reduces the need to tax consumption early in the life cycle and has a positive first-order welfare effect that can be important in magnitude. And such a tax can induce young people to acquire more human capital than would otherwise have been the case in the presence of a liquidity constraint.

Sixth, Zhu (1992) extends the Ramsey growth model by incorporating uncertainty into the model. Government spending is modeled as a stochastic process. In addition, there is a shock to the technology. Agents must choose their savings before the shocks are observed each period. It is shown that the tax rate on capital income in the long-run is not necessarily zero.

Finally, Krusell, Quadrini, and Rios-Rull (1996) incorporate the political process into the model. Voter–consumers differ in their labor endowment or productivity and solve the same sort of dynamic decision problem as in Judd and Chamley's model; however, in addition they vote on next period's tax rate, and tax revenue is used for redistributive purposes. A number of surprising results emerge. For example, it is shown that, even though consumption taxation is less distorting, output under an income tax will be greater than under the consumption tax because voters under the median voter hypothesis will prefer that a higher level of revenue is collected under the consumption tax than under the income tax.

In the next section we present Atkinson and Stiglitz's static optimal taxation model and methodology, and their application to the case of intertemporally additive preferences. This will not only provide some additional insight for the results discussed later in this chapter, but will also provide the reader with background for the less familiar primal problem where the government chooses quantities instead of prices. In Section 4.3 we present the Ramsey growth model with endogenous labor supply and derive Chamley's main result. In

Section 4.4 we extend Chamley's result to the case studied by Correia where there is a second factor in elastic supply. Section 4.5 extends the model by discussing the endogenous growth model and Robert Lucas's result. Atkinson and Stiglitz's methodology is used extensively to derive these results. Section 4.6 presents several caveats to the zero capital income tax rate result, and Section 4.7 concludes the chapter.

4.2. The optimal tax methodology of the primal problem

In this section we will first study the methodology employed by Atkinson and Stiglitz (1972), since it is somewhat distinct, and one of their main results involving additive preferences. They study a static model and pose the government's optimal tax problem as a primal problem in quantities rather than the usual dual problem in prices and hence in the tax rates themselves. This will provide some background for the work of Judd, Chamley, and Lucas discussed in the next section.

Consider a simple static economy where labor is used to produce n commodities. For simplicity the technology is linear, which serves to fix producer prices. We will let labor be the numeraire. There is one consumer whose preferences are given by $U(x, 1 - L)$, where $x = (x_1, x_2, \ldots, x_n)'$ is the column vector of commodities, $1 - L$ is leisure, and L is labor supply. The utility function is twice continuously differentiable, quasi-concave, and monotonically increasing in all its arguments. The consumer's budget constraint is $wL = \sum_i q_i x_i$, where $q_i = p_i + t_i$ is the consumer price of good i, p_i is the constant producer price, and t_i is the commodity tax rate imposed on good i. The consumer chooses x and L to maximize utility subject to the budget constraint. The first-order conditions are

$$U_j = \lambda q_j, \quad \text{for } j = 1, 2, \ldots, n, \tag{4.1a}$$

$$U_L = \lambda, \tag{4.1b}$$

where U_j is the marginal utility of good j, U_L is the marginal utility of leisure, and λ is the marginal utility of income.

To pose the government's decision problem, substitute (4.1) into the consumer's budget constraint to obtain

$$LU_L(x, 1 - L) - \sum_i x_i U_i(x, 1 - L) = 0. \tag{4.2}$$

The government's budget constraint is

$$g = \sum_i t_i x_i,$$

where g is exogenous government spending. Using the definition of prices and the consumer's budget equation, this can be written as

$$g = \sum_i t_i x_i = \sum_i q_i x_i - \sum_i p_i x_i = wL - \sum_i p_i x_i. \tag{4.3}$$

The government chooses (x, L) to maximize $U(x, 1 - L)$ subject to (4.2) and (4.3). Write the Lagrangean as

$$U(x, 1 - L) + \mu(LU_L - \sum_i x_i U_i) + \gamma(wL - \sum_i p_i x_i - g),$$

where μ and γ are the multipliers.

It is straightforward to show that the first-order conditions are

$$U_j - \mu U_j - \gamma p_j + \mu(LU_{Lj} - \sum_i x_i U_{ij}) = 0,$$

$$-U_L + \mu U_L + \gamma + \mu(\sum_i x_i U_{iL} - LU_{LL}) = 0.$$

Define $H^k = (LU_{Lk} - \sum_i x_i U_{ik})/U_k$ to be the sum of the elasticities of marginal utility with respect to good k and $H^L = (\sum_i x_i U_{iL} - LU_{LL})/U_L$ to be the sum of the elasticities of marginal utility with respect to labor. The first-order conditions imply

$$\theta_j = t_j/q_j = [(\gamma - \lambda)/\lambda](H^j - H^L)/(1 - H^L). \qquad (4.4)$$

This is the main result derived by Atkinson and Stiglitz (1972).

Two special cases of (4.4) are of some importance. First, if $H^L = 0$ and $U_{ij} = 0$ for all $i \neq j$, then (4.4) implies the inverse elasticity rule first derived by Ramsey (1927); that is, the greater the elasticity of demand, the lower the tax rate should be, ceteris paribus. Second, suppose labor supply is perfectly inelastic, i.e. that $-H^L$ converges to infinity. Then

$$\theta_j/\theta_k = (t_j/q_j)/(t_k/q_k) = (H^j/H^0 - 1)/(H^k/H^0 - 1) \rightarrow 1,$$

which implies that uniform taxation is optimal.

One important application of additivity is the life cycle framework. Atkinson and Stiglitz assert that, if we interpret the n commodities as consumption over n periods, utility is additive according to

$$V(L) + \sum_{t=1}^{n} U(x_t),$$

and if $r > 0$ so that a rising consumption profile is optimal for the consumer, then

$$\theta_t/\theta_{t+j}(<, =, >)1 \quad \text{as} \quad H^t(<, =, >)H^{t+j},$$

by (4.4), with $j = t$ and $k = t + j$.[1] Thus, for example, if the elasticity of marginal utility is constant, then it is optimal to impose a proportional consumption tax. However, if the elasticity of marginal utility is increasing in consumption and the consumption profile is rising over the life cycle, it is optimal to impose a higher tax rate in the future. In that case, the consumption tax must be supplemented with an interest income tax.[2] This result tends to conform nicely with the result derived in the overlapping generations model of the last chapter. Of course, if the elasticity is decreasing in consumption and the consumption profile is rising over the life cycle, then it is optimal to subsidize interest income.

It is instructive to consider two examples quite popular in the literature. First, suppose $U = \ln(c)$. Then $H^t = 1$ and $\theta_t = \theta$ for $t = 1, 2, \ldots, n$. Next, suppose utility is isoelastic, $U = c^{1-\sigma}/(1 - \sigma)$. Now $H^t = \sigma$ and once again, $\theta_t = \theta$. In both cases, uniform taxation is optimal.

There are two possible shortcomings of this analysis. First, it is partial equilibrium in the sense that it ignores the position of the economy relative to the golden rule expansion path. As we saw in the last chapter, this can be quite important in determining the properties of the optimal tax system. Second, the representative consumer experiences a finite horizon known with perfect certainty. In the next section we will study a model where the agent experiences an infinite horizon. Confronting an infinite horizon can sometimes be a proxy for facing an horizon of uncertain length.

4.3. Optimal taxation in the Ramsey growth model: the zero tax result

In this section we will introduce a discrete version of the Ramsey growth model studied by Judd (1985) and Chamley (1986).[3] Time is discrete and the economy lasts for ever. There is one good available, which can be consumed or stored as capital for use in production in the future. All private agents behave in an atomistic way, taking aggregate variables as beyond their own control. Private inputs of capital (K) and labor (L) are combined to produce output (Y) according to a neoclassical, constant-returns-to-scale, production function, $Y_t = f(K_t, L_t)$, which is twice differentiable, concave, and monotonically increasing in both inputs. A large number of identical, competitive firms produce the consumption good. Profit maximization implies that

$$f_K = r, \tag{4.5}$$

$$f_L = w, \tag{4.6}$$

where subscripts denote partial derivatives. The economy is populated by a large number of identical consumers. Each consumer lives for ever.

For simplicity, we will assume there is one consumer who behaves atomistically. The representative consumer's preferences are given by

$$\sum_{t=0}^{\infty} \beta^t U(c_t, 1 - L_t), \tag{4.7}$$

where $U(\ )$ is the period utility function. It is twice continuously differentiable, quasi-concave, and monotonically increasing in both consumption (c) and leisure $(1 - L)$ each period, where $\beta = 1/(1 + \rho)$ is the discount factor, and ρ is the rate of time preference. The agent's budget constraint is given by

$$w_t(1 - t_{wt})L_t + [1 + r_t(1 - t_{rt})]a_t - a_{t+1} - c_t = 0, \quad \text{for } t > 0, \tag{4.8}$$

where $a = k + b$ is asset accumulation, k is capital accumulation, b is the stock of one-period government bonds, r is the real return on investment, w is the wage rate, and t_r and t_w are the taxes on capital and labor income, respectively, as before. The consumer chooses infinite sequences $\{c_t, L_t, k_{t+1}, b_{t+1}\}$ to maximize (4.7) subject to (4.8), taking a_0 as given. For an interior solution, the first-order conditions are given by

$$U_c(c_t, 1 - L_t) = \beta[1 + r_{t+1}(1 - t_{rt+1})]U_c(c_{t+1}, 1 - L_{t+1}), \tag{4.9a}$$

$$U_L(c_t, 1 - L_t) = w_t(1 - t_{wt})U_c(c_t, 1 - L_t), \tag{4.9b}$$

where (4.9a) governs the optimal intertemporal consumption decision and (4.9b) governs the optimal labor supply decision. The sequence of equations (4.9) governs the sequence of decisions involving consumption, labor supply, and asset accumulation.

The government collects taxes imposed on labor and asset income in order to finance spending (g) each period. The government's budget constraint is given by

$$g_t + (1 + r_t)b_t = b_{t+1} + r_t t_{rt} a_t + w_t t_{wt} L_t, \quad \text{for } t > 0, \tag{4.10}$$

where b_t is one-period government debt that pays the net market return.

To close the model, note that the resource constraint is given by

$$f(k_t, L_t) + k_t = k_{t+1} + c_t + g_t, \quad \text{for } t > 0. \tag{4.11}$$

All agents behave atomistically and competitively.

There are several ways to derive the main zero tax rate result in this literature. However, both Judd and Chamley used the method employed by Atkinson and Stiglitz and we will follow them in discussing their result. The first step is to write the government's decision problem in terms of quantities rather than net prices. To this end, iterate on (4.8) using backward substitution and substitute (4.9) into the resulting equation for net prices to obtain

$$\Gamma = \sum_{t=0}^{\infty} \beta^t [L_t U_L(c_t, 1 - L_t) - c_t U_c(c_t, 1 - L_t)]$$

$$+[1 + f_k(k_0, L_0)(1 - t_{r0})]k_0 U_c(c_0, 1 - L_0) = 0. \tag{4.12}$$

This is known as the *implementability constraint*. It ensures that the consumer behaves optimally as the economy evolves along the growth path after the tax policy has been imposed and that the consumer's budget constraint is not violated on the optimal growth path.

The government chooses quantities to maximize (4.7) subject to the resource constraint and the implementability constraint. The Lagrangean can be written as

$$\sum \beta^t \{U(c_t, 1 - L_t) + \alpha_t[f(k_t, L_t) + kt - k_{t+1} - c_t - g_t]\} + \mu_0\Gamma,$$

where α_t and μ_0 are the multipliers.

First, notice that if t_{r0} can be chosen optimally we obtain

$$-rk_0 U_c(c_0, 1 - L_0)\mu_0 \geq 0.$$

If $t_{r0} > 0$, then $\mu_0 = 0$. However, in that case the implementability constraint is irrelevant. Differentiating the Lagrangean with respect to c_t, L_t, and k_{t+1} we obtain, respectively,

$$U_c(c_t, 1 - L_t) = \alpha_t,$$
$$U_L(c_t, 1 - L_t) = \alpha_t f_L(k_t, L_t),$$

and

$$\alpha_t / \alpha_{t+1} = \beta(1 + f_k).$$

In a steady state, it follows that

$$U_c(c_t, 1 - L_t)/U_c(c_{t+1}, 1 - L_{t+1}) = 1 = \beta(1 + f_k)$$
$$U_L(c_t, 1 - L_t)/U_c(c_t, 1 - L_t) = f_L.$$

These are the first-best conditions from the social planner's problem. Thus, if t_{r0} can be chosen optimally, the first-best allocation can be supported as a competitive equilibrium. The reason is due to the fact that k_0 is fixed at the beginning of the planning horizon and thus t_{r0} acts like a non-distorting tax. If a non-distorting tax is available, distorting taxes should not be employed. We will assume that $t_{r0} = 0$ to eliminate this possibility, following the literature.

To obtain the main result, differentiate the Lagrangean with respect to k_{t+1} to obtain

$$\alpha_t \beta^t = \alpha_{t+1} \beta^{t+1} [1 + f_k(k_{t+1}, L_{t+1})]. \tag{4.13}$$

In a steady state this implies that $1 = \beta(1 + f_k)$. Since consumption and labor supply are constant in a steady state, we have from the consumer's decision problem, $1 = \beta[1 + f_k(1 - t_r)]$. This will coincide with (4.13) in a steady state only if $t_r = 0$. Thus, interest income should not be taxed in a steady state.

As noted by Chamley, this result can be extended to the case where there are many consumption goods available and where there are many capital stocks as well. With many consumption goods available, it is still optimal not to tax capital income, although it may be optimal to tax commodities differentially at a point in time. The result also extends to the case where agents are heterogeneous as long as the government uses the same discount rate for each type. Interestingly enough, the result does not depend on an infinite interest elasticity of savings. Judd and Chamley both consider more general models where the discount rate is endogenous and at the optimum is equal to the rate of return on capital in a steady state. It follows from this that the interest elasticity of savings is not necessarily infinite in the long run. Thus, the magnitude of the interest elasticity of savings is not critically important in determining whether or not a tax on capital is optimal. And Judd derives the result in the context of a two-class economy where there are workers who do not save and capitalists who do. So the zero tax result does not require a homogeneous population.

Chamley also studies the dynamic path of the economy for the special case of isoelastic preferences. He shows that for this case there exists a time period τ such that for $t < \tau$ high taxes are imposed on capital but for $t \geq \tau$ the tax rate on capital income is zero. The high tax on capital early in the horizon is equivalent to lumpsum taxation since the capital stock early in the planning horizon in his continuous time model is fixed. In the isoelastic case the transition to the asymptotic zero tax rate is instantaneous. Prior to time τ the lumpsum nature of the tax dominates the distortion of the capital accumulation decision. However, after τ the opposite is the case.

There is an interesting case where the zero tax result does not hold up. In the last chapter we motivated the infinite horizon model by assuming that agents experienced a finite life themselves but cared about the welfare of the offspring. This leads to a model where the parent alive at time t behaves as if she confronts an infinite horizon planning problem. Essentially, this delivers a utility function similar to (4.7). However, if the parent actually cares about the size of the bequest itself, in the sense that the bequest enters the parent's utility function as a separate argument, then the long run zero tax result will not go through. In that case, it once again becomes optimal to impose a tax on interest income.[4] As we will see in Chapter 11, the empirical evidence on bequests does not support the model of pure altruism, where the parent cares about the welfare of the offspring as the sole motive for bequeathing resources to the next generation. Parents may instead care explicitly about the level of the bequest, or there may be a strategic motive involved in making a bequest; for example, the parent may attempt to use the bequest in order to elicit certain behavior from the offspring. In either case, this long-run result will not go through and taxing capital income may be optimal.

In Judd's (1985) two-class model of workers and capitalists, the interest income tax may be shifted substantially to workers. A small increase in the capital income tax rate will induce a decrease in capital accumulation that lowers the wage received by the workers under certain conditions. The incidence of the tax may be substantially shifted to workers in the short run as the economy converges to a steady state. However, Judd also provides a case where workers desire an increase in the tax rate. This occurs because under certain conditions the income effects dominate and the capitalists save more at the margin in that particular case and this raises the wage.

Judd shows that the optimal capital income tax rate vanishes in the limit even if the social planner cares only about the welfare of the workers. It follows that the capital income tax cannot be used to effect redistribution in the long run. Thus, the long-run result does not depend on efficiency considerations alone. Of course, as Judd admits, the obvious problem with this long-run result is that it is not known how long it will take for the economy to converge, or how much redistribution will take place as the economy converges.

In an interesting contribution, Kemp, Long, and Shimomura (1993) argue that the economy modeled by Judd and Chamley may not converge to a steady state. Indeed, they show that the steady state may be unstable, and that even if it is stable the optimal tax rate on capital may follow a spiral about the steady state, rather than converge to it, depending on the parameters of the model. They provide a numerical example where the economy follows a closed orbit in which the capital income tax rate alternates endlessly from positive to negative. (See section A of the Appendix to their paper.) Furthermore, they argue that, if the government wants to redistribute from capitalists to workers, it may not best for the economy to converge to a steady state where such redistribution cannot take place. Instead, it may be preferable for the economy to enter a closed orbit where capital income is taxed and redistributed to workers, thus sacrificing some long-run efficiency for short-run equity.

In a more recent contribution, Judd (1999) allows for many public goods, some of which may affect the technology of private production, non-stationary production functions, and human capital. He invokes two key principles from the optimal commodity tax literature: the uniformity of the optimal tax rates under certain conditions, and the prohibition of taxing intermediate goods such as capital under the production efficiency result of Diamond and Mirrlees (1971a). Judd shows that, if the marginal social value of government wealth is uniformly bounded, the average distortion introduced by the capital income tax is zero *on average* over any long period of time, regardless of whether or not the economy actually converges to a steady state equilibrium. Furthermore, if the economy does converge to a steady state, the optimal tax rate on capital is zero. Judd extends the model to include human capital investments and presents an example where it is optimal to tax labor income, physical capital is exempt from taxation, and human capital investments are subsidized.

Judd also points out that a variety of current consumption tax proposals would shift taxation from physical capital to human capital by taxing labor income more heavily without any real justification. He argues there is no aggregate efficiency reason for shifting the burden of taxation from physical to human capital. Thus, advocates of a consumption tax should perhaps also support a subsidy for human capital development as part of their consumption tax proposals.

We can mention one possible caveat to the Judd–Chamley zero tax result right away. Suppose the government fixes its expenditures to be equal to a constant fraction of GNP according to $g = \gamma f(k)$ for all t, for some positive constant γ, where $0 < \gamma < 1$. Indeed, the ratio of government spending to GNP in many countries has been relatively stable in the postwar era. In that case, (4.13) becomes

$$\alpha_t \beta^t = \alpha_{t+1}\beta^{t+1}[1 + (1 - \gamma)f_k].$$

In a steady state this implies that $(1 - \gamma)f_k = \rho$. However, from the consumer's decision problem, we have $(1 - t_r)f_k = \rho$ since the consumer takes government spending as given. Hence, it follows that $t_r = \gamma > 0$ in a steady state. Therefore, if the government chooses its spending to be equal to a constant fraction of GNP, it is optimal to tax capital income at a rate equal to that constant fraction in the long run.

4.4. An extension of the model: untaxed factors

Correia (1996) pointed out, in an interesting extension of Judd and Chamley's analysis, that there may be other factors of production supplied in an elastic fashion that cannot be taxed. Additional restrictions on the government's ability to tax the various factors of production may imply that it is optimal to tax capital income in a steady state.

To see this, suppose there is a third factor of production, a, and the representative agent's endowment of this factor is a^*. Preferences at time t are given by $U(c_t, 1 - L_t, a^* - a_t)$, and our earlier assumptions apply. Output is produced according to $f(k_t, L_t, a_t)$.

Profit maximization implies (4.5) and (4.6) once again. In addition, we obtain the condition $f_a = p_t$, where p is the price of renting the third factor. Utility maximization on the part of the consumer leads to the same conditions as before. We also have

$$U_a(c_t, 1 - L_t, a^* - a_t) = p_t U_c(c_t, 1 - L_t, a^* - a_t), \qquad (4.14)$$

where $U_a = \partial U / \partial a$.

Correia assumes that the third factor cannot be taxed or, more generally, that it cannot be taxed optimally. This requires that an additional condition be imposed on the government's optimal policy choices, namely, (4.14). The Lagrangean for the government's restricted decision problem is

$$\sum \beta^t \{ U(c_t, 1 - L_t, a^* - a_t) + \alpha_t [f(k_t, L_t) + k_t - k_{t+1} - c_t - g_t]$$
$$+ \phi_t [U_a(c_t, 1 - L_t, a^* - a_t) - f_a(k_t, L_t, a_t) U_c(c_t, 1 - L_t, a^* - a_t)] \}$$
$$+ \mu_0 \Omega,$$

where the implementability constraint is given by

$$\Omega = \sum \beta^t [L_t U_L(c_t, 1 - L_t, a^* - a_t) - c_t U_c(c_t, 1 - L_t, a^* - a_t)$$
$$+ a_t U_a(c_t, 1 - L_t, a^* - a_t)] + [1 + f_k(k_0, L_0, a_0)(1 - t_{r0})]$$
$$k_0 U_c(c_0, 1 - L_0, a^* - a_0) = 0.$$

Differentiate the Lagrangean with respect to k_{t+1} to obtain,

$$-\alpha_t \beta^t + \alpha_{t+1} \beta^{t+1} (1 + f_k) - \phi_{t+1} f_{ak} \beta^{t+1} = 0. \qquad (4.15)$$

In a steady state we can rearrange this equation to obtain

$$\alpha(f_k - \rho) = \phi f_{ak}. \tag{4.16}$$

At the optimum, $\alpha > 0$ and $\phi > 0$. And from the consumer's decision problem, we know that $1 = \beta[1 + f_k(1 - t_r)]$ or $f_k - \rho = t_r f_k$. Combining this information, (4.16) implies

$$t_r = \phi f_{ak}/\alpha f_k.$$

Therefore, it follows that the sign of t_r is equal to the sign of f_{ak}. If a and k are complements (substitutes), then $f_k > (<) \rho$ and $t_r > (<)0$. In the former case it is optimal to tax capital income even though the horizon is infinite.

The intuition is that taxing or subsidizing capital indirectly affects the untaxed factor. If the third factor and capital are complements, a tax on capital is an optimal way of taxing the third factor, and conversely if they are substitutes. Of course, assuming there is an untaxed factor is somewhat arbitrary. The general point, however, is that if there is such a restriction on the government's ability to impose the tax structure over time, it may not be optimal to impose a zero tax rate on capital. Whether capital should be taxed or subsidized is an empirical issue that must be decided on a case-by-case basis depending on the sign of f_{ak}.

4.5. Results from the endogenous growth model

Since the papers by Romer (1986) and Lucas (1988), the endogenous growth model has become a popular framework for explaining long-run growth. In these models the growth rate itself is endogenous, as the name suggests. Thus, the growth rate can be affected by policy and, more specifically, by the government's tax policy. As it turns out, the growth rate of the economy can be reduced dramatically by imposing taxes that affect the accumulation of any factor that stimulates the growth rate at the margin. There is also some recent empirical evidence in support of the model (see Kneller, Bleaney, and Gemmell 1999).

First, we present a simple version of the endogenous growth model, the Ak model, and then we discuss Lucas's model. The technology is linear and only capital is used in production according to $y_t = Ak_t$. The utility function of the representative agent with an infinite horizon is given by $\sum \beta^t U(c_t)$ for simplicity. The consumer's budget constraint is given by

$$[1 + r_t(1 - t_{rt})]k_t - k_{t+1} - c_t = 0.$$

The Euler equation of the consumer's decision problem is

$$U_c(c_t)/U_c(c_{t+1}) = \beta[1 + r_{t+1}(1 - t_{rt+1})] = \beta[1 + A(1 - t_{rt+1})],$$

where the last equality follows from profit maximization so that $r = A$.

On a balanced growth path, output per worker, capital per worker, and consumption per worker all grow at the same rate. Suppose $U = \ln(c)$. Then the growth rate is given by

$$\gamma_c = c_{t+1}/c_t - 1 = \beta[A(1 - t_r) - \rho].$$

Furthermore, the resource constraint can be written as

$$Ak_t + k_t - k_{t+1} - c_t - g_t = 0,$$

which can be rewritten as

$$\gamma_k = (k_{t+1} - k_t)/k_t = A - (c_t + g_t)/k_t.$$

Since A is constant and the lefthand side of the last equation is constant on a balanced growth path, it follows that $(c_t + g_t)/k_t$ must also be constant on a balanced growth path. Thus, $c, g,$ and k all grow at the same rate, and therefore the common growth rate is determined by $\beta[A(1 - t_r) - \rho]$. It then follows that the growth rate is decreasing in the capital income tax rate. In that case, it is not optimal to tax capital income in the long run.

Lucas (1988, 1990) extended this model by incorporating human capital in order to explain postwar data for the United States, and his main conclusion was that income from capital should not be taxed at all because such taxation can permanently reduce the growth rate. It is worth quoting him at length:

When I left graduate school in 1963, I believed that the single most desirable change in the US tax structure would be the taxation of capital gains as ordinary income. I now believe that neither capital gains nor any of the income from capital should be taxed at all.[5]

This is quite a remarkable statement, and is based on his study of the endogenous growth model. So it is worth discussing his analysis in some detail. We will present a discrete time version of his model to maintain the notation presented earlier.

Preferences are represented by the discounted sum of utilities over an infinite horizon as before,

$$\sum_{t=0}^{\infty} \beta^t U(c_t, 1 - L_t - e_t), \tag{4.17}$$

where L is labor supplied to the labor market in exchange for a wage rate, and e is time spent engaged in the pursuit of acquiring human capital. The resources constraint is

$$f(k_t, L_t h_t) + k_t - c_t - k_{t+1} - g_t = 0, \tag{4.18}$$

where h is the stock of human capital, Lh is effective labor, and $f(\ )$ is a neoclassical CRS technology. The stock of human capital evolves according to

$$h_t = h_{t-1} + s(e_{t-1})h_{t-1}, \tag{4.19}$$

where $s(\ )$ is concave.

Profit maximization leads to equations similar to (4.5) and (4.6), namely, $w_t = f_L(k_t, L_t h_t) = \partial f / \partial L_t h_t$, and $r_t = f_k(k_t, L_t h_t) = \partial f / \partial k_t$. Utility maximization by the consumer also leads to conditions similar in spirit to those presented earlier in this chapter. There are three margins of choice: the intertemporal consumption allocation decision, the labor supply decision, and the allocation of time between working and acquiring additional human capital.

Lucas then extends the zero tax result to the case where the economy converges to the balanced growth path rather than a steady state where growth stops. If the economy converges to a balanced growth path where output per capita, consumption per capita, capital per capita, and human capital per capita all grow at the same rate, capital should not be taxed in the long run. He then shows how the growth rate can be affected by taxation. If preferences are isoelastic according to $U(c_t, 1 - L_t - e_t) = [c_t(1 - L_t - e_t)]^{(1-\sigma)} / (1 - \sigma)$, the marginal product of capital is equal to $\rho + \sigma v$, where v is the growth rate of consumption; that is, $f_k = \rho + \sigma v$ on a balanced growth path. It follows that capital should not be taxed if the economy converges to a balanced growth path in the long run. Note that this remains true even when agents accumulate human capital as well. Therefore, the consumption tax dominates the general income tax if the economy is on a balanced growth path in Lucas's endogenous growth model.

Finally, assuming that the United States is a closed economy on a balanced growth path, Lucas parameterizes his model in order to simulate what would happen if the optimal Ramsey taxes were imposed. The experiment essentially involves reducing the tax imposed on capital income while the labor income tax rate adjusts so as to maintain the government's budget. In addition, government spending per unit of human capital and government transfers per unit of human capital are fixed. Complete elimination of the capital income tax would increase the per capita capital stock by about 34 per cent, increase per capita consumption by about 4.2–6 per cent, depending on whether or not labor supply is endogenous, improve welfare by 5.5 per cent, reduce labor supply by 2 per cent when it is endogenous, and increase the labor income tax rate only from 40 to 46 per cent (see case B depicted in Lucas 1990: 305, tables 2–4). Interestingly enough, the numerical results do not seem to depend on much in the model aside from the marginal product of capital condition and the curvature of the production function.

These results tend to confirm the early work by Feldstein, Boskin, Bradford, and Summers, among others, discussed in the last two chapters. However, several caveats should be mentioned. First, most of the optimal taxation literature assumes that the government is absolutely committed to its tax policy. This, however, ignores the potential time inconsistency problem; after the government has implemented a tax system that eliminates the tax on capital, it always has an incentive to renege on that policy by taxing the current stock of capital at a high rate since this is tantamount to imposing a non-distorting tax on a fixed factor.

Second, it is assumed that the only opportunity cost of acquiring human capital is forgone earnings; other costs, such as school building and maintenance costs, teacher salaries, and incidental out-of-pocket costs, are not included, yet may be significant in the aggregate. In addition, Lucas also assumes that government spending does not affect production. As we will see in the next section, if government spending can improve the marginal productivity of capital investment, then a tax on capital may be part of the government's optimal policy in the long-run.

In an interesting contribution, Kim (1998) calculates the impact of tax policy on growth by comparing the United States to Korea using a computer simulation model. He sets up a model of endogenous growth similar to Lucas's model involving human and physical capital, where goods produce the human capital rather than time, and includes a full range of government policies and additional private securities, such as bonds and equities. The model is calibrated to mimic the behavior of the actual economies. Kim finds that about 30 per cent of the difference in growth can be attributed to differences in tax systems. Interestingly enough, differences in the labor income tax account for 20 per cent of the difference in growth rates. In addition, Kim also calculates only a modest effect from eliminating all taxes on growth in the United States.

Pecorino (1993) extended Lucas's model by assuming three sectors in the economy—a consumption goods sector, a physical capital sector, and a human capital sector—and focusing his attention on the positive effects of the tax structure on the growth rate. The main extension is that both labor (time) and capital are combined to produce human capital, whereas Lucas assumed that only time was involved. Using a Cobb–Douglas technology for each sector and isoelastic preferences, Pecorino simulates the balanced growth path of the model under different tax policies and assumptions. In particular, he shows that the effect of taxation on the equilibrium path depends on the factor intensity of the consumption goods sector relative to the capital goods sector.

Several important points emerge from Pecorino's study. If tax rates on capital and consumption are chosen to maximize growth, then the factor used more intensively in the consumption sector should be taxed at a higher rate. Second, when labor supply is endogenous, capital depreciation is constant across sectors, and the technology differs only by a scaling parameter across sectors, then equal taxation of human capital and physical capital will maximize growth. Third, when labor supply is endogenous, the growth maximizing tax rates are skewed toward taxing physical capital. Finally, Pecorino simulates replacement of the income tax with a consumption tax when there is no depreciation and the technologies are the same across sectors. The growth rate increases from 1.53 to 2.53 per cent and welfare improves by about 3.4 per cent of consumption under such a reform.

Hendricks (1999) argued that large growth effects of taxation could be due to two important assumptions typically made in the recent literature: that the representative decisionmaker has an infinite horizon in the model, and that human capital accumulation only requires time. He uses an OG model and assumes that the representative agent experiences a finite horizon, that human capital production includes goods inputs as well as time, and that goods inputs into the production of human capital are tax deductible. He then simulates his model and shows that the growth effect of eliminating all taxes is much smaller than the usual result. Furthermore, he parameterizes an OG model, where the representative agent experiences a finite planning horizon, and the Ramsey growth model, where the agent experiences an infinite horizon, so the two models simulate the same steady state, and he shows that the growth effects of taxation are higher in the infinite horizon model. The small growth effects that Hendricks calculates for the OG model are consistent with the US experience in the postwar era, a period that saw a dramatic increase in income tax revenue coupled with only a small change in the growth rate. Hendricks also shows that the growth effects increase if human capital training is subsidized.

The results of Kim, Pecorino, and Hendricks suggest that the impact of taxation on the economy's growth rate may be very model-specific. It may depend critically on the length of the representative agent's planning horizon and the manner in which human capital accumulation is modeled. In addition, the taxation of labor income may be more important than previous researchers had thought, although Judd is an exception. In the next section we will present a number of other important caveats.

4.6. Caveats

Aiyagari (1995) argued that individuals face shocks and incomplete insurance markets which may cause borrowing constraints to become binding in some periods of their horizon. In his model, this has the effect of breaking up an infinite horizon into finite segments. Agents may save as a precaution against experiencing a large negative income shock that would cause the constraints on borrowing to be binding. Such precautionary savings are inefficient. Aiyagari shows that the optimal capital income tax rate should be strictly positive as a result. In simulations of his model he shows that observed capital income tax rates can be generated by the model. This may provide an explanation for why we observe taxes on capital.

Jones, Manuelli, and Rossi (1993) study a sequence of endogenous growth models involving human capital accumulation and productive government spending. In the first model they assume there are two types of capital, physical capital and human capital, and that both forms of capital enter the model in a symmetric fashion. They then show that it is actually optimal for the government not to tax either form of capital in the long run. Instead, the government should impose high tax rates early in its planning horizon (since the capital stocks are fixed in the short run), run a budget surplus, and then lower tax rates to zero asymptotically and use the surplus to finance future government spending. Consumption per capita, physical capital per capita, and welfare all increase as a result of imposing the optimal Ramsey tax debt system.

These results are extended in a second model by assuming that human capital accumulation is asymmetric; it requires time as an input and this is an untaxed activity. It is still optimal for the tax rate on physical capital to go to zero eventually. However, this is also true of the tax rate imposed on labor earnings—both income tax rates approach zero asymptotically. Interestingly enough, high tax rates on consumption and physical capital are optimal early in the planning horizon. However, a subsidy to human capital is also optimal early in the planning horizon, followed by a positive tax rate later. For their choice of functional forms and parameters, all tax rates eventually approach zero and future spending is financed out of the surplus produced early in the horizon.

Finally, they incorporate productive public spending into a special case of the model. It is assumed that private capital is the only input to producing output, for simplicity; in other words, labor is not used. They assume that public capital, however, improves the productivity of private investment. The agent's constraints are given by

$$\sum [(1 - \tau_{rt})k_t - c_t - x_t] \geq 0$$

and

$$k_{t+1} = (1 - \delta)k_t + G(x_t, g_t),$$

where x is investment, δ is the depreciation rate, and $G(\ )$ is the private capital produced by the investment. It is assumed that $G(\ )$ is homogeneous of degree one in both inputs, is concave, and is differentiable. Government spending (g) improves the productivity of investment. They show that in some cases the limiting tax rate on capital is not zero. The intuition is that if government spending is productive profits are generated, and the tax on capital is an indirect tax on those profits.

Milesi-Ferreti and Roubini (1998) included three sectors in an endogenous growth model: a sector that produces the consumption good, a sector that produces human capital, and a sector that produces leisure, where capital and time are both required. The system is block-recursive when leisure is produced via a constant-returns-to-scale (CRS) technology and the production of leisure does not affect the growth rate. They also derive the result that all taxes on labor and capital should be zero in the long-run equilibrium.

The main problem with the optimal Ramsey policy of introducing high tax rates early in the horizon in order to generate a surplus is that it assumes politicians will not use the surplus for wasteful public spending projects once it has been built up. One might be somewhat skeptical of such an assumption in a democracy. If there is a probability that politicians in the future might spend the surplus in a wasteful manner, this might reduce the incentive to impose high tax rates now in order to generate a surplus. Second, it assumes that consumers experience an infinite planning horizon. Realistically, however, this will not be so. It follows that some agents will experience the high tax rates early on, but not the low taxes later on, and will be worse off relative to another policy which smoothes tax rates out over time.

Another extension of the analysis is to assume that markets are incomplete. Hubbard and Judd (1986) also raise the issue of liquidity constraints and argue that such constraints may have the effect of making a tax on interest income optimal, ceteris paribus. In US data it would appear that about 19–20 per cent of the population is liquidity constrained in the sense that they cannot borrow when young. Using a version of the Ramsey growth model, Hubbard and Judd impose the additional constraint that the agent's stock of assets be non-negative for the entire horizon. Simulations using a Cobb–Douglas technology and isoelastic preferences indicate that the capital stock is about 35 per cent higher when there is a liquidity constraint for about 19 per cent of the population than when there is not. They then argue that a switch from an interest income tax to a wage tax reduces the consumption of liquidity constrained individuals and thus creates a first-order welfare loss for this group. The intuition is that the liquidity constraint acts like a pre-existing distortion and thus creates a first-order welfare effect, whereas the usual tax distortions are of second-order importance. This first-order loss must be compared with the second-order loss in welfare associated with the direct distortion of the intertemporal consumption decision for agents who are not liquidity constrained. In some cases there can be a net welfare loss associated with a tax reform that switches from interest taxation to wage or consumption taxation.

In his discussion of Hubbard and Judd's paper, Hall (1986) argued that families can mitigate the problems associated with liquidity constraints by lending across generations. In addition, if the problem has not been solved within the family, then perhaps the problem really does not exist for the government to solve through its choice of tax policy. Summers (1986) in his comment on Hubbard and Judd's paper was also very skeptical about the main results and suggested (among other points) that, if liquidity constraints were really a problem, then perhaps a policy focused directly on the constraint would be more appropriate. For example, if young people cannot borrow in order to attend college because they are liquidity constrained, then perhaps a low interest student loan program is a more appropriate policy to employ in alleviating the constraint. Tax policy can then be free to raise revenue for general spending purposes.

However, Browning and Burbidge (1990) argue that the case involving liquidity constraints was not really stated clearly by Hubbard and Judd. They claim that the real problem is that the constraint may cause individuals to acquire too little human capital. They study a partial equilibrium model of an individual who confronts a borrowing restriction in the first period of a T-period horizon, where T is finite. Labor supply is fixed and the agent wishes to acquire human capital in the first period. They simulate their model assuming isoelastic preferences and show that the optimal tax structure typically involves a positive tax on interest income and a very low tax rate on consumption. In the absence of human capital and the liquidity constraint, a consumption tax is optimal since labor supply is fixed in their model. However, if the agent is liquidity constrained, it is optimal for the government to supplement a consumption tax with an interest income tax because this increases wealth early in the horizon by reducing the agent's tax liability when the liquidity constraint is binding, in the absence of human capital. This result is strengthened if the individual cannot borrow to finance the acquisition of human capital, thus further weakening the case for the consumption tax.

Zhu (1992) studies a stochastic version of the Ramsey growth model. The representative consumer cares about consumption and leisure in each period. The technology for producing the one consumption good is neoclassical. However, there are two sources of shocks to the economy: shocks can occur to the technology (z) and to government spending (g). The consumer maximizes expected lifetime utility. Consumers must make their savings decision before the shocks at time t, g_t and z_t are realized but must choose their labor supply at time t thereafter. Output is produced according to $f(k_t, L_t; z_t)$ where $\{z_t\}$ is a stochastic process. The government chooses tax rates on capital and labor income and decides how much state-contingent debt to issue. Markets clear and expectations are realized in equilibrium. In this setting Zhu shows that there is no presumption that the optimal *ex ante* capital income tax rate is zero, nor is there a presumption that it is zero in the long run.

Krusell, Quadrini, and Rios-Rull (1996) model the choice of a tax base within the context of a framework that includes political choices made by majority voting. They note that most industrial economies rely more heavily on income-based taxes than on consumption taxes and argue that there must be a reason for this. They seek the answer within the political mechanism. In their model, people differ in their labor endowment and solve a dynamic problem similar in spirit to the Ramsey model used by Judd and Chamley. In addition, people vote each period for the tax system next period, and thus the tax system and level of government spending are chosen by majority rule. They assume a single peakedness condition on preferences that is sufficient to imply that the median voter will be decisive. Voter–consumers are confronted by two possible tax systems, a pure consumption tax and a general income tax, and the revenue is redistributed equally among the population.

Krusell, Quadrini, and Rios-Rull simulate the steady state equilibrium of their model and come to some rather interesting conclusions. First, consumption taxation generates *lower* steady state output than income taxation. The consumption tax in their model is less distorting than the income tax, so voters choose a higher level of government redistribution and hence a greater level of taxation under the consumption tax. Second, the consumption tax generates lower output than the labor income tax, because the consumption base is broader for redistributive purposes and thus voters choose a higher consumption tax rate than under the labor income tax. Third, if capital income taxation is the only source of revenue, a wider distribution of wealth will generate high tax rates and large distortions as a result. A number of other interesting cases are considered and some of the results are somewhat surprising. For example, adding a general income tax to an economy in a steady state with consumption taxes can improve welfare. This is of some empirical interest, because many countries began their fiscal systems by introducing consumption based taxes first in the form of retail sales taxes, and then added an income tax later.

Judd (1997) considers the case where there is imperfect competition and shows that, while taxes on pure profits, wage income, and consumption are positive, capital income should generally not be taxed and under certain conditions should be subsidized. This result relies on two other well known results. First, it is well known that a monopolist will charge a price that is greater than marginal cost. The distortion created by such a firm can be alleviated through a subsidy if lumpsum taxation is available. Second, Diamond and Mirrlees (1971a, b) showed that only final goods should be subject to taxation, not intermediate goods. Judd combines these two ideas to argue that capital employed by a firm with market power should be subsidized since it is an intermediate good and thus the tax on such capital should be negative. However, this means that the income tax structure is still necessary in order to subsidize capital. Essentially, the capital income subsidy acts like an anti-trust policy. It serves to reduce the inefficiency associated with monopoly that can lead to lower capital intensity of production and lower output.

Guo and Lansing (1999) extend Judd's monopoly model by incorporating capital depreciation, a depreciation allowance, and endogenous government expenditures. They show that the optimal capital income tax rate balances the "underinvestment" effect, resulting from the existence of the monopoly noted by Judd, against the taxation of economic profits, the "profit" effect. If the government can impose the optimal profit tax, the negative "underinvestment" effect dominates and the tax on capital income is negative. However, if the government cannot impose the optimal profit tax, say, because corporations can disguise their cashflow, then it must rely on an imperfect tax instrument, the income tax, and the tax on capital may be positive as a result. They also show that, if the government introduces an accelerated depreciation allowance for capital, then the capital subsidy is not needed and the taxation of capital becomes optimal once again. Finally, the higher the level of spending by the government, the greater the need for tax revenue. This tends to accentuate the "profit" effect, making it more likely that the optimal tax on capital is positive.

The main problem with this general argument involving monopoly is that in many cases the classification of a commodity as an intermediate good or as a final commodity is somewhat arbitrary. Is a personal computer a final good that should be taxed, or an intermediate good that should be subsidized? If it is used in the home, one might be tempted to classify it as a final good. However, if it is used at a place of business, or if it is used in a "home office," then it might be classified as an intermediate good. Unfortunately, people might try to avoid a tax on final goods by purchasing personal computers for home use through their business, thus evading the tax. The same is true for a broad range of commodities, including automobiles, telephones, and furniture. The government would have to design rules and regulations to define exactly what is an intermediate good and put into place an enforcement mechanism. The administrative costs of introducing such a policy might be high enough to preclude undertaking the policy.

Finally, in Chapter 8 we will show that it is optimal to tax capital income in the Ramsey growth model if output causes a negative externality to the environment. If the representative consumer cares about the quality of the environment and that quality is decreasing in output per worker and hence in capital per worker, then the tax on capital in the long run may be justified as a Pigouvian externality tax.

4.7. Conclusion

In this chapter we discussed the more recent literature on optimal taxation that relies heavily on the Ramsey model, or versions of the model, where the representative agent experiences an infinite planning horizon. Within the context of Ramsey type models, Arrow and Kurz (1970), Judd (1985), Chamley (1986), and later Lucas (1990) argued that in the long run it was not optimal to tax capital income. This is especially true in the endogenous growth model employed by Lucas, because a tax on interest income generated from capital tends to permanently reduce the growth rate of the economy, with enormous implications for consumption and welfare. And Jones, Manuelli, and Rossi (1993) showed that it was suboptimal to tax either physical or human capital in the long run in a model where both forms of capital contribute to growth. Essentially, the government imposes high tax rates on both forms of capital early in its planning horizon, runs a surplus, and then lowers both tax rates asymptotically to zero and uses its surplus to finance future government spending.

A number of caveats to this basic zero tax rate result of not taxing capital in the long run were studied as well. These caveats include: government spending set equal to a fraction of GNP, precautionary savings resulting from incomplete insurance markets, productive public spending that enhances private investment, liquidity constraints, uncertainty and incomplete markets, the existence of monopoly, and negative externalities that adversely affect the environment. These extensions of the basic model all tend to indicate that exempting capital from taxation, or in some cases subsidization, may be suboptimal and that the general case for the consumption tax is very weak. This is in accord with the results of the early literature on the OG model studied in the last chapter. Therefore, we are tempted to conclude that it is most likely the case that it is suboptimal to impose a zero tax rate on capital income in a second-best environment even in the long run.

One final caveat to the Arrow–Kurz–Judd–Chamley–Lucas result that we should point out involves the taxation of capital on the transition path. Most of the debate has been about taxation in the long run. However, it is typically optimal to tax physical capital on the transition path to the long-run steady state equilibrium in versions of the Ramsey growth model, or to tax capital heavily at the beginning of the planning horizon in order to exploit the so-called capital levy. Indeed, the present value of capital income taxes paid on the transition path can be quite large even if the optimal long-run tax rate is zero. So the case for completely exempting capital income from taxation is rather weak in models of a closed economy.

NOTES TO CHAPTER 4

1. Notice that if the utility function is additive, $H^t = -c_t U_{cc}(c_t)/U_c(c_t)$, where $x_1 = c_1$, $x_2 = c_2$, and so on.
2. See Atkinson and Stiglitz (1972, page 214).
3. See also the recent paper by Atkeson, Chari, and Kehoe (1999).
4. To quote Chamley (1986), "Note that the result does not hold when the level of bequest is an explicit argument in the direct utility function." See the last paragraph on page 612.
5. This is, indeed, the first sentence of his seminal paper that was presented as the Hicks Lecture.

5

International Taxation of Capital

5.1. Introduction

In this chapter we will study the problem of consumption and capital taxation when resources are mobile.[1] When the economy is closed, relative prices are determined within the boundaries of the economy. When resources are taxed in that context, it is likely that agents will be less likely to supply the resource. Thus, taxation can cause agents to save and invest less, supply less labor, buy less of an asset, accumulate a smaller stock of a natural resource, and so on. We would expect this to raise the before-tax prices of these factors and shift some of the burden of the tax to other sectors of the economy.

Agents may also supply less of a factor when taxed in the context of an open economy where resources are mobile. However, there is an important new effect which must be considered when the economy is open: resources may leave the economy for another economy. This may be especially true when the policy is a tax imposed on capital. When the economy is open and capital is internationally mobile, arbitrage conditions must hold in equilibrium; and the after-tax returns must equalize across the different potential locations for the investment.[2] The same will be true of any resource when it is mobile. We will focus our attention on capital.

This raises the possibility that it may be very difficult to tax internationally mobile capital, and this is, indeed, one of the main issues studied in this chapter. The analysis of the last chapter, for example, may be moot if it is impossible for the government to tax capital income at all. On the other hand, the government may respond to such a situation by limiting the mobility of capital through the use of capital controls, or signing a tax treaty with other countries in order to tax it.

In the next section we will discuss some of the general principles of direct taxation when capital is mobile. When capital is mobile it may come under the jurisdiction of other taxing authorities in addition to the tax authority of the agent's own country. It follows that more than one government may attempt to tax a transaction or flow of capital income. There are two general principles of direct taxation in open economies: the residence principle and the source principle. Under the residence principle, the worldwide income of the resident is subject to tax regardless of its source. Under the source principle, all income generated within the territory of the economy is subject to tax regardless of who owns it.

Double taxation becomes a real possibility when capital is mobile across countries. Over time, two general methods have evolved to limit this problem. Credit can be given for foreign taxes paid, or a deduction can be allowed instead. Most countries operate under the credit provision and thus allow an investor credit up to the domestic tax rate for foreign tax paid. Investors prefer crediting to deducting since it yields a higher rate of return after taxes and provides greater assistance from double taxation.

For example, suppose the capital income tax rate is 50 per cent in the United States and 30 per cent in Canada. Under the credit system, an investor in the United States would pay 30 per cent per unit of capital income to the Canadian government on an investment in Canada and 20 per cent ($0.20 = 0.5 - 0.3$) to the US government on the same unit of capital income. The investor keeps 50 per cent of a unit of capital income after taxes have been paid; the overall tax rate is 50 per cent. Under the deduction method, foreign tax paid is deducted from taxable income instead. Thus, the US investor would pay 30 per cent to the Canadian government on an investment in Canada and 50 per cent of the remaining 70 per cent, or an additional 35 per cent ($(1 - 0.30) \times 0.50$), to the US government. Under this method the investor pays an overall tax rate of 65 per cent and thus nets only 35 per cent on a unit of income after taxes.

In Section 5.3 we present several models of the taxation of internationally mobile capital and study some of the predictions of the models. We first discuss the arbitrage or portfolio effect in a static model of capital allocation. A change in a tax rate may directly affect the arbitrage condition immediately setting up an incentive for agents to adjust their portfolios. For example, increasing the tax rate on domestic capital will lower the domestic after-tax return and induce agents to shift investment abroad. We next allow the savings decision to be endogenous; this adds greater complexity and ambiguity to the comparative statics exercises. We also study several incidence experiments involving the imposition of the residence principle, the source principle, and a consumption tax within the context of an OG model of two countries with perfect capital mobility.

In Section 5.4 we discuss some of the principles of optimal taxation in open economies. First, we describe the early work of Hamada (1966), Feldstein and Hartman (1979), and Bond and Samuelson (1989) on the optimality of credits or deductions and the existence of an equilibrium. Hamada set up a policy game between two countries choosing to tax capital income and argued that the credit system was preferred if neither country has market power in the world economy since it leads to a more efficient allocation of capital. However, Feldstein and Hartman showed that the deduction method might be preferred if the capital exporting country was a "Stackelberg leader" in the policy game. Bond and Samuelson showed that a Nash equilibrium does not exist under the credit method but does exist under the deduction method when countries are small and do not have any market power. Therefore, it follows that it may be difficult for a country to sustain the credit system.

Next, we discuss the results of Razin and Sadka (1991a, b) and Gordon (1992), who argued that it may be impossible for a small open economy to tax capital because of capital flight and tax evasion behavior. Taxing capital under the residence principle requires monitoring of the foreign source income of the resident. If this cannot be done, only domestically generated income can be taxed—the source principle. However, under the production efficiency result of Diamond and Mirrlees (1971a), it is not optimal to tax income at its source. This follows because taxing foreign-owned income will lead to capital flight, and labor or other immobile factors will bear the burden of the tax. Since immobile factors will bear the burden anyway, it is best to tax them directly rather than distort the capital allocation decision. This leaves taxing domestically owned capital. However, domestic investors may illegally evade the tax by investing in foreign companies, which then reinvest the funds back in the domestic economy, thus effectively evading the tax. Of course, taxpayers may honestly disclose their taxable income from foreign sources, thus eliminating this problem altogether.

Finally, we present the results of Horst (1980), Findlay (1986), and Keen and Piekkola (1997), who showed that source taxation may be optimal under certain conditions. The production efficiency result implicitly requires income transfers across countries and the taxation of pure profits. If such transfers are not forthcoming, or if pure profits cannot be taxed optimally, the production efficiency result will no longer hold. In that case, taxing capital flows may be optimal since such a tax serves as a substitute for the transfers across countries. The problem then becomes one of monitoring income.

In Section 5.5 we discuss the issue of policy coordination and present the results of Kehoe (1989), who argued that cooperation among countries, whereby several countries band together to reduce disparities in their respective tax systems, may not improve welfare. A tax treaty may be a simple way of allowing a group of countries to tax capital when none of the individual countries would be able to in the presence of capital mobility. Agents may try to avoid taxation by shifting their capital to countries that promise a low tax rate on capital income. A treaty attempts to minimize this possibility, thus allowing a collection of countries to tax capital collectively when none might be able to alone. Kehoe combines this idea with the time inconsistency problem of taxing capital income and shows that countries will tend to overtax capital under the cooperative solution.

In Section 5.6 we discuss the assumption that capital is mobile on empirical grounds. Feldstein and Horioka (1980) first challenged the view that capital was perfectly mobile. They analyzed a cross section data set of OECD countries and showed there was a significant positive correlation between domestic saving and domestic investment. If capital is perfectly mobile, savers will seek the highest return (adjusted for risk) worldwide, and this should produce a zero correlation between domestic saving and investment. However, Feldstein and Horioka found that the correlation was positive and significant. Other analysts noticed that rate-of-return differentials existed across countries, and it also appeared that international portfolio diversification was well below what reasonable models of international finance predicted.

This strongly suggests that capital is not perfectly mobile across countries and that investors may prefer to invest locally rather than globally. A number of possible explanations for this have been put forth. Unfortunately, none have yet evolved into the conventional wisdom. This is somewhat disquieting, since it is possible that incorporating a deep reason for capital immobility into a theoretical model may affect the optimal taxation of capital income. In any case, this may be an area of potentially fruitful research for future work.

In Section 5.7 we discuss the implications of capital mobility for the debate on the consumption tax. It turns out that, while allowing for capital mobility greatly complicates matters, it does not necessarily lead to the presumption that it is optimal to exempt capital income from taxation. It follows that allowing the economy to be open does not necessarily lead to the implication that the consumption tax is optimal per se. Section 5.8 briefly concludes the chapter.

5.2. Some basic principles of direct taxation

Following the convention in this literature, we will assume there is a home country and a foreign country and denote variables in the foreign country with an asterisk. Furthermore, we will present our discussion in terms of the home country, following tradition. (Readers are encouraged to see Frenkel, Razin, and Sadka (1991), for example, and the references contained in their discussion, for greater coverage of this topic, including the treatment of indirect taxes).

There are two basic principles of direct taxation when the economy is open to resource flows across its boundaries: the *residence* or worldwide principle, and the *source* or territorial principle. Under the residence principle, the home country government taxes the income of its residents regardless of the source of the income. A resident pays tax on capital income from domestic sources in the home country and on capital income from abroad, while foreigners are exempt from tax on capital income generated in the home country. Under the source system, all income generated within the home country is taxed by the government in the home country. Thus, residents and foreigners who own capital in the home country pay tax on the income from that capital, while residents of the home country do not pay tax on income they receive from abroad. Ignoring depreciation, taxing all income under the source principle is akin to taxing GDP, while taxing all income under the residence principle is akin to taxing GNP.

A country can apply one principle to all sources of income or it can apply different principles to different sources of income. For example, consider the hybrid system where the home country applies the source principle to labor income and the residence principle to capital income. In that case, all labor income generated in the home country is taxed, including the labor income of foreigners residing in the home country; however, only residents would pay tax on capital income generated within the home country and from abroad, while the income generated from capital invested in the home country by foreigners would be exempt.

A certain consistency in the tax treatment of capital must occur if arbitrage opportunities are to be eliminated. If both countries adopt the same principle, then double taxation of capital will not occur and such arbitrage opportunities will not exist when capital is freely mobile. However, if the two countries adopt different principles, or hybrid principles, this may create significant arbitrage opportunities which may make an equilibrium impossible to achieve.

To see this, we must define the tax rates that each country can impose on capital income flows. Let $t_r(A, B)$ represent the capital income tax rate imposed in the home country on taxpayer A where the source of income is B, where $A = R$, NR represents resident (R) or nonresident (NR), and $B = D$, F represents a domestic (D) source or a foreign (F) source of income. Thus, the home country can impose tax rates $t_r(R, D)$, $t_r(R, F)$, and $t_r(NR, D)$; the home country can tax the domestic capital income of its residents, the foreign capital income of its residents, and the capital income of nonresidents stemming from investments in the home country, respectively. Similarly, the foreign country can impose $t_r^*(R, D)$, $t_r^*(R, F)$, and $t_r^*(NR, D)$. Under the residence principle, the home country would choose $t_r(R, D) = t_r(R, F)$, and $t_r(NR, D) = 0$, while under the source principle, the home country would choose $t_r(R, D) = t_r(NR, D)$, and $t_r(R, F) = 0$, and similarly for the foreign country.

First, suppose both countries employ the residence principle. The resident of the home country can invest at home and earn $1 + r[1 - t_r(R, D)]$, or can invest in the foreign country and earn $1 + r^*[1 - t_r(R, F)]$. The two must be equal in order to eliminate any profitable arbitrage possibilities, implying

$$r[1 - t_r(R, D)] = r^*[1 - t_r(R, F)]. \tag{5.1}$$

If the two sources of income are taxed at the same rate, it follows immediately that $r = r^*$. The same is true from the foreign country's perspective. A resident in the foreign country can earn $1 + r^*[1 - t_r^*(R, D)]$ by investing domestically in the foreign country, or can earn $1 + r[1 - t_r^*(R, F)]$ by investing abroad in the home country. Arbitrage requires that the two be equal. If the foreign country taxes the two at the same rate, then $r^* = r$. It follows that, if both countries employ the residence principle, the resulting system will be consistent in the sense that $r = r^*$ in both countries.

Under the source principle, the resident of the home country can earn $1 + r[1 - t_r(R, D)]$ at home and $1 + r^*[1 - t_r^*(NR, D)]$ from an investment in the foreign country. Arbitrage requires that the two must be equal. Thus,

$$r[1 - t_r(R, D)] = r^*[1 - t_r^*(NR, D)]. \tag{5.2}$$

Similarly, in the foreign country,

$$r^*[1 - t_r^*(R, D)] = r[1 - t_r(NR, D)]. \tag{5.3}$$

If $t_r(R, D) = t_r(NR, D)$ and $t_r^*(R, D) = t_r^*(NR, D)$, then the two arbitrage conditions (5.2) and (5.3) are consistent.

More generally, the investor in the home country can earn $r[1 - t_r(R, D)]$ from an investment at home, or $r^*[1 - t_r^*(NR, D) - t_r(R, F)]$ from an investment in the foreign country, since the foreign country can tax capital invested in the foreign country and the home country can tax the same transaction. Thus,

$$r[1 - t_r(R, D)] = r^*[1 - t_r^*(NR, D) - t_r(R, F)]. \tag{5.4}$$

Similarly in the foreign country,

$$r^*[1 - t_r^*(R, D)] = r[1 - t_r(NR, D) - t_r^*(R, F)]. \tag{5.5}$$

Equations (5.4) and (5.5) must hold for an equilibrium to exist. It follows from these two equations that the following condition must hold:

$$[1 - t_r(R, D)][1 - t_r^*(R, D)] = [1 - t_r(NR, D) - t_r^*(R, F)][1 \\ -t_r^*(NR, D) - t_r(R, F)]. \tag{5.6}$$

Equations (5.1)–(5.3) are special cases of this.

Conflicts can arise if the two countries impose different systems. Suppose the home country taxes its own residents only on their domestic income and the foreign country imposes no taxes on capital at all. Then (5.6) becomes $[1 - t_r(R, D)] = 1$, which can hold only if the home country exempts the capital income of its residents. To see this, note that in the foreign country $r = r^*$. In the home country $r[1 - t_r(R, D)] = r^*$. Obviously, these two conditions cannot both hold simultaneously when $t_r(R, D) > 0$. The same is true if the two countries adopt different pure systems. However, credits or deductions can be used to alleviate the problem associated with double taxation. For example, many countries allow a credit for foreign taxes paid.

When the home country allows a credit for foreign taxes paid, it is essentially transferring tax revenue to the foreign country. Suppose the home country imposes the residence principle, the foreign country imposes the source principle, the tax rate is 30 per cent at home, and 25 per cent in the foreign country. Without credits or deductions, the resident of the home country would pay 25 per cent to the foreign country on any investment income generated there plus an additional 30 per cent on the same income to the home country. The after-tax return on an investment at home pays $0.70r$ for a home country resident, while an investment in the foreign country pays $(1 - 0.25 - 0.3)r^* = 0.45r^*$. However, if the home country provides a full credit for tax paid abroad, then the investor at home will pay 30 per cent tax on investment income generated at home and 30 per cent tax on investments abroad, where 25 per cent goes to the foreign country and 5 per cent goes to the home country. The credit converts the system to a residence based tax for the home investor. The home country collects tax only on the difference in tax rates, though. The home country would collect $0.30r$ on investments at home and $0.05r^*$ on investments abroad. Most countries do not credit above their own tax rate, however. Thus, a full definition of the residence system would also include full crediting for foreign taxes paid. Of course, under the source principle no crediting is required, since residents are not taxed on their foreign source income.

Countries can also allow a deduction for foreign taxes paid, rather than a credit. For example, if $r^* t_r^*(NR, D)$ is the tax per unit of investment in the foreign country imposed on the home country investor, the tax imposed on this same unit of investment by the home country under the deduction method is $t_r(R, F)[r^* - r^* t_r^*(NR, D)]$, where $r^* - r^* t_r^*(NR, D)$ is the tax base per unit of investment after deducting the tax paid by the investor to the foreign country. The after-tax return to a unit of investment under the deductions method is

$$[1 - t_r(R, F)][1 - t_r^*(NR, D)] - t_r(NR, D)]r^* = [1 - t_r(R, F)][1 - t_r^*(NR, D)]r^*,$$

and the investment is essentially taxed twice. Thus, the investment decision is distorted by both taxes under the deduction method. It follows that the credit method alleviates the double taxation problem more fully than the deduction method. We will compare the optimality of the two methods in Section 5.4.

The different tax systems may have different incidence effects as well. Ihori (1991) considered a revenue-neutral tax reform from a capital income tax to a consumption tax under each system and showed that the incidence of the reform would generally differ depending on which system is initially in place. Normally, we would expect agents to save more at the margin when the capital income tax rate is lowered. We can label this a "supply side" effect because it means that more capital will become available. Second, there may also be an "arbitrage" effect. If some assets are taxed at the margin but others are not and the tax rate is lowered, agents will adjust their portfolios by accumulating more of an asset whose relative after-tax return has increased and less of any asset whose relative return has fallen.

Under the residence principle, the before-tax rates of return must equalize across countries. It follows that a reduction in the interest income tax will induce only a supply side effect, not an arbitrage effect, since the tax rates do not enter the arbitrage equation. On the other hand, after-tax rates of return must equalize under the source principle. Therefore, a change in the interest income tax rate in one country will induce an arbitrage effect in addition to the supply side effect. It follows that, if one country introduces a reform that increases the consumption tax rate while simultaneously reducing the capital income tax rate so as to maintain revenue, the response of the economy under one principle will generally differ from the response under a different principle. We will study this in more detail in the next section.

5.3. Taxing mobile capital

In a closed economy it is well known that a tax on capital income may be partly shifted to other factors, such as labor. However, Bovenberg (1986) and Gordon (1986) showed that the burden of a tax on capital will be *completely* shifted to labor if the economy is small relative to the world capital market and capital is perfectly mobile.

Imagine that capital is perfectly mobile but labor is not. In that case, the return to capital is determined by the world economy and is thus exogenous to a small, open economy. Under the usual assumptions of competitive markets and profit maximization, the wage will be positively related to the amount of capital per worker available to the domestic economy. If the government imposes a tax on capital and capital is mobile, capital will move to a "safe haven" to avoid the tax and the before-tax wage will fall, thus shifting the burden of the tax entirely to labor. The elasticity of capital with respect to the tax would be infinite. Therefore, whether the economy is open or not is critically important to the incidence of the tax system and the choice between two tax systems.

In the early literature that modeled optimizing agents and endogenous investment decisions, Frenkel and Razin (1986a, b, 1989) and van Wijnbergen (1986) studied two-period models. Bovenberg (1986, 1989) used a version of the Ramsey growth model adapted to an open economy framework, where the representative consumer experiences an infinite planning horizon. Frenkel, Razin, and Symansky (1990) presented a T-period model including a linear technology that fixes producer prices; however, they conducted their theoretical analysis in a simplified two-period version of the model. Sibert (1985, 1990) and Ihori (1991) presented results in the context of a two-country OG model with a neoclassical technology, where agents experience a two-period planning horizon. In what follows we will study several highly stylized models of open economies to provide examples of the kind of analysis undertaken in this literature.

5.3.1. A static model of the allocation of capital

Consider a world economy composed of two countries, the home country and the foreign country. Suppose there is one good produced via capital and labor according to a well behaved, neoclassical technology. Let y be output produced at home, y^* be output produced in the foreign country, k be capital per worker in the home country, k^* be capital per worker in the foreign country, and let output be produced according to $y = f(k)$ and $y^* = f^*(k^*)$, where $f(\ )$ and $f^*(\ )$ satisfy the Inada conditions. Capital and output are perfectly mobile across countries, while labor is immobile.

There is one consumer in each country. The preferences of each consumer are represented by a well defined utility function that satisfies the usual assumptions, $U(c)$ and $U^*(c^*)$ in the home and foreign country, respectively. The consumer in the home country is endowed with one unit of labor, which is supplied in a perfectly inelastic fashion to the labor market in exchange for a wage, and k^e units of capital, which can be invested at home or in the foreign country. The consumer in the foreign country is endowed with one unit of labor and k^{e*} units of capital. The consumer at home can invest capital at home (k) or in the foreign country (x), and similarly for the consumer in the foreign country.

First, consider the residence principle and suppose both countries apply it to capital income. We will assume that the home country introduces a consumption tax. The budget constraint for the consumer in the home country is

$$w + [1 + r(1 - t_r)]k + [1 + r^*(1 - t_r)]x + T = c(1 + \theta), \qquad (5.7)$$

where w is the wage, r is the return to investing at home, r^* is the return to investing abroad, $t_r(R, D) = t_r(R, F) = t_r, t_r(NR, D) = 0, \theta$ is the consumption tax rate, and T is a lumpsum rebate of the tax revenue. The consumer chooses consumption and the allocation of capital to maximize utility subject to (5.7), and $k^e = k + x$. The first-order conditions imply that

$$r = r^*, \qquad (5.8)$$

and before-tax rates of return must be equal if $k, x > 0$. Under profit maximization, $r = f_k(k)$ and $r^* = f_k^*(k^*)$, where a subscript associated with a function denotes a derivative. It follows that $f_k(k) = f_k^*(k^*)$.

To close the model, notice that in equilibrium $x + x^* = 0$; capital imports must equal capital exports. It follows from this that

$$k^e + k^{e*} = k + k^*. \qquad (5.9)$$

Equations (5.8) and (5.9) determine (k, k^*). Since none of the tax rates enter either equation, we can conclude that the capital income tax and the consumption tax do not affect the allocation of capital under the residence system if both countries adopt that principle.

Next, consider the source principle. The budget constraint of the consumer in the home country is

$$w + [1 + r(1 - t_r)]k + [1 + r^*(1 - t_r^*)]x + T = c(1 + \theta), \qquad (5.10)$$

where $t_r(R, D) = t_r(NR, D) = t_r, t_r(R, F) = 0$, and $t_r^* = t_r^*(R, D) = t_r^*$ (NR, D), and $t_r^*(R, F) = 0$. The first-order conditions imply that

$$r(1 - t_r) = r^*(1 - t_r^*). \qquad (5.11)$$

Under profit maximization, this becomes

$$f_k(k)(1 - t_r) = f_k^*(k^*)(1 - t_r^*). \qquad (5.12)$$

Equation (5.9) also holds. Once again, the consumption tax does not affect the allocation of capital: only the taxes imposed on capital flows by the two countries will affect the allocation of capital across countries.

It is straightforward to show that an increase in the capital income tax rate imposed by the home country under the source principle will reduce capital invested in the home country and increase capital invested abroad when compensated through a lumpsum rebate of all revenue to the taxpayer it was collected from. This will hold more generally if the revenue is used to finance public spending that does not directly affect private capital investments. This result underscores the point made by Ihori (1991) that the two tax systems can have different incidence effects. Finally, it also leads to a discussion of spillover effects.

Under the source principle, the foreign consumer's budget constraint is

$$c^* = w^* + [1 + r^*(1 - t_r^*)]k^* + [1 + r(1 - t_r)]x^* + T^*.$$

Applying the arbitrage condition, the tax rebate, and $k^{e*} = k^* + x^*$, the budget constraint can be written as

$$c^* = w^* + (1 + r^*)k^{e*},$$

where $w^* = f^*(k^*) - r^*k^*$ and $r^* = f_k^*(k^*)$. It follows that the indirect utility function of the foreign consumer is

$$U^* = U^*(w^* + (1 + r^*)k^{e*}).$$

Differentiating, we obtain

$$dU^*/dt_r = U_c^*((dw^*/dt_r) + k^{e*}(dr^*/dt_r)) = U_c^*(c^*)x^*f_{kk}^*(dk^*/dt_r), \quad (5.13)$$

where $U_c^* = dU^*/dc^*$, and where we have used $k^{e*} = k^* + x^*, dw^*/dt_r = -k^* f_{kk}^*$, and $dr^*/dk^* = f_{kk}^*$. The spillover effect of the change in the home country's tax policy is captured by $x^*(dk^*/dt_r)$. Since capital invested in the foreign country increases with the tax rate in the home country, the sign of the spillover effect in (5.13) is minus the sign of x^*.

If capital flows from the home country to the foreign country, $x^* < 0$, and the home country increases its tax rate on capital income originating in the home country under the source principle, the consumer in the foreign country is better off. The increase in her wage as capital flows into the foreign country offsets the drop in the return on capital in the foreign country to make her better off. In this case, the spillover effect is positive. Alternatively, if $x^* < 0$, a decrease in the return on capital lowers the cost of importing capital and serves to make the agent in the foreign country better off. On the other hand, if capital flows from the foreign country to the home country, then $x^* > 0$, and the spillover effect is negative.

If the home country reduces its tax on capital and increases the consumption tax rate to raise the same amount of revenue, then under the source principle this will produce a negative spillover effect for any countries that receive a net flow of capital from the home country. In this case the shift to the consumption tax, while beneficial for the home country, may not be beneficial for the foreign country. This could cause the foreign country to retaliate by adjusting its tax policy.

5.3.2. *An overlapping generations model of international taxation*

Following Sibert (1985, 1990) and Ihori (1991), we will assume there are two countries, the home country and the foreign country. At time t, N_t agents are born in each country and $N_t = 1$ for simplicity. Each agent lives for two periods and is endowed with one unit of labor in the first period and none in the second. The technology is neoclassical: $y = f(k)$ and $y^* = f^*(k^*)$ denote output in the two countries. Firms producing the one consumption good maximize profit. Thus, in a steady state $r = f_k(k)$ and $r^* = f_k^*(k^*)$. From this, we know that $k(r)$ and $dk/dr = k_r = 1/f_{kk} < 0$, and similarly for the foreign country. The steady state wages are given by $w = f(k) - rk$ and $w^* = f^*(k^*) - r^*k^*$. Thus, $w(r) = f(k(r)) - rk(r)$, with $dw/dr = w_r = -k$, and similarly for the foreign country.

The preferences of the representative consumer in the home country are given by $U(c_{1t}, c_{2t})$, where c_{jt} is consumption in period of life j. The utility function satisfies the usual assumptions. The budget constraints are given by

$$w_t - k_{t+1} - x_{t+1} - (1 + \theta)c_{1t} = 0,$$
$$\{1 + r_{t+1}[1 - t_{t+1}(R, D)]\}k_{t+1} + \{1 + r_{t+1}^*[1 - t_{t+1}(R, F)$$
$$-t_{t+1}^*(NR, D)]\}x_{t+1} - (1 + \theta)c_{2t} = 0.$$

Arbitrage will require that the after-tax returns equalize across investments similar to (5.8) or (5.11), depending on which tax system is introduced. Assuming an interior solution and arbitrage, collapse the budget constraints to obtain

$$w_t/(1 + \theta) - c_{1t} - q_2 c_2 = 0.$$

Under the residence based tax, $q_2 = 1/[1 + r(1 - t_r(R, D))]$ and arbitrage requires $r = r^*$. Under the source based tax, $q_2 = 1/[1 + r(1 - t_r(R, D)]$ and arbitrage requires $r[1 - t_r(R, D)] = r^*[1 - t_r^*(NR, D)]$.

First, consider the case where there is no consumption tax imposed in either country and both countries collect taxes under the residence based system. The saving functions that solve the decision problems in the respective countries are given by $S(w(r), r(1 - t_r))$ and $S^*(w^*(r), r(1 - t_r^*))$. Saving in the home country is equal to $k + x$, while saving in the foreign country is $k^* + x^*$. A steady state equilibrium occurs where $x + x^* = 0$. Thus, the steady state equilibrium must satisfy

$$S(w(r), r(1 - t_r)) + S^*(w^*(r), r(1 - t_r^*)) = k(r) + k^*(r), \qquad (5.14)$$

where we have used $r = r^*$.

Imagine that the home country increases its tax rate at the margin and rebates the revenue back to the taxpayer. We can differentiate (5.14) with respect to the tax rate in the home country to obtain

$$dr/dt_r = rS_{ru}/D, \qquad (5.15)$$

evaluated at the initial no-tax equilibrium, where S_{ru} is the compensated derivative of the saving function with respect to the net interest rate and $D = (1 - t_r)S_r - kS_w - k_r + (1 - t_r^*)S_{r*}^* - k^*S_{w*}^* - k_r^*$. If $D > 0$, the world equilibrium is stable. Therefore, if saving is increasing in the interest rate in both countries, the world interest rate will increase with the capital income tax rate imposed in the home country. Furthermore, since the wage rate is decreasing in the interest rate, both wages will fall with the capital income tax rate. Therefore, the tax imposed by the home country will cause a spillover effect in the foreign country, and vice versa.

It is instructive to compare the response to the tax experiment in the open economy to the response in the closed economy. Let $D_H = (1 - t_r)$ $S_r - kS_w - k_r$ and $D_F = (1 - t_r^*)S_r^* - k^*S_w^* - k_r^*$. If $D_H, D_F > 0$, then the equilibrium in each country is stable when both economies are closed to capital flows. It is straightforward to show that the response in the closed economy is $(dr/dt_r)_{closed} = (rS_{ru}/D_H)$. We can rewrite (5.15) as

$$(dr/dt_r)_{open} = (D_H/D)(dr/dt_r)_{closed}.$$

It follows immediately that the response in the open economy is smaller in magnitude than the response on the closed economy since $0 < D_H/D < 1$. The intuition for this result is that in the closed economy the tax induces a decrease in saving and investment, which causes the real interest rate to rise. However, in an open economy the agent in the home country reduces her accumulation of both domestic and foreign assets. This spreads some of the reduction in capital to the foreign country. Of course, for a small open economy, $dr/dt_r = 0$.

Another way to see this is to recall that $S(w(r), r(1 - t_r)) = k(r) + x$ and $S^*(w^*(r^*), r^*(1 - t_r^*)) = k^*(r^*) + x^*$. Differentiate both to obtain

$$D_H(dr/dt_r)_{open} = rS_{ru} + dx/dt_r,$$
$$D_F(dr^*/dt_r)_{open} = dx^*/dt_r.$$

We can rewrite the first equation as

$$(dr/dt_r)_{open} = (dr/dt_r)_{closed} + (1/D_H)dx/dt_r.$$

The tax causes net capital exports to fall and thus implies that the open-economy response is smaller in magnitude than the closed-economy response.

Also notice that the current account is defined as

$$x = S(w(r), r(1 - t_r)) - k(r). \tag{5.16}$$

Differentiating, we obtain

$$dx/dt_r = D_H(dr/dt_r) - rS_{ru}. \tag{5.17}$$

The second term, $-rS_{ru}$, captures the direct effect of the tax, while the first term in (5.17) captures the indirect effect. The first term is clearly positive. An increase in the interest rate induces greater saving and investment in the home country and this will cause the current account to improve. On the other hand, the direct effect of the tax on capital is to lower saving, and this may cause the current account to worsen. Using (5.15) in (5.17), we obtain

$$dx/dt_r = -rS_rD_F/D < 0. \tag{5.18}$$

The direct effect of the tax outweighs the indirect effect, causing a deterioration in the current account.

Next, consider the case where both countries introduce the source principle. In that case (5.11) holds. In equilibrium the following condition must hold:

$$S(w(r), r(1 - t_r)) + S^*\left(w^*(r), r^*\left(1 - t_r^*\right)\right) = k(r) + k^*(r^*), \tag{5.19}$$

in addition to (5.11).

Suppose the home country raises its tax rate slightly and rebates the revenue as before. Differentiate the system of (5.11) and (5.19) and solve to obtain

$$dr/dt_r = r(D_H + S_rD_F)/D, \tag{5.20a}$$

$$dr^*/dt_r = r(kS_w + k_r)/D. \tag{5.20b}$$

If the equilibrium in each country is stable when closed, the interest rate in the home country is increasing in the capital income tax rate. However, it is possible for the interest rate in the foreign country to fall as capital shifts to the foreign country. This will occur if the demand for capital in the home country is more elastic to the interest rate than saving is to the wage. A comparison of (5.15) and (5.20) underscores the point that the incidence of taxation may differ between the two principles.

Finally, Ihori (1991) introduces a consumption tax into the OG model presented above and studies the incidence of a tax reform from capital income taxation to the consumption tax, holding tax revenue constant under both systems. Under the residence system there is only a supply side effect associated with the reform because before-tax interest rates are the same across countries. A reduction in the capital income tax rate causes consumers to save more and this reduces the world interest rate, while the consumption tax in this model only causes income effects. However, there is also an arbitrage effect under the source system since after-tax returns must be equal instead. A reduction in the capital income tax rate in the home country under the source principle will not only cause consumers to save more, but will also cause them to shift capital from the foreign country to the home country. This makes it possible for the two interest rates to move in opposite directions when the tax reform is introduced in the source based system. The home-country interest rate may fall while the foreign-country interest rate may rise.

5.4. Principles of optimal taxation when capital is mobile

In a closed economy, the government can introduce taxes on labor, capital, commodities, and transactions in general to finance its expenditures. In most analyses of the optimal tax problem, it is imagined the government chooses tax rates taking into account the behavioral response to the proposed tax system and the equilibrium conditions governing behavior at the aggregate level. In a sense, both phenomena can restrain the government's behavior.

Unfortunately, as we have seen in Chapters 3 and 4, the set of policy instruments available to the government can affect the policy outcome. For example, if the government can use its debt policy to maintain the economy on the optimal growth path, it may not be optimal for the government to tax capital income under certain conditions when private agents have a finite planning horizon.[3] However, if debt policy is not available and the competitive economy is under-capitalized, it might be optimal to tax capital income. Paradoxically, when agents have a finite planning horizon, they receive most of their capital income at the end of the horizon. Imposing a capital income tax causes them to save more and move the economy closer to the optimal growth path. The point is that the set of government instruments available may have an impact on the outcome.

When we shift the focus of attention to the open-economy tax problem, there are additional constraints on the government's choice of policy. We have already mentioned that capital mobility can impose a severe restraint on the government. In addition, the tax instruments that are available may depend on what the government can observe. If it can observe capital flows between countries, it may wish to impose taxes on those flows. Third, the government in one country may want to take into account the possible response of governments in other countries to its policy. For example, if one country introduces a policy with a negative spillover effect, it might expect retaliation from the other countries that are adversely affected by its policy. Such potential retaliation can impose a restriction on the government's policy. Related to this is the issue of whether the government in choosing its policy takes the policies of other governments as beyond its control or behaves as a "Stackelberg leader" in the policy game. The leader can usually extract additional utility when choosing policy. Finally, there is the issue of whether optimal policy design should be considered from the vantage point of the individual country or the collection of countries as a whole.

5.4.1. Early research

Hamada (1966) introduced a model of two countries choosing tax rates and showed that the credit method is preferred to the deduction method by both the capital exporting country and the capital importing country. This is because the credit method yields a more efficient allocation of capital than the deduction method. This result was derived by comparing the non-cooperative Nash equilibrium under the deduction method, where both countries choose their tax policy taking the other country's policy as given, with the cooperative outcome, when the credit method is used instead. Musgrave (1969) suggested that the deduction method induced an anti-trade bias because of the double taxation problem. Furthermore, a capital exporting country will prefer deductions to credits since the credit method gives up more revenue to the host country of the investment than does the deduction method. A capital importing country will prefer credits to deductions for the same reason.

Feldstein and Hartman (1979) assume that the capital exporting or home country is a "Stackelberg leader" and the capital importing or foreign country is a "follower" in the policy game. A firm in the home country combines capital and labor via a neoclassical technology domestically and can set up a foreign subsidiary. The firm chooses how much capital to allocate to domestic production and how much to allocate to its subsidiary. The subsidiary produces in the foreign country using a different technology. The home country taxes the domestic profit while the foreign country taxes the profit of the subsidiary before repatriation. The home country also taxes the profit earned abroad but allows a credit or deduction for foreign taxes paid. Capital is freely mobile, and arbitrage eliminates any rate-of-return differentials.

The home country chooses tax rates and credits to maximize national income taking into account the behavior of the foreign country. In the special benchmark case where the foreign wage is unaffected by the investments of the home country, Feldstein and Hartman prove that the "full tax after deduction" method is optimal. The home country taxes domestic profit and profit earned abroad at the same rate but allows a full deduction for taxes paid to the foreign country. Thus, the marginal product of capital used at home is the same as the marginal product of capital invested abroad.

They then extend this result to the case where investment in the foreign country affects the local wage rate in the foreign country. Their main result is that it is actually optimal for the home country to tax foreign profits at a higher rate than domestically generated profit when the tax policy in the foreign country is fixed. The intuition is as follows. If all subsidiaries behaved as a single monopsonist and reduced their collective demand for labor in the foreign country, profit would rise for the usual reason, namely, that the monopsonist can increase its profit by exercising its market power. Of course, no individual subsidiary can do this alone. However, the home country government can achieve this result by taxing foreign profit at a higher rate than domestic profit. This serves to restrict capital investment in the foreign country and reduce the demand for labor.

Feldstein and Hartman show that this result goes through in the Cobb–Douglas case and in the CES case under a minor restriction on the parameters when the foreign country also chooses its tax rates optimally as a "follower" by taking the tax policy of the home country as given. Presumably, this differential taxation of capital income would survive an extension of the model to allow for taxation of labor income as well, since the basis for the result is the home country exploiting its market power *vis-à-vis* the foreign country. Thus, the consumption tax would not be optimal when the capital exporting country has market power.

Bond and Samuelson (1989) extend this analysis by considering a non-cooperative game played by two rival governments where neither country has any market power. Each country chooses a tax rate to impose on an investment made by the home country investor in the foreign country. From our earlier notation, the home government taxes the investment income at rate $t_r(R, F)$, while the foreign country taxes the same unit of income at rate $t_r^*(NR, D)$. To keep matters simple, the economy lasts one period, both governments can observe the foreign investment income, the domestic capital income earned by a resident is not taxed, and both countries choose the tax rate to maximize their own national income.

Let F_K represent the marginal product of capital in the home country and F_K^* represent the marginal product of capital in the foreign country. Under the deduction method, arbitrage for the investor in the home country implies

$$F_K = [1 - t_r(R, F)][1 - t_r^*(NR, D)]F_K^*.$$

Under the credit method, we have instead

$$F_K = \left\{1 - \max[t_r(R, F), t_r^*(NR, D)]\right\}F_K^*,$$

where the home country credits up to its own tax rate but not above it. It follows that the effective tax rate is the larger of $t_r(R, F)$ or $t_r^*(NR, D)$ under the credit method.

Bond and Samuelson show that no Nash equilibrium exists under the credit system where tax rates are positive and there is a capital flow between the two countries. More specifically, they show that in a Nash equilibrium capital flows between the two countries are zero; the taxes eliminate trade in capital in the presence of a credit. The intuition is that each country attempts to set its tax rate at least as high as the other country to gain the benefit of restricting trade in capital; the foreign country attempts to obtain more tax revenue, while the home country attempts to limit this. The tax rate that emerges from this strategic interaction is so high that no capital flows between the two countries. On the other hand, this does not occur under the deduction method and a Nash equilibrium exists under that method. The main conclusion of their study is that the credit method, but not the deduction method, has an anti-trade bias. In addition, national income is higher for both capital exporting and capital importing countries under the deduction method.

Mintz and Tulkens (1996) model the interaction between two small countries relative to the world capital market. They provide a taxonomy of tax systems depending on the general features of the system. They show that a residence based system adopted by both countries is optimal but cannot be supported as an equilibrium. This tends to support the results of Bond and Samuelson.

5.4.2. Optimal taxation with production efficiency

Bond and Samuelson consider only a very narrow range of tax policies and behavior for the two governments. In more complicated models, other considerations may become important. One such consideration is the notion of production efficiency, first introduced in the context of optimal tax theory by Diamond and Mirrlees (1971a). Heuristically, the choice of the optimal tax system involves the choice between producer and consumer prices, the difference being the tax rates, with the proviso that the government be able to tax pure profit. Tax rates are chosen to maximize consumer welfare subject to various constraints, such as government budget. The Diamond–Mirrlees result states that the economy should be on the aggregate production possibility frontier when the optimal tax rates are chosen. If the economy were inside the frontier, the government could adjust consumer prices so as to induce a move to the frontier, increasing the consumption possibility of some good. Since utility is monotonically increasing in consumption, this move would improve welfare. Therefore, the initial set of taxes could not have been optimal to begin with.

Under this concept, it is suboptimal to tax capital under the source principle. A tax on capital when it is perfectly mobile will be borne by immobile factors such as land, labor, or natural resources. So it is better to tax those factors directly, because taxing them indirectly by taxing capital income at source distorts the capital allocation decision across countries—although, as noted by Gordon (1992), taxing labor may induce some taxpayers, especially the self-employed, to redefine their labor income as a flow of capital income instead, thus avoiding the labor income tax.

The government could avoid this distortion by imposing the capital income tax under the residence principle while allowing a deduction or credit for foreign taxes paid and exempting foreign owned capital income generated domestically. However, this raises the problem of monitoring the tax base. Monitoring becomes critically important in discussing taxation in the presence of mobile resources. The government must be able to monitor the tax system it imposes because some agents may try to illegally evade some of their tax liability otherwise. Razin and Sadka (1991a) forcefully argue that it is especially difficult to monitor international capital flows. For example, when the home country imposes a tax on residents' income under the residence principle, it must be able to monitor the behavior that generates that particular tax base. However, it is unlikely that it will be able to observe income from foreign sources. Therefore, taxpayers have an incentive to underreport income from such sources, making it difficult, if not impossible, for the government to impose the residence principle in practice. Of course, this assumes that taxpayers are basically dishonest and will attempt to illegally evade some of their tax liability whenever possible.

The government can try to tax the domestic capital income of its residents, exempting foreign source income and foreign owned income generated domestically. However, this raises two issues. First, the government must take into account the real possibility of capital flight: investors may shift funds abroad to escape the tax. This is especially problematic if the economy is small relative to the world market. In addition to this, domestic investors may try to evade taxes on their domestic capital income by cleverly investing in foreign intermediaries who then reinvest in the domestic economy. Thus, Razin and Sadka (1991a) and Gordon (1992) argue that the optimal tax on capital income is zero.

Razin and Sadka also raised the interesting possibility that the government can use capital controls to aid it in taxing capital income. In particular, Gordon argued that capital controls coupled with the use of double taxation credits allow governments to tax capital income and, moreover, can be used to explain the system we observed in the past until the 1980s. In a model similar to that of Bond and Samuelson but where saving and labor supply decisions are endogenous, Gordon showed that a Nash equilibrium will not exist, which supports the result obtained by Bond and Samuelson. However, he also showed that an equilibrium that supports the double taxation convention of crediting foreign taxes paid will exist if one country is a "Stackelberg leader" and a capital exporter, while all the other countries are capital importers.

The intuition is as follows. Suppose the capital exporting leader imposes a residence based tax but allows a full credit for foreign taxes paid. Further, assume that individual investors are not allowed to invest abroad themselves but must do so through a corporation that is strictly monitored so that it cannot evade its proper tax liability. A country that imports capital will have an incentive to follow the "Stackelberg leader" and set its tax rate equal to the leader's tax rate. It doesn't pay to choose a lower rate since this will simply cost it tax revenue. It also doesn't help to choose a higher rate, since the credit does not extend above the level set by the exporter's tax rate. If the leader raises its tax rate, the other countries will follow suit and raise theirs. So a positive tax rate that maximizes the leader's payoff, while taking into account the behavior of the followers, will survive the strategic behavior of the various players in the policy games.

The "leader" can then set the worldwide tax rate. The capital importing countries are essentially induced to tax capital at its source and thus are choosing a source based system. However, because of the double taxation convention of crediting foreign paid taxes, the investment decision of investors in the capital exporting country is not distorted since the credit converts the source based system to a residence based system from their perspective. Also, the investors do not have an incentive to evade taxes by investing abroad as long as the capital importing country chooses the same tax rate as the capital exporting leader chooses.

Gordon argues that this theory can explain the observed prevalence of the double taxation convention coupled with the taxation of capital income when capital is mobile. Unfortunately, his argument relies on one country playing the role of leader. Gordon argues that prior to the mid 1980s a natural candidate for the leader would have been the United States. However, after the mid to late

1980s the USA became a capital importer instead. It is unclear which country can play the role of leader now. In that case we should observe an abandonment of the convention. Yet many countries continue to use it, so it is unclear whether or not countries are choosing their tax policies optimally, and, if they are, whether or not Gordon's theory is correct.

Essentially, we can summarize the analysis by stating that, if there are no restrictions on the distorting tax instruments available to the governments in the world economy, no restrictions on international transfers, and pure profits can be taxed optimally, then production efficiency remains optimal. In that case, before-tax rates of return should be equal across investments. This requires that the residence principle be employed. Capital income taxes at source are suboptimal. However, if the government cannot readily observe the foreign income of its residents, and residents can avoid tax by investing in foreign subsidiaries who reinvest at home, then it may be best not to tax capital income at all.

Implicitly, it is assumed in this analysis that pure profits can be taxed optimally and that there are optimal lumpsum transfers taking place across countries. It is well known that production efficiency will not hold if profits cannot be taxed optimally. In addition, in the Diamond–Mirrlees analysis there is only one government budget constraint. However, the production efficiency result also requires transfers across countries because each country has its own government budget constraint. The lumpsum transfers across countries serve to link countries up through their respective government budget constraints in a way that makes the production efficiency result applicable. In the next section we will relax the assumptions that there are lumpsum transfers across countries and pure profit taxes. As we will see, taxation at source may then become optimal.

5.4.3. Optimal taxation without production efficiency

Horst (1980) derived a simple rule governing the optimal taxation of capital income in a partial equilibrium, supply and demand framework. He assumed that both supply and demand for capital were elastic and derived an elasticity formula that generalizes several interesting special cases. For example, if the supply of capital in both the capital importing and the capital exporting country is fixed, then the residence principle is optimal. On the other hand, if the demand for capital is fixed in both countries, then the source principle is optimal. Double taxation of capital income with a deduction for foreign taxes paid is optimal if the supply of capital in the capital exporting country is fixed and the demand for capital in the capital importing country is fixed.

Findlay (1986) extended this analysis by studying a simple model where there are two countries, a capital importing country and a capital exporting country. There are two tax instruments available to the capital importing country, a tax imposed on domestically owned capital and a tax on foreign owned capital income. The capital exporting country can impose a tax on capital invested at home and a tax on capital income earned abroad. It can also choose to provide tax relief for taxes paid abroad. Each country chooses policy taking the policy of the other country as beyond its control.

Given the choices of the capital exporting country, Findlay showed that it is optimal for the capital importing country to impose a lower tax on income from foreign owned capital than on income from domestically owned capital. To see why, consider two extreme cases. First, imagine that the supply of domestically owned capital in the capital importing country is inelastic. Then it is best to tax domestically owned capital and exempt foreign owned capital. Next, suppose that the marginal product of domestic capital in the importing country is fixed. Then the country's tax revenue can be raised in a nondistorting manner by taxing both sources of capital income at the same rate. In general, the economy will lie in between the two extreme cases. Thus, it is best from the perspective of the capital importing country to tax domestically owned capital at a higher rate than foreign owned capital. He also showed that it is optimal for the capital exporting country to tax domestically invested capital income at a higher rate than foreign income from abroad.

Finally, Findlay showed that it is optimal to tax capital flows between countries from a world perspective. Imagine that a social planner will choose three possible tax rates to impose on the two countries: a tax on domestically owned capital in each country and a tax imposed on the capital income flow between the two countries. The revenue is collected by the planner and distributed to the two countries. He shows that the optimal tax structure mimics that which is chosen separately by the two countries under the deduction method. It follows that some double taxation is optimal. The intuition for this result is that there are no actual transfers between the two countries in a competitive equilibrium. The taxation of capital income flowing between the two countries mimics the effect of the transfers.

The connection between transfers across countries, the taxation of pure profits, and the production efficiency result was highlighted by Keen and Piekkola (1997). See also Wildasin (1977). They allow for restrictions on the taxation of pure profits and consider the optimal tax problem from a worldwide perspective. When lumpsum taxes are precluded, they derive two results. First, the earlier result of Horst, where the taxation of international capital flows is governed by a formula involving supply and demand elasticities, still holds; indeed, Keen and Piekkola provide a more general formula where the Horst rule drops out as a special case when lumpsum taxes are fully available. Second, pure profit taxes are critically important. If the profit tax is low in the capital importing country, a source based tax is optimal; source taxation mimics the profit tax. On the other hand, when pure profit taxes are fully utilized, the residence principle is optimal. It follows that, if pure profits cannot be fully taxed, the residence principle will not be generally be optimal.

One conclusion that can be drawn from this literature is that production efficiency requires lumpsum transfers across countries and the optimal taxation of profits. While there are limited transfers taking place in Europe, such transfers are more the exception than the rule worldwide. It is also notoriously difficult to tax pure profits. In many cases corporations can redefine a cashflow to disguise it and thus escape a profit tax. Therefore, production efficiency from the world's perspective may not be optimal. This allows for the possibility that source based taxation may be part of an optimal tax package. Taxation of capital flows can then substitute for the taxation of profits and transfers across countries in a second-best solution.

Governments may also try to tax capital by imposing capital controls. Razin and Sadka (1991b) consider a model of a two-period, small open economy and show that, if the government cannot observe the foreign source income of its residents, it may be able to improve welfare by imposing capital controls on the flow of capital out of the country. Thus, a capital export control acts like a lumpsum redistribution from domestic taxpayers to the government. The domestic tax base expands and this may allow the government to tax domestic capital at a lower rate, ceteris paribus, than would otherwise have been the case. This, of course, assumes that the government can observe the flow of capital out of the country.

5.5. Policy coordination

Given that different countries will be imposing their tax policies simultaneously, it is of some interest to know whether the group of countries as a whole can benefit from coordinating their policies. Indeed, coordinating policy provides the impetus for European consolidation. However, if countries are able to coordinate their policy, the actual nature of the policy game being played between the governments and the private sector becomes important.

Consider a world economy composed of two countries and imagine that the two countries wish to achieve a cooperative solution. Suppose the governments solve this problem of choosing infinite sequences of tax rates on the income from labor, capital, and foreign source capital by posing the joint decision problem at the beginning of the coincidental planning horizon, deriving the optimal policy rules, and then simply implementing the proposed policy rules as time proceeds. If private agents have a finite planning horizon, if the governments share information about foreign investments and are absolutely committed to their joint policy rules, and if the production efficiency result holds, then residence based taxation will be optimal and it will generally be optimal to tax capital income. However, if the governments can reoptimize later on in the horizon, they will also generally find it optimal to deviate from the previously optimal plan—the cooperative solution will not generally be time consistent.

In particular, Kehoe (1989) argued that policy coordination may not be optimal if governments attempt to exploit the so-called capital levy, studied in greater detail in Chapter 6. The capital levy problem is as follows. When the government chooses the time path of its taxes to maximize the utility of its residents subject to its budget constraints over time, it will take into account the elasticity of savings, as we have seen in Chapters 3 and 4. However, at each moment in time the capital stock is fixed. If the government takes this into account when choosing the optimal tax rates, it will be tempted to tax the fixed capital stock at a very high rate. Indeed, this is what a straightforward application of the Ramsey rule tells it to do: tax fixed factors at a high rate. So at the beginning of its planning horizon, the government has an incentive to promise to impose low taxes on capital income in the future because capital accumulation is somewhat elastic. However, if it can reoptimize when the future arrives, it will be tempted to break its earlier promise and tax capital at a high rate. The cooperative tax policy where countries coordinate their policy is subject to this inconsistency.

Kehoe suggests that capital flight can temper this sort of "time inconsistency" problem. A single government that attempts to exploit the capital levy by raising taxes on capital domestically invested will induce investors to move their capital elsewhere. However, if governments get together to coordinate their policies, they may collectively try to exploit the capital levy by imposing high tax rates on capital. Therefore, cooperation may not be optimal.

Kehoe considers a simple two period setup where there are two countries in the world economy and a representative agent in each. Production occurs only in the second period according to a linear technology. The agent is endowed with y units of the one consumption good available and one unit of labor in the second period. The preferences of the agent in country j are given by $U^1(c_{j1}) + \beta U^2(c_{j2}, 1 - L_j)$, where c_{jk} is consumption in period k, $1 - L_j$ is leisure, and L_j is labor supply. The agent can allocate savings between a home investment k_{jh} and foreign investment k_{jf}. The government imposes a tax on labor and a tax on capital income on the residence principle in order to finance a government expenditure. It is also assumed that, if both governments choose equal tax rates, investors invest only in their own economy for simplicity.

The timing of the action in the model is as follows. First, private agents decide how much to save and consume in the first period. Second, the government in each country chooses its tax rates. Third, private agents choose how to allocate their capital across countries. The private agents work and receive their capital income in the second period and consume the proceeds of their income. Finally, the governments collect taxes and provide a public good.

First, Kehoe examines the non-cooperative equilibrium and proves that both governments will choose not to tax capital at all in a Nash equilibrium. Thus, the consumption tax is optimal in this specialized framework. However, Kehoe also proves that, if the two countries cooperate by choosing their tax policies to maximize the sum of their utilities subject to their separate budgets, they will choose a 100 per cent tax on capital since the countries as a group will try to exploit the capital levy. In addition to this, it is also shown that welfare is greater in the non-cooperative equilibrium than in the cooperative equilibrium.

We will study the nature of the policy game in greater detail in Chapter 6. We will compare the open loop game, where the government chooses its tax policy once and for all at the beginning of its planning horizon, with the closed loop game, where the government chooses its policy sequentially each period. The government in the latter policy game will try to exploit the so – called capital levy because each period the capital stock is fixed by past decisions. This is intimately related to the time consistency problem. In the former game, the government chooses its policy at the beginning of its horizon and then simply implements the previously chosen policy as time proceeds. The open loop game is extensively studied in the literature summarized in Chapters 3 and 4.

One last remark is appropriate. If private agents can illegally evade some of their capital income tax liability, this may thwart the government's ability to exploit the capital levy. In that case, cooperation may be better than not cooperating. We will also discuss tax evasion in Chapter 6.

5.6. Is capital internationally mobile?

Much of the foregoing analysis assumed that capital was perfectly mobile. However, if that assumption is false, then the results need to be seriously modified. Indeed, if capital is not mobile, a strong case can be made for taxing capital income based on the results of Chapters 2 and 3.

Feldstein and Horioka (1980) first challenged the view that capital was internationally mobile. Domestic saving will presumably seek the highest rate of return and domestic investment will be financed by investors on a worldwide basis. They argued that if this is the case then there should be no correlation between domestic saving and domestic investment; in addition, we should also observe an equalization of rates of return across countries, after adjusting for risk. However, Feldstein and Horioka present evidence that this is not so. In particular, they estimate a simple linear equation that relates the gross domestic investment GDP ratio (I/Y) to the gross domestic saving GDP ratio (S/Y) using a panel data set of OECD countries from 1960 to 1974:

$$(I/Y) = \alpha + \beta(S/Y).$$

The estimated parameter for the entire sample is $\beta = 0.887$. For various five-year subperiods the estimates range from 0.872 to 0.909. Of course, if capital is perfectly mobile $\beta = 0$. Later in the paper they also control for simultaneity bias and obtain virtually the same result. This basic result was confirmed later by Feldstein (1983) and Dooley, Frankel, and Mathieson (1987). For a skeptical review see Tesar (1991).

More recently, Hussein (1998) used time series analysis on OECD data for the period 1960–93. He finds that the ratio of domestic saving to GDP and the ratio of domestic investment to GDP are both integrated of order 1, meaning that both series are stationary not in levels but in their first difference. Second, he estimates a linear equation similar to that of Feldstein and Horioka using dynamic OLS that controls for possible endogeneity bias and autocorrelation problems that may exist in the data. In eleven of the twenty-three OECD countries, the estimated coefficient is greater than 1 for the full set of observations; in five cases it is significantly greater than 1 at the 5 per cent level of confidence. For Iceland the coefficient (0.91) is not significantly different from 1. In only one case—Germany—is the coefficient insignificantly different from 0; and in six additional cases the coefficient is greater than 0.70. This would tend to support the earlier conclusion that domestic saving and investment are highly correlated.[4]

A number of authors have attempted to explain the apparently low degree of capital mobility, or the empirical result obtained by Feldstein and Horioka, or both. Westphal (1983) suggested that, if a country successfully used its tax policy to target its current account, it could easily produce a positive correlation between saving and investment in the data.[5] Murphy (1984) argued that large countries would normally receive a large amount of their own saving as new investment even though capital is mobile and that this might bias the empirical results. Golub (1990) maintained that a country's domestic saving and investment could be highly correlated even though capital flows freely if capital outflows are matched by equally large inflows, and the net flow data used by Feldstein and Horioka may mask this. Finn (1990) suggested that there are productivity shocks that might affect both saving and investment, thus causing a positive correlation between the two. Gordon and Bovenberg (1996) argued that capital mobility may be inhibited if foreign investors know less about the local foreign economy than domestic investors and would pay too much for domestic assets as a result of this asymmetric information. Coakley and Kulasi (1997) suggested that an estimate of $\beta = 1$ would not necessarily be evidence of a lack of capital mobility but would follow as an implication of the current account being solvent in the long run. Exchange rate risk and uncertainty about local inflation and future tax policy may be other reasons for investors to be wary of investing abroad.

Whatever the explanation is, it is apparent that capital is not perfectly mobile across countries. There would also appear to be a lack of international portfolio diversification (see Lewis 1995). Unfortunately, the reason for the apparent immobility of capital across countries and the lack of diversification may have an important impact on the optimal policy a government should pursue, and mistakes may occur if this is not recognized. For example, if the local government believes that uncertainty about future tax policy is the reason for a lack of foreign investment, it may take certain actions to assure potential investors that policy is favorable toward investment and to reduce the uncertainty by imposing supportive laws that are difficult to change. However, if some other reason accounts for the lack of mobility, this policy may have little effect on investment.

5.7. Discussion

The literature on international taxation is very large, and we have attempted to cover quite a bit of ground in this chapter. In this section we will discuss the implications of the foregoing analysis for the consumption tax debate. Of course, whether or not the consumption tax is itself optimal depends on whether or not capital income should be taxed, and, if it should be taxed, on whether or not the government can actually impose a tax on capital when capital is mobile. The case for exempting capital income is very weak in the context of a closed economy. However, allowing the economy to be open raises the issue of optimality again, since it is unclear whether the production efficiency result holds in the context of the world economy.

It is perhaps instructive to consider a simple model of two countries. Consumers gain utility from a consumption good. The consumption good can be produced using capital and labor. Preferences and the technology are both well behaved. One country, say the home country, will be exporting capital to the other country, the foreign country. The home country has a choice of imposing a tax on the domestic capital income of its residents, the foreign source income of its residents, or the labor income of its residents. The foreign country has the choice of taxing the domestic capital income of its residents, the foreign owned capital income generated in its territory by the investment flowing to it from the home country, or the labor income of its residents. More generally, we may observe cross-hauling of capital across countries where agents in both countries make investments in the other country involving different kinds of capital. In that case, both countries may tax domestically generated capital income, foreign owned capital income, and foreign source capital income.

If the production efficiency result holds from a worldwide perspective, then the residence principle is preferred to the source principle; pretax rates of return should be equalized. The capital exporting country then has the choice of taxing the saving or the labor income of its residents, possibly at different rates. It will generally be optimal to tax labor and saving income at different rates under the Ramsey rule of optimal tax theory if agents have a finite planning horizon.[6] The capital importing country has the same incentive under the residence principle. Therefore, if private agents have a finite planning horizon, there is no presumption that a consumption tax will be optimal relative to an income tax that includes a tax on capital income, even if capital is mobile. The critical issue then is whether or not capital income, especially foreign source income, can be observed.

Next, suppose that production efficiency is no longer optimal because transfers between countries or profit taxes are not available. In that case we cannot rule out the optimality of taxing capital income at the source. The capital importing country then has the choice of taxing foreign owned capital income, in addition to taxing domestically owned capital income and labor, possibly at different rates, when it chooses its policy optimally. The capital exporting country then must decide whether or not to allow a credit for foreign paid taxes. In general, a full credit may be allowed, which converts the source tax in the capital importing country to a residence based tax from the perspective of the home country investor. There is still no presumption, however, that a consumption tax is optimal in either country relative to an income tax that includes a tax on capital income when private agents have a finite planning horizon.

The critical assumption is that capital income can be observed. So once again we return to the monitoring problem, which also exists in a closed economy. In the context of a closed economy, the government can audit taxpayers and try to catch tax evaders. In the open economy context, the government must generally rely on foreign governments to provide it with information about the foreign source income of its residents, or must rely on the honesty of its residents to correctly disclose their true income. If such information is not forthcoming, it may be difficult for the government to monitor the capital income of its residents and hence impose a tax on it.

The presumption in the literature appears to be that investors are far more sophisticated than the tax authorities and can escape the taxation of their investment income if they so choose. In the extreme case where all capital income tax liability can be evaded, the consumption tax becomes optimal almost by default. However, if taxation is so pernicious that it generates such incredible evasion behavior, then agents would also have an incentive to evade taxes on their consumption and the government would be unable to collect any tax revenue.

Three comments are in order. First, this assumes that taxpayers are necessarily going to illegally evade their tax liability whenever possible. Yet many taxpayers declare their income truthfully. Second, widespread tax evasion may lead governments to impose severe capital controls, as pointed out by Razin and Sadka. Third, this may also lead governments to sign tax treaties in order to tax capital income. Capital controls and tax treaties may lead to a lower level of welfare on average than if taxpayers had simply declared their capital income truthfully and accepted a moderate tax on capital. In a sense, this is a Prisoner's Dilemma problem. If everyone would declare their income honestly, the government could impose taxes at a moderate level. However, each individual may have an incentive to evade her personal liability. As more taxpayers try to evade their taxes, the government is forced to impose capital controls.

Many analysts have pointed out that sophisticated taxpayers may be able easily to avoid or illegally evade their capital income tax liability. As taxpayers become more sophisticated, tax avoidance becomes more of a problem without coordination with foreign countries. However, the tax authorities too may become more sophisticated. To be sure, police organizations like Scotland Yard, Interpol, and the FBI have become much more sophisticated in catching "high tech" criminals and terrorists in the last decade. Clearly, the tax authorities have a strong incentive to become more sophisticated as well. One could easily imagine a situation in which the government required investors to make financial investments through a "clearing house" that monitors outgoing capital. An electronic tag could be placed on a flow of capital which would track it to a particular foreign country and report back to the clearing house whenever income is received from that investment.[7] Indeed, such electronic surveillance might make international agreements obsolete; the capital exporting country would not need to rely on other countries at all.[8]

In addition, there appears to be considerable evidence that capital is not perfectly mobile across countries. If this is true, capital income may be easier to observe than was previously thought. If so, it will become a target for taxation, and the implications of the closed economy models may still be relevant when the economy is open to capital flows.

5.8. Conclusion

We have discussed the general principles of direct taxation when the economy is open to capital flows and have applied them to the taxation of capital. First, we defined the basic principles of direct taxation: the residence principle and the source principle. Second, we studied several incidence results where the open economy response differed from the closed economy response and also differed according to which tax principle was imposed. Third, we discussed the results on optimal taxation when the economy is open and considered the policy coordination problem relative to the capital levy. Finally, we looked at the empirical evidence on capital mobility.

In general, it is fair to say that matters become more complex when the economy is open for a number of reasons, including capital flight, retaliation by other countries, and general tax evasion. The key issue involves monitoring foreign source capital income.

However, allowing capital to be mobile does not necessarily imply that the consumption tax is preferred to the income tax under a variety of circumstances. Governments will most likely find it optimal to tax capital, to restrict its mobility in order to tax it, or to sign tax treaties enabling them to impose a tax on it with impunity from capital flight. As private investors become more sophisticated, we would expect governments also to become more sophisticated in tracking the flow of capital.

NOTES TO CHAPTER 5

1. For general surveys of this area, see Frenkel, Razin, and Sadka (1991), Frenkel and Razin with Yuen (1996), Giovannini (1989), and the papers in Razin and Slemrod (1990). We will be concerned only with the literature on international taxation. There is an equally large literature on taxation in local economies that raises some of the

same issues involving tax competition; see e.g. Mintz and Tulkens (1986) or Wildasin (1988).

2. Sometimes these conditions are labeled "no arbitrage" conditions because when they hold there is no incentive for an agent to shift her capital from one investment opportunity to another.

3. See Atkinson and Sandmo (1980) and King (1980).

4. Hussein tests the hypothesis of perfect correlation between the two variables. The results indicate that only five countries satisfy this hypothesis. He concluded that this is evidence against the Feldstein–Horioka hypothesis. However, Feldstein and Horioka did not claim that the correlation was perfect: the claim was that, if capital were perfectly mobile, the correlation should be zero. The main problem with Hussein's analysis is the short time span of observations. It is difficult to undertake the dynamic OLS procedure with only 33 observations when leads and lags of the first difference of the regressors must be included in the estimated equation.

5. A current account deficit induced by an increase in investment might call forth a tax increase that reduces consumption and increases saving. Saving and investment would be positively correlated as a result, even if capital is perfectly mobile.

6. This will also be true in the Ramsey growth model on the transition path to the steady state and in the endogenous growth model as the economy moves toward the balanced growth path. However, it will not be optimal to tax capital income in the long run in either the Ramsey growth model or the endogenous growth model.

7. Some software companies place hidden tags in their software to protect their copyright. The tag sends a signal via the Internet back to the company whenever the buyer of the software boots the software up. The company then knows if its software is being used on a computer other than the one it was initially registered on.

8. The issue of monitoring capital income electronically is similar in spirit to scrambling television signals to force television viewers to pay for the programs they watch. Fifty years ago such scrambling was impossible. However, as the technology evolved it eventually became feasible. Now it is commonplace. Electronic monitoring of capital flows will almost certainly eventually become feasible.

6

Taxation and the Time Consistency Problem

6.1. Introduction

Kydland and Prescott (1977) first discovered the existence of an inconsistency that may arise in the open loop policy game between the government and agents in the private sector when the government is a dominant player or "Stackelberg Leader" in the policy game. At the beginning of its planning horizon, a benevolent government may choose a policy rule that maximizes a social welfare function subject to a variety of constraints including its budget constraint and the behavior of the private sector. Indeed, much of the literature discussed in Chapters 3 and 4 studied the properties of such rules. The rule tells the government how to set its policy parameters now and in the future. Unfortunately, when the future arrives the government may decide to deviate from its initial policy rule. If it does, its initial rule is said to be time-inconsistent. Furthermore, private agents may anticipate this and behave in a way that generates a suboptimal equilibrium.[1]

A famous example of this sort of inconsistent policymaking outcome is the so-called *capital levy problem*. It is optimal for the government at the beginning of its planning horizon to promise to tax capital income at a low rate in the future if saving is highly interest elastic because this will provide private agents with an incentive to save and invest. This is a simple application of the famous Ramsey rule of optimal tax theory discussed in Chapter 3. However, when the future arrives, the capital stock is fixed by past saving decisions and thus becomes a fixed factor. The Ramsey rule tells us to tax fixed factors at higher rates than factors that are responsive to prices. If the government can reoptimize when the future arrives, it will reapply the Ramsey rule and that rule will tell it to tax fixed factors like the current capital stock at a high rate.[2] Unfortunately, private agents may anticipate that the government's policy will be inconsistent, perhaps because the government has reneged on its policy promises in the past, and so may save less than the optimal amount. The resulting equilibrium will be suboptimal as a result.

Numerous examples of inconsistent decisionmaking exist. Kydland and Prescott (1977) suggest that it is not optimal for people to live in a floodplain but once they are there it becomes optimal to have the Army Corp. of Engineers build dikes and levees. Initially, before anyone is living on the floodplain, the government's optimal rule is to refuse to build levees in order to keep people from moving to it. However, people will not believe the rule and will move to the floodplain anyway because they know the government will build the dikes and levees if there are people living on it. Of course, after people actually move to the floodplain it becomes optimal for the government to build dikes and levees to protect against flooding. Thus, its initial rule is time-inconsistent.

Fischer (1980) provides the example of an exam. Initially, it is optimal for the professor to give a final exam at the end of the course since the goal is to provide students with an incentive to study. However, just before the exam the professor should cancel it, because the students will have already learned the material. Unfortunately, the students may anticipate this and will not study as a result. So the professor then decides to give the exam and everyone is worse off as a result. Schelling's (1980) book contains a wonderful example called the Kidnapper's Dilemma. A kidnapper has kidnapped a victim but is having second thoughts. The victim promises not to tell on the kidnapper or reveal his identity to the police if he lets her go. However, the kidnapper understands that once he releases the victim she may renege on her promise. So he chooses not to let her go, and the standoff continues.

A simple way of stating the general problem is to say that the government may have an incentive to renege on its policy promises because of the structure of the policy game. Another way of stating the problem is to say that the current government cannot bind future governments to its policies, although one can interpret the "future" government as the "current" government when the future arrives. The problem arises because the government has a dynamic decision problem to solve and plays the role of a "Stackelberg Leader" in the policy game with the private sector.

Most of the work on optimal taxation in dynamic economic environments considered in Chapters 3 and 4 has ignored this problem. Indeed, researchers have continued to study optimal tax policy in the context of the so-called open loop policy game, where the government chooses its optimal policy rule at the beginning of its planning horizon and is absolutely committed to the rule as time proceeds. Unfortunately, the open loop policy rule is generally time-inconsistent; the government will typically have an incentive to deviate from the rule. In addition to this, the calculation of the excess burden of a tax system may also be inconsistent. First, under a lifetime calculation of the deadweight loss, the excess burden of a general income tax will be larger if the calculation is made *before* the saving decision has occurred than after, as long as saving responds to the tax. Second, a calculation of the excess burden of a general income tax at a point in time will be smaller than a lifetime excess burden calculation because some saving decisions are fixed at a point in time.

In the open loop policy game, the government chooses its optimal policy rule for its entire planning horizon, at the beginning of its horizon, taking into account the behavioral response of the private sector to its policy over time. As time proceeds, the government simply implements its initially optimal choices for its policy parameters as long as it is absolutely precommited to those choices. In the closed loop policy game, each player solves a decision problem each period. In particular, the government can reoptimize every period in the closed loop policy game. If the government's decision problem is recursive, the distinction between the two game forms will not matter.[3] However, the economic behavior of the agents in the private sector will generally depend on *future* government policy through their expectations. If the government takes the behavioral response of the private agents into account in choosing its optimal policy rule and agents' expectations are forward looking, the government's decision problem will no longer be recursive. The government's choices at the beginning of its planning horizon for its future policy will be time-inconsistent when its decision problem fails to be recursive.[4]

In the closed loop policy game, the government solves a decision problem each period. It chooses its policy optimally, taking the behavioral response by private agents into account and its past choices as given. The closed loop policy game is time-consistent because the agents are rational in a sequential sense.[5] Each period the government and the agents in the private sector solve a decision problem and each agent knows the problem the other agent is solving. The government can make a promise about its future policy. However, if that promise is not consistent with the decision problem the private agents believe it will be solving in the future, private agents will not believe the promise.

As mentioned, the literature studied in Chapters 3 and 4 has focused attention on the open loop policy game and has studied the operating characteristics of the optimal tax policy rule. This requires two critical assumptions: either taxing the initial capital stock is ruled out or the tax rate imposed on the initial capital stock is fixed; and the government is absolutely committed to its open loop policy rule. The argument in support of focusing attention on optimal policy rules like this rather than on the time-consistent tax policy is that the time consistency problem stems from a lack of commitment on the part of the government. It has been suggested by Kydland and Prescott (1980), among others, that we study the properties of various policy rules, find one with reasonable characteristics, and then find a way of persuading the government to implement the rule and fully commit to maintaining it. Unfortunately, in a representative democracy a constitution can be amended or reinterpreted. For example, the income tax was passed in the United States during the Civil War but was not renewed in 1872. It was passed again in 1894 but was struck down by the Supreme Court in 1895 in Pollack *v.* Farmer's Loan and Trust Co. Finally, the 16th Amendment to the Constitution of the United States was passed in February 1913, and within the year Congress passed the income tax.[6]

Thus, much of the debate about the optimal open loop tax policy may be beside the point if the best policy rule cannot be implemented in a democracy.

The fact that the pure cashflow consumption tax, which does not tax capital income, has not been fully implemented successfully or replaced the income tax in any country to date may be due to its time inconsistency. This is one interpretation of the cases posed by India and Sri Lanka, which both introduced the tax but rescinded it shortly after passing it. Of course, other reasons could also have been involved.

In the next section we will discuss the general nature of recursive decisionmaking, the open loop policy game, and the closed loop policy game. In Section 6.3 we will study the capital levy and derive the result that it is optimal for the government to tax capital at a high rate if it can reoptimize. Thus, in the closed loop game, where each agent solves a decision problem in each period of the game, the government will impose a high tax rate on capital income and agents will save little in anticipation.

In Section 6.4 we will show that, if capital income tax evasion is possible, the *supply of capital for tax purposes* becomes elastic even though the actual supply of capital may be fixed by past saving decisions. Under certain conditions we show that it is optimal to tax labor at a higher rate than capital in the closed loop policy game. In addition, we show that an optimal reform of the tax system after the capital has been accumulated may not entail raising the tax rate on capital because of tax evasion. Therefore, the existence of capital income tax evasion may lead to a bias in favor of the consumption tax. This is similar to the government trying to tax capital income in a world market where capital is internationally mobile. If capital can flee to a safe haven, it becomes difficult for a single government to tax capital. Thus, illegal tax evasion, which makes the supply of capital for tax purposes responsive to tax policy even after the capital has been accumulated, has much the same effect on the government's ability to tax capital income as mobility has.

Section 6.5 discusses the effect of equity. Imposing the capital levy may lead to an undesirable income distribution, as noted by Rogers (1986). The implication is that taxing labor income or consumption may be favored over a tax on capital because of a concern for equity if labor income is more unequally distributed than capital income. This may lead to a bias toward the consumption tax. On the other hand, if capital income is more unequally distributed than labor income, it may be optimal to tax capital at a higher rate than would otherwise have been the case. Batina (1991) derived the actual rules governing such taxation in the sequential closed loop game when people differ only in their marginal labor productivity. In the last period of the government's planning horizon, the optimal tax rates will mimic those derived in static models such as in Dixit and Sandmo (1977). The wage tax rate will reflect efficiency and the concern for equity. Earlier in the planning horizon, however, the government must also take into account the effect its tax rates will have on the state of the economy in the future. This can lead to imposing higher tax rates on capital income early in the planning horizon. We extend this to the case where agents differ in their first-period endowments rather than in their marginal productivity. Section 6.6 concludes the chapter.

6.2. Recursive decisionmaking and policy games

6.2.1. *A single decisionmaker*

In control theory, variables are typically classified as either state variables or control variables. A state variable provides a description of the position of the system at a given point in time. State variables are usually stocks, for example capital stock, although this is not always the case. A control variable is a variable typically chosen by the decisionmaker; and it can influence the future state of the system. In many cases there are different ways of describing the state of the system, so the dichotomy between the two types of variables is not always unique.

Consider a decisionmaker in a two-period setting. Let y_t represent the state variable and x_t the control variable at time t. The objective function is

$$U(x_1) + U(x_2) + V(y_2), \tag{6.1}$$

and the so-called transition functions, or laws of motion, for the state variable are given by

$$y_1 = f(y_0, x_1), \tag{6.2}$$

$$y_2 = f(y_1, x_2). \tag{6.3}$$

The initial state, y_0, is given. The agent wishes to choose the controls so as to maximize (6.1) subject to (6.2), (6.3), and y_0 given. In the open loop decision problem the agent chooses the controls at the beginning of the planning horizon; as time proceeds, the agent simply implements the plan chosen at the beginning of the horizon. In the closed loop decision problem, the decisionmaking occurs sequentially through time as the decisionmaker solves a control problem each period. If the decision problem is recursive, so that the objective function and constraints at a moment in time depend only on current and past choices but not future ones, the two solutions will coincide.

We will consider the open loop decision problem first. Suppose all choices are made at the beginning of the first period and consider an interior solution to the decision problem. Substitute the two constraints into the objective function and differentiate to obtain the first-order conditions

$$U_x(x_1) + f_x(y_0, x_1) V_y(f(f(y_0, x_1), x_2)) f_y(f(y_0, x_1), x_2) = 0, \tag{6.4}$$

$$U_x(x_2) + V_y(f(f(y_0, x_1), x_2)) f_x(f(y_0, x_1), x_2) = 0, \tag{6.5}$$

where subscripts associated with functions denote derivatives. Equation (6.4) governs the optimal choice of x_1, while (6.5) governs the choice of x_2. The solution to this system, (6.4) and (6.5), is a function of the initial state y_0,

$$x_1 = X_0^{1o}(y_0), \tag{6.6}$$

$$x_2 = X^{2o}(y_0), \tag{6.7}$$

where the superscript o denotes the open loop problem.

Alternatively, the agent can solve the problem sequentially in stages as in the closed loop problem. Consider the decision problem confronting the agent at the beginning of the second period. She wishes to maximize $U(x_2) + V(y_2)$ through her choice of x_2, subject to (6.3), taking the current state, y_1, as given at the beginning of the second period. The first-order condition can be written as

$$U_x(x_2) + V_y(f(y_1, x_2))f_x(y_1, x_2) = 0. \tag{6.8}$$

This equation can be solved to obtain

$$x_2 = X^{2c}(y_1), \tag{6.9}$$

where the superscript c denotes the closed loop decision problem. The state y_2 is determined by $y_2 = f(y_1, X^{2c}(y_1))$. Equation (6.9) instructs the decisionmaker exactly what to do in the second period as a function of the state variable y_1. The payoff is $U(X^{2c}(y_1)) + V(f(y_1, X^{2c}(y_1)))$.

In the first period of the horizon, the decisionmaker knows how she will act in the second period contingent on the state y_1. She chooses x_1 to maximize

$$U(x_1) + U(X^{2c}(y_1)) + V(f(y_1, X^{2c}(y_1)))$$

subject to the current state y_0 being taken as given, and (6.2). The first-order condition is

$$U_x(x_1) + V_y(f(y_1, x_2))f_y(y_1, x_2)f_x(y_0, x_1) = 0, \tag{6.10}$$

where we have used the first-order condition from the second period to simplify. This equation and (6.2) can be used to solve for x_1 as a function of the current state,

$$x_1 = X^{1c}(y_0) \tag{6.11}$$

Since the first-order conditions of the two problems match up, the solutions will match up. Thus, $(x_{1o}, x_{2o}) = (x_{1c}, x_{2c})$. To see this, compare (6.4) with (6.10) and (6.5) with (6.8). Equation (6.11) coincides with (6.6). Finally, notice that in the closed loop decision problem, $y_1 = f(y_0, X^{1c}(y_0))$. Substitute this into (6.9) to obtain $x_2 = X^{2c}(f(y_0, X^{1c}(y_0)))$. This will coincide with (6.7) from the open loop decision problem. The dynamic programming approach to the decision problem that uses backward recursions, (6.8) and (6.10), will yield the same outcome as the open loop approach as long as the decision problem is recursive.

However, if the decision problem is not recursive, the two methods may lead to different outcomes. Strotz (1956) was the first to recognize this problem. To see how this can occur, consider a simple example similar to one presented by Pollack (1968). Suppose there is a decisionmaker who has a T-period horizon and who chooses the consumption profile $(C_1, C_2, \ldots, C_T)$ to maximize $U(C_1, C_2, \ldots, C_T)$ subject to $E_t + K_{t-1} = C_t + K_t$, for $t = 1, \ldots, T$, where

$K_0 = 0$, E_t is the endowment in period t, C_t is consumption in period t, K_t is saving, and the interest rate is zero for simplicity. Pollack assumes that tastes at a point in time are determined by current and future consumption since bygones are bygones and the past cannot be changed.

Consider the decisionmaker at the beginning of the planning horizon. In the open loop decision problem she will choose C_j to satisfy

$$\partial U(C_1, C_2, \ldots, C_T)/\partial C_j = \partial U(C_1, C_2, \ldots, C_T)/\partial C_{j+1}$$

However, at time j, bygones are bygones, and the objective function is $U(C_j, C_{j+1}, \ldots, C_T)$. In that case, the first-order condition for C_j when chosen at time $t = j$ is

$$\partial U(C_j, C_{j+1}, \ldots, C_T)/\partial C_j = \partial U(C_j, C_{j+1}, \ldots, C_T)/\partial C_{j+1}.$$

In general, this condition will not yield the same solution as the previous condition for C_j when C_j is chosen at time $t = 1$. Notice that the problem does not arise if preferences are time-separable, i.e. $\sum_i U(C_i)$, since the first-order condition in both cases is given by

$$\partial U(C_j)/\partial C_j = \partial U(C_{j+1})/\partial C_{j+1}.$$

As another example, consider an agent who lives for two periods, is endowed with one unit of labor in both periods, chooses labor supply optimally, cares about consumption and leisure, but in the first period also cares about his future consumption. The objective function at the beginning of the first period is

$$U^1(C_1, 1 - L_1, C_2) + U^2(C_2, 1 - L_2),$$

where $U^1(C_1, 1 - L_1, C_2)$ is first-period utility, $U^2(C_2, 1 - L_2)$, is second-period utility, and $\partial U^1/\partial C_2 > 0$. The agent is happier today if he expects to consume more in the future. The budget constraints are $L_1 = C_1$, and $L_2 = C_2$, where we have assumed that the wage rate is equal to 1 and there is no capital, for simplicity.

In the open loop decision problem the agent chooses a consumption and labor supply plan (C_1, L_1, C_2, L_2) at the beginning of the first period to maximize $U^1(C_1, 1 - L_1, C_2) + U^2(C_2, 1 - L_2)$ subject to the two budget constraints. The first-order condition for C_2, when chosen at the beginning of the first period, can be written as

$$\partial U^1/\partial C_2 + \partial U^2/\partial C_2 = \partial U^2/\partial H_2,$$

where $H_2 = 1 - L_2$ is leisure in the second period. However, at the beginning of the second period the agent chooses (C_2, L_2) to maximize $U^2(C_2, 1 - L_2)$ subject to $L_2 = C_2$, since bygones are bygones. The first-order condition for C_2, when chosen at the beginning of the second period, is

$$\partial U^2/\partial C_2 = \partial U^2/\partial H_2.$$

Clearly, the solution to this equation will not coincide with the solution of the first-order condition for C_2 when C_2 is chosen at the beginning of the first period unless $\partial U^1 / \partial C_2 = 0$. Thus, the open loop decisions will generally differ from the closed loop decisions in this model.

The common element in these two examples is that the agent's objective function at a moment in time depends on *future* control variables. This makes the problem nonrecursive. The same problem can arise if the law of motion of the state variable at a moment in time depends on future controls as well. When the decision problem is not recursive the decisionmaker will deviate from her original plan if she can reoptimize in the future. Since the original plan is no longer optimal when the future arrives, the agent is said to suffer from "Strotz Myopia."

6.2.2. *A dynamic game*

A similar sort of inconsistency can arise in a game between two or more players if one of the players is a "Stackelberg leader" or "dominant" player in the game and the other player, the "passive player" or "follower," is forward looking. Consider the following setup. Suppose there are two players, A and B, and player A chooses $x = (x_1, x_2)$, while B chooses $z = (z_1, z_2)$. The common objective function is

$$U(x_1, z_1) + U(x_2, z_2) + V(y_2),$$

where y is a state variable as before. The constraints are

$$y_1 = f(y_0, x_1, z_1) \quad \text{and} \quad y_2 = f(y_1, x_2, z_2),$$

and the initial state y_0 is taken as given, as before. We will assume that A is the dominant player in the game and B is the passive player. The passive player takes the dominant player's decisions as exogenous to his own. However, the dominant player takes the behavioral response of the passive player into account when solving her decision problem.

In the open loop game, the dominant player first figures out how the passive player will play the game by solving the passive player's decision problem. The dominant player then incorporates this information into her decision problem. The Ramsey rule is a classic example of this where the government essentially solves the decision problems being faced by the private sector and incorporates this information into its own decision problem.

It is straightforward to show that the following equations govern the passive player's decisions in the open loop game:

$$U_z(x_1, z_1) + f_z(y_0, x_1, z_1) V_y(f(y_1, x_2, z_2)) f_y(y_1, x_2, z_2) = 0, \qquad (6.12)$$

$$U_z(x_2, z_2) + V_y(f(y_1, x_2, z_2)) f_z(y_1, x_2, z_2) = 0. \qquad (6.13)$$

These are similar in spirit to the equations governing the open loop decision problem above, (6.4) and (6.5), amended to include z. Substitute the transition equation for y_1 and solve (6.12) and (6.13) to obtain

$$z_1 = Z^{1\circ}(y_0, x_1, x_2), \tag{6.14}$$

$$z_2 = Z^{2\circ}(y_0, x_1, x_2). \tag{6.15}$$

Equations (6.14) and (6.15) describe how the passive player will play the game as a function of the choices made by the dominant player and the initial state of the system. The important point to notice is that the decision made by the passive player in the first period regarding z_1 depends on the future action chosen by the dominant player, x_2.

The dominant player's decision problem in the open loop policy game is to choose (x_1, x_2) to maximize the objective function subject to the two transition equations and the behavior of the passive agent. By substituting the transition equations and (6.14) and (6.15) into the objective function, we obtain

$$U(x_1, Z^{1\circ}(y_0, x_1, x_2)) + U(x_2, Z^{2\circ}(y_0, x_1, x_2))$$
$$+V(f(f(y_0, x_1, Z^{1\circ}(y_0, x_1, x_2)), x_2, Z^{2\circ}(y_0, x_1, x_2))).$$

It is instructive to derive the first-order condition for x_2,

$$U_x(x_2, z_2) + V_y(y_2)F_x(y_1, x_2, z_2)$$
$$+[U_z(x_1, z_1) + V_y(y_2)f_z(y_1, x_2, z_2)f_z(y_0, x_1, x_2)](\partial z_1/\partial x_2)$$
$$+[U_z(x_2, z_2) + V_y(y_2)f_z(y_1, x_2, z_2)](\partial z_2/\partial x_2) = 0. \tag{6.16}$$

The dominant player takes the behavioral response of both z_1 and z_2 to x_2, namely $\partial z_1/\partial x_2$ and $\partial z_2/\partial x_2$, into account at the *beginning* of the planning horizon.

We can solve the first-order conditions to obtain

$$x_1 = X^{1\circ}(y_0) \quad \text{and} \quad x_2 = X^{2\circ}(y_0) \tag{6.17}.$$

The equilibrium of the game is described by (6.14), (6.15), and (6.17).[7] Notice that the objective function in period 1 for the dominant player,

$$U(x_1, Z^{1\circ}(y_0, x_1, x_2)),$$

now depends on a future control variable, namely, x_2. Therefore, the dominant player's decision problem will not be recursive and this is why the time consistency problem arises.[8]

In the closed loop game, A is still a dominant player and B is still passive. We will assume that A moves first each period, taking into account how agent B will respond. B's decision problem is still recursive. At the beginning of the second period B chooses z_2 to maximize

$$U(x_2, z_2) + V(f(y_1, x_2, z_2)),$$

taking x_2 and y_1 as given. The first-order condition is (6.13) once again. Solving,

$$z_2 = Z^{2c}(y_1, x_2) \tag{6.18}.$$

A chooses x_2 to maximize $Ux_2, Z^{2c}(y_1, x_2)) + V(f(y_1, x_2, Z^{2c}(y_1, x_2)))$, taking y_1 as given. The first-order condition is

$$U_x(x_2, Z^{2c}(y_1, x_2)) + V_y(y_2)f_x(y_1, x_2, Z^{2c}(y_1, x_2)) + [U_z(x_z, Z^{2c}(y_1, x_2))$$

$$+ V_y(y_2)f_z(y_1, x_2, Z^{2c}(y_1, x_2))](\partial z_2/\partial x_2) = 0. \tag{6.19}$$

This can be solved to obtain

$$x_2 = X^{2c}(y_1). \tag{6.20}$$

Comparing (6.19) with (6.16), it is immediate that the solution for x_2 in the two games will differ because of the first term in (6.16), namely,

$$[U_z + V_y f_y f_z](\partial z_1/\partial x_2),$$

unless $\partial z_1/\partial x_2 = 0$. In general, however, $x_2^c \neq x_2^0$ since x_2^0 will include the response of z_1 to the control x_2.

For completeness, we need to describe what happens in the first period. The passive player will use (6.12) to choose z_1. The solution is $z_1 = Z^{1c}(y_0, x_1, x_2)$. The dominant player will choose x_1 to maximize

$$U(x_1, Z^{1c}(y_0, x_1, x_2)) + U(x_2, Z^{2c}(f(y_0, x_1, Z^{1c}(y_0, x_1, x_2)), x_2) +$$

$$V(f(f(y_0, x_1, Z^{1c}(y_0, x_1, x_2)), x_2, Z^{2c}(f(y_0, x_1, Z^{1c}(y_0, x_1, x_2)), x_2))),$$

where $x_2 = X^{2c}(y_1)$. The solution is $x_1 = X^{1c}(y_0)$.

The open loop outcome $(x_1^0, x_2^0, z_1^0, z_2^0)$ is sometimes described as the pre-commitment equilibrium since in order for it to be an equilibrium the government cannot be allowed to reoptimize: it must be absolutely precommitted to its policy rule (6.17). This is the basis for most of the research on optimal tax theory described in Chapters 3 and 4 which studies optimal tax policy rules. However, if the government does reoptimize, it will typically deviate from the initial choice for x_2 by choosing x_2 to satisfy (6.19) instead of (6.16). If private agents anticipate this, then we are in the realm of the closed loop policy game, and the outcome $(x_1^c, x_2^c, z_1^c, z_2^c)$ will result instead. In that case, the open loop outcome is said to be time inconsistent.[9] The problem arises for two interrelated reasons. First, the passive player in the game, the private sector, has forward looking expectations, and second, the dominant player, the government, takes the behavioral response of the passive player into account. In the next section we will apply this idea to the taxation of capital.

6.3 The capital levy problem

Following Batina (1992), consider a simple model similar in spirit to Fischer (1980). The economy lasts two periods. In the first period, capital is accumulated.

In the second period, capital and labor are combined to produce the one good available according to a linear technology. This serves to fix relative prices. We could also have assumed the economy was small relative to the world economy without affecting our results. There is a large group of taxpayers and firms, each of which behaves competitively. To simplify, we will assume only one taxpayer and one firm. Both behave competitively.

The taxpayer's preferences are given by

$$U = u^1(c_1) + u^2(c_2, 1 - L) \tag{6.21},$$

where c_j is consumption in period j and L is labor supply. The taxpayer is endowed with e units of the single good available in the first period and one unit of labor in the second period. This initial endowment can be consumed or saved. The savings in the first period becomes the capital used in production in the second period. The government is unable to tax leisure or the first-period endowment. The taxpayer's budget constraints are given by

$$e - c_1 - s = 0, \tag{6.22}$$
$$[1 + r(1 - t_r)]s + w(1 - t_w)L - c_2 = 0, \tag{6.23}$$

where s is savings, r is the interest rate, w is the wage, t_r is the tax on interest income, and t_w is the tax on labor earnings, as in previous chapters.

At the beginning of the first period in the open loop game, the taxpayer chooses consumption, labor supply, and savings to maximize (6.21) subject to (6.22) and (6.23). The first-order conditions are similar to those presented in previous chapters such as Chapter 2 and need not be presented again. The solution to the taxpayer's decision problem is a savings function and a labor supply function that can be written, respectively, as

$$S(e, w_n, r_n) \quad \text{and} \quad L(e, w_n, r_n), \tag{6.24}$$

where $w_n = w(1 - t_w)$ and $r_n = r(1 - t_r)$. Similarly, the indirect utility function at the beginning of the planning horizon can be written as

$$v = V^1(e, w_n, r_n). \tag{6.25}$$

It is straightforward to show that $\partial v / \partial t_w = -\lambda_2 wL$ and $\partial v / \partial t_r = -\lambda_2 rs$, where λ_2 is the marginal utility of exogenous income in the second period, I, evaluated at $I = 0$.

In the open loop policy game, the government chooses first by picking a tax rule for setting tax rates in the second period. As in the previous section, it takes the behavior of the private agents into account in choosing the optimal tax rates; in other words, it takes the responses in (6.24) into account. Its constraint in the second period is given by

$$w t_w L(e, w_n, r_n) + r t_r S(e, w_n, r_n) = G, \tag{6.26}$$

where G is the exogenous revenue requirement. The government's decision problem is to choose tax rates to maximize $V(e, w_n, r_n)$ subject to its constraint (6.26). The first-order conditions are given by

$$-\lambda_2 wL + \alpha(wL - w^2 t_w L_w - rt_r wS_w) = 0, \qquad (6.27a)$$

$$-\lambda_2 rs + \alpha(rs - rwt_w L_r - r^2 t_r S_r) = 0, \qquad (6.27b)$$

where α is the multiplier for the government's budget constraint, and the uncompensated behavioral responses are given by $L_w = \partial L/\partial w_n$, $L_r = \partial L/\partial r_n$, and so on. We can rearrange (6.27) to obtain a formula similar in spirit to the corresponding formula derived in Chapter 3 for the Ramsey rule.

The general solution to (6.26) and (6.27) will depend on the parameters (e, w, r, G). This is the optimal, second-best tax system, assuming that the economy is either small relative to the world capital market or on the golden rule path. In general, it will typically be optimal to tax both capital and labor income, as we have seen from Chapters 3 and 4.

What happens if the government can reoptimize at the beginning of the second period? First, we have to describe the private agent's decision problem at the beginning of the second period. Essentially, capital is fixed. So the taxpayer chooses (c_2, L) to maximize $u(c_2, 1 - L)$ subject to (6.23), taking s and the government's tax policy as given. The solution can be written as

$$C^2(w_n, r_n, s) \quad \text{and} \quad L(w_n, r_n, s), \qquad (6.28)$$

and the indirect utility function in the second period is $V^2(w_n, r_n, s)$. The important point to notice at this stage is that when s is fixed the interest income tax becomes a lumpsum tax and causes only an income effect as a result. Thus,

$$\partial L/\partial t_r = -rsL_I,$$

where $L_I = (\partial L/\partial I)$ denotes an income effect.

The Lagrangean for the government's decision problem at the beginning of the second period is

$$V^2(w_n, r_n, s) + \alpha[wt_w L(w_n, r_n, s) + rt_r s - G].$$

Differentiating yields,

$$-\lambda_2 wL + \alpha(wL + w^2 t_w L_w) = 0, \qquad (6.29a)$$

$$-\lambda_2 rs + \alpha(rs + wt_w rsL_I) = 0. \qquad (6.29b)$$

The Slutsky equation for L_w is given by $L_w = L_{wu} + L_{II}$ where $L_{wu} > 0$ is the compensated labor supply response to the net wage. Using this in (6.29a), we have

$$wL(\alpha - \lambda_2 + \alpha wt_w L_I) + \alpha w^2 t_w L_{wu} = 0. \qquad (6.30)$$

However, (6.29b) implies that $\alpha - \lambda_2 + \alpha w t_w L(\partial L/\partial I) = 0$. Equation (6.30) then implies that $\alpha w^2 t_w L_{wu} = 0$. Since $\alpha > 0$, $w > 0$, and $L_{wu} > 0$, it follows that $t_w = 0$ and only capital income should be taxed.

Fischer (1980) calculated a Cobb–Douglas example that illustrates the gain to be had from binding the government to its optimal open loop tax policy. In the first-best equilibrium he calculated the following:

$$c_1 = 1.424, \quad c_2 = 1.922, \quad L = 0.519, \quad s = 1.576, \quad U = 0.759.$$

In the open loop or precommitment equilibrium, he obtained instead

$$c_1 = 1.726, \quad c_2 = 1.553, \quad L = 0.419, \quad s = 1.274, \quad U = 0.706.$$

However, in the time-consistent or closed loop equilibrium, we have

$$c_1 = 2.014, \quad c_2 = 1.417, \quad L = 0.646, \quad s = 0.986, \quad U = 0.625.$$

Relative to the open loop equilibrium, consumption is biased toward the beginning of the life cycle, savings are significantly lower (29 per cent), labor supply in the second period is significantly higher (54 per cent), and utility is somewhat lower (13 per cent) in the closed loop or time-consistent equilibrium. The taxpayer essentially substitutes greater labor supply in the future for lower capital accumulation today as a way of financing future consumption in response to the possible time inconsistency of the government's tax policy in the future.

How does this relate to the issue of whether or not the consumption tax is optimal? At the beginning of the planning horizon the consumption tax, or an income tax that taxes capital at an exceptionally low rate, may appear to be optimal if capital accumulation is highly responsive to the tax rates. However, if the government can reoptimize later in its planning horizon, imposing a high tax rate on capital will appear to be optimal if capital is in fixed supply. A government that promises to implement the consumption tax in the future will have a strong incentive to raise taxes on capital later when the future arrives. Therefore, the consumption tax policy may be time inconsistent. In addition to this, taxpayers may save less in anticipation of this inconsistency, leading to a suboptimal outcome. The upshot of this discussion is that the gain in welfare to be had from shifting to the consumption tax may change as time proceeds and may be lower if the government's tax policy is time inconsistent.

6.4. Capital income tax evasion

In this section we will extend Fischer (1980) by allowing for capital income tax evasion, following Batina (1990b). We will follow the classic paper on tax evasion by Allingham and Sandmo (1972) and extend it to a dynamic framework.[10] The economy is closed and lasts for two periods, as before. There is one consumption good produced via a linear technology. There is a large number of private agents. Each private agent receives an endowment of the consumption good in the first period (e) and can either consume it (c_1) or save it (s) as before. In the second period each agent chooses how much to work (L) and how much capital income to report to the tax authorities (rx), where r is the interest rate and x is reported capital. In general, $x \neq s$. Labor income (wL) is correctly reported to the tax authorities by the worker's employer, where w is the wage as before.[11]

Following the literature on tax evasion, there are two states of nature. In the first state the tax evader is caught with probability p, and in the second state the tax evader escapes detection with probability $1 - p$. In the aggregate, a proportion p of the tax evaders are caught and when caught an evader pays a penalty of π on unreported capital income $(r(s - x))$.

The representative agent's expected utility function is of the form

$$E(U) = U(c_1) + pU_1(c_{21}, 1 - L) + (1 - p)U_2(c_{22}, 1 - L),$$

which satisfies the usual assumptions of monotonicity and concavity, where p is the probability of being caught evading, and c_{2j} is second-period consumption in state of nature j. The agent's budget constraints are

$$c_1 = e - s,$$
$$c_{21} = w(1 - t_w)L + (1 + r)s - rt_r x - \pi r(s - x),$$
$$c_{22} = w(1 - t_w)L + (1 + r)s - rt_r x.$$

The agent chooses consumption, labor supply, savings, and reported capital so as to maximize $E(U)$ subject to the budget constraints. We will assume that the agent is at an interior solution.

The capital income tax distorts the tax evasion decision in our model. To see this, notice that the first-order condition with respect to reported capital implies that

$$pU_{1c}/(1 - p)U_{2c} = t_r/(\pi - t_r).$$

An increase in the tax rate increases the MRT depicted on the righthand side, making it more expensive to report capital income at the margin.[12]

The government's expected tax revenue is given by

$$E(R) = wt_w L + rt_r x + p\pi r(s - x),$$

where $p\pi r(s - x)$ is the penalty revenue collected from evaders who are caught. If expected revenue is increasing in reported capital, then $t_r > p\pi$. The tax revenue is collected by a tax authority who takes the government's tax evasion policy and the tax evasion penalty π as given.

In the *open loop policy game* the tax authority chooses its tax policy (t_w, t_r) first so as to maximize welfare subject to collecting a given amount of expected revenue. The government is absolutely committed to this policy rule in the open loop game and cannot revise it later in the game. Private agents then solve their decision problems, taking the government's tax policy as given. Finally, the government simply implements the policy chosen earlier in the game.

The optimal open loop tax policy rule is characterized by

$$wt_w(rxL_{twu} - wLL_{tru}) + rp\pi(rxS_{twu} - wLS_{tru})$$
$$= r(t_r - p\pi)(wLX_{tru} - rxX_{twu}), \qquad (6.31)$$

where $A_{twu} = (da/dt_w)_u$, and $A_{tru} = (da/dt_r)_u$ for $a = L, s, x$ are utility compensated tax effects. (The interested reader is referred to the Appendix for a derivation of these results.)

Equation (6.31) is an extension of the optimal tax formula derived by Atkinson and Sandmo (1980) and King (1980) and discussed in Chapter 3 to the case where the taxpayer can also choose how much capital income to truthfully declare to the tax authority. It also extends Fischer (1980) by including capital income tax evasion. And it extends Allingham and Sandmo (1972) to a dynamic framework. Essentially, (6.31) equates the marginal excess burden per dollar of tax revenue collected across the two taxes. It should be noted that in the open loop game the government will take into account the responses of the taxpayer's savings, labor supply, and capital income declaration decisions in choosing its optimal open loop tax rate policy.

If $p = 1$ and $\pi = 0$, then $x = s$ and (6.31) will mimic the optimal tax formula presented in Chapter 3 for the overlapping generations model in a steady state when the economy is on the golden rule path. When $p < 1$ and > 0, then $x < s$ for p low enough, and there will be additional terms in the optimal tax formula, as depicted in (6.31). The government should choose $t_r = p\pi$, which we will label the minimal interest income tax rate, if

$$rxL_{twu} - wLL_{tru} = 0, \qquad (a)$$

and if

$$(rxS_{twu} - wLS_{tru}) = 0. \qquad (b)$$

The earlier result in Chapter 3 implied that, if a condition similar in spirit to (a) was true, then it was optimal not to tax capital income. With successful tax evasion, however, (a) and (b) are jointly sufficient to imply the same result. However, the fact that there is a second condition for sufficiency in this case makes it somewhat less likely that the consumption tax will be optimal in the presence of tax evasion in the open loop game.

The special case where saving is completely unresponsive to tax policy is of some interest. In that case we obtain

$$wt_w(rxL_{twu} - wLL_{tru}) = r(t_r - p\pi)(wLX_{tru} - rxX_{twu}). \qquad (6.31')$$

This equation is similar in spirit to (3.22) in Chapter 3 when the economy is on the golden rule path, where saving is replaced by reported capital income. However, the solution may be radically different from (3.22) since reported capital income may be much more responsive to the tax rates than to actual saving.

In the *closed loop policy game* taxpayers choose saving first, the government chooses its tax policy next, and, finally, taxpayers choose their labor supply and reported capital *after* the government's tax policy has been chosen. The resulting equilibrium is sequentially rational in the sense that each agent does the best for itself at each point in the game. We could add another stage to the game at the beginning by having the government move first in choosing a promise to make about its future policy; for example, the government might promise to impose the optimal open loop policy later in the game. Then in the second stage of the game, private agents would decide how much to save. In the third stage the government would then impose its policy and, lastly, in the fourth stage private agents would decide how much to work. If the promise made by the government in the first stage of the game is not consistent with the solution to its decision problem later in the game, it will not be believed by the taxpayers when they are choosing how much capital to accumulate.

The optimal closed loop policy rule is characterized by

$$(\mu - \alpha)wL = \alpha[w^2 t_w L_{twu} + r(t_r - p\pi)X_{twu}], \tag{6.32}$$

$$(\mu - \alpha)rx = \alpha[wt_w L_{tru} + r(t_r - p\pi)X_{tru}], \tag{6.33}$$

where $\mu = \lambda_1 + \lambda_2 + \alpha[wt_w L_I + r(t_r - p\pi)X_I]$ is the social marginal utility of income, λ_j is the private marginal utility of income in state of nature j, $\alpha > 0$ is the Lagrange multiplier for the government's expected revenue constraint, and $A_I = da/dI$ denotes an income effect for $a = L, x$.

Furthermore, we can combine (6.32) and (6.33) to obtain the optimal closed loop tax policy rule,

$$wt_w(wLL_{tru} - rxL_{twu}) = r(t_r - p\pi)(rxX_{twu} - wLX_{tru}), \tag{6.34}$$

which is essentially (6.31′). The interpretation of (6.34) is similar in spirit to the interpretation of (6.31′); the tax rates are chosen so as to equate the marginal excess burden per dollar of tax revenue collected across the two taxes, except that in this case saving does not respond to the tax rates.

In the special case where there is no tax evasion, the capital income tax causes only an income effect. When this is true (6.33) implies that $\mu = \alpha$; that is, the capital income tax rate should be chosen so that the social marginal utility of income is equal to the social value of relaxing the government's budget constraint, as pointed out by Batina (1992). This follows because in the absence of tax evasion the capital levy is a nondistorting tax since capital is in fixed supply when the tax rate is chosen. Given that $\mu = \alpha$ from (6.33), (6.32) implies $w^2 t_w L_{twu} = 0$, and thus, $t_w = 0$; in other words, imposing a distorting tax on labor is suboptimal when there is a nondistorting tax available, namely the capital levy. Indeed, if $E(R) \geq rs$, capital income should be confiscated before any labor income is taxed.

These results will not generally hold in the presence of capital income tax evasion. To see this, consider the case where the cross price effects are zero. Equation (6.34) becomes

$$t_w L_{twu}/L = (t_r - p_\pi)X_{tru}/x. \tag{6.35}$$

Since it can be shown that $L_{twu} = (dL/dt_w)_u < 0$ and $X_{tru} = (dx/dt_r)_u < 0$, it follows immediately from (6.35) that t_w and $t_r - p_\pi$ must both be positive in order to raise a positive amount of tax revenue. More generally, if $X_{twu} > 0$ and $L_{tru} > 0$, or if the own tax effects dominate the cross tax effects, then the labor income tax rate will be positive, $t_w > 0$, and it will not be optimal to rely solely on the capital levy.

It is also possible for the labor income tax rate to be greater than the capital income tax rate in the closed loop game if tax evasion behavior is responsive enough to tax policy. To see this, suppose the cross effects are zero. Set $t_w = \phi t_r < 1$ for some $\phi > 1$, substitute ϕ_r for t_w in (6.35), and rearrange to obtain

$$t_r/p_\pi = (X_{tru}/x)/(X_{tru}/x - \phi L_{twu}/L).$$

It is immediate that $t_r > p_\pi$ since $L_{twu} < 0$ and the denominator is negative. Hence $0 < t_r < t_w < 1$ is consistent with our special case of (6.32) and (6.33).

Finally, in order to compare the open loop and closed loop tax rates, consider a tax reform undertaken by the government after capital has been accumulated and is in fixed supply where tax rates change so that expected revenue is constant. Denote the response of indirect utility to the reform by dv/dt_r and evaluate the result at the open loop equilibrium. If $dv/dt_r > (<)\ 0$, then the closed loop capital income tax rate is greater (less) than the open loop tax rate. And, if $dv/dt_r = 0$, the two tax rates are equal. The precise condition governing the response of welfare to the reform is given by

$$dv/dt_r = (wLrx/D)[wt_w(L_{tru}/rx - L_{twu}/wL)$$
$$+ r(t_r - p_\pi)(X_{tru}/rx - X_{twu}/wL)], \tag{6.36}$$

evaluated at the *open loop equilibrium*, where $D = wL + wt_w L_{tw} + r(t_r - p_\pi)$ $X_{tw} > 0$, and $A_{tw} = (da/dt_w)$ for $a = L, x.$[13]

The government should rely more on the capital income tax rate and less on the wage tax rate in the closed loop equilibrium, the greater the responsiveness of compensated labor supply to the wage tax. On the other hand, the government should rely more on the wage tax rate and less on the capital income tax rate, the greater the responsive of compensated reported capital to the capital income tax rate. The cross tax effects are ambiguous, however; $X_{twu} = (dx/dt_w)_u > (<)\ 0$ and $L_{tru} = (dL/dt_r)_u < (>)\ 0$ work in the direction of making $dv/dt_r < (>)\ 0$.

Using the open loop policy rule (6.31) in (6.36), we can restate (6.36) as

$$dv/dt_r = (rxrp\pi/D)wt_w[S_{twu} - (wL/rx)S_{tru}] \qquad (6.37).$$

It is immediate that dv/dt_r $(<, =, >)$ 0 if and only if $(ds/dt_w)_u$ $(<, =, >)$ $(wL/rx)(ds/dt_r)_u$, where $(ds/dt_w)_u = S_{twu}$ and $(ds/dt_r)_u = S_{tru}$. The term $S_{twu} - (wL/rx)S_{tru}$ is theoretically ambiguous just as the righthand side of (6.36) is. Thus, the issue becomes an empirical one and we cannot rule out the case where $dv/dt_r < 0$ on theoretical grounds.[14] Therefore, it is possible for the capital income tax rate to be lower in the closed loop equilibrium without precommitment than in the open loop equilibrium with precommitment. This occurs because of tax evasion; if the capital income tax distorts the capital income tax evasion decision, the capital levy is no longer a lumpsum tax even though the actual amount of capital is fixed by previous savings decisions. Therefore, greater reliance on the capital income tax instrument may not improve welfare if evasion behavior is highly responsive to the tax.

All of this is to say that the consumption tax may be "almost optimal" in the presence of capital income tax evasion in the sense that only a small tax on capital may be feasible. In the closed loop equilibrium minimal capital income taxation occurs when $t_r = p\pi$ since no net revenue is collected from reported capital income tax. This is actually optimal when

$$L_{tru}/rx = L_{twu}/wL,$$

from (6.34). This is very similar in spirit to the earlier result in Chapter 3. When virtually the same labor supply elasticities are either equal to one another or both zero, the consumption tax is optimal when the economy is on the golden rule growth path. The same conclusion is almost true in the presence of capital income tax evasion. When the same elasticities are either both zero or equal to one another and the economy is on the optimal growth path, the minimal capital income tax is optimal, namely, set $t_r = p\pi$.

6.5. Equity concerns

If the population of taxpayers is heterogeneous, equity becomes an issue. It is entirely possible that a benevolent government that takes equity into account might not wish to impose high taxes on capital income even when efficiency considerations would imply that it is optimal to do so in the closed loop policy game. Thus, a concern for equity may conflict with efficiency in determining the optimal tax structure in the closed loop policy game and may serve to limit the capital levy problem.

Rogers (1986) considers a two-period model where people differ in their initial holdings of capital in the first period, that is their initial endowment, and in their labor productivity at the margin. She discusses the open loop policy rule and optimal deviations from it if the government is able to "reform" the tax system later in its planning horizon at the beginning of the second period. The formula governing the optimal tax reform in deviating from the initial policy rule has three terms in it.[15] The first term captures the efficiency effect associated with the capital levy and is the same as the analysis when taxpayers are identical. This term works in the direction of raising the interest income tax rate. The other terms capture the effect of the different sources of heterogeneity and the government's concern for equity.

The effect of incorporating equity into the model depends on the source of the inequality. In choosing its optimal tax policy reform at the beginning of the second period, the government redistributes away from the relatively most unequally distributed resource toward the more equally distributed resource. When capital is more unequally distributed, Rogers argues that a higher tax rate on capital income coupled with a lower tax rate on labor is optimal. The opposite will be true when labor is more unequally distributed. However, Rogers did not derive the optimal tax policy rules in the closed loop, time-consistent policy game.

Batina (1991) derived the time consistent tax policy for a government with a two-period horizon when private agents differ only in their marginal labor productivity. The government chooses tax policy (t_w, t_r) each period for that period alone, taking into account the behavioral response of taxpayers in that period. Private agents then choose their control variables taking the government's policy as given. This sequence of action repeats itself in the second period. It is assumed that all agents know how the policy game is to be played.

In the last period of the horizon, the results are very similar to those derived in a static linear income tax model. The wage tax rate should be chosen to satisfy the formula

$$t_w = -\text{cov}(\mu, wL)/\alpha w^2 L_{ww}^*, \tag{6.38}$$

where $\text{cov}(\mu, wL)$ is the covariance between μ and wL, $L_{ww}^* = \Sigma_i (\partial L_i/\partial w_n)_u > 0$ is the aggregate compensated wage effect on labor supply, $\mu_i = \lambda_i + \alpha w t_w (\partial L_j/\partial I)$ is the social marginal utility of income for taxpayer i, λ_i is the private marginal utility of income, and α is the multiplier for the government's budget constraint. The numerator of (6.38) captures the concern for equity, while the denominator captures the efficiency effect. Equation (6.38) is similar to the formula derived by Dixit and Sandmo (1977) in a static model. Clearly, if the covariance between the social marginal utility of income and labor earnings is negative, the tax rate on labor income in the last period of the government's horizon will be positive. It is not optimal for the government to rely solely on the capital levy when balancing equity with efficiency.

Earlier in the planning horizon, the government must take into account the fact that its current policy will affect the state of the economy and that this will, in turn, affect utility and the tax base in the following period. It can be shown that a formula similar to (6.38) holds but includes a second term which captures the effect of the current period's tax policy on the state of the economy next period, and hence the future tax base and welfare. Intuitively, if capital accumulation is increasing in the net wage in the aggregate, as seems likely, then it is optimal to set the wage tax rate earlier in the planning horizon *lower* than would otherwise have been the case because of this "state of the economy" effect. It is still optimal to tax wage income early in the horizon if the static effect captured by (6.38) outweighs the effect of the tax rate on the state of the economy. By induction, this will be true for any earlier period in the planning horizon for a finite horizon of any length. This result provides a counterexample to those who would argue that labor earnings be subject to a high tax rate for equity reasons. Wage taxation may be low to stimulate capital accumulation and improve the state of the economy and hence the tax base in the future.

To extend this, consider the case where agents differ only in their first-period endowment, not their marginal productivity. There are N agents who differ only in e and we can rank-order them in the following way: $e_1 > e_2 > e_3 > \ldots > e_N$. The game is solved sequentially using backward recursions and is time-consistent by construction. We will also assume that preferences are time-separable; that is, $U(c_{1_j}) + U(c_{2_j}, 1 - L_j)$ for all $j = 1, 2, \ldots, N$ private agents.

At the beginning of the second period, agent j chooses (c_{2_j}, L_j) to maximize $U(c_{2_j}, 1 - L_j)$ subject to her constraint,

$$w_n L_j + (1 + r_n)s_j - c_{2_j} = 0,$$

taking $(1 + r_n)s_j$ as given. The solution is a pair of functions (c_{2_j}, L_j) given by

$$C^{2j}\big(w_n, (1 + r_n)s_j\big) \quad \text{and} \quad L^j\big(w_n, (1 + r_n)s_j\big).$$

The indirect utility function is given by

$$V\big(w_n, (1 + r_n)s_j\big). \tag{6.39}$$

Moving backward, the government next chooses its tax policy. It chooses (t_w, t_r) to maximize a utilitarian sum of utilities that depend on (6.39), $\Sigma_i \phi_i v_i$, where the ϕ_i are social weights. Its budget constraint is

$$w t_w \Sigma_i L_i + r t_r \Sigma_i s_i = G, \tag{6.40}$$

where G is government spending, which is assumed to be exogenous.

Finally, in the first stage of the game taxpayers choose their savings knowing how policy will be chosen in the second stage of the game. Agent j chooses s_j to maximize $U(e_j - s_j) + V\big(w_n, (1 + r_n)s_j\big)$. The first-order condition is standard and will be omitted.

Two comments are in order. First, t_w will cause the usual substitution and income effects as before. However, now t_r will cause only an income effect. It is straightforward to show that $\partial L_j/\partial t_r = -r s_j(\partial L_j/\partial I)$, where $\partial L_j/\partial I$ denotes an income effect. Second, because preferences are time-separable, it is straightforward to show that $\partial L/\partial e_j < 0$ and $\partial s_j/\partial e_j > 0$ from the perspective of the first period, if the marginal utility of second-period consumption is nondecreasing in leisure, i.e. if $U_{L2} = U_{2L} \geq 0$. Thus, we also have the rankings

$$L_1 < L_2 < \ldots < L_N \quad \text{and} \quad s_1 > s_2 > \ldots > s_N.$$

This follows, since tastes are the same, all agents have the same marginal productivity, and all agents face the same market prices.

The Lagrangean for the government is

$$\sum_i \phi_i V(w_n, (1 + r_n)s_j) + \alpha[wt_r + \sum_i L^i(w_n, (1 + r_n)s_j) + rt_r \sum_i s_i - g],$$

where α is once again the multiplier. The first-order conditions can be written as

$$\sum_i (\mu_i - \alpha) rs_i = 0, \qquad (6.41)$$

$$\sum_i (\mu_i - \alpha) wL_i = \alpha w^2 t_w L_{ww}, \qquad (6.42)$$

where $\mu_i = \phi_i \lambda_{2i} + \alpha wt_w(\partial L_i/\partial I)$ is the social marginal utility of second-period income, λ_{2i} is the private marginal utility of second-period income, and $L_{ww}^* = \sum_i (\partial L_i/\partial w_n)_u$ is the sum of the compensated responses which captures the distortion of the wage tax. Equation (6.41) governs the optimal tax rate on interest income, while (6.42) governs the optimal wage tax rate.

To keep matters simple, suppose there are two types, A and B. If $e_A > e_B$, then $L_A < L_B$ and $s_A > s_B$. It follows that $wL_A/rs_A < wL_B/rs_B$. Equation (6.41) implies that

$$(\mu_A - \alpha)/(\alpha - \mu_B) = s_B/s_A.$$

The righthand side of this condition is positive. Therefore, it follows that t_r should be chosen so that $(\mu_A - \alpha)$ and $(\mu_B - \alpha)$ are of opposite sign. Suppose the marginal responses are the same. Then $\mu_i = \lambda_i$. Notice from (6.39) that the first argument is the same across agents. However, the second argument differs. If marginal utility is decreasing in capital income, $\lambda_A < \lambda_B$ and hence $\mu_A < \mu_B$. It also follows that $\mu_A < \alpha < \mu_B$.

After simplifying, (6.42) can be written as

$$t_w = (\mu_B - \alpha) rs_B(wL_A/rs_A - wL_B/rs_B)/\alpha w_2 L_{ww}^*,$$

using (6.41). Wage taxation is consistent with the interest income tax if $\mu_B > \alpha > \mu_A$. This formula is again similar in spirit to one derived by Dixit and Sandmo (1977) in a static setting. The numerator captures a concern for equity, while the denominator captures the efficiency effect.

The fact that $t_w > 0$ under reasonable conditions implies that it may not be optimal for the government to rely solely on the capital levy when equity is of concern. The tax rates are chosen so as to adjust the distribution of income and raise revenue by balancing equity with efficiency when the tax policy game is played sequentially. The agent who is well endowed with capital in the first period will save more and thus be better endowed with capital in the second period.

However, the "capital rich" agent will choose to supply less labor than the "capital poor" agent. Ironically, this will serve to shift some of the burden of the capital levy from the "capital rich" agent to the "capital poor" agent through the wage tax rate, because the "capital poor" agent happens to be "labor rich," while the "capital rich" agent is "labor poor." Thus, a concern for equity may shift some of the tax burden of the capital levy from a "capital rich" agent to a "capital poor" agent.

6.6. Conclusion

We have studied the mechanics of the policy game between the government and the private sector and how they relate to the choice of the tax base. Two methods of posing the interaction between the taxpayer and the government were studied, the open loop policy game and the sequential or closed loop game. In the open loop game the government chooses an optimal policy rule at the beginning of its planning horizon. The rule is a contingency plan for choosing tax rates in the future. As time proceeds the government simply implements the specific tax rates it knew would be optimal at the beginning of its planning horizon. The Ramsey rule is an example of this sort of decisionmaking. The literature on optimal tax theory has tended to focus its attention on this type of policy game and has made tremendous progress in studying the operating characteristics of different rules, most notably the Ramsey rule.

On the other hand, the government may not be absolutely committed to its policy rule and may choose to deviate from the initially optimal rule. Alternatively, a new government not bound by past policy promises may come into power. One way of modeling this is to have the policy game played sequentially, where both the government and the taxpayers solve a decision problem each period rather than at the beginning of the time horizon. This is the closed loop policy game. If the basic structure of the game is recursive so that each decision-maker's control problem depends only on past state variables and controls, then the two solution concepts will deliver the same equilibrium outcome. However, if the control problem of some of the decisionmakers, notably the government, is not recursive, so that it depends on future state variables and controls, then the outcome of the two games will generally differ. This is the essence of the time consistency problem.

The welfare cost of the tax system and the optimal tax policy may differ dramatically between the two games. The capital levy is an example where the outcome differs. If capital accumulation is highly elastic, it may be optimal not to tax capital income at all under the optimal, open loop tax rule. In that case the consumption tax is the optimal policy to pursue at the start of the planning horizon. However, if the government is replaced by a new government, or is able to reoptimize itself, it will notice that the current stock of capital is in fixed supply. Reapplying the Ramsey rule will lead to the imposition of a high tax on capital. This means that the income tax will dominate the consumption tax under a simple welfare cost calculation at any given point in time because the capital stock is fixed by past decisions at a point in time. This is known as the capital levy problem, and it may explain the prevalence of income taxation and why no country has ever replaced its income tax with the cashflow consumption tax.

Of course, there may be countervailing behavior on the part of the private sector that serves to temper the capital levy problem. Capital flight whereby investors seek a safe haven for their capital is one possibility that we studied in Chapter 5. Two additional examples were studied in this chapter, namely capital income tax evasion and a concern for equity on the part of the government. Under both, it is optimal to tax labor income at a higher rate than would otherwise have been the case under reasonable conditions. If taxpayers can evade some of their capital income tax liability and the behavior involved in reporting capital to the tax authorities is highly responsive to the tax, labor income taxation becomes a more attractive option. Second, taxing capital at a high rate may cause an unfavorable response in the income distribution which can be avoided by taxing labor.

It is, of course, possible for the closed loop tax rule to mimic the open loop rule when these other considerations are taken into account, in the sense that the "optimal" tax on capital may be quite low. It may be optimal under the open loop policy rule to tax capital at a low rate because saving is highly responsive to tax policy.[16] It might also be optimal to tax capital at a low rate under the sequential policy game but for very different reasons, for example tax evasion, equity, or capital flight. Thus, tax evasion and equity may work in the direction of making the consumption tax policy preferable to the income tax in a realistic setting where decisions are made sequentially.

Finally, we should mention the important paper by Chari and Kehoe (1990). They derive the result that the open loop tax policy, which they refer to as the Ramsey tax policy, can be introduced by the government in a sequential game if policy is a function of the entire history of the game each period and if the government's horizon is infinite. The reason for this is similar in spirit to the results from the game theory literature on trigger strategies. If two players play the Prisoner's Dilemma game, for example, cooperation can emerge in a repeated game setting with an infinite horizon if both players play a trigger strategy. Under such a strategy, both players begin by cooperating. If one player deviates from cooperation, the other player punishes the first player by playing non-cooperatively for ever in the "penalty phase" of the game. If the discount rate for both players is low enough, cooperation can emerge as an equilibrium because the cost of deviating is too high.

In the tax policy game studied by Chari and Kehoe, taxpayers do not punish the government per se since they are playing the game passively rather than strategically; that is, taxpayers are behaving atomistically by being price and policy takers. However, if the government begins by playing the open loop tax policy but then deviates at some point in the future, taxpayers will revert to the closed loop solution to their decision problem and will accumulate less capital. Welfare will be lower as a result than if the open loop policy rule had been adhered to by the government. If discount rates are low enough, the open loop tax policy can be implemented successfully in the infinite horizon sequential game they consider.

Our main comment is that governments in democracies appear to have very short horizons and high discount rates, and many governments appear to behave in a sequential manner. Examples of politicians reneging on their policy promises are legion. It is, of course, important to study and develop our knowledge of the "best" open loop policy rules. However, we should also recognize the inherent difficulty of getting self-interested politicians, who will experience only a short, finite time in office themselves, to pass the necessary legislation and then getting them to stick to the policy rule without deviating. The second aspect of this problem lies in getting future governments to go along with previous policy decisions; in most countries the current government has great difficulty binding future governments to its policies. This suggests that studying sequential policy-making in realistic settings such as capital mobility, tax evasion, and equity concerns may be of greater use in designing actual tax policy than studying open loop rules—although it should be recognized that the characteristics of open loop rules and the tools and techniques used in studying them can teach us much about policy design.

APPENDIX 6A: THE OPEN LOOP POLICY GAME

In the open loop game with precommitment the government moves first and chooses its tax rates taking into account the manner in which savings, labor supply, and reported capital will respond. Then the taxpayers choose savings, labor supply, and reported capital taking tax policy as given.

The representative taxpayer chooses consumption, savings, labor supply, and reported income to maximize expected utility subject to the budget constraints. We can solve the first-order conditions of the taxpayer's decision problem for an interior solution to obtain the functions $L^o(t_w, t_r)$, $S^o(t_w, t_r)$, and $X^o(t_w, t_r)$ for labor supply, savings, and reported capital, respectively. The comparative statics are easily derived from the first-order conditions. The responses $L_{tw} = (dL/dt_w)$, $L_{tr} = (dL/dt_r)$, and so on, are generally ambiguous. However, the compensated own tax effects can be shown to be negative; for example, $L_{twu} = (dL/dt_w)_u < 0$.

The taxpayer's expected indirect utility function depends on the tax rates and is given by

$$V^o(t_w, t_r, I_1, I_2) = U(c_1) + pU_1(c_{21}, 1 - L) + (1 - p)U_2(c_{22}, 1 - L)$$
$$+ \lambda_1(w_1 - s - c_1) + \lambda_1[I_1 + w_nL + (1 + r)s - rt_rx - \pi r(s - x) - c_{21}]$$
$$+ \lambda_2[I_2 + w_nL + (1 + r)s - rt_rx - c_{22}],$$

where $I_1 = I_2 = 0$, and where we have the following derivative results:

$$dV^o/dI_1 = \lambda_1 > 0, \quad dV^o/dI_2 = \lambda_2, \quad dV^o/dt_w = -(\lambda_1 + \lambda_2)wL,$$
$$dV^o/dt_r = -(\lambda_1 + \lambda_2)rx.$$

The government's decision problem is to choose (t_w, t_r) to maximize $V^o(\ )$ subject to its expected revenue constraint, $E(R) = wt_w L(\ ) + rt_r X(\ ) + \pi r(S(\ ) - X(\ ))$. The first-order conditions can be written as

$$-(\lambda_1 + \lambda_2)wL + \alpha wL + \alpha[wt_w L_w + r(t_r - p\pi)X_w + rp\pi S_w] = 0,$$
$$-(\lambda_1 + \lambda_2)rx + \alpha rx + \alpha[wt_w L_r + r(t_r - p\pi)X_r + rp\pi S_r] = 0,$$

evaluated at the open loop equilibrium. Define the social marginal utility of income in the open loop game as

$$\mu = \lambda_1 + \lambda_2 + \alpha[wt_w L_I + r(t_r - p\pi)X_I + rp\pi S_I],$$

where L_I, X_I, S_I denote income effects. Using the definition of the social marginal utility of income, we can rewrite the first-order conditions to the government's decision problem as

$$(\mu - \alpha)wL = \alpha[wt_w L_{wu} + r(t_r - p\pi)X_{wu} + rp\pi S_{wu}],$$
$$(\mu - \alpha)rx = \alpha[wt_w L_{ru} + r(t_r - p\pi)X_{ru} + rp\pi S_{ru}].$$

These equations can be collapsed by eliminating the terms in $(\mu - \alpha)$ to obtain (6.31).

APPENDIX 6B: THE CLOSED LOOP POLICY GAME

In the closed loop policy game without precommitment, the taxpayer moves first by choosing savings and first-period consumption. Then the government chooses its tax policy, taking savings as given. Finally, the taxpayer chooses labor supply and reported capital, taking tax policy as given.

Working backwards, in the third stage of the game the taxpayer chooses (L, x) to maximize expected utility,

$$pU^1[w_n L + (1 + r)s - rt_r x - \pi r(s - x), 1 - L] + (1 - p)U^2[w_n L$$
$$+ (1 + r)s - rt_r x, 1 - L],$$

taking $(1 + r)s, p, \pi, t_w,$ and t_r as given. We can write the solution as $L^c(t_w, t_r)$ and $X^c(t_w, t_r)$, which will have a slightly different form from the functions derived under the open loop game. The expected indirect utility function is given by

$$V^c((1 + r)s, p, \pi, t_w, t_r) = pU_1(c_{21}, 1 - L) + (1 - p)U_2(c_{22}, 1 - L) + \lambda_1[w_n L$$
$$+ (1 + r)s - rt_r x - \pi r(s - x) - c_{21}]$$
$$+ \lambda_2[w_n L + (1 + r)s - rt_r x - c_{22}],$$

where $\partial V^c/\partial t_w = -(\lambda_1 + \lambda_2)wn$ and $\partial V^c/\partial t_r = -(\lambda_1 + \lambda_2)rx$.

The government chooses its tax policy taking s as given, but taking into account the response of labor supply and reported capital. It chooses its tax policy to maximize V^c

subject to its expected revenue constraint and the aforementioned behavioral responses. The first-order conditions are given by

$$- (\lambda_1 + \lambda_2)wL + \alpha wL + \alpha[wt_w L_w + r(t_r - p\pi)X_w] = 0,$$
$$- (\lambda_1 + \lambda_2)rx + \alpha rx + \alpha[wt_w L_r + r(t_r - p\pi)X_r] = 0.$$

Define the social marginal utility of income in the closed loop game as

$$\mu = \lambda_1 + \lambda_2 + \alpha[wt_w L_I + r(t_r - p\pi)X_I].$$

Using this in the first-order conditions delivers the optimal feedback rule for the government's tax policy in the sequential game.

NOTES TO CHAPTER 6

1. For general surveys of the time consistency problem, see Persson and Tabellini (1990) and Chari, Kehoe, and Prescott (1989).
2. President George Bush's promises about tax policy are a good case in point. Bush served as vice president for eight years in the two Reagan administrations and voters had little information about what he would do as president. As a presidential candidate in 1988, he made the following pledge at the Republican National Convention: "Read my lips, no new taxes!". However, he went back on that promise in the 1990 budget deal with the Democrats, which raised taxes dramatically in order to lower the deficit. Afterwards, in an attempt to recover before the 1992 election campaign, Bush promised to lower capital gains taxes. However, his proposal was met with skepticism and he lost the subsequent election.
3. A decision problem will be recursive if the objective function and constraints depend only on current control and state variables and past controls and states, but not on future controls or states. A state variable provides a description of the position of the system, such as capital stock, while a control variable is typically chosen by the decisionmaker, for instance savings.
4. In the language of game theory, the strategies played in the policy game's open loop equilibrium will not be subgame-perfect. See Fudenberg and Tirole (1991) on subgame perfection.
5. It is also subgame-perfect.
6. See Goode's (1969) excellent book on the income tax.
7. The equilibrium need not be unique. We will ignore this problem, as does most of the literature on optimal taxation.
8. The passive player's problem is recursive since the passive player takes the dominant player's decisions as exogenous to his own. He chooses z to maximize the following function:

$$U(X^{1o}(y_0), z_1) + U(X^{2o}(y_0), z_2) + V(f(f(y_0, X^{1o}(y_0), z_1), f(y_0, X^{2o}(y_0), z_1), z_2)).$$

Notice that the current objective function in the first period for B, $U(X^{1o}(y_0), z_1)$, depends only on current and past controls and states, not on future controls or states.

9. Fischer (1980) presents an example of a "surprise" equilibrium where the taxpayer is fooled into believing the open-loop rule will be implemented. Clearly, this cannot be a true equilibrium if the private sector can catch on to the government's inconsistent behavior.

10. See Cowell (1990) for a good survey of the literature on tax evasion. Boadway and Keen (1998) study a two-period model where the representative private agent chooses how much to save in the first period and how much capital income to report in the second period. The government chooses the capital income tax rate and the probability of detecting evaders. There is no labor in the model. They show that evasion is optimal if the government cannot commit to its capital income tax policy. A sufficient condition is for saving to be increasing in the after-tax interest rate. Renstrom (1998) studies a model where there are self-employed and non-self-employed agents, and only the former can evade their taxes. He shows that maximum enforcement is never optimal when the government cannot commit to its tax policy, and that evasion can reduce the maximum tax rate the government can impose on the capital of the self-employed.

11. The Treasury Department calculates that approximately 99.5 per cent of all wages and salaries in the United States are correctly reported for people filing income tax returns, while only 94 per cent of interest and dividend income is correctly reported by filers and only 88.3 per cent of capital gains are reported. See Department of Treasury (1992). The calculation is for 1987.

12. See Clotfelter (1983) and Poterba (1987) for evidence that higher marginal tax rates increase noncompliance at the margin.

13. Under a tax reform where tax revenue is held constant, one of the tax rates becomes endogenous so the government's budget will balance. In our analysis the labor income tax rate serves this purpose. If the behavioral responses to the tax rates are small in magnitude, then $D > 0$ and $dt_w/dt_r < 0$; that is, the tax rates move in the opposite direction for a fixed amount of expected revenue. This rules out "Laffer curve" phenomena where $dt_w/dt_r > 0$ for a given $E(R)$.

14. Unfortunately, empirical work to date cannot be used to decide this issue. One would need to estimate compensated responses like $S_{ru} = (ds/dt_r)_u$ and cross effects like $S_{wu} = (ds/dt_w)_u$. This would require estimating a system of labor supply, savings, *and* tax evasion behavior that included not only the tax rates as explanatory variables but also the tax evasion policy parameters (p, π). This would be a challenging estimation problem and to our knowledge has not been done.

15. See equation (12) in Rogers's (1986) insightful paper.

16. Although see our discussion of the controversy over the subsidization of savings in the United States in the 1980s through use of Individual Retirement Accounts (IRAs) and 401(k) plans in Chapter 3. The evidence from the 1980s in the United States may be interpreted as suggesting that the timing of financial transactions may be very elastic, while the level of savings may not respond as dramatically to tax policy.

7

Taxation and Privately Produced Public Goods

7.1. Introduction

In this Chapter we will study several models of charity and privately produced public goods and examine the incidence of income and consumption taxation. Acts of charity, donations to religious organizations, and private contributions to goods that have "public" characteristics are commonplace in many countries. It is generally believed that when private agents contribute to a pure public good a suboptimal amount of the public good will be produced, because each individual donor ignores the effect of her action on the other donors, and as a result the aggregate level of the public good will be lower than would be socially desirable. However, in some instances the private sector may be able to solve problems the public sector cannot, especially when public funds are not as readily available as they once were in some countries. Public policy, especially tax policy, may have an important impact on these private efforts, and that is the focus of our attention in this chapter.

There is a variety of motives for making contributions to charity and public goods. One such motive is a purely selfish one: the donor cares about the size of the gift donated to charity—the larger the donation, the greater the benefit to himself. In such a model, the donor will ignore the economic circumstances of the ultimate recipient of the donation. Thus, any *change* in those circumstances will be ignored by the donor; for example, if a recession were to occur, he would ignore the possibility that more people might lose their jobs and require economic assistance. The donor will respond only to a change in his own circumstances. The key variables that determine the size of the donation in this regard are the donor's own wealth or income and the "effective" price of donating, which adjusts the donor's cost of contributing to charity for the tax bracket he is in. A "supply of charity" function in a utility maximizing framework can be easily derived, linearized, and econometrically estimated. This entails estimating a regression of charitable donations on the donor's income or wealth, the "effective price" of donating to charity, and some demographic variables. It is typically discovered that donations are a "normal" good and the "effective" price elasticity is less than one in magnitude and sometimes no different from zero.[1] This model has served as the workhorse model of the empirical literature and is very similar in its properties to the bequest-as-consumption model we will study in Chapter 11.

Another motive for contributing to charity or a public good is that the donor cares about the ultimate recipient's welfare or consumption. In that case the donor will take the recipient's income, cost of consuming, and any other relevant variable into account in choosing the optimal donation. In this setup the donor *will* respond to significant changes in the recipient's economic environment. The implications for policy may differ between the two models in ways that are very similar to the different models of bequeathing we study in Chapter 11. For example, the consumption tax will distort the donor's donation decision in exactly the opposite way in the two models, in a manner very similar to the models of bequests in Chapter 11. More specifically, the donor will take into account the fact that the recipient will have to pay the consumption tax in the second model but not in the first. This will mean that the consumption tax will be neutral in exactly the opposite set of circumstances in the two models.[2]

Surprisingly little empirical research has been done on private contributions to public goods using disaggregated data. This is due to a lack of high quality data. Most work has used aggregate data gleaned either from surveys or income tax records. However, Kingma (1989) studied donations to National Public Radio stations in the United States, and, more recently, Smith, Kehoe, and Cremer (1995) studied donations to a rural health care facility in the United States. The main conclusions are that there is less than one-for-one crowding out, and that the elements that might affect the decision to donate are not the same as those that affect the decision of *how much* to give. For example, income played an important role in the decision of how much to give but not in the decision of whether or not to give in the study by Smith, Kehoe, and Cremer. This is evidence against the neutrality theorem in the literature.[3]

We will also extend the privately produced public good model by including endogenous labor supply in the model. The labor supply response can be especially important when studying the incidence of different tax systems. There can also be an interesting interaction between the different economic decisions when a tax system is imposed.

We will also include voluntary labor in the model. Agents can donate money, time (can volunteer labor), or both. As it turns out, both the income tax and the consumption tax will distort the decision to donate labor time. It is also shown that donated labor is decreasing with wage: wealthy individuals earning a high wage are less likely to donate labor than poor agents earning a low wage, ceteris paribus. This raises the interesting possibility that wealthy agents may donate cash to a privately produced public good while poor agents may donate labor. We provide an example where a wealthy agent donates cash while a poor agent donates time. It is shown that the consumption tax induces wealthy individuals to donate less cash and poor agents to donate more of their time, thus inducing a subtle shifting of the provision of the public good from the rich to the poor in response to the consumption tax.

We will also extend the Ramsey growth model by including a privately produced public good. The representative agent can accumulate capital and contribute to a public good. We will be particularly interested in the interaction between the capital income tax and the contribution decision. In the Ramsey growth model the competitive economy will evolve along the modified golden rule path. However, the equilibrium will be suboptimal because of the existence of a pure public good and the so-called free rider problem. Whether a particular tax system exacerbates the suboptimality problem or partially alleviates it will be of special concern.

Finally, we pose the problem of reconstructing the government's finances. It is imagined that the government has run large fiscal deficits in the past but now wishes to balance its budget. We are specifically interested in whether or not the consumption tax can help alleviate the crisis. We model the solution to the budgetary crisis as a non-cooperative game played among special interest groups, each of which contributes to the solution in a way that can be interpreted as making a contribution to a public good. Individual interest groups pay net taxes to the government but receive general benefits in spending from the government in return. Taxes paid by the group reduce utility while transfers from the government and general government spending increases it. The tax a group pays can be interpreted as being chosen by the group when it decides to politically support the government's policy. In a long run non-cooperative equilibrium the government chooses a policy that interest groups support, and each group contributes taxes that finance the government's policy.

We show that in equilibrium the group's optimal net tax contribution to the government is an increasing function of the group's income, a decreasing function of total government spending, and a decreasing function of the group's own taste for private consumption over public spending. It is shown that the consumption tax may *reduce* the group's desire to contribute to the solution of the fiscal crisis. A preferred way of reducing the deficit may be to cut general government spending.

The chapter is organized in the following way. In the next section we study a prototypical static model of a charity where there are different motives for making donations. The incidence of an income tax and a consumption tax is examined and the effects of the taxes on contributions to charity are derived and discussed. In Section 7.3 we extend the model of Section 7.2 to that of a privately provided public good by including an endogenous labor supply decision, and we study the impact of the income tax and the consumption tax on the resulting Nash equilibrium in the donations game. In Section 7.4 we study the case of voluntary donations of labor and focus attention on a two-class model. The rich provide one public good by making cash contributions, while the poor supply another public good through their donations of labor. In

Section 7.5 we examine the case of a privately provided public good in the Ramsey growth model with capital accumulation and study the interaction between the different tax systems, the privately produced public good, and the accumulation of capital. Section 7.6 we examines the problem of reconstructing the government's budget and shows that the consumption tax may exacerbate the fiscal crisis. In Section 7.7 we briefly discuss the results of Ihori and Itaya on the fiscal reconstruction process using a consumption tax. And Section 7.8 concludes.

7.2. A model of charity

There are $n+1$ agents, where $n \geq 2$. The first n agents are donors and the $(n+1)$th agent is the recipient. All behave atomistically in the sense that each feels she cannot influence the behavior of any of the other individual agents. On the other hand, each of the donors contributes to charity that is received by the recipient. There is one consumption good available. The ith donor is endowed with w_i units of the consumption good. The recipient is not endowed with the good but must receive it from the donors. It costs q units of the consumption good to convert the consumption good into a transfer.

The preferences of the ith donor are given by $U^i(c_i, \alpha c_{n+1}, (1-\alpha)t_i)$, where c_i is the donor's own consumption of the good, c_{n+1} is the consumption of the recipient, and t_i is the transfer made by donor i to the recipient. We will assume that the utility function is twice continuously differentiable, quasi-concave, and monotone increasing. The ith agent's budget constraint is given by

$$w_i - c_i - qt_i = 0. \tag{7.1}$$

The recipient's budget constraint is

$$\sum_i t_i = c_{n+1}, \tag{7.2}$$

where $\Sigma_i t_i$ is the sum of the transfers made to the recipient.

There are different motives for making a transfer to the recipient, and the choice of motive will affect the decision problem and ultimately the incidence of the consumption tax. One motive for making a charitable transfer is because it makes the donor feel good—the larger the transfer, the better the donor feels. To capture this motive, set $\alpha = 0$ in the utility function. The preferences of the donor become $U_i(c_i, 0, t_i)$ and the donor's decision problem is to choose (c_i, t_i) to maximize $U^i(c_i, 0, t_i)$ subject to (7.1). The donor does not consider how the donation is used by the recipient.

In this version of the model, we can substitute (7.1) into the utility function for an interior solution and differentiate to obtain

$$U_c^i(w_i - qt_i, 0, t_i) - qU_t^i(w_i - qt_i, 0, t_i) = 0, \tag{7.3}$$

where $U_c^i = \partial U^i / \partial c_i$ is the marginal utility of consumption and $U_t^i = \partial U^i / \partial t_i$ is the marginal utility of the transfer. This model has been extensively used in the empirical literature on charity.

We can solve (7.3) to obtain the "charity function" in this model for agent i,

$$t_i = C^i(w_i, q). \tag{7.4}$$

It is straightforward to show that $C_w^i > 0$ and $C_q^i = C_{qu}^i - t_i C_w^i$ is the Slutsky equation.[4] The empirical work suggests that charity in this model is a normal good and that the elasticity with respect to q is significantly less than zero but greater than -1, although in some studies the price elasticity is not different from zero.[5]

The main implication of the model is that the donor will ignore the economic circumstances of the recipient when choosing the charitable donation. Thus, if the recipient receives more income from some other source, the donor will not adjust his transfer at all. For example, in this model the government can tax the donors and set up its own transfer program for the recipient. Some donors may reduce their own charitable transfer to the recipient in response to the tax they pay. However, the net impact will be a net increase in the transfer received by the recipient as long as the income elasticity of the charitable transfer is less than 1, an empirically reasonable assumption.

However, if the motive for making the transfer to the recipient is based on caring about the level of the recipient's consumption or his welfare then the donor may take into account the additional constraint (7.2) as well. Set $\alpha = 1$. Then the preferences of the donor become $U^i(c_i, c_{n+1}, 0)$. The agent in this model cares altruistically about the recipient and chooses (c_i, t_i) to maximize this utility function subject to (7.1) and (7.2), taking as given the behavior of the recipient and the other donors. Substitute the constraints into the utility function and differentiate to obtain the following first-order condition for an interior solution:

$$U_T^i(w_i - qt_i, t_i + T_{-i}, 0) - qU_c^i(w_i - qt_i, t_i + T_{-i}, 0) = 0, \tag{7.5}$$

where $U_T^i = \partial U^i / \partial T$, $T_{-i} = \Sigma_{j \neq i} t_j$ is everyone else's transfer to the recipient apart from donor i's, and $T = T_{-i} + t_i = \Sigma_j t_j$. We can solve the first-order condition to obtain the "charity function" in this model:

$$t_i = CC^i(w_i, q, T_{-i}). \tag{7.6}$$

This is similar in spirit to the classic duopoly game, where each firm's reaction function depends in part on the other firm's output. Here, each donor's transfer depends on the sum of the other donor's transfers.

It can be shown that the donor's response to a change in w_i or q is of the same form as before. However, now the donor will respond to a change in the circumstances of the recipient. In particular, if t_k increases for some reason (for example), then donor i will respond by reducing t_i, $\partial t_i / \partial t_k < 0$.

Furthermore, several neutrality results occur in this model when $\alpha = 1$ but not in the first model where $\alpha = 0$.[6] First, a redistribution of income among donors will have no effect on the ultimate equilibrium. Donors who pay a higher tax lower their transfer to the recipient by exactly the same aggregate amount as donors who receive a transfer under the redistribution scheme. The level of the transfer received by the recipient is unaffected by the redistribution policy as long as the donors involved are at an interior solution to their decision problems. To see this, suppose the government imposes a tax on donor k and transfers the proceeds to donor g. It can be shown that donor k will reduce his transfer to the recipient by exactly the same amount that donor g increases his transfer. Therefore, there is no net effect on the recipient of this redistribution.

Second, a lumpsum tax imposed on donors by the government that is transferred to the recipient will also have no impact on the equilibrium as long as the donors are at an interior solution to their respective decision problems after the policy is imposed. Donors who pay the tax reduce their transfer to the recipient by exactly the same aggregate amount as the additional transfer given to the recipient by the government. The transfer received by the recipient is the same as before the policy. Indeed, the recipient is unaffected by the policy in both propositions. Of course, neither of these propositions will be true if charitable contributions are characterized by (7.4) instead of (7.6).

The main effect of the pure form of the consumption tax, where general consumption is taxed but not charitable transfers, is to raise the price of general consumption relative to transfers. The main effect of such a tax will depend on the motive for making a charitable transfer. The model where $\alpha = 0$ will predict that the consumption tax will remain neutral with regard to the decisionmaking embodied in the model if the charitable transfer is taxed at the consumption tax rate. This is because general consumption (c) and the transfer (t) both enter the $\alpha = 0$ model in exactly the same way, once in the utility function and once in the budget constraint. However, the model where $\alpha = 1$ makes the exact opposite prediction: when $\alpha = 1$ the consumption tax will be neutral only when the transfer is not taxed at the consumption tax rate. This is because the donor in this model will take into account the fact that the recipient will also pay the consumption tax when the donation is consumed.

To see this in detail, consider the general model and the ith agent's decision problem,

$$\max U^i([w_i - (1 + \theta_t)qt_i]/(1 + \theta_i), \alpha(t_i + T_{-i})/(1 + \theta_{n+1}), (1 - \alpha)t_i),$$

where θ_i is a consumption tax rate paid by donor i, θ_t is a consumption tax imposed on the transfer, and θ_{n+1} is the tax rate paid by the recipient. For simplicity, we will assume that the consumption tax revenue is rebated to the taxpayer from which it is collected, so the only change is in relative prices.

We have not included this transfer in the budget constraint to reduce notational clutter. The first-order condition is

$$-(1 + \theta_t)qU^i_c/(1 + \theta_i) + \alpha U^i_T/(1 + \theta_{n+1}) + (1 - \alpha)U^i_t = 0.$$

When $\alpha = 0$, we have

$$-(1 + \theta_t)qU^i_c/(1 + \theta_i) + U^i_t = 0.$$

The tax is neutral only when $\theta_t = \theta_i$. In that case, θ_{n+1} does not affect the donor's decisions. On the other hand, when $\alpha = 1$, we have instead

$$-(1 + \theta_t)qU^i_c/(1 + \theta_i) + U^i_T/(1 + \theta_{n+1}) = 0.$$

Now the tax will be neutral only when $\theta_t = 0$ and $\theta_i = \theta_{n+1}$. Essentially, if the transfer is taxed as the consumption of the donor and then again when the recipient consumes the transfer, it is being taxed twice. The second tax is ignored by the donor in the first model but is taken into account in the second model.[7]

Of course, if labor supply is endogenous, any version of the consumption tax will distort the labor–leisure choice. Since the tax will distort that decision, it is no longer a lumpsum, nondistorting tax and the optimal policy design problem may include distortion of the transfer decision as well in spreading out the excess burden of the tax. The difficulty is that in an economy with heterogeneous agents, some will be type $\alpha = 0$, some will be type $\alpha = 1$, some will be $0 < \alpha < 1$ types, and some may be at a corner solution for some set of parameters but not for others. If heterogeneity exists in this manner, it will be difficult, if not impossible, for the government to discriminate across the different types. In that case, it will become somewhat difficult for the government to know how to optimally distort the transfer decision. If the government thinks that most people are type $\alpha = 0$ when they are really type $\alpha = 1$, for example, it will choose the wrong tax rate when taxing charitable transfers, and this will lead to a suboptimal outcome.

Finally, it is of some interest to determine how the equilibrium responds to the distorting consumption tax in this context. When $\alpha = 0$, the consumption tax is neutral when the transfer is taxed at the same rate as consumption. The donor's response to a non-neutral tax when $\alpha = 0$ is fairly easy to derive; transfers to the recipient rise with the tax rate under a lumpsum rebate of the revenue back to the taxpayer because the tax favors transfers over general consumption. We would then expect donors to give more in response to the non-neutral tax and the recipient to be better off as a result.

When $\alpha = 1$, the tax is not neutral when the transfer is taxed at the consumption tax rate because the donor takes the double taxation of the donation into account. When $\theta_t = \theta_i = \theta_{n+1}$, we have the first-order condition,

$$U^i_T/U^i_c = (1 + \theta_t)q.$$

Now an increase in the consumption tax rate at the margin makes transfers more expensive relative to general consumption because they are being taxed twice, once when the donor makes the transfer and a second time when the recipient uses the transfer to consume. The transfer will fall with the tax rate under a lumpsum rebate of the revenue, and we would expect the recipient to be worse off as a result. Whether or not this is true in equilibrium requires an equilibrium condition.

For simplicity, assume that $n = 2, \theta_i = \theta$, and the donors play the static "donation game" as Nash players, described above. Then we have

$$t_1 = CC^1(w_1, q, \theta, CC^2(w_2, q, \theta, t_1)) \tag{7.7}$$

in equilibrium. Differentiating, we obtain[8]

$$dt_1/d\theta = (CC^1_{\theta u} + CC^2_{\theta u})/(1 - CC^1_T CC^2_T),$$

where $CC^j_{\theta u} = (dt_j/d\theta)_u$ is the pure substitution effect under a lumpsum rebate of the tax revenue to the taxpayer. If $1 > CC^1_T CC^2_T$, the Nash equilibrium in the donation game is stable. Therefore, if $CC^1_{\theta u} < 0$, transfers to the recipient fall with the tax. Thus, $dT/d\theta = \Sigma_j dt_j/d\theta < 0$ as well and the recipient is unambiguously worse off as a result. This follows because the double taxation of the transfer is taken into account by the donor in this case.

7.3. A model of a privately produced public good

In this section we will develop a somewhat more general version of the model of the last section by including labor supply and we will study the case of a privately produced public good where $\alpha = 1$. There are $n \geq 2$ private agents. There are two goods, one consumption good and one privately produced public good. The ith agent is endowed with one unit of labor. The preferences of the ith private agent are represented by $U^i(c_i, 1 - h_i, G)$, where c_i is the agent's consumption of the private good, h_i is her labor supply, $1 - h_i$ is her leisure, and G is her consumption of the public good, where G is defined as

$$G = \Sigma_j g_j. \tag{7.8}$$

Equation (7.8) is similar in spirit to (7.2). The technology for producing the two goods is linear, which serves to fix producer prices. Thus, the resource constraint is given by

$$\Sigma_i w_j h_j - \Sigma_j c_j - q\Sigma_j g_j = 0, \tag{7.9}$$

where w_i is i's wage rate and q is the cost of converting the consumption good into the public good.

In the competitive equilibrium, the ith agent chooses (c_i, h_i, g_i) to maximize utility subject to the budget constraint

$$w_i(1 - t_w)h_i - (1 + \theta)c_i - (1 + \theta_g)qg_i = 0, \tag{7.10}$$

and subject to the definition (7.8), taking as given g_j for all $j \neq i$, where θ is the general consumption tax rate, θ_g is the tax rate imposed on contributions to the public good, and t_w is the labor income tax rate. The first-order conditions are given by

$$w_i(1 - t_w)U_c^i/(1 + \theta) - U_L^i = 0, \tag{7.11a}$$

$$U_G^i - q(1 + \theta_g)U_c^i/(1 + \theta) = 0. \tag{7.11b}$$

We can define the following "prices,"

$$\phi_{wi} = w_i(1 - t_w)/(1 + \theta) \quad \text{and} \quad \phi_q = q(1 + \theta_g)/(1 + \theta). \tag{7.12}$$

These "prices" will help in determining the incidence of the different tax systems. The definitions in (7.12) allow us to write the solution to the decision problem as

$$h_i = H^i(\phi_{wi}, \phi_q, G_{-i}), \tag{7.13a}$$

$$g_i = \Gamma_i(\phi_{wi}, \phi_q, G_{-i}), \tag{7.13b}$$

where $G_{-i} = \Sigma_{j \neq i} g_j$ is the sum of everyone but person i's contribution to the public good.

If the substitution effect dominates, $H_w^i = dh_i/d\phi_{wi} > 0$. The empirical evidence on labor supply tends to support this conclusion: the own wage effect on labor supply is small in magnitude, but positive.[9] Furthermore, if the substitution effect dominates the income effect in contributions to the public good, then $\Gamma_q^i = dg_i/d\phi_q < 0$. There is also some empirical evidence that supports this conclusion.[10] In addition, there are strong arguments that can be made that $\Gamma_{G-i}^i = dg_i/dG_{-i} < 1$; that is, if everyone contributes more to the public good, agent i will contribute less.

Unfortunately, there is no evidence available that we know of for the derivatives H_q^i, H_{G-i}^i, and Γ_w^i. However, in Appendix 7A it is shown that

$$H_q^i < 0, H_{G-i}^i < 0, \quad \Gamma_w^i > 0$$

under reasonable assumptions, for example separability. A higher price of contributing to the public good reduces contributions. If everyone else contributes more to the public good, donor i will reduce his contribution. Finally, a higher wage will induce the donor to increase his contribution to the public good.

How does the agent respond to the different taxes? First, consider the labor income tax. The income tax lowers the price ϕ_{wi} and thus provides a disincentive to work. Since $H_w > 0$, we would expect the agent to work less at the margin in response to the tax. In addition, we would expect contributions to the public good to fall since $\Gamma_w > 0$. Both prices are affected by the consumption tax if contributions to the public good are not taxed. In that case, both prices fall with the tax, thus causing two price effects. First, since $H_w > 0$ and $\Gamma_w > 0$, the agent will work less and contribute less to the public good as a result of ϕ_{wi} being lower.

And, second, since $\Gamma_q < 0$ and $H_q < 0$, we would also expect the agent to contribute more to the public good and work more as well because of the second effect. On net, the response is ambiguous. However, if the own price effects dominate the cross price effects, labor supply will fall and contributions to the public good will rise. On the other hand, if contributions to the public good are taxed at the consumption tax rate, then only ϕ_{wi} is affected by the consumption tax; we would then expect the agent to work less and contribute less to the public good since $H_w > 0$ and $\Gamma_w > 0$.

It is common in the literature to consider the symmetric game where all agents are identical in order to close the model. In that case we can define a Nash equilibrium with identical agents as a pair (c, g) that satisfies the following two equations:[11]

$$g = \Gamma[\phi_w, \phi_g, (n-1)g], \tag{7.14a}$$

$$nwH[\phi_w, \phi_g, (n-1)g] = nc + qng. \tag{7.14b}$$

First, consider the case where labor supply is fixed at $h = 1$. Then (7.14a) determines the equilibrium value of g. Differentiating, we have

$$dg/dq = \Gamma_g/[1 - (n-1)\Gamma_{G-i}], \tag{7.15a}$$

$$dg/d\phi_w = \Gamma_w/[1 - (n-1)\Gamma_{G-i}], \tag{7.15b}$$

$$dg/d\phi_g = \Gamma_g/[1 - (n-1)\Gamma_{G-i}]. \tag{7.15c}$$

As discussed in the literature on privately produced public goods, if $1 > (n-1)\Gamma_{G-i}$, the equilibrium will be stable.[12] Furthermore, since $\Gamma_g < 0$, it follows immediately that the equilibrium level of the public good is decreasing in the cost q and the price ϕ_g. However, the response with respect to ϕ_w and hence the response to the wage, is ambiguous. It seems reasonable to assume that $\Gamma_w > 0$. If this assumption is correct, then the equilibrium level of the privately produced public good will increase with the wage.

More generally, when labor supply can be chosen optimally, we must differentiate both equations in (7.14). The response of the public good is given by

$$dg/dw = \Gamma_w/\Delta,$$
$$dg/dq = \Gamma_q/\Delta,$$

where $\Delta > 0$ implies the equilibrium is stable (see the Appendix). Since $\Gamma_w > 0$ and $\Gamma_q < 0$, the equilibrium contribution to the public good is increasing in the wage rate and decreasing in the cost of making a contribution. Unfortunately, the response of consumption is ambiguous. Finally, the response of labor supply is given by

$$dh/dw = H_w + (n-1)H_{G-i}\Gamma_w/\Delta,$$
$$dh/dq = H_q + (n-1)H_{G-i}\Gamma_q/\Delta.$$

Since $H_w > 0$, $H_{G-i} < 0$, and $\Gamma_w > 0$, the direct effect, H_w, and the indirect effect, captured by $(n-1)H_{G-i}\Gamma_w/\Delta$, work in opposite directions. Obviously, if the direct effect dominates, then the equilibrium level of labor supply is increasing in the wage. Similarly, if the direct effect dominates in the second price effect involving q, then the equilibrium level of labor supply is decreasing in the cost of contributing to the public good.

How can we apply these results to the different tax systems? The key to understanding the effect of a tax is the manner in which the "prices" are affected by the tax experiment. Consider a tax experiment involving a lumpsum rebate of the tax revenue. Clearly, the labor earnings tax will only alter the price ϕ_w and will reduce the incentive to work. We would expect the equilibrium level of labor supply to fall with the labor earnings tax. In addition to this, the equilibrium contribution to the public good will also fall in response to the labor earnings tax under reasonable conditions.

On the other hand, the consumption tax will lower both prices if the contribution to the public good is not taxed at the consumption tax rate. If the own price effects dominate, this will provide an incentive to work less and contribute more to the public good. In this case we would expect labor supply to fall with the consumption tax rate and the equilibrium level of the public good to increase with the tax rate. Of course, if the contribution to the public good is also taxed at the same rate as consumption, the consumption tax will only distort the labor supply decision and reduce the incentive to work in much the same manner as the labor earnings tax.

7.4. Volunteer labor

In this section we will briefly consider a model of volunteer labor in the spirit of the last section. Suppose the representative agent is endowed with one unit of labor. She either works or donates labor. Let a_i denote the amount of labor she donates to a voluntary effort in providing a public good. Examples include volunteering at the local school, working in a soup kitchen providing help to the needy, manning a telephone at a telethon designed to raise money for a worthy cause, helping place sandbags to shore up a dike or levy in the face of a flooding river, and donating blood.[13] Assume that utility is given by $U^i(c_i, A)$, where $A = \Sigma_i a_i$ is the aggregate amount of time donated, and is also taken to be a measure of the public good. The budget constraint is $w_i(1 - a_i) - c_i = 0$, where $1 - a_i$ is labor supply. The agent chooses (c_i, a_i) to maximize utility subject to the budget constraint, taking everyone else's contribution $A_{-i} = \Sigma_{j \neq i} a_j$ as given. The first-order condition is

$$U_A^i - w_i U_c^i = 0.$$

For an interior solution to the agent's decision problem, the solution to the first-order condition is the "donated labor" function, and it is given by

$$a_i = D^i(w_i, A_{-i}).$$

The derivative properties of this function are given by

$$da_i/dw_i = [U_c + (1 - a_i)(wU_{cc} - U_{Ac})]/(U_{AA} - 2wU_{cA} + w^2 U_{cc})$$
$$= (da_i/dw_i)_u + (1 - a_i)(da_i/dI_i),$$
$$da_i/A_{-i} = (wU_{cA} - U_{AA})/(U_{AA} - 2wU_{cA} + w^2 U_{cc}) = -(1 - da_i/dI_i),$$

where $da_i/dI_i = (wU_{cc} - U_{Ac})/(U_{AA} - 2wU_{cA} + w^2 U_{cc})$ is a pure income effect and I_i is lumpsum income evaluated at $I_i = 0$. The first term in the price derivative, $(da_i/dw_i)_u$, is the pure substitution effect and is negative; a higher wage causes substitution away from donated time toward market work. The second term in the price derivative is an income effect and can be positive or negative. If the income effect is negative or small in magnitude, then $D_w^i = da_i/dw_i < 0$, and an increase in the wage lowers donated labor. An increase in everyone else's contribution to the public good causes the agent to reduce his contribution if $1 > da_i/dI_i$. If donated labor is an inferior good or if the income effect is small in magnitude, then $D_{A-i}^i = da_i/dA_{-i} < 0$.

It is of particular importance to consider a corner solution in this case. If the agent does not donate time, then $U_A^i/U_c^i < w_i$ and the market value of time is greater than the psychological value of donating time. It is straightforward to show that donated time is decreasing in the wage rate; the more valuable is one's market time, the smaller is the incentive to donate time to the public good. So, ceteris paribus, we would expect agents earning a higher wage to be less likely to donate their labor than agents earning a lower wage.

The opportunity cost of donated time is w_i. After taxes, this is given by

$$w_i(1 - t_w)/(1 + \theta).$$

In this framework both the labor earnings tax and the consumption tax have the same effect on donating time; both taxes increase the incentive to donate time by reducing the value of market time. Thus, a shift from one tax to the other may have no effect on donated time in this framework.

An equilibrium with identical agents can easily be defined as in the last section. A Nash equilibrium is an amount of donated labor a^* that satisfies

$$a^* = D[w/(1 + \theta), (n - 1)a^*],$$

in the presence of the consumption tax. Under a lumpsum rebate of the tax revenue, we obtain the following result, evaluated at the initially undistorted equilibrium:

$$da^*/d\theta = -wD_{wu}/[1 - (n - 1)D_{A-i}] > 0,$$

where $D_{wu} < 0$ is a compensated price effect. Since donated labor is decreasing in the wage and $1/(n - 1) > D_{A-i}$ for stability, it follows that the consumption tax would induce greater donations of labor. The intuition is that the tax favors donated labor over market labor.

We can extend this model by including two privately provided public goods, G and A, where G is produced from cash contributions while A is produced by donated labor. A is decreasing in the wage rate, while G is increasing in the wage, as discussed in the last section. This raises an interesting application of the corner solution in contributions to one of the public goods. For example, since g is increasing in the wage while a is decreasing in the wage, an interesting case to consider is one where wealthy agents provide G by donating cash, while poor agents provide A by donating labor. Assume there are n_r identical rich agents and n_p identical poor agents. Rich agents solve the decision problem of the last section of this chapter appended to include $A = n_p a$ in their utility functions as a separate argument, while poor agents solve the decision problem of this section appended to include $G = n_r g$ as a separate argument in their utility functions. Thus, for the representative rich agent, the choice functions are

$$h = H(w_r, q, (n_r - 1)g, n_p a), \qquad (7.16a)$$

$$g = \Gamma(w_r, q, (n_r - 1)g, n_p a). \qquad (7.16b)$$

For the representative poor agent, we have instead

$$a = D(w_p, (n_p - 1)a, n_r g). \qquad (7.17)$$

The question then becomes one of ascertaining the derivatives $H_A = dh/dA$, $\Gamma_A = dg/dA$, and $D_G = da/dG$. If the utility of the rich agent is separable between the private and public goods, that is if $U^r = u(c_r, 1 - h_r) + v(G, A)$ and the cross-partial derivatives U_{CL} and V_{GA} are positive, then $H_A, \Gamma_A > 0.$[14] It is also straightforward to show that $D_G > 0$ under the same separability conditions. Therefore, under these conditions it follows that A and G are positively correlated.

Now consider the impact of the labor earnings tax where the revenue is rebated in a lumpsum manner to the agent it is taken from. A labor earnings tax paid by both types of agent lowers the net wage. Equations (7.16b) and (7.17) constitute two equations in (g, a). Differentiating and solving, we obtain

$$dg/dt_w = -[w_r \Gamma_w (1 - (n_p - 1)D_{A-i}) + w_p D_w n_p \Gamma_A]/\Delta,$$

$$da/dt_w = -[w_p D_w (1 - (n_r - 1)\Gamma_{G-i}) + w_r D_G n_r \Gamma_w]/\Delta,$$

where $\Delta = [1 - (n_r - 1)\Gamma_{G-i}][1 - (n_p - 1)D_{A-i}] - n_p n_r \Gamma_A D_G > 0$ for stability. The first term in each equation is the direct effect of the tax, while the second term is the indirect effect. The latter effect captures the spillover impact of the other public good. For example, the term $w_p D_w n_p \Gamma_A$ in the first equation captures the indirect effect of the tax on G through A.

If the direct effects outweigh the indirect effects, the rich agents will reduce their contribution to the public good G, while the poor agents will increase their contribution to the public good A in response to the imposition of the labor income tax.[15] It follows that the labor income tax may produce a subtle shifting of the burden of providing public goods from the rich to the poor. The rich agent may be better off as a result while the poor agent may be worse off.

The consumption tax has exactly the same effect in this model if the rich agents' cash contributions are taxed at the consumption tax rate. However, if cash donations to the public good are not taxed at the same rate as general consumption, and direct effects dominate, then both public goods increase in response to the tax. The specific responses are given by

$$dg/d\theta = -[(w_r\Gamma_w + q\Gamma_q)(1 - (n_p - 1)D_{A-i}) + w_pD_wn_p\Gamma_A]/\Delta,$$

$$da/d\theta = -[w_pD_w(1 - (n_r - 1)\Gamma_{G-i}) + D_Gn_r(w_r\Gamma_w + q\Gamma_q)]/\Delta.$$

If the direct effects dominate cross price effects, $(w_r\Gamma_w + q\Gamma_q) < 0$. It follows that $dg/d\theta > 0$ and $da/d\theta > 0$. For the rich agents donating to the public good, G becomes a favored activity under the consumption tax which taxes only general consumption c_r but not g. For the poor agents, the consumption tax reduces the value of working at the margin and the agent shifts time from market oriented work to donated labor as before.

7.5. The Ramsey growth model with a privately produced public good

In this section we will study the interaction between a privately produced public good, capital accumulation, and the different tax systems. Consider the Ramsey growth model extended to include a privately produced public good. Population is constant and there are n private agents. There are two goods available, a private consumption good and a privately provided public good. The consumption good is produced via a neoclassical constant-returns-to-scale production function, $y_t = f(k_t)$, that satisfies the usual assumptions. The consumption good can be converted into the public good at a constant cost of q per unit. The preferences of the representative consumer are given by

$$\sum_{t=0}^{\infty} \beta^t U(c_t, G_t), \tag{7.18}$$

which also satisfies the usual assumptions, where c is general consumption and G is the public good, as before. Contributions to G determine its value according to (7.8). Since agents are identical, $G = ng$. The representative agent's budget constraint is given by

$$w_t + [1 + r_t(1 - t_{rt}) - \delta]k_t - k_{t+1} - (1 + \theta)c_t - (1 + \theta_g)qg_t = 0, \tag{7.19}$$

where k is capital per worker, w is the wage, r is the return to capital, δ is the depreciation rate, t_r is the tax rate imposed on capital, θ is the consumption tax rate, and θ_g is the consumption tax rate imposed on contributions to the public good.

The representative agent chooses a sequence $\{c_t, k_{t+1}, g_t\}$ taking as given the other agents' choices. The first-order conditions are

$$U_{ct} = \lambda_t(1 + \theta),$$
$$U_{Gt} = \lambda_t q(1 + \theta_g),$$
$$\lambda_t = \beta[1 + r_{t+1}(1 - t_r) - \delta]\lambda_{t+1}.$$

In a steady state these equations imply

$$U_G(c, ng) - [q(1 + \theta_g)/(1 + \theta)]U_c(c, ng) = 0, \qquad (7.20)$$
$$r(1 - t_r) = \rho + \delta. \qquad (7.21)$$

This last equation serves to fix the capital per worker ratio since the righthand side of (7.21) is fixed and t_r is exogenous. In a steady state, profit maximization and constant returns to scale imply $r = f_k(k)$ and $f(k) = rk + w$. Using this information in the budget constraint, we obtain

$$f(k) = \delta k + (1 + \theta)c + (1 + \theta_g)qng + t_r f_k(k)k. \qquad (7.22)$$

We will consider experiments where the revenue is lumpsum rebated back to the consumer in the same period it was taken from him. This will allow us to focus on the substitution effects of the policy. First, consider the case where the government imposes an interest income tax. It is immediate from (7.21) that capital per worker is a declining function of the tax rate. We can thus write it as a function of the parameters according to $k(t_r; \delta, n, \rho)$, where $\partial k/\partial t_r = k_{tr} < 0$. Abbreviating this function as $k(t_r)$, we can use this function in (7.20) and (7.22) to obtain the following two equation system in (c, g):

$$U_G(c, ng) - qU_c(c, ng) = 0,$$
$$f(k(t_r)) = \delta k(t_r) + c + qng,$$

under the interest income tax. Differentiating the system, we obtain the following results.

$$dg/dt_r = (r - \delta)k_{tr}(qU_{cc} - U_{Gc})/\Delta, \qquad (7.23a)$$
$$dc/dt_r = (r - \delta)nk_{tr}(U_{GG} - qU_{Gc})/\Delta, \qquad (7.23b)$$

where $\Delta = n(U_{GG} - 2qU_{cG} + q^2 U_{cc}) < 0$. If $U_{Gc} \geq 0$, then g and c both decrease with the tax rate since $r - \delta = rt_r + \rho > 0$. Capital per worker also decreases with the tax rate.

Next, consider the consumption tax. It follows from (7.20) that the consumption tax will distort the decision between consuming the private good and contributing to the public good if $\theta_g \neq \theta$, as before. Assume this is the case. Also, it follows from (7.21) that k is fixed at k^* so that capital per worker is unaffected by the consumption tax in the long run. First, consider the case where

$\theta_g = 0$. We can write the resulting system of (7.20) and (7.22) in a steady state equilibrium as

$$U_G(c, ng) - [q/(1 + \theta)]U_c(c, ng) = 0,$$
$$f(k^*) = \delta k^* + c + qng,$$

under a lumpsum rebate of the revenue. Differentiating the system, we obtain

$$dg/d\theta = -qU_c/\Delta, \qquad (7.24a)$$
$$dc/d\theta = qU_c/\Delta. \qquad (7.24b)$$

General consumption falls with the consumption tax rate, while contributions to the public good increase since the privately produced public good is favored over general consumption by the tax.

Finally, consider the case where $\theta_g > 0$ and differs from θ. The impact of θ_g under a lumpsum rebate of the revenue to the taxpayer is the same as the impact of q. It is straightforward to show that general consumption increases with θ_g while contributions to the public good fall.

7.6. The reconstruction of the public's finances

Many countries are suffering from large government deficits. This is due to the general slowdown of economic growth, the Asian crisis, and the fact that politicians in democracies use debt to maintain or increase spending for political purposes without having to raise taxes. Many governments are attempting to return to a situation of fiscal responsibility by reducing public spending and raising taxes. For obvious reasons, the former tends to be stressed rather than the latter. However, when taxes are raised one of the more popular taxes is the consumption tax. For example, Japan introduced a consumption tax in 1989 and recently increased the tax rate in order to raise more revenue in the reconstruction process. Whether this was a wise move is one question we will address. In the United States a wide array of consumption based excise taxes on cigarettes, alcohol, and gasoline and a wide variety of user fees, for example admission to the national parks, were increased dramatically in the late 1980s and early 1990s in order to raise revenue to balance the budget.

Futagami (1989) explored a dynamic game between the government and the private sector. He studied the optimal timing of implementing a consumption tax to reconstruct the government's budget in a Solow type growth model. Alesina and Drazen (1991) presented a simple model of stabilization where the stabilization is delayed by a war of attrition. They derived the expected time of stabilization as a function of the parameters of the economy. Ihori (1996b) and Ihori and Itaya (1998) compared the open loop policies of the game with those of the feedback solution and investigated the normative role of taxes and transfers in internalizing the free rider problem.

In this section we will develop a simple dynamic game between the government and the private sector for a small country experiencing a foreign debt problem. There are different interest groups that are willing to experience an increase in their net tax payment to attain a fiscal reconstruction of the government's budget. We focus on the positive aspects of the process and will also examine the role the consumption tax can play in that process.

We imagine the economy is small and open. There are $n \geq 2$ agents or groups. Each group cares about its own group-specific privileges involving the net tax it pays to the government and possibly total government spending. It is also assumed that the government has been running large deficits in the past and that a dynamic game is being played between the government and the private sector. Special interest groups in the private sector choose whether or not to support a particular policy of reconstructing the government's budget by "voluntarily" paying higher net taxes in order to receive the joint benefit of reduced interest on the debt.

Group i is endowed with y_{ti} units of the consumption good at time t. Its preferences at time t are given by the utility function $U^i(\gamma_i c_{ti}, (1 - \gamma_i)M_t)$, where c_{ti} is the consumption of group i at time t, M_t is government spending at time t, and $1 \geq r_i \geq 0$ is constant. The utility function is twice differentiable, quasi-concave, and weakly monotone increasing in each argument. Over time, group i's preferences are represented by

$$\Omega_i = \sum_{t=0}^{\infty} \beta^t U^i[\gamma_i c_{ti}, (1 - \gamma_i)M_t]. \tag{7.25}$$

The group cares about its own consumption, from which it alone benefits, and about total government spending, from which all interest groups benefit. The higher γ_i is, the more the group cares about its own consumption relative to total government spending. Its budget constraint at time t is

$$y_{ti} = c_{ti} + T_{ti}, \tag{7.26}$$

where T_{ti} is a lumpsum *net tax* paid by group i at time t equal to its tax minus any group-specific transfers. Thus, the tension is between the group's benefit in paying a low net tax versus receiving large benefits through public spending.

The government's budget constraint is

$$\Sigma_j T_{tj} + B_{t+1} = (1 + r)B_t + M_t, \tag{7.27}$$

where B_t is the government's external indebtedness at time t, and r is the exogenously given world interest rate. Furthermore, there is a restriction imposed on the government's path of spending over time,

$$M^* = rB_t + M_t, \tag{7.28}$$

where M^* is a constant. This restriction states that government spending plus the government's interest payments on its past debt must be equal to a constant. Thus,

$$M_{t+1} - M_t = -r(B_{t+1} - B_t);$$

in words, an increase in government debt at time t must induce a decline in government spending at time $t + 1$.

In the non-cooperative, open loop game with commitment, group i chooses a sequence $\{c_{ti}, T_{ti}, M_t, B_{t+1}\}$ to maximize (7.25) subject to (7.26), (7.27), and the restriction (7.28). The policy that satisfies the first-order conditions of this control problem will be supported by group i in the open loop equilibrium of the game. The first-order conditions are given by

$$\gamma_i U_{cti} = \alpha_t,$$
$$(1 - \gamma_i) U_{Mti} = \alpha_t + \mu_t,$$
$$\alpha_t - \beta(1 + r)\alpha_{t+1} = r\beta\mu_{t+1},$$

where α is the multiplier for (7.27), μ is the multiplier for (7.28), $U_{cti} = \partial U/\partial c_{ti}$, and so on. The first condition governs the optimal choice of the tax payment. The second condition governs the optimal choice of government spending. The third condition governs the optimal choice of foreign debt.

In a long run steady state equilibrium these conditions imply that

$$(1 - \gamma_i) U_{Mi}/\gamma_i U_{ci} = \rho/r. \tag{7.29}$$

The lefthand side is the marginal rate of substitution between general government spending and consumption while the righthand side is the marginal rate of transforming government spending into private consumption.

There are two special cases of interest. First, suppose $\gamma = 1$. In this case, group i is completely selfish and does not care about total government spending at all, only its net contribution to the government's budget. Unfortunately, this provides it with disutility. In that case the first-order conditions imply $U_{cti} = 0$. Thus, $c_{ti} = y_{ti}$ and $T_{ti} = 0$, and the group is unwilling to contribute to the solution of the budget crisis. Second, suppose $\gamma_i = 0$. In this case, we have instead $U_{Mti} = 0$. Group i is completely unselfish and $y_{ti} = T_{ti}$ and $c_{ti} = 0$ as a result. Here the group is willing to put forth a maximum effort to solve the budget crisis.

By combining the first-order conditions, we obtain the following equation in the long run:

$$(1 - \gamma_i) U_{Mi}(\gamma_i(y_i - T_i), (1 - \gamma_i)M) - (\rho/r)\gamma_i U_{ci}(\gamma_i(y_i - T_i),$$
$$(1 - \gamma_i)M) = 0. \tag{7.30}$$

Equation (7.30) determines the net tax T_i the group is willing to pay in the long run to help ease the budget crisis. It is a function of $(\gamma_i, y_i, M, \rho/r)$. If we assume that the utility function is additively separable, differentiating, we obtain the following results:

$$dT_i/d\gamma_i = [U_M + (1 - \gamma_i)U_{MM} + (\rho/r)(U_c + \gamma_i U_{cc})]/(\rho/r)\gamma_i U_{cc},$$

$$dT_i/dM = -(1 - \gamma_i)^2 U_{MM}/(\rho/r)\gamma_i U_{cc} < 0,$$

$$dT_i/dy_i = \gamma_i(\rho/r)U_{cc}/(\rho/r)\gamma_i U_{cc} = 1 > 0,$$

$$dT_i/d(\rho/r) = \gamma_i U_{ci}/(\rho/r)\gamma_i U_{cc} < 0,$$

where we have dropped some of the i subscripts for brevity.

If $\varepsilon_M = -(1 - \gamma)U_{MM}/U_M < 1$ and $\varepsilon_c = -\gamma U_{cc}/U_c < 1$, then $U_M + (1 - \gamma)U_{MM} = U_M(1 - \varepsilon_m) > 0$ and $U_c + \gamma U_{cc} = U_c(1 - \varepsilon_c) > 0$. It follows from this that the tax is decreasing in γ_i; the group is less willing to contribute to the government's budget the more it cares about its own consumption. Second, the tax is decreasing in M; the larger the level of government spending, the lower the tax the group is willing to pay and the more it wants to free-ride. Third, the tax is increasing in income. Finally, if the ratio of the rate of time preference to the foreign interest rate increases, the group is less willing to contribute to solving the budget crisis. So, for example, if the foreign interest rate on the external debt increases, the group is more willing to contribute to solving the crisis.

We can now define a long-run equilibrium. A long-run equilibrium is a pair (M^+, B^+) that satisfies

$$\Sigma_j T(M^+; \gamma_j, y_j, \rho/r) = rB^+ + M^+,$$

$$M^* = rB^+ + M^+.$$

Note that optimization by the individual groups is built into the definition since we have substituted the function $T(\ )$ in for the variable T. Substitute the second equation into the first to obtain

$$\Sigma_j T(M^+; \gamma_j, y_j, \rho/r) = M^*.$$

This equation determines M^+ as a function of the parameters $\gamma_1, \ldots, \gamma_n$, $y_1, \ldots, y_n, \rho/r$, and M^*. It is straightforward to show that M^+ is increasing in γ for $d\gamma_i = d\gamma > 0$ for all i, decreasing in M^*, and increasing in r. Once M^+ is determined, B^+ is determined by the second condition in the definition of the equilibrium. Thus, B^+ is decreasing in γ, increasing in M^*, and decreasing in r.

An interesting application of the model is to a small developing country borrowing from abroad at the world interest rate. The model predicts that, in the long run internal political solution to the budgetary crisis, the mix of debt and government spending will shift away from government spending and toward carrying a larger stock of foreign debt if the foreign interest rate is lower. This is somewhat ironic; it is typically unbridled government borrowing from abroad that gets many small developing countries into budgetary trouble to begin with. When the country renegotiates its loans and receives aid from the IMF, this often involves a lower interest rate being charged. However, a lower interest rate may make special interest groups less interested in solving their internal political problems and this may make solving the crisis harder to accomplish.

We can ask what will happen if the government institutes a consumption based tax to a group's willingness to pay for reconstructing the government's budget. Will the group be more or less willing to contribute to alleviating the financial crisis if the consumption tax is imposed by the government? With a consumption tax, group i will support the policy that maximizes

$$\Omega_i = \sum_{t=0}^{\infty} \beta^t U^i (\gamma_i c_{ti}, (1 - \gamma_i)M_t),$$

subject to (7.26) adjusted for taxes according to $y_{tj} - T_{tj} - (1 + \theta)c_{tj} = 0$, and the government budget constraint,

$$\Sigma_j T_{tj} + \theta \Sigma_j c_{tj} + B_{t+1} = (1 + r)B_t + M_t,$$

and subject to (7.28). Notice that $T_{tj} + \theta c_{tj}$ is group c's contribution to the government's budget in the presence of the extra consumption tax.

Since $c_{tj} = (y_{tj} - T_{tj})/(1 + \theta)$ under the consumption tax, we can write the government's budget constraint as

$$(1 + r)B_t + M_t = \Sigma_j T_{tj} + [\theta/(1 + \theta)]\Sigma_j(y_{tj} - T_{jt}) + B_{t+1},$$
$$= \Sigma_j T_{tj}/(1 + \theta) + [\theta/(1 + \theta)]\Sigma_j y_{tj} + B_{t+1}.$$

Using this as the government's budget constraint in group i's political decision problem, the first-order conditions of group i's problem imply the following equation in the long run:

$$(1 - \gamma_i)U_{Mi}(\gamma_i(y_i - T_i)/(1 + \theta), (1 - \gamma_i)M) - (\rho/r)\gamma_i U_{ci}(\gamma_i(y_i - T_i)/ (1 + \theta), (1 - \gamma_i)M) = 0.$$

Differentiating we obtain,

$$dT_i/d\theta = -c_i < 0,$$

under the assumption that preferences are additively separable. Thus, the consumption tax may make it more difficult for the government to obtain political support for solving the financial crisis. An increase in the consumption tax rate reduces wealth and raises the cost of consumption relative to contributing to the reconstruction of the government's budget. This reduces group i's willingness to contribute to the reconstruction of the government's budget. It also follows from this last result that $d(T_j + \theta c_j)/d\theta = 0$ and the consumption tax rate is neutral with regard to the group's total net tax.

The equilibrium level of M under the consumption tax policy, M^c, is given by

$$\Sigma_j T(M^c; \gamma_j, y_i, \rho/r, \theta) = M^*.$$

Differentiating, we have

$$dM^c/d\theta = [1/(1 + \theta)]^2 [\Sigma_i(Ti - T_{i\theta}) - y_i)]/\Sigma_i T_{iM}.$$

The denominator is negative, while the numerator is ambiguous. The second term, $-\Sigma_i y_i$, is negative while the first term, $\Sigma_i(T_i - T_{i\theta})$, is positive. If the consumption tax reduces group i's willingness to contribute to the solution of the problem and this effect dominates, then government spending in the long run will fall and the stock of foreign debt will rise. However, carrying a larger stock of debt may make solving the crisis more difficult.

The consumption tax may not be the best way of reconstructing the government's budget in the long run. A preferred way may be to cut the spending target M^*. There are two reasons for this. First, reducing M^* forces downward pressure on both the stock of foreign debt and domestic government spending. However, the main benefit of reducing the target is that it may increase each group's willingness to contribute taxes to the solution of the deficit problem. This added benefit may be politically important in solving the crisis.

7.7. Using the consumption tax for fiscal reconstruction

Ihori and Itaya (1998) showed that an increase in the consumption tax will not alleviate a fiscal crisis. The reason is that the tax will simply lead to an increase in group-specific transfers and thus will simply increase the size of the government, rather than reduce the stock of outstanding indebtedness. Becker and Mulligan (1998) showed that more efficient tax systems that rely on broad based taxes with fairly flat rate structures are also associated with larger government. A shift to a tax system with lower marginal deadweight loss reduces the incentive for taxpayers to put pressure on the government to reduce its size. Instead, such a tax system leads to greater government.

The intuition behind these results concerning the income and consumption taxes is essentially the same as in Bernheim (1986) and Boadway, Pestieau, and Wildasin (1989), although they use static models to make their points. The key assumption for these results is that every interest group can "see through" the government's budget constraint in the sense that they recognize that the policy parameters must be chosen so as to satisfy this constraint whatever decisions are taken by the interest groups. This assumption of "no budgetary illusion" may be justified in a situation where the number of groups is small.

We can also investigate the normative role of consumption tax policy for alleviating fiscal crises. Under what circumstances would raising the consumption tax rate be effective for fiscal reconstruction? We now consider the case where the fiscal authorities uniformly transfer some portion of the consumption taxes, ε, to every special interest group.

It can be shown that the consumption tax policy has real effects so long as ε is positive. In order for the economy to attain the Pareto-efficient allocation at the steady state open loop solution, the optimal consumption tax rate, θ^o, should be set according to

$$\theta^o = n/\varepsilon,$$

for $n > 1$. This is increasing with the number of interest groups and decreasing with the portion of consumption taxes to be used for lumpsum redistribution. The positive externality is spread over more groups as the number of groups increases. A higher consumption tax rate is required to internalize it.

General consumption taxes are sometimes regarded as a powerful measure that can be used to raise a large amount of tax revenue since the base is very broad. This is a revenue effect. We have shown in Section 7.6 that this revenue effect does not work well in alleviating the crisis. It mainly serves to make the size of the government larger. However, the consumption tax also changes the relative price of private consumption in terms of voluntary taxes, thereby making private consumption less attractive and inducing substitution from c to G. This is the substitution effect.

When ε is low, the government deficit is likely to be offset by revenues from consumption taxes. It follows that the marginal benefit of fiscal reconstruction for each interest group is low, and hence would not be likely to induce any interest group to abandon its privilege easily. The revenue effect is mostly offset by an increase in group-specific privileges. This explains why raising consumption taxes may result in a larger government. The consumption tax policy works well only if some of the consumption tax revenues are uniformly returned to the interest groups involved. Hence, the lower ε is, the higher θ^o must be to reduce the marginal cost of abandoning the existing privileges resulting from the substitution effect.

7.8. Conclusion

Charity and private contributions to public goods are important features of most economies. A large number of people choose to donate their time and their money to what they regard as worthy causes. The effect of public policy, especially tax policy, on their behavior may be of some importance.

There are several motives for donating time and money, and the specific motive is important in determining how a particular donor will react to public policies including taxation. We examined two such motives, one where the donor cares about the actual amount donated and another where the donor cares about the ultimate recipient's consumption. We showed that the incidence of tax policy may differ depending on the motive for donating.

We extended the basic model in several ways. First, we included labor supply and studied the interaction between supplying labor and donating cash transfers to a public good. We also extended the model by including donated labor. If donated labor is decreasing in the wage, wealthy individuals may donate cash while poor individuals may donate their labor instead. We provided an example where the wealthy agent reduces his contribution to the public good while the poor agent increases his contribution in response to the consumption tax. Thus, one implication of the consumption tax may be that it will shift the provision of a privately produced public good from the wealthy to the poor.

We also incorporated contributions to a privately produced public good into the infinite horizon Ramsey growth model and studied the incidence of the interest income tax and the consumption tax. The interest income tax reduces capital accumulation, consumption, and contributions to privately produced public goods in the long run equilibrium. The consumption tax that exempts contributions to the public good has no effect at the margin on capital accumulation, reduces consumption, and increases cash contributions to the public good.

Finally, many governments are attempting to reconstruct their budgets by reducing their fiscal deficits and some governments are using consumption taxes to do so, most notably Japan. Indeed, many small developing countries have experienced problems involving large foreign debt and need to reconstruct their budgets as well.

This process can be modeled as individual special interest groups each contributing to a public good, the reconstruction of the government's budget. It is shown that the consumption tax may make it more difficult to solve the budget crisis and that reducing spending targets may be a preferred way of solving the budgetary problem. This may explain part of the Japanese government's difficulty in reconstructing its budget even though it recently raised the consumption tax rate. If special interest groups are particularly upset with the imposition of the consumption tax, it is possible they will be less willing to contribute taxes to the solution of the crisis. This would not lead to a decrease in the stock of debt in the future, thus making it more difficult to solve the budgetary crisis in the long run.

APPENDIX 7A: THE PRIVATELY PRODUCED PUBLIC GOODS MODEL
WITH LABOR SUPPLY

The optimization problem of the representative agent for an interior solution without taxes can be stated as

$$\max U(wh_i - qg_i + I, 1 - h_i, g_i + G_{-i}),$$

evaluated at $I = 0$, where I is a source of lumpsum income. Equations (7.11) are the first-order conditions for the problem. Totally differentiating, we obtain the following substitution effects:

$$\Gamma_q^i = (dg_i/dq)_u = U_c(U_{LL} - 2qU_{cL} + w^2 U_{cc})/J < 0,$$
$$\Gamma_w^i = (dg_i/dw)_u = U_c(wU_{Gc} - U_{GL} - wqU_{cc} + qU_{cL})/J,$$
$$H_q^i = (db_i/dq)_u = -U_c(wU_{Gc} - U_{GL} - wqU_{cc} + qU_{cL})/J,$$
$$H_w^i = (db_i/dw)_u = -U_c(U_{GG} - 2qU_{cG} + q^2 U_{cc})/J > 0,$$

where $J = (U_{GG} - 2qU_{cG} + q^2 U_{cc})(U_{LL} - 2qU_{cL} + w^2 U_{cc}) - (wU_{Gc} - U_{GL} - wqU_{cc} + qU_{cL})^2 > 0$. Clearly, $\Gamma_q^i < 0$ and $H_w^i > 0$. In addition, $\Gamma_w^i > 0$ and $H_q^i < 0$ if $(wU_{Gc} - U_{GL} - wqU_{cc} + qU_{cL}) > 0$. One sufficient condition for this is that utility be additively separable. However, if $U_{Gc}, U_{cL} > 0$, then $wU_{Gc} > U_{GL}$, which is somewhat less restrictive than additive separability.

In addition, it can be shown that

$$\Gamma_{G-i}^i = dg_i/dG_{-i} = -(1 - qdg_i/dI),$$
$$H_{G-i}^i = db_i/dG_{-i} = qdb_i/dI.$$

If $qdg_i/dI < 1$, then $\Gamma_{G-i}^i < 0$. The second result involving labor supply is entirely new to the literature, to our knowledge. If leisure is a normal good, then labor supply is decreasing in the aggregate contributions of the other agents, $H_{G-i}^i < 0$.

In equilibrium with identical agents we have the following conditions,

$$g = \Gamma[w, q, (n-1)g],$$
$$c + qg = wH[w, q, (n-1)g].$$

The response of the public good to the wage and the cost of contributing is given by differentiating the system and solving to obtain

$$dg/dw = \Gamma w/\Delta,$$
$$dg/dq = \Gamma q/\Delta,$$

respectively. Since $\Gamma_w > 0$ and $\Gamma_q < 0$ under our assumptions, and $\Delta > 0$ for stability, it follows that $dg/dw > 0$ and $dg/dq < 0$. The response of consumption is ambiguous. Finally, the general equilibrium responses of labor supply to the wage and the cost of contributing to the public good are given by

$$db/dw = H_w + (n-1)H_{G-i}\Gamma_w/\Delta,$$
$$db/dq = H_q + (n-1)H_{G-i}\Gamma_q/\Delta.$$

The direct effects, H_w and H_q, work in the opposite direction of the indirect effects, $(n-1)H_{G-i}\Gamma_w/\Delta$ and $(n-1)H_{G-i}\Gamma_q/\Delta$. If the former dominate, then $db/dw > 0$ and $db/dq < 0$.

NOTES TO CHAPTER 7

1. See Clotfelter (1984).

2. Typically, in the privately provided public goods literature it is assumed the agent cares about her own consumption and the total amount of the public good available and makes a contribution to the total amount available. For an early statement of the "subscriptions" model, see Malinvaud (1972); for the more recent literature, see Warr (1982, 1983), Roberts (1984, 1987), Bergstrom, Blume, and Varian (1986), Andreoni (1988, 1990), Boadway, Pestieau, and Wildasin (1989), Buchholz (1993), and Buchholz and Konrad (1993).

3. Warr (1982, 1983) was first to show that donations are independent of the distribution of income in the so-called subscriptions model where donors care about the total amount donated by everyone. Government contributions to the public good financed by lumpsum taxes can also be perfectly crowded out by a one-for-one decline in private contributions in such a model. See also Shibata (1971).

4. Differentiate (7.3) to obtain,

$$(U_{tt}^i - 2qU_{ct}^i - q^2 U_{cc}^i)dt_i + (U_{tc}^i - qU_{cc}^i)dw_i - [U_c^i + t_i(U_{tc}^i - qu_{cc}^i)]dq = 0,$$

and solve. The response, $dt_i/dw_i > 0$ if $U_{tc}^i \geq 0$.

5. For a recent example see Smith, Kehoe, and Cremer (1995), who find the tax price to be statistically insignificant.

6. See Shibata (1971), Warr (1982, 1983) and Roberts (1984) for early discussions of these propositions, and later Ihori (1992).

7. Notice that if $\theta_{n+1} = 0$ and $\theta_t = \theta i$ for $i = 1, 2, \ldots, n$, then the tax is neutral in both models. This possibility has not been recognized in the literature to our knowledge.

8. Differentiate to obtain

$$(1 - CC_T^1 CC_T^2)dt_1 = (CC_{\theta u}^1 + CC_{\theta u}^2)d\theta,$$

and simplify. Under a lumpsum rebate of the revenue there will only be substitution effects associated with the tax. Thus, $CC_{\theta u}^1$ and $CC_{\theta u}^2$ capture the response to the tax at the margin.

9. See the discussion of the empirical work on labor supply in Chapter 3.

10. See Clotfelter (1984).

11. It is well known that the equilibrium will not be optimal. Each agent will ignore the impact his action has on the other agents. A Pigouvian subsidy is typically called for as a solution to this problem.

12. See e.g. Warr (1983) and Bergstrom, Blume, and Varian (1986).

13. Another example would be mowing one's lawn and maintaining one's yard, certainly a time-intensive activity if ever there was one. Maintaining one's property makes the property more attractive to the neighbors, thus providing a public good.

14. By differentiating the system of (7.11) and solving,

$$\Gamma_A = dg/dA = -v_{GA}(u_{LL} - 2wu_{cL} + w^2 u_{cc})/J,$$

$$H_A = dh/dA = qv_{GA}(u_{cL} - wu_{cc})/J,$$

where $J > 0$ is the determinant of the system. See Appendix 7A. If $v_{GA} > 0$ and $u_{cL} \geq 0$, then it follows that $\Gamma_A > 0$ and $H_A > 0$.

15. This follows because $\Gamma_w[1 - (n_p - 1)D_{A-i}] > 0$ and $D_w[1 - (n_r - 1)\Gamma_{G-i}] < 0$.

8

The Environment and Tax Policy

8.1. Introduction

Research on the interaction of production, consumption, economic growth, and the environment has increased dramatically in recent years. In this chapter we will study the way income and consumption taxes may affect economic decisions that may interact with the environment. More specifically, we will study an overlapping generations model of a renewable resource and a second model of an environmental stock externality, a version of the Ramsey growth model.

Mourmouras (1993) studied an overlapping generations model with a renewable resource where the growth rate of the resource stock is constant; that is, the regeneration function of the resource is a constant. He shows that competition may lead to over depletion of the resource stock and hence to lower welfare relative to both a Rawlsian social welfare criterion and a sustainability criterion which disallows declining utility across generations. Mourmouras argues that the first-best allocation cannot be attained even when the government has access to perfectly nondistorting taxes and transfers because of the asymmetric assignment of the property right to the resource. In addition, he shows that it is *necessary* in his model for the government to confiscate the resource from the initial old generation that owns it and to compensate the owners by issuing them fiat money in order for the competitive economy-cum-government policy to achieve the first-best solution.

Batina and Krautkraemer (1996) assumed that the regeneration function of the resource was a smooth, concave function of the amount of the resource carried over as an asset. The knife edge property evident in Mourmouras's model disappears as a result. However, it is still possible for the private economy to accumulate too much of the resource as an asset. This remains true even if there is physical capital in the model; too much of both assets may be accumulated. They showed that the introduction of another asset, such as fiat money or one-period government bonds, that pays the socially optimal rate of return will allow the government to decentralize the optimal allocation. In the interesting case where the resource stock also has an amenity value, a Pigouvian subsidy will not work alone. It must be accompanied by a policy, for example government debt, that keeps the competitive economy on the optimal expansion path.

Babu *et al.* (1997) study an OG model that includes a nonrenewable resource that causes a harmful pollution externality. It is shown that, if individual agents take into account the pollution caused when they extract and use some of the resource to produce the consumption good, then the Hotelling rule governing the price of the resource needs to be modified to include the externality.[1] They also derive the optimal Pigouvian tax on resource use by firms and show that the tax will be increasing over time if the marginal product of capital is larger than the externality effect. However, if agents behave atomistically and do not take their individual impact on the environment into account, then the Hotelling rule and the typical Pigouvian externality tax apply.

Some economists have suggested that pollution taxes can yield a double dividend; pollution taxes can internalize various harmful externalities associated with pollution and can be used to lower other distortionary taxes. Bovenberg and Mooij (1994) show that pollution taxes may reduce welfare in the presence of pre-existing distortions. Bovenberg and van der Ploeg (1994) study the optimal second-best taxation and public spending rules when environmental taxes and public goods that hurt the environment are included in the model. Special cases are studied and some limited comparative statics are undertaken. For example, it is shown that there will be a higher "dirt" or pollution tax imposed on polluting goods, a lower tax on labor earnings, greater public abatement, and a cleaner environment if there is an increase in the representative agent's taste for the environment. Finally, Bovenberg and Smulders (1995) study environmental externalities within an endogenous growth model and derive necessary conditions that permit balanced growth to occur in the presence of a pollution externality.

John *et al.* (1995) study an OG model where consumption causes a harmful externality to the environment and they contrast the policies pursued by a short-lived government with those of a long-lived government. The long-lived government can internalize eternality problems that a short-lived government cannot. Farzin (1996) studies the case of an interlinked resource and environmental stock externality coupled with a threshold effect, and it is shown how the Pigouvian tax policy must be modified to take this interaction into account. However, the simulations of the model are very sensitive to the choice of the parameters. Unfortunately, the model is partial equilibrium in nature and the specific behavior of the individual consumers and firms is not modeled. Finally, Mohtadi (1996) assumes that the environment is harmed by capital accumulation and studies the optimal output tax and regulatory policy in the context of a version of the Ramsey growth model.

We will generalize this work in several ways as we study the impact of the different tax systems on renewable resources and harmful stock externalities. The decision problem that agents face will be completely specified. Labor supply will also be included as an endogenous element of the models. When studying the stock externality we will assume that both consumption and production cause a harmful externality to the environment. This can have an important impact on optimal policy design.

The specific purpose of this chapter is to study the impact of the income and consumption tax policies on the environment. Tax policy affects the environment in a number of interesting ways, some direct and some indirect. For example, a carbon tax imposed on the consumption of gasoline is directly designed to reduce driving and hence pollution and thereby to improve the quality of the environment. On the other hand, allowing an exemption that includes writing off an investment in a fleet of delivery trucks against a firm's tax liability can indirectly have a detrimental effect on the environment if trucks pollute the environment more than other available forms of transport, such as light rail. No single model can capture all of these effects in a cogent, tractable manner. We will concentrate on two environmental issues and how the income and consumption taxes might affect them: a renewable resource and a general pollution externality.

First, we will examine an overlapping generations model of a renewable resource and derive a version of Hotelling's rule regarding the evolution of the price of the resource. Examples of renewable resources include timber, fish stocks, clean air and water, natural habitats and local ecosystems, and perhaps even the ozone layer. In the context of the overlapping generations model, it is possible that the competitive economy may acquire too much of a renewable resource as an asset. This is similar in spirit to Diamond's (1965) result that capital over-accumulation cannot be ruled out under competition since there is no single decisionmaker who can decide how much capital to accumulate in the aggregate under competition. It is shown that the interest income tax will distort the resource asset accumulation decision by distorting the intertemporal consumption decision.

It is also shown that the consumption tax will be neutral toward the intertemporal consumption decision. However, when the model is extended to allow the resource to have an amenity value, then the consumption tax will favor the resource as an asset. For example, land with timber on it is a more pleasant place to camp, fish, and enjoy the natural habitat than land that has been clear cut. We show that the consumption tax will distort the decision to acquire the resource as an asset if it has an amenity value. An increase in the consumption tax rate compensated to maintain disposable income will induce the agent to acquire more of the resource stock as an asset. This result needs to be tempered if labor supply is endogenous since the consumption tax will distort the labor supply decision. It is then possible for the demand for the resource as an asset to fall with an increase in the consumption tax rate because of its interaction with labor supply.

Second, we will study a version of the Ramsey growth model that includes both a consumption externality and a production externality that adversely affect the environment. We will derive the conditions characterizing the social planner problem where the planner takes the externalities into account and compare them with those of the competitive equilibrium. It will be optimal for the government to tax both labor and capital income in order to allow the competitive equilibrium to support the first-best optimum. This is in marked contrast to the results that stem from the classic Ramsey growth model. Judd (1985) and Chamley (1986) showed that it was suboptimal to tax capital income in the long run and Lucas (1990) extended this result to an endogenous growth model, as explained in Chapter 4. However, the environment and the possible externalities associated with pollution are ignored in these models.

We will show that it becomes optimal to tax capital in the long run when the act of production causes a harmful externality to the environment. Indeed, the tax on capital in the presence of such externalities acts as a classic Pigouvian externality tax. In addition to this, the optimal tax on labor income in a steady state will also be positive and its magnitude will depend on the magnitude of both externalities at the margin. This is because labor causes both a consumption externality and a production externality. If the agent works more, production increases and this causes a harmful production externality in our setup. In addition to this, if the agent works more, she will also consume more and this will also cause a harmful consumption externality.

Third, we will study an important special case of the Ramsey externality model where the quality of the environment evolves according to a linear equation and where individual agents can undertake an action that helps improve the environment. If agents behave atomistically by taking aggregate variables like the quality of the environment as given, then their consumption decisions and their decision to help improve the environment will be socially suboptimal. We show, however, that the consumption tax can be used to take care of both externalities at once and allow the competitive equilibrium to support the socially optimal allocation. Of course, if production also causes harm to the environment, then the consumption tax alone will not suffice and a tax on capital will again be optimal.

The chapter is organized in the following way. We present an overlapping generations model of a renewable resource in the next section. The optimality of the competitive equilibrium is considered and in Section 8.3 we study the impact of the interest income tax and the consumption tax in that model. Section 8.4 considers a version of the Ramsey growth model extended to include externalities, where both consumption and production cause harm to the environment. The income and consumption tax policies are considered in Section 8.5. It is shown that it is optimal to tax capital in the long run, in contrast to the results of Judd (1985), Chamley (1986), and Lucas (1990), for example, because the tax on capital acts as an optimal Pigouvian externality tax. It is also shown that it is optimal to tax labor income as well. Thus, one conclusion is that, when production and consumption both generate an externality, the consumption tax per se is not necessarily optimal. Section 8.6 looks at an important case where private agents can take an action to help the environment. It is shown that the consumption tax can adjust behavior at the margin so as to allow the competitive equilibrium to support the socially optimal allocation in a steady state. Section 8.7 discusses the case where there is "clean" consumption which does not harm the environment and "dirty" consumption which does. If the government can distinguish between the two, the competitive economy with a Pigouvian tax policy can support the optimum; if it cannot, a flat-rate consumption tax will not allow the government to support the optimum. Section 8.8 concludes the chapter.

The main reason for using the OG model when studying the resource issue is that it opens up the intriguing possibility that private agents may over-accumulate assets including the resource. This cannot occur in the Ramsey growth model. And there are two reasons for using the Ramsey growth model in studying the externalities issue. First, Judd, Chamley, and Lucas have derived certain propositions involving the optimal taxation of capital in that model that may be affected by the existence of an externality. Second, the Ramsey model does not allow inefficient over-accumulation to occur and this allows us to focus our attention on the externality issue without getting sidetracked.

8.2. An overlapping generations model of a renewable resource

Time is discrete, $t = 1, 2, \ldots$, and the economy lasts for ever. The economy is initially endowed with R_1 units of a renewable resource. Population is constant. At time t, $N_t = 1$ agents are born and each lives for two periods, young and old. Young agents are endowed with one unit of labor while old agents are not endowed with anything. There is one consumption good available produced by a neoclassical constant-returns-to-scale technology using some of the resource and labor according to $Y_t = F(X_t, L_t)$, where Y is output, X is the amount of the resource used and depleted in production, and L is labor. $F(X, L)$ is twice continuously differentiable, monotone increasing, CRS, and satisfies the Inada conditions.

The total stock of the resource available at time t is R_t and it can either be used in production or stored as an asset for use later. Thus,

$$R_t = X_t + A_t, \tag{8.1}$$

where A is the amount of the resource stored as an asset. The resource regenerates itself naturally. If A_t of the resource is stored at time t, then $A_t + G(A_t)$ becomes available at time $t + 1$, where $G(\ )$ is the regeneration function. We will assume that $G(\ )$ is twice continuously differentiable, $G(A) \geq 0$ for $A > 0$, $G(A)$ is strictly concave, $G(0) = 0$, and there exists $A+ > 0$ such that $G_A(A+) = 0$, where $dG/dA = G_A$. There also exists an $A++ > A+$ such that $G_A(A++) < 0$. This is depicted in Figure 8.1.[2]

The preferences of the representative agent in generation t are represented by a well behaved utility function according to $U(c_{1t}, c_{2t})$, where c_{jt} is consumption in

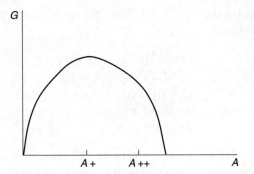

Figure 8.1. The regeneration function

period of life j for a member of generation t. We will assume $U(\ )$ is twice continuously differentiable, quasi-concave, and monotone increasing.

The initial old care only about their second-period consumption, $U(c_{20})$, which is concave, increasing, and twice continuously differentiable. They own R_1 units of the initial resource. Under competition they sell X_1 units of the resource to firms who use them in production. A_1 units are sold to the young at time $t = 1$ for them to hold as an asset.

The aggregate resource constraint at time t is given by $Y_t = N(c_{1t} + c_{2t-1})$. This can be written in per capita terms as

$$f(X_t/L_t) = c_{1t} + c_{2t-1}, \tag{8.2}$$

where $f(X_t/L_t) = F(X_t/L_t, 1)$. Finally, the evolution of the resource follows a simple nonlinear difference equation,

$$R_{t+1} = A_t + G(A_t) = R_t - X_t + G(R_t - X_t), \tag{8.3}$$

where the last equality uses equation (8.1).

The social planner's problem in a stationary state is to choose (c_1, c_2, X, A) to maximize $U(c_1, c_2)$ subject to (8.1)–(8.3). Since we seek an interior solution, we will simplify matters by substituting for X. We can write the Lagrangean for the social planner's problem as

$$U(c_1, c_2) + \phi(f(G(A)/L) - c_1 - c_2),$$

where ϕ is the multiplier.[3] The first-order conditions are given by

$$U_1 = \phi,$$
$$U_2 = \phi,$$

and

$$\phi f_X G_A / L = 0.$$

Since the constraint will be binding at an interior equilibrium, $\phi > 0$. And since $f_X > 0$ and $L > 0$, it follows that $G_A(A^o) = 0$ at the optimum from the third condition. We also have $U_1/U_2 = 1$. Thus, the social optimum must satisfy the following conditions:

$$U_1\left(c_1^o, c_2^o\right)/U_2\left(c_1^o, c_2^o\right) = 1, \tag{8.4a}$$
$$f(G(A^o)) = N\left(c_1^o + c_2^o\right), \tag{8.4b}$$
$$G_A(A^o) = 0, \tag{8.4c}$$
$$X^o = G(A^o), \tag{8.4d}$$
$$R^o = X^o + A^o. \tag{8.4e}$$

where $L = 1$, and a superscript o denotes the optimal allocation. Dynamic efficiency is represented by the conditions $G_A = 0$ and $U_1/U_2 = 1$ when evaluated at the planner's optimal allocation. We have abstracted from the problem of static efficiency by assuming that the population is normalized at unity.

Under competition, the consumer chooses a consumption profile and decides how much of the resource to accumulate as an asset to smooth consumption over her life cycle. More formally, she solves

$$\max U(c_{1t}, c_{2t})$$
$$\text{s.t. } w_t - c_{1t} - q_t A_t = 0,$$
$$q_{t+1}(A_t + G(A_t)) - c_{2t} = 0,$$

where w is the wage and q_t is the price of the asset at time t. The first-order conditions imply[4]

$$U_1/U_2 = q_{t+1}(1 + G_A)/q_t.$$

Firms maximize profit by renting labor and buying the resource in order to produce output that is in turn sold to both the young and the old at time t. Profit per worker is

$$\pi = f(X_t/L_t) - q_t X_t/L_t - w_t.$$

Profit maximization at time t implies $f_X = q_t$. Hence

$$w = f(X_t/L_t) - q_t X_t/L_t = f(X_t) - q_t X_t,$$

by CRS and $L_t = 1$.

We seek a stationary equilibrium path where $A_t = A > 0$ and $q_t = q > 0$. The stationary competitive equilibrium is determined by the following system:

$$U_1\left(c_1^c, c_2^c\right)/U_2\left(c_1^c, c_2^c\right) = 1 + G_A(A^c), \tag{8.5a}$$
$$c_1^c = w^c - q^c A^c, \tag{8.5b}$$
$$c_2^c = q^c(A^c + G(A^c)), \tag{8.5c}$$
$$q^c = f_X(X^c), \tag{8.5d}$$
$$w = f(X^c) - q^c X^c, \tag{8.5e}$$
$$X^c = G(A^c), \tag{8.5f}$$
$$R^c = X^c + A^c, \tag{8.5g}$$

where the superscript c denotes the allocation under competition. Since there is no mechanism under competition that forces $G_A = 0$, the competitive equilibrium will generally be suboptimal. Indeed, it is possible that $G_A(A^c) < 0$, whereby too much of the resource has been accumulated.

We can easily extend this result to the case where there is physical capital. Suppose output depends on K, X, and L according to $F(K, X, L)$, where $F(\ )$ exhibits constant returns to scale, i.e. CRS, and assume that physical capital depreciates at rate δ. It is straightforward to show, by studying the stationary decision problem of the social planner as we did above, that the steady state optimum is characterized by the following set of equations:

$$U_1/U_2 = 1,$$
$$G_A = 0,$$
$$F_K = \delta,$$
$$X^o = G(A^o),$$
$$R^o = X^o + A^o,$$
$$F = \delta K^o + c_1^o + c_2^o,$$

where $L = 1$. The condition $F_K = \delta$ corresponds to the golden rule in this model.

Under competition, however, we obtain the following conditions instead:

$$U_1/U_2 = 1 + F_k - \delta,$$
$$F_k - \delta = G_A,$$
$$X^c = G(A^c),$$
$$R^c = X^c + A^c,$$
$$F = \delta K^c + c_1^c + c_2^c.$$

The second condition is an arbitrage requirement between the two assets, physical capital and the resource.[5] Again, there is no mechanism under competition that prohibits over-accumulating capital of both kinds. Thus, $G_A < 0$ may occur under competition. This point is due to Batina and Krautkraemer (1996).

Finally, we can consider the case where the resource also has an amenity value. Suppose A_t enters the agent's utility function at time t, $U(c_{1t}, c_{2t}, A_t)$. The socially optimal allocation must satisfy the following conditions in a steady state:[6]

$$U_1/U_2 = 1,$$
$$U_A/U_2 = -f_x G_A,$$
$$X^o = G(A^o),$$
$$R^o = X^o + A^o,$$
$$f(G(A^o)) = c_1^o + c_2^o.$$

Thus, $G_A < 0$ at the optimum if $\partial U/\partial A = U_A > 0$. More of the resource will be accumulated as an asset if it has an amenity value than if not. Under competition, it is straightforward to show that the conditions governing the equilibrium are

$$U_1/U_2 = 1 + G_A + U_A/f_X U_2,$$
$$q^c = f_X,$$
$$X^c = G(A^c),$$
$$R^c = X^c + A^c,$$
$$f(X^c) = c_1^c + c_2^c.$$

There is no reason to believe that the first equation under competition will match up with the first two equations of the social planner's allocation. Therefore, there is no reason to expect the allocation associated with the competitive equilibrium to be optimal except by coincidence.

8.3. The effects of taxation

We can pose the question of what impact the different tax systems might have on a competitive equilibrium that includes a renewable resource using the model of the last section. First, suppose there is an asset income tax imposed where asset income is taxed at rate t_r. The agent's second-period budget constraint becomes

$$q_{t+1}[A_t + (1 - t_r)G(A_t)] - c_{2t} = 0.$$

The only effect of this on the model is to alter the first-order condition of the consumer's decision problem, which becomes

$$U_1/U_2 = 1 + (1 - t_r)G_A \qquad (8.6)$$

in a stationary equilibrium. It is straightforward to show that $dA/dt_r < 0$, under a lumpsum rebate of the revenue in the same period when the revenue was collected so as to maintain the agent's disposable income in that period.

If there is physical capital in the model, there are several cases to consider. First, suppose the gross income from both assets is taxed at the same rate, t_r. The consumer's budget constraints in a stationary equilibrium are

$$c_1 = w - qA - s$$

and

$$c_2 = (1 + r - \delta)s + q(A + G(A)) - t_r(rs + qG),$$

where s is saving in physical capital, r is the return on capital, and δ is the depreciation rate of capital. The arbitrage condition in this case is given by $r(1 - t_r) - \delta = (1 - t_r)qG_A(A)$, or $(r - qG_A)(1 - t_r) = \delta$. Differentiating the arbitrage condition yields

$$dA/dt_r = -(r - qG_A)/(1 - t_r)qG_{AA} > 0.$$

The demand for the resource asset increases with the tax rate on gross asset income because it is favored relative to physical capital since there is no write-off for depreciation.

Second, if depreciation can be completely written off, the consumer's budget constraints are

$$c_1 = w - qA - s$$

and

$$c_2 = (1 + r - \delta)s + q(A + G(A)) - t_r[(r - \delta)s + qG].$$

The arbitrage condition is $r - \delta = qG_A(A)$, and the mix between the two assets will not be affected at the margin since they are treated symmetrically.

Third, if the resource is taxed as an asset but physical capital is not, the budget constraints are

$$c_1 = w - qA - s$$

and

$$c_2 = (1 + r - \delta)s + q(A + G(A)) - t_r qG.$$

The arbitrage condition becomes $r - \delta = qG_A(A)(1 - t_r)$. Differentiating, we obtain

$$dA/dt_r = G_A/(1 - t_r)G_{AA} < 0.$$

If physical capital is favored, the demand will switch from the resource to capital, given r.

Finally, if physical capital is taxed but the resource is not, then we have instead

$$c_1 = w - qA - s,$$

and

$$c_2 = (1 + r - \delta)s + q(A + G(A)) - t_r rs.$$

The arbitrage condition is $r(1 - t_r) - \delta = qG_A$. Differentiating,

$$dA/dt_r = -r/qG_{AA} > 0.$$

If the resource is favored, demand for the resource will increase.

We can conclude that the capital income tax will distort the decision of which asset to hold if the assets are not treated symmetrically. In particular, if the resource is favored, demand for it will increase, given the gross return to physical capital.

The consumption tax has no impact at the margin but causes an income effect only if the resource is simply an asset. To see this, notice that under the consumption tax the budget constraints in the absence of physical capital are given by

$$w_t - (1 + \theta)c_{1t} - A_t = 0$$

and

$$A_t + G(A_t) - (1 + \theta)c_{2t} = 0.$$

The first-order condition to the consumer's decision problem in a stationary state is given by

$$U_1/U_2 = 1 + G_A.$$

It follows that the consumption tax causes only an income effect but no harmful substitution effects since the tax rate does not enter the marginal rate of transformation on the righthand side of the equation. This will remain true if there is physical capital in the model as well.

On the other hand, if the consumption tax is progressive, then we have instead,

$$U_1/U_2 = (1 + G_A)(1 + \theta_1)/(1 + \theta_2).$$

The MRT will equal $1 + G_A$ only if the taxpayer is in the same tax bracket in different periods. We would expect income to fall after retirement. Thus, $\theta_2 < \theta_1$. In that case, the consumption tax will increase the MRT on the righthand side and provide the taxpayer with an incentive to increase the ratio c_2/c_1 by saving more.

If there is an unobservable amenity value associated with the resource, matters are somewhat different. Suppose there is an amenity value to the resource that is not taxed under the consumption tax policy so that the utility function is given by $U(c_{1t}, c_{2t}, A_t)$ for the representative agent in the tth generation. The budget constraints are as before. Thus, the first-order condition governing the choice of the resource as an asset under competition is given by

$$U_A(1 + \theta) - U_1 + (1 + G_A)U_2 = 0,$$

where the arguments of the marginal utilities are

$$c_{1t} = (w_t - A_t + T_{1t})/(1 + \theta)$$

and

$$c_{2t} = (A_t + G(A_t) + T_{2t+1})/(1 + \theta).$$

The terms T_{jk} are lumpsum rebates of the tax revenue collected within the period. Under a lumpsum rebate of the revenue, it can be shown that $dA/d\theta > 0$ when evaluated at the initial equilibrium. The intuition is that the consumption value of the amenity is favored over general consumption by the consumption tax policy, which cannot tax the unobservable amenity value of the resource.

If we extend the model by including labor supply, then the labor supply decision will be distorted by the consumption tax and this may serve to induce the agent to reduce his acquisition of the resource as an asset even if it has an additional amenity value associated with it. To see this, let the utility function be given by $U(c_{1t}, c_{2t}, 1 - L_t, A_t)$ where L is labor supply and $1 - L$ is leisure. Consumption is defined by

$$c_{1t} = (w_t L_t - A_t + T_{1t})/(1 + \theta),$$
$$c_{2t} = (A_t + G(A_t) + T_{2t+1})/(1 + \theta).$$

In addition to the previous equation governing the choice of the resource asset, we also have the following equation governing the choice of labor supply:

$$U_L = [w/(1+\theta)]U_1.$$

The consumption tax will distort the labor supply decision, as in earlier chapters.

At the margin, a small increase in the consumption tax rate will have two effects. First, "amenity consumption" is favored over general consumption as before and we would expect an increase in demand for the resource when the consumption based tax is imposed because of this. However, an increase in the consumption tax rate lowers the "net wage rate" $w/(1+\theta)$. This makes leisure more attractive than working and will serve to reduce both forms of consumption. The net response of the asset now becomes ambiguous as a result. It can be shown that the response of the asset is given by the following expression if the revenue is rebated in a lumpsum manner and the response is evaluated at the initial equilibrium $\theta = 0$:

$$dA/d\theta = -w(dA/dw)_u - U_A J/H,$$

where $(dA/dw)_u$ is a compensated cross price effect, and $U_A J/H$ is the "favored amenity consumption" effect, where $J = w^2 U_{11} - 2w U_{1L} + U_{LL} < 0$, and $H > 0$ is the Hessian matrix.

The response of labor supply is also ambiguous. It is possible for labor supply to *increase* with the tax if the "favored amenity consumption" effect is large enough in magnitude. This is in contrast to the case where there is no amenity value associated with the resource; labor supply unambiguously decreases in response to the consumption tax when the resource has no amenity value.

8.4. A Ramsey growth model with environmental externalities

In this Section we will present a model that introduces a stock externality involving pollution associated with consumption and production into the Ramsey growth model. Time is discrete and the economy lasts forever: $t = 0, 1, 2, \ldots$ Population is constant and normalized to one. There is a single consumption good available produced via a neoclassical, constant-returns-to-scale technology, $y_t = f(k_t, L_t)$, where y is output, k is capital per worker, and L is labor hours, and where $f(\ )$ is twice continuously differentiable, concave, and satisfies the Inada conditions.

There is a single representative consumer who experiences an infinite horizon. She is endowed with k_0 units of capital at the beginning of the horizon and with one unit of labor each period. Her period utility function is $U(c_t, 1 - L_t, e_t)$, where c is consumption, $1 - L$ is leisure, and e is a measure of the quality of the environment, and where $U(\ )$ is twice continuously differentiable, quasi-concave, and monotonically increasing. We will also assume that $\partial U/\partial c = U_c \to 0(\infty)$

as $c \to \infty(0)$, given a finite value for e and when $0 < L < 1$, and that $\partial U/\partial e = U_e \to 0(\infty)$ as $e \to \infty(0)$, for finite c and $0 < L < 1$. The consumer discounts future utility with the discount factor $\beta = 1/(1 + \rho) < 1$, where ρ is the rate of time preference, as in previous chapters. Preferences over time are represented by

$$\sum_{t=0}^{\infty} \beta^t U\big(c_t, 1 - L_t, e_t\big). \tag{8.7}$$

The resource constraint or law of motion for capital for the economy at time t is

$$k_t(1 - \delta) + f\big(k_t, L_t\big) - k_{t+1} - c_t - g_t = 0, \tag{8.8}$$

where g_t is government consumption, assumed not to affect utility or the technology, and δ is the depreciation rate, $0 < \delta < 1$. Finally, all agents behave competitively by taking prices and variables at the aggregate level as given and beyond their control.

The distinguishing feature of the model involves the evolution of the quality of the environment. The quality of the environment will be treated as a stock variable. We will assume that both the act of consumption and the act of production produce an externality that harms the environment. The "stock" of the quality of the environment evolves according to the following law of motion:

$$e_{t+1} = G\big(e_t, c_t, y_t\big). \tag{8.9}$$

We will assume the individual consumer or firm behaves atomistically and takes the quality of the environment as given and beyond her control; consumers and firms take the sequence $\{e_t\}$ as given. We will also assume that $G(\ )$ is differentiable and that $0 < G_e < 1$, where $G_e = \partial e_{t+1}/\partial e_t$, $G_c = \partial e_{t+1}/\partial c_t < 0$, and $G_y = \partial e_{t+1}/\partial y_t < 0$. The better the quality of the environment today, the better it will be tomorrow, ceteris paribus. The greater consumption or output per worker is today, the greater the damage to the environment today and the lower the quality of the environment will be tomorrow. In a steady state where c and y are constant, the quality of the environment settles down to a constant according to $e = G(e, c, y)$.[7]

Following the literature on optimal taxation in dynamic models, we will also assume that the economy converges to a stable steady state, where $e, c, k > 0$ and $1 > L > 0$. We will compare the conditions in such an equilibrium with the steady state allocation stemming from the planner's problem. We will show that the optimal tax on capital in the long run is strictly positive in the presence of a production externality and that the tax on labor will generally depend on both the consumption and production externalities at the margin. Also, following the literature, we will ignore the time consistency problem. (See Chapter 6 for an analysis of this problem.)

8.5. The main results of the Ramsey pollution externalities model

8.5.1. *First-best solution*

First, consider the social planner's problem characterizing the first-best in the presence of externalities. The social planner chooses a sequence $\{c_t, L_t, k_{t+1}, e_{t+1}\}$ to maximize (8.7) subject to the laws of motion (8.8) and (8.9), taking k_0 and e_0 as given. Let λ_t be the multiplier for (8.8) and let α_t be the multiplier for (8.9). λ is the social value of capital at the margin and α is a measure of the social value of a marginal improvement in the quality of the environment. Since (8.9) will hold as an equality, $\alpha > 0$. In addition, we will study an interior steady state equilibrium where $c > 0$, $1 > L > 0$, $k > 0$, and $e > 0$. Therefore, $\lambda > 0$ as well.

The first-order conditions for the planner's problem are[8]

$$U_{ct} = \lambda_t - \beta\alpha_{t+1}G_{ct}, \tag{8.10a}$$
$$U_{Lt} = f_{Lt}\lambda_t + \beta\alpha_{t+1}f_{Lt+1}G_{yt+1}, \tag{8.10b}$$
$$\beta U_{et+1} = \alpha_t - \beta\alpha_{t+1}G_{et+1}, \tag{8.10c}$$
$$\lambda_t = \beta(1 + f_{kt+1} - \delta)\lambda_{t+1} + \beta\alpha_{t+1}G_{yt+1}f_{kt+1}, \tag{8.10d}$$

where $\partial U/\partial c_t = U_{ct}$ is the marginal utility of consumption, $\partial U/\partial L_t = U_{Lt}$ is the marginal utility of leisure, $f_{kt+1} = \partial f(k_{t+1}, L_{t+1})/\partial k_{t+1}$, and $\partial f(k_t, L_t)/\partial L_t = f_{Lt}$. The terms G_c and G_y on the righthand side of the equations (8.10a, b, d) are new to the literature on taxation in Ramsey models and are due to the consumption and production externalities.

In equation (8.10a) λ can be interpreted as the "price" of consumption in the absence of the consumption externality. When the externality is present, however, consumption causes harm to the environment at the margin, $G_c < 0$. Since α is the social value of the environment at the margin, αG_c is the social value of the harmful consumption externality, and $-\alpha G_c > 0$ is the increment in the "price" of consumption resulting from to the consumption externality. Similarly, in (8.10b) $\alpha\beta G_y$ is the social value of the marginal production externality arising from working one more hour. Since $\alpha\beta G_y < 0$, the social value of labor at the margin is less than would have been the case had there not been an externality; that is, $f_{Lt}\lambda_t + \beta\alpha_{t+1}f_L G_{yt+1} < f_{Lt}\lambda_t$.

Finally, in the absence of a production externality, λ_t is the marginal opportunity cost of forgoing one unit of consumption today and $\lambda_{t+1}\beta(1 + f_{kt+1} - \delta)$ is the marginal consumption benefit tomorrow discounted to the present. However, when there is a harmful production externality, the social value of the benefit of forgoing consumption is reduced by $\beta\alpha_{t+1}G_{yt+1}f_{kt+1} < 0$.

It follows from (8.10a) and (8.10c) that in a steady state

$$U_c(c, 1 - L, e)/\beta U_e(c, 1 - L, e) = (\lambda/\alpha - G_c)/(1 - \beta G_e). \tag{8.11}$$

It follows from (8.10d) that

$$(f_k - \delta - \rho)\lambda/\alpha = -G_y f_k. \tag{8.12}$$

Since (8.9) is binding in a steady state, $\alpha > 0$. Since $f(k, L) = \delta k + c + g$ in a steady state, the shadow price of capital is positive as well. Thus, $\lambda/\alpha > 0$.[9] Therefore, for an interior solution to the planner's problem in a steady state, $f_k - \delta - \rho > 0$. Denote $(k/L)^g$ as the golden rule level of capital per worker hour; $f_k((k/L)^g) = \delta + \rho$. It follows from (8.12) that the optimal steady state level of capital per worker hour in the presence of a production externality, $(k/L)^o$, is less than the golden rule level; $(k/L)^o < (k/L)^g$; that is, $f_k((k/L)^o) - f_k((k/L)^g) = -G_y f_k((k/L)^o)\alpha/\lambda > 0$ implies that $(k/L)^o < (k/L)^g$.

Finally, from (8.10a) and (8.10b),

$$U_L/U_c = f_L(\lambda/\alpha + \beta G_y)/(\lambda/\alpha - \beta G_c) \tag{8.13}$$

in a steady state. The marginal rate of substitution between leisure and consumption is equal to the marginal product of labor multiplied by a factor that relates each externality at the margin to the ratio of the shadow prices of capital and the environment,

$$\Phi = (\lambda/\alpha + \beta G_y)/(\lambda/\alpha - \beta G_c).$$

Since G_c, $G_y < 0$, it follows that $\Phi < 1$.

The socially optimal allocation must satisfy the following system of equations in a steady state:

$$U_c(c^o, 1 - L^o, e^o)/U_e(c^o, 1 - L^o, e^o)$$
$$= [\lambda^o/\alpha^o - \beta G_c(e^o, c^o, y^o)]/[1 - \beta G_y(e^o, c^o, y^o)],$$
$$U_L(c^o, 1 - L^o, e^o)/U_c(c^o, 1 - L^o, e^o)$$
$$= f_L[\lambda^o/\alpha^o - \beta G_y(e^o, c^o, y^o)]/[\lambda^o/\alpha^o - \beta G_c(e^o, c^o, y^o)],$$
$$f(k^o, L^o) - \delta k^o - c^o - g = 0,$$
$$e^o = G(e^o, c^o, y^o),$$
$$[f_k(k^o, L^o) - \delta - \rho]\lambda^o/\alpha^o = -G_y(e^o, c^o, y^o)f_k(k^o, L^o).$$

This system determines $(c^o, e^o, n^o, k^o, \lambda^o/\alpha^o)$. Following the literature, we will assume that the steady state exists and is stable.

8.5.2. *The competitive equilibrium*

In a competitive equilibrium firms maximize profit and pay factors the appropriate factor price. Thus, $r = f_k$ in a steady state and $w = f_L$, where w is the wage and r is the real interest rate or marginal product of capital per worker. It follows from the assumption of constant returns in the technology that $f(k, L) = rk + wL$ in a steady state.

The consumer chooses consumption and labor supply profiles and a sequence for capital to maximize (8.7) subject to the private budget constraint,

$$w_t(1 - t_{wt})L_t + [1 + r_t(1 - t_{rt}) - \delta]k_t - k_{t+1} - c_t = 0, \tag{8.14}$$

taking $\{e_t\}$, k_0, prices, and tax rates as given, where t_{wt} is the labor income tax rate, and t_{rt} is the capital income tax rate. The first-order conditions of the consumer's decision problem are

$$U_{ct} = \lambda_t, \tag{8.15a}$$
$$U_{Lt} = \lambda_t w_t (1 - t_{wt}), \tag{8.15b}$$
$$\lambda_t = \beta[1 + r_{t+1}(1 - t_{rt+1}) - \delta]\lambda_{t+1}. \tag{8.15c}$$

The government's budget constraint is $t_{wt}w_t L_t + t_{rt}r_t k_t = g_t$. It is imagined that the government wishes to spend g_t at time t and we will take the infinite sequence $\{g_t\}$ as given. The government chooses sequences $\{t_{wt}, t_{rt}\}$ to maximize (8.7) subject to the resource constraint, the behavior of the private sector as embodied in (8.15), its own budget constraint, and the evolution of the quality of the environment, equation (8.9). Government expenditures g are used to provide a public good that does not influence the incentives of the individual agents at the margin.

We can now derive our main results for this section of the chapter. Under competition, (8.15c) in a steady state implies that $f_k(1 - t_r) - \delta = \rho$, or

$$f_k - \delta - \rho = t_{rt}f_k. \tag{8.16}$$

This matches up with the social planner's problem if the tax rate on capital is set according to

$$t_r = -G_y \alpha/\lambda > 0, \tag{8.17}$$

where α/λ is determined by (8.12). The intuition is straightforward: capital should be taxed at the margin if output and hence capital causes a harmful externality.

Next, consider the wage tax. From (8.15a) and (8.15b),

$$U_L/U_c = w(1 - t_w) = f_L(1 - t_w).$$

Thus, t_w should be chosen so that

$$f_L(1 - t_w) = f_L(\lambda/\alpha + \beta G_y)/(\lambda/\alpha - \beta G_c),$$

or

$$t_w = -\beta(G_y + G_c)/(\lambda/\alpha - \beta G_c). \tag{8.18}$$

Since $\lambda/\alpha >$ and $G_c < 0$, the denominator of this expression is positive. The numerator is also positive since $(G_y + G_c) < 0$. The intuition for this result is that the wage tax rate picks up two effects. Consumption causes a harmful externality and the wage tax is similar to a consumption tax in this model. Thus, taxing labor reduces the consumption externality by reducing consumption. Second, labor supply also causes a production externality, and this leads to imposing a Pigouvian tax on labor as well.

In the special case where there is only a consumption externality, that is where $G_y = 0$, then $t_r = 0$, $t_w = -\beta G_c/(\lambda/\alpha - \beta G_c) > 0$, and λ/α is determined by $U_c/U_e = (\lambda/\alpha)/(1 - \beta G_c)$. In the special case where there is only a production externality, $G_c = 0$, then $t_r = -G_y \alpha/\lambda > 0$, $t_w = -\beta G_y/(\lambda/\alpha) > 0$, and λ/α is determined by $U_c/U_e = (\lambda/\alpha)/(1 - \beta G_y)$.

8.6. Private actions to clean up the environment

In this section we will examine the effect policy can have when private agents take actions that help to improve the environment, following Ihori (1999b). It will be shown that one policy instrument, the consumption tax, can adjust the private agent's economic behavior at the margin so as to take care of two externality problems simultaneously. Two separate instruments are not necessary in this special case.

We will continue to study a version of the Ramsey growth model. Output is produced using capital and labor, $y = f(k)$ is output per worker, and k is capital per worker. There is one representative agent who behaves competitively by taking aggregate variables and prices as given. We will assume that period utility is given by $U(c_t, h_t, e_t)$, where h is an action the agent can take that helps the environment. In addition, we will assume that the environment follows a simple linear law of motion,

$$e_{t+1} = E + \phi e_t - \gamma c_t + \mu h_t, \tag{8.19}$$

where ϕ, γ and μ are positive parameters, and $0 < \phi < 1$. If $c = h = 0$, or if $\mu h = \gamma c$, the environment will converge to $E/(1 - \phi)$, which can be interpreted as a pristine level of quality for the environment.[10] More generally, in a steady state, $e = E/(1 - \phi) + (\mu h - \gamma c)/(1 - \phi)$. We will focus on an equilibrium where $E > \gamma c - \mu h$.

The social planner's problem is to choose sequences of consumption, help for the environment, capital, and the environment to maximize $\Sigma \beta^t U(c_t, h_t, e_t)$ subject to (8.19), and the law of motion for capital per worker,

$$f(k_t) + (1 - \delta)k_t - k_{t+1} - c_t - qh_t = 0,$$

taking as given k_0 and e_0, where q is the cost of turning help for the environment into an actual improvement in the environment at the margin. It is straightforward to show that the first-order conditions imply

$$f_k(k) = \delta + \rho, \tag{8.20a}$$
$$U_h/U_c = q - \beta\Omega(U_e/U_c), \tag{8.20b}$$

where $\Omega = (\gamma + q\mu)/(1 - \beta\phi) > 0$,

$$f(k) - \delta k = c + qh, \tag{8.20c}$$

and

$$e = (E + \mu h - \gamma c)/(1 - \phi). \tag{8.20d}$$

The planner takes into account two important elements in choosing the optimal allocation: (1) consumption will hurt the environment, and (2) help to the environment will improve it.

Under competition, the consumer chooses a sequence $\{c_t, h_t, k_{t+1}\}$ to maximize $\Sigma \beta^t U(c_t, h_t, e_t)$ subject to

$$w_t + (1 + r_t - \delta)k_t - k_{t+1} - c_t - qh_t = 0,$$

taking the infinite sequence $\{e_t\}$ as given. The first-order conditions will imply that

$$f_k(k) = \delta + \rho \tag{8.21a}$$

and

$$U_h/U_c = q. \tag{8.21b}$$

In addition to this, the budget constraint can be written as

$$f(k) - \delta k = c + qh, \tag{8.21c}$$

and the environment in equilibrium is given by

$$e = (E + \mu h - \gamma c)/(1 - \phi). \tag{8.21d}$$

The first point to notice is that the capital stock under competition will match up with that of the social planner. This is because we have assumed that output and capital do not pollute the environment. The second point is that (8.21b) clearly does not match up with (8.20b). This is for two reasons. First, atomistic agents will ignore the pollution effect of private consumption. Second, the agent will also ignore the fact that help to the environment in the aggregate will improve the environment.

The consumption tax can play an interesting role in this setting. If we impose a consumption tax on c but not h, (8.21) becomes $U_h/U_c = q/(1 + \theta)$. If the government chooses θ according to

$$\theta = \Omega \beta (U_e/U_c)[q - \beta \Omega(U_e/U_c)] > 0, \tag{8.22}$$

and uses the revenue in a non-systematic way, then the competitive equilibrium will support the socially optimal allocation. Of course, if production also harms the environment, then the consumption tax alone will not suffice. However, it is of some interest that a consumption tax can be justified if it deters harmful consumption externalities to the environment.

8.7. Clean consumption and dirty consumption

We will now extend the model of the last section to include two types of consumption: "clean" consumption, which does not cause pollution, and "dirty" consumption, which does. Ihori (1999a, b) showed that a Pigouvian consumption tax imposed on polluting consumption is not enough to internalize the pollution externality since it also distorts the relative price of clean versus dirty consumption and the relative decision to spend on cleaning up the environment. He showed that the optimal allocation may be supported by competition if separate taxes are imposed on clean and dirty consumption. A general consumption tax will not work. However, expenditures to clean up the environment must be exempt from taxation. In that case taxes on both types of consumption make spending on cleaning up the environment a preferred form of spending.

Suppose there are n identical consumers. Let cc_t represent the representative agent's clean consumption at time t and dc_t be her dirty consumption at time t. Her period utility function is $U(cc_t, dc_t, e_t)$. We will assume for simplicity that a unit of clean consumption can be turned into p units of dirty consumption and that p is constant.

The social planner's problem is to choose an infinite sequence $\{cc_t, dc_t\}$ and sequences for capital and the environment that maximize social welfare,

$$\sum_{t=0}^{\infty} n\beta^t U(cc_t, dc_t, e_t),$$

subject to

$$k_{t+1} = f(k_t) + (1 - \delta)k_t - ncc_t - pndc_t - qnh_t,$$
$$e_{t+1} = E + \phi e_t - \gamma ndc_t + \mu nh_t.$$

The first-order conditions imply that

$$f_k(k) = \delta + \rho, \tag{8.23a}$$
$$n\beta U_e / U_{cc} = q(1 - \beta\phi)/\mu, \tag{8.23b}$$
$$U_{dc}/U_{cc} = p + q\gamma/\mu. \tag{8.23c}$$

Since we assumed that the environment does not affect the technology and production directly, the golden rule will hold in this model. Second, (8.23b) governs the optimal choice for the environment and is a version of the Samuelson rule for a pure public good. Finally, (8.23c) governs the optimal tradeoff in consumption of the private goods. We also have the steady state versions of the two constraints,

$$f(k) = \delta k + n_{cc} + npdc + nqh, \tag{8.23d}$$
$$e = (E - n\gamma dc + n\mu h)/(1 - \phi). \tag{8.23e}$$

To solve the system, notice that k is determined by (8.23a). Equations (8.23b–e) then determine (cc, dc, e, h).

Under competition, agent i chooses $\{cc_{it}, dc_{it}, h_{it}, a_{it}\}$ to maximize utility $\Sigma_t \beta^t U(cc_{it}, dc_{it}, e_t)$ subject to

$$w_{it} + (1 + r_t - \delta)a_{it-1} - a_{it} - (1 + \theta_{cc})cc_{it} - (1 + \theta_{dc})pdc_{it}$$
$$- (1 + \theta_h)qh_{it} + T = 0,$$

taking the sequence $\{e_t\}$ as given, where a is asset accumulation, θ_{cc} is a consumption tax rate imposed on clean consumption, θ_{dc} is a consumption tax rate imposed on dirty consumption, θ_h is a consumption tax rate imposed on cleaning up the environment, and T is a lumpsum rebate of the tax revenue collected.

Under the assumption that the consumer takes the environment as exogenous to her decisions, the first-order conditions imply

$$r = \delta + \rho, \tag{8.24a}$$
$$U_{dc}/U_{cc} = p(1 + \theta_{dc})/(1 + \theta_{cc}), \tag{8.24b}$$

and $h = 0$, since there is only a cost associated with private efforts at cleaning up the environment and no corresponding benefit in this case. Equation (8.24b) governs the tradeoff between clean and dirty consumption.

To close the model, firms produce the clean consumption good according to a CRS technology and maximize profit, hence $r = f_k$. In addition, $na = k$ and $cc_i = cc$, $dc_i = dc$, $h_i = h$, $a_i = a$, in a steady state equilibrium. Thus, (8.24a) matches up with the golden rule level of capital, (8.23a). And the consumer converts some of the clean consumption good into dirty consumption at a price of $p(1 + \theta_{dc})/(1 + \theta_{cc})$ per unit trading off clean for dirty consumption according to (8.24b).

Can the Pigouvian tax policy support the optimal allocation in this case? First notice that the constraints (8.23d, e) will also hold under competition. Second, the competitive economy will be on the golden rule path. Third, notice that if $\theta_{cc} = 0$ and $\theta_{dc} = q\gamma/p\mu$, (8.24b) will match up with (8.23c) so the mix of clean and dirty consumption will be optimal. However, the competitive economy will not be able to support the optimal allocation under a Pigouvian tax policy since there is no condition corresponding to (8.23b). Contributions to the public good environmental quality will generally be suboptimal; too much will be spent on clean and dirty consumption and too little will be spent on help for the environment. The Pigouvian tax cannot stimulate private contributions to the quality of the environment in this case since there is no *private* benefit from contributing to the environment.

Next, consider the case where the consumer believes she can influence the environment. One possibility is that people believe they can influence the local environment by picking up litter from roads and highways, recycling newspaper, bottles, and cans, cooking with clean burning fuels, and so on, and the general environment is made up of a collection of local environments. In this case, the individual takes the law of motion for the environment into account in solving her decision problem. The Lagrangean for the decision problem is

$$\sum_{1=0}^{\infty} \beta^t \{ U(cc_{it}, dc_{it}, e_t)$$
$$+ \lambda_{it}[w_{it} + (1 + r_t - \delta)a_{it} + T - (1 + \theta_{cc})cc_t - p(1 + \theta_{dc})dc_t$$
$$- q(1 + \theta_h)h_t - a_{it+1}]$$
$$+ \alpha_t[E + \phi e_t - \gamma(n-1)dc_{it} - \gamma dc_{it} + \mu(n-1)h_t + \mu h_{it} - e_{t+1}]\},$$

where $(n-1)dc_t$ is everyone but person i's dirty consumption and $(n-1)h_t$ is everyone but person i's cleanup efforts. The first-order conditions imply the golden rule and

$$U_{dc}/U_{cc} = p(1 + \theta_{dc}) + q\gamma(1 + \theta_h)/\mu, \tag{8.25a}$$

$$\beta U_e/U_{cc} = q(1 + \theta_h)(1 - \beta\phi)/\mu(1 + \theta_{cc}). \tag{8.25b}$$

Now if $\theta_{cc} = 0$, $\theta_h = 1/n - 1$, and $\theta_{dc} = q\gamma(n-1)/np\mu$, then the competitive equilibrium can support the optimum because (8.25a) matches up with (8.23c), (8.25a) matches up with (8.23b), the economy is on the golden rule path, and the two constraints hold with equality.

Finally, we can ask: what happens if clean and dirty consumption are observationally equivalent? After all, a newspaper that is recycled can be considered "clean" consumption while a newspaper thrown away in the trash that eventually finds its way to a land fill might be considered "dirty" consumption. It might be impossible to know beforehand whether an individual consumer will recycle the newspaper or throw it away in order to charge the appropriate price. One might impose a system of refundable deposits where the consumer receives a small rebate for returning the item to the seller. For example, returning soda bottles for a deposit is very popular in many states in the United States. However, this can become difficult to implement if too many commodities are involved.

Suppose the government is constrained so that $\theta_{cc} = \theta_{dc} = \theta$. Then (8.25) can be written as

$$U_{dc}/U_{cc} = p + q\gamma(1 + \theta_h)/\mu(1 + \theta), \tag{8.26a}$$

$$n\beta U_e/U_{cc} = nq(1 + \theta_h)(1 - \beta\phi)/\mu(1 + \theta). \tag{8.26b}$$

Unfortunately, this will not allow the government to support the optimum. To see this, notice that (8.26a) matches up with (8.23c) if and only if $\theta = \theta_h$. However, if this is true, the righthand side of (8.26b) is $nq(1 - \beta\phi)/\mu$, which is larger than the righthand side of (8.23b). If help to the environment is taxed at the same flat rate, the tax rates do not enter (8.26) at all. It follows that the flat-rate consumption tax cannot support the optimum in this case. This is due to the fact that the negative spillover effect of dirty consumption should be taxed as well so as to stimulate abatement activities.

8.8. Conclusion

We studied two major issues in the economics of the environment and how each interacted with the tax system, renewable resources, and harmful stock externalities. With regard to renewable resources, it is possible for the competitive economy to acquire too large a stock of the resource as an asset. Self-interested individual decisionmakers will acquire assets to smooth their consumption, and certain arbitrage conditions must hold across assets. However, there is nothing that prohibits agents from saving too much in both assets, thus driving down the return below the socially optimal level. This is similar in spirit to a point made by Diamond (1965).

The general income tax that taxes capital income will lower the return to acquiring assets and may improve welfare if it moves the competitive economy closer to the optimal expansion path. On the other hand, the consumption tax will not distort the decision to hold the asset at the margin. The exception to this is when the resource asset has an additional amenity value that provides the agent with utility. Then the consumption tax favors "amenity consumption" of the asset over general consumption.

Unfortunately, the acts of consumption and production may cause harmful damage to the environment that may need to be addressed by government policy. We showed that it is optimal for the government to tax capital in the long run if production causes a harmful externality to the environment. Labor should also be taxed, and the labor tax rate will depend on both the consumption and production externalities. This is in marked contrast to Judd (1985), Chamley (1986), and Lucas (1990), who showed that capital should not be taxed in the long run in the Ramsey growth model without externalities.

We also considered the case where private agents themselves can make contributions to cleaning up pollution. A consumption externality will not be internalized if private agents behave atomistically. If private agents take into account the impact their economic behavior has on the environment, then a differential consumption tax that taxes "dirty" consumption, exempts "clean" consumption, and subsidizes expenditures on cleaning up the environment, can support the optimum. However, it may be impossible for the government to distinguish "clean" from "dirty" consumption. A general, flat-rate consumption tax will not allow the competitive economy to support the optimal allocation. Additional policy tools will be necessary. Of course, if there are other sources of pollution, such as production, additional policy tools may be necessary for this reason as well.

One conclusion of this analysis is that one can derive conditions under which capital should be taxed in order to alleviate an externality. It obviously follows that the pure form of the consumption tax is not optimal in the presence of production externalities such as those studied in this chapter. Imposing the consumption tax in the presence of harmful externalities may reduce consumption and thus alleviate some of the possibly harmful effects of consumption on the environment. However, a general consumption tax will not allow the competitive economy to support the optimum if the government cannot distinguish between "clean" and "dirty" consumption.

NOTES TO CHAPTER 8

1. Under the famous Hotelling rule, the price of the resource rises at the rate of interest. If $p(t)$ is the price of the resource at time t and r is the interest rate on a risk-free asset, the Hotelling rule is $p(t+1)/p(t) = 1 + r$. Babu *et al.* (1997) show that there is an extra term in the equation if agents take into account the negative impact of their extraction of the resource on the environment.

2. A commonly used growth function is the logistic growth function $G(A) = b(1 - A/M)$, where M is the carrying capacity of the environment and b is the intrinsic growth rate (Clark 1976). Mourmouras (1993) and Kennedy (1994) study a special case of our model where G is a constant proportion of A; e.g., $G = mA$ where $m > 0$ is constant. This leads to a "knife edge" property for the equilibrium expansion path.

3. This follows since $X_t = R_t - A_t$ and $R_{t+1} = A_t + G(A_t)$ become $X = R - A$ and $R = A + G(A)$ in a steady state. Thus, $X = R - A = A + G(A) - A = G(A)$.

4. Agents behave atomistically. However, it appears from (8.5a) that the individual agent takes the impact of his choice of A on the return at the margin, G_A, into account. It is best to think of the following example in this regard. Imagine the decision of an agent who owns a plot of land with timber on it. The agent must decide how much of the timber to harvest (X) and how much to save for the future (A). In making this choice, however, the agent will affect the ability of his land to regenerate timber *at the margin*; if more is harvested A is lower and G_A will be higher, but if less is harvested A is larger and G_A will be lower. It is certainly possible for the land to be unable to support timber in the future if too much is harvested now.

5. With physical capital in the model we obtain a version of the famous Hotelling rule, $q_{t+1} = q_t(1 + r_{t+1} - \delta)/(1 + G_A)$, which states that the resource price next period depends on the price today times the ratio of the opportunity cost to the benefit of the resource as an asset.

6. Set up the Lagrangean, $U(c_1, c_2, A) + \lambda[f(G(A)/L) - c_1 - c_2]$.

7. John *et al.* (1995) assume a linear version of (3) that depends negatively on consumption and positively on an action taken by the government to reverse environmental damage. See also Ihori (1999a), who allows private agents to take an action that can affect the environment. Agents in his model are not atomistic, strictly speaking.

8. We can write the Lagrangean as
$$\Sigma \beta^t \{ U(c_t, 1 - L_t, e_t) + \lambda_t[(1 - \delta)k_t + f(k_t, L_t) - k_{t+1} - c_t] + \alpha_t[G(e_t, c_t, f(k_t, L_t)) - e_{t+1}] \}.$$

9. Alternatively, $U_L > 0$ for an interior solution in a steady state. And $\alpha > 0$ since (8.9) is strictly binding. From (8.10b), $U_L = f_L(\lambda + \beta \alpha G_y) > 0$, so $f_L(\lambda + \beta \alpha G_y) > 0$. Since $f_L > 0$ when $k, L > 0$, it follows that $\lambda/\alpha > -\beta G_y > 0$ since $G_y < 0$. Thus, $\lambda/\alpha > 0$ at an interior solution in a steady state.

10. John *et al.* (1995) assume that the environment is determined by $e_{t+1} = (1 - b)e_t - \gamma c_t + \mu m_t$, in our notation where $b < 1$, $\gamma, \mu > 0$, and m is a tax imposed on agents by the government used to help the environment. Notice that if $c = m = 0$, the environment gradually decays. This seems somewhat problematic.

9

Durable Goods and Taxation

9.1. Introduction

In this chapter we will examine the impact of the capital income tax and the consumption tax on the demand for durable goods. There are two areas of the literature that are related to the work in this chapter: the literature on fixed assets like land, and the literature on housing. The literature that models a fixed asset like land typically assumes that land is productive in the sense of being important to the production of the consumption good contained in the model. It then proceeds to study the so-called capitalization effect; the price of land can jump instantaneously when fiscal policy is altered and this can re-distribute the burden of a change in policy. It is usually assumed that the stock of land is fixed and provides no amenity value. We will show this can have repercussions for the incidence of a consumption tax. In the literature on housing it is usually assumed that the stock of housing "produces" a service flow which benefits the owner of the house but is not required in the production of the output of the consumption good. Again, the price of housing can jump instantaneously when the economic environment is perturbed and this can have ramifications for tax policy.

More specifically, in a rather surprising contribution, Feldstein (1977) showed that a tax on land could be partially shifted to capital as people adjust their asset portfolios in the context of a simple intertemporal model. In fact, he showed it is even possible for the price of land to increase with the tax imposed on land. This was a surprising result since land in his model is a fixed factor and previously it was thought that a fixed factor would bear the full burden of any tax imposed on it. However, Calvo, Kotlikoff, and Rodriguez (1979) showed that this result would not go through if generations were connected via cash transfers within the family because the family would neutralize the change in tax policy by altering the cash transfer connecting generations. When the price of land adjusts to the new tax policy, the old generation receives either an additional capital gain or a loss. If bequests are positive before and after the change in tax policy, Calvo *et al.* showed that the family can neutralize the capitalization effect of the tax by altering the bequest.

Chamley and Wright (1987) put this area of the literature on a solid foundation by carefully modeling the fixed factor, land, in the context of a general equilibrium overlapping generations model and derived the stability conditions of the long run equilibrium. They studied the incidence of a wage tax and a tax on the dividend from the land and presented several interesting results. For example, it is possible for the long run price response to differ from the immediate price response.

Other analysts have studied the capitalization effects of incorporating a fixed asset like land into a dynamic model as well. Eaton (1988) showed that a permanent increase in foreign investment can lower welfare if the influx of foreign capital causes land prices to increase. Fried and Howitt (1988) studied the effects of government deficits on the current account, the interest rate, and welfare in an overlapping generations model with a fixed asset, land. As it turns out, the capitalization effect acts much like government debt in redistributing income across generations. Ihori (1990) investigated the incidence of a land tax in the presence of inflation. Taxing land can lead perversely to an increase in the price of land. However, if the price of land falls, the reduction in the welfare of the old generation may be reduced somewhat if inflation also diminishes.

The tax treatment of housing, a durable good, has also been extensively studied.[1] Most of the work we are aware of is partial equilibrium in nature. Skinner (1996) studied a simple two-period partial equilibrium model of housing demand and empirically estimated the efficiency cost of subsidizing housing in the United States. This includes the cost of intergenerational transfers that occur because of the increase in the price of housing when it receives favorable tax treatment. He finds that the dynamic efficiency cost of the subsidy is four to five times previous welfare cost estimates.[2]

The upshot of both these different branches of the literature is that there may be capitalization effects when there is another asset in the economy (in addition to physical capital) that need to be taken into account when studying the incidence of policy. In particular, the dynamics of the model can become much more complicated when a fixed asset is included. Some tax policies will be immediately capitalized into the price of land, for example, and this can affect the way the policy influences the economy and who will ultimately bear the burden of any particular fiscal policy.

In the next section we will present an overlapping generations model with land and describe the main effects of income and consumption taxation in the model. The interest income tax on capital will provide an incentive to shift the portfolio toward land, thus possibly raising the price of land in the long run. On the other hand, the consumption tax has no effect at the margin; it only produces income effects. However, if land provides utility and thus produces an amenity value, then the consumption tax will distort decisionmaking at the margin. Essentially, land becomes a favored form of consumption under the consumption tax and agents will have a greater incentive to acquire the fixed asset. Including an amenity value to the fixed asset is new to the literature in this area, to our knowledge.

We also extend the model to include rich and poor agents and assume there is a fixed cost to holding land. This captures the additional costs associated with owning land, for example the costs of filing the title to the property, surveying the property, searching for liens against the property, and so on. As a result, only the rich will hold land in equilibrium. The return to land must be higher than the return to capital in order to get agents to hold land. In this model the poor accumulate capital only in their portfolios. We show that the poor generally bear most of the burden of a tax on capital while the consumption tax is generally nondistorting. Some of the capital income tax can be shifted, however, if a reduction in capital per worker reduces the marginal product of labor and hence the labor income of the rich and also reduces the marginal productivity of the land owned by the rich.

In Section 9.3 we present an OG model and assume that the durable good can be accumulated as an asset in addition to providing utility based on the service flow of the stock. Agents acquire the durable good when they are young and enjoy the service flow from the durable good. They can choose to maintain the stock as well. In the second period of life when they are old they can sell the possibly depreciated durable. This model is a generalization of the models currently appearing in the literature. Both taxes are discussed in this model.

Section 9.4 studies the land model with maintenance expenditures. This model generalizes the land model described in Section 9.2 by including maintenance of the land. It also generalizes the model of Section 9.3 by allowing resale of the durable good, in this case land, and by allowing the durable good to be productive. The incidence of the consumption tax will depend critically on whether the purchase of land and the maintenance of it are included in the consumption tax base.

In Section 9.5 we extend the Ramsey growth model to include a durable good where there is no resale market for the durable good. The consumer can convert some of the consumption good into a durable good, and she derives utility from the service flow of the stock of the durable good. We study the incidence of the interest income tax and a consumption tax in the long run when a durable good is included in the model. In general, the predictions of the Ramsey growth model are typically much sharper than those of the OG model.

Finally, in Section 9.6 we will discuss the tax prepayment method applied to the durable good. Under prepayment the asset is essentially ignored in the calculation of the tax base. It is not included when the asset is initially purchased, nor is the income from the asset included later on. We show that under prepayment the flat-rate consumption tax will be neutral, as discussed in Chapter 1. However, we show that, if the tax is progressive, then the decision to purchase the durable good will be distorted by the tax. In addition, the decision to maintain the durable good will also generally be distorted by the consumption tax under prepayment.

9.2. A model with land

9.2.1. Taxes in the land model

Time is discrete and the economy lasts for ever. Each period N_t identical agents are born and each lives for two periods, young and old. We will normalize by assuming $N_t = 1$ for all t. The initial old generation owns the initial capital stock and the stock of land. The supply of land is fixed at A units. There is one consumption good produced according to a neoclassical CRS technology that uses land (A), labor (L), and capital (K) to produce output. Output per worker is given by $y_t = f(k_t, A/L)$, where k is capital per worker and A/L is land per worker. Denote the factor prices r, w, and v for the real interest rate, the wage, and the return to land, respectively. After profit maximization, each will equal its respective marginal product. Preferences are represented by $U(c_{1t}, c_{2t})$, which satisfies the usual assumptions, where c_{jt} is consumption in period of life j for the representative agent in generation t.

The consumer chooses consumption and how much capital and land to accumulate to maximize utility subject to the following constraints:

$$w_t - (1 + \theta)c_{1t} - k_{t+1} - (1 + \theta_A)p_t A = 0,$$
$$[1 + r_{t+1}(1 - t_r)]k_{t+1} + (p_{t+1} + v_{t+1})A - (1 + \theta)c_{2t} = 0,$$

where p_t is the price of a unit of land at time t, w is the wage, r is the interest rate, θ is the consumption tax rate, θ_A is the consumption tax rate imposed on land purchases, and t_r is the interest income tax rate, as before. For simplicity we will assume the tax revenue is rebated back to the consumer in the period it is collected. (The lumpsum rebates have been omitted for brevity.)

Arbitrage must hold if both assets are held; thus,

$$1 + r_{t+1}(1 - t_r) = (p_{t+1} + v_{t+1})/(1 + \theta_A)p_t. \tag{9.1}$$

The first-order condition governing the intertemporal consumption decision is standard and is omitted; the interest income tax will distort that decision while a flat-rate consumption tax will not. Notice that the interest income tax rate enters the arbitrage condition. It follows that the interest income tax will distort the portfolio decision. Also, notice that the consumption tax will distort the portfolio decision unless land is exempt from the tax as well. The interest income tax reduces the return to capital and would provide an incentive to shift from capital to land in the portfolio. On the other hand, the consumption tax that includes land in the base would also reduce the value to holding land and would cause a shift in the opposite direction.

We can represent the solution to the consumer's control problem by a savings function, $S(w_t, r_{t+1}(1 - t_r))$, after the tax revenue is rebated. In equilibrium this is equal to $k_{t+1} + p_t A$:

$$S(w_t, r_{t+1}(1 - t_r)) = k_{t+1} + p_t A.$$

Since $r = f_k(k, a) = \partial f / \partial k$ and $a = A/L$ is fixed, we can solve to get $k(r)$, where $dk/dr = k_r = 1/f_{kk} < 0$. Furthermore, since $v = f_a(k, a) = \partial f / \partial a$ and $k(r)$, it follows that $v(r) = f_a(k(r), a)$. Thus, $v_r = f_{ak}k_r < 0$ if $f_{ak} > 0$. Finally, the wage is given by $w(r) = f(k(r), a) - v(r)a - rk(r)$ and $w_r = -k - av_r$, which is also negative if the first term dominates. It seems reasonable to assume that the wage and return to land are positively related to the level of physical capital, and hence negatively related to the real interest rate, since additional capital will make the other two factors more productive at the margin. Thus, $w_r, v_r < 0$ seems reasonable.

With this information, we can rewrite the equilibrium condition as

$$S(w(r_t), r_{t+1}(1 - t_r)) = k(r_{t+1}) + p_t A. \tag{9.2}$$

Equations (9.1) and (9.2) constitute a two equation system in (r, p). Chamley and Wright (1987) calculated the eigenvalues of the system and studied the local stability properties of the equilibrium. In particular, they showed that one eigenvalue is stable and one is unstable. Thus, the system appears to be saddlepoint stable.

First, consider the interest income tax. In a stationary equilibrium the price of land settles down to a constant and the arbitrage condition imples that $r(1 - t_r) = v(r)/p$ or $p = v(r)/r(1 - t_r)$. Use this in (9.2) to obtain the condition governing the stationary equilibrium,

$$S(w(r), r(1 - t_r)) = k(r) + Av(r)/r(1 - t_r).$$

Under a lumpsum rebate of the revenue, we obtain the following long run incidence result:

$$dr/dt_r = r(S_r + pA)/E > 0, \tag{9.3}$$

where $E = S_r - k_r + w_r S_w - Av_r/r + Ap/r$. The denominator of this derivative is positive if $S_r > 0$, $k_r < 0$, $v_r < 0$, and $w_r S_w$ is small in magnitude. The numerator contains two terms. The first term embodies the typical result involving capital accumulation, namely that the tax affects the saving decision adversely and capital accumulation falls as a result. The second term captures a capitalization effect and is also positive in sign. It follows that the interest rate increases with the tax rate, $dr/dt_r > 0$.

In addition, the long run response of the price of land is

$$dp/dt_r = v/r - (v/r^2)(dr/dt_r). \tag{9.4}$$

This response is generally ambiguous. The first term captures the direct effect of the change in the tax on the price, which is an arbitrage effect, while the second term captures the indirect effect, which involves a change in the before-tax interest rate. Combining terms, we can rewrite (9.4) as

$$dp/dt_r = (v/r)(w_r S_w + k_r + Av_r/r)/E$$

The demand for capital per worker is downward sloping, so $k_r < 0$. If $w_r, v_r < 0$, it follows that the price falls with the interest income tax rate. However, we cannot rule out the case where the price rises. If, for example, $v_r > 0$ and Av_r/r is large in magnitude, it is possible for the price of land to rise with the tax rate.

The consumption tax that exempts land is nondistorting in this model. So to make the problem interesting, suppose that land is included in the tax base. Then the arbitrage condition in equilibrium is

$$1 + r = (1 + v/p)/(1 + \theta_A). \tag{9.5}$$

Using this, we can write the equilibrium condition,

$$S(w(r), r) = k(r) + Av(r)/[(1 + \theta_A)(1 + r) - 1]. \tag{9.6}$$

We can treat the steady state version of (9.2) and (9.5) as a two-equation system in (r, p), or we can differentiate (9.6) directly. Differentiating the system, we obtain

$$dr/d\theta_A = -(1 + r)A/\Delta < 0, \tag{9.7}$$
$$dp/d\theta_A = -(1 + r)(S_r + w_r S_w - k_r)/\Delta < 0, \tag{9.8}$$

evaluated at the initial equilibrium, where $\Delta = (v/p^2)(S_r + w_r S_w - k_r) + A(1 - v_r/p)$. If $S_r + w_r S_w - k_r > 0$, the equilibrium is stable in the absence of land. Furthermore, if $v_r < 0$ and the equilibrium is stable in the absence of land, then $\Delta > 0$. It follows that the interest rate and the price of land both fall when the consumption tax is imposed.

The intuition is that when the consumption tax is imposed there is an incentive to buy less land and acquire more capital. The interest rate falls as a result. As the demand for land falls, so too does the price of land.

9.2.2. Extension: land with an amenity value

We can extend the model by allowing the agent to care for the land itself. If the model is taken literally, farmers produce corn that can be used as seed for future planting or can be eaten. The farmer might very easily care about the land itself. Newspapers and newsmagazines in the United States, for example, are replete with stories depicting the "love of the land" and the "life of the family farm," especially when such farms are forced out of business. The same is true in other countries, such as Japan and France. To capture this we will assume the agent cares about the stock of land, A. The stock of land thus enters the utility function as a separate argument according to $U(c_{1t}, c_{2t}, A)$. Once again, we will make the usual assumptions regarding the utility function.

Under the interest income tax, the first-order conditions in equilibrium are

$$U_1/U_2 = (1 + r_n),$$
$$U_A/U_2 = pr_n - v,$$

where $r_n = r(1 - t_r)$. The tax distorts both the intertemporal consumption decision and the portfolio decision. However, the arbitrage condition presented earlier does not hold as long as the marginal utility of the land is strictly positive. Let $q_n = pr_n - v$. This is the net opportunity cost of acquiring land in a stationary equilibrium. The first-order conditions and the definition of second-period consumption given by the wealth constraint,

$$c_2 = (1 + r_n)(w - c_1) - q_n A,$$

can be solved to obtain the demand for first-period consumption and the demand for land,

$$C(w, r_n, q_n) \quad \text{and} \quad A(w, r_n, q_n).$$

The supply physical capital can then be defined as

$$S(w, r_n, q_n) = w - C(w, r_n, q_n) - A(w, r_n, q_n).$$

The supply of capital will be increasing in the wage if first-period consumption and the demand for land increase with the wage but the sum of responses is less than one in magnitude, that is if $C_w + A_w < 1$, where $\partial C / \partial w = C_w$ and $\partial A / \partial w = A_w$. The supply of capital will also be increasing in the after tax interest rate and the net cost of acquiring land if first-period consumption and the demand for land are decreasing in the after tax interest rate and the net cost of acquiring land.

From the technology and profit maximization, we can write the wage and rental on land as functions of the interest rate, $w(r)$ and $v(r)$. We can then write the equilibrium conditions in the following manner:

$$S(w(r), r(1 - t_r), pr(1 - t_r) - v(r)) = k(r),$$
$$A = A(w(r), r(1 - t_r), pr(1 - t_r) - v(r)).$$

These equations determine the stationary values of (r, p) as a function of t_r after a lumpsum rebate of the tax revenue.

Unfortunately, the response of the endogenous variables to the tax rate in this case is ambiguous. The higher tax rate reduces the return to acquiring physical capital and thus reduces the opportunity cost of acquiring land. This induces a shift in the portfolio from capital toward land. It also gives the agent an incentive to acquire less of both assets by saving less. The portfolio and saving effects work in the direction of reducing capital and raising the real interest rate. The demand for land increases because of the portfolio effect but decreases because of the saving effect. Finally, factor returns for labor and land will also respond, and this causes the outcome of the response to be ambiguous.

If the consumption tax is imposed and land is exempt from the tax, the first-order conditions of the representative consumer's decision problem are

$$U_1 / U_2 = 1 + r,$$
$$U_A / U_2 = (pr - v)/(1 + \theta).$$

The decision to buy land is now distorted by the tax. Indeed, land is a favored activity. Under a lumpsum rebate of the revenue, an increase in the consumption tax rate is similar to the substitution effect associated with a decrease in the opportunity cost of land. The agent has an incentive to acquire more land as a result. However, the response of first-period consumption is ambiguous. So it is possible for capital accumulation to increase or decrease.

The equilibrium must satisfy the following,

$$S(w(r), r, q/(1 + \theta)) = k(r),$$
$$A = A(w(r), r, q/(1 + \theta)),$$

where $q = pr - v(r)$. Unfortunately, the response of both the interest rate and the price of land will be ambiguous, as in the previous case, for the same reason.

Next, suppose land is taxed at the consumption tax rate when the initial purchase is made. The second condition above becomes

$$U_A/U_2 = p(1 + r) - (p + v)/(1 + \theta),$$

and the portfolio decision is still distorted. Now, since the selling price of the land is reduced by the tax, there is an incentive to hold less land in the portfolio than before. Since the amount of land is fixed in supply, the price of land will fall as a result of this effect. However, the total amount of assets accumulated will also be affected, and this will again make the net response to the tax ambiguous.

9.2.3. Extension: a two-class model

Suppose there are two agents born in each generation, one who is endowed with one unit of labor and one who is endowed with $h > 1$ units of labor. The population is stationary. Suppose further there is a fixed cost of acquiring land, F; it is costly to survey the land, check the title to it, and search for any liens on the property. The marginal return to the land must be greater than the return to capital in order for people to hold land. For simplicity we will assume that $w < F < wh$. In this case the well endowed agent will hold only land in her portfolio, while the less well endowed agent will hold only capital. The savings function for the former agent is $S(wh, (1 + v/p)/(1 + \theta_A); F)$ in equilibrium, while the savings function for the latter agent is $S(w, r_n)$, where $(1 + v/p)/(1 + \theta_A) > 1 + r_n$.

The labor of the two agents is perfectly substitutable in the production of the consumption good. Thus, $w(r)$ and $v(r)$ still describe the wage and rental on land. The equilibrium separates accordingly:

$$S(w(r)h, (1 + v(r)/p)/(1 + \theta_A); F) = A, \tag{9.9}$$
$$S(w(r), r_n) = k(r). \tag{9.10}$$

Equation (9.10) is similar to the equilibrium condition in Diamond's (1970) model without land. Equation (9.9) describes the equilibrium if the interest rate were fixed or if were the only asset in the model.

From this, it follows that the interest rate is increasing in the interest income tax rate for the same reason as it is in Diamond's model. Second, the consumption tax has no effect on the interest rate even if land is taxed. The consumption tax rate does not enter (9.10). Third, both the interest income tax and the consumption tax reduce the price of land albeit through different channels. To see this, differentiate (9.9) to obtain

$$dp/dt_r = [(w_r S_w + v_r S_Q/p)/(v S_Q/p^2)] dr/dt_r,$$
$$dp/d\theta_A = [(w_r S_w + v_r S_Q/p)/(v S_Q/p^2)] dr/dt_r - (1 + v/p)/[v/p^2(1 + \theta)],$$

where $S_Q = \partial S/\partial(1 + v/p) > 0$. The coefficient for the response of the interest rate is positive if saving is increasing in the net return to holding land, and if the term in S_w is small in magnitude. The response of the price of land to the interest income tax contains only an indirect effect that works through the interest rate, while the response to the consumption tax also contains a direct effect. The second term in the second equation captures the direct effect of the consumption tax when land is included in the base. Both effects work in the same direction, causing the price to fall.

9.3. Durable goods

9.3.1. *The basic model*

In this section we will consider a durable good with resale value, such as a car or a house. This model is related to the land model of Section 9.2 when $v = 0$. We will extend the model by allowing the quality of land to deteriorate. However, we will also assume that maintenance expenditures can maintain the quality of the land.

Again, time is discrete and the economy lasts for ever. There is one consumption good and a durable good. Population is constant and normalized to one. An agent lives for two periods, young and old. The representative agent is endowed with w units of the consumption good in the first period of life and none in the second. In the first period the agent can consume some of the good immediately (c_1), store some of it for consumption next period (k), use some of it to buy the durable good ($p_t D_t$), and at the end of the period make a maintenance expenditure to improve the durable good (qm). In the second period the agent just consumes her income. The agent's budget constraints are given by

$$w - c_{1t} - k_t - p_t D_t - qm_t = 0,$$
$$(1 + r)k_t + p_{t+1} D_{t+1} - c_{2t} = 0,$$

where $r > 0$ is the constant return to storage.

Preferences are given by $U(c_{1t}, c_{2t}, s_1 D_t, s_2 D_{t+1})$, which satisfies the usual assumptions. The third argument in the utility function is the utility the consumer derives from the services of the durable good in the first period of life before the durable good requires any maintenance, $S_1 = s_1 D_t$, where $s_1 > 0$ is a constant. The last argument is the utility the consumer obtains from the services of the durable good in the second period of life after maintenance has improved the stock but before the agent sells the durable good, $S_2 = s_2 D_{t+1}$. The durable good evolves according to

$$D_{t+1} = (1 - \delta)D_t + m_t. \tag{9.11}$$

The consumer maximizes utility subject to the budget constraints and the law of motion for the durable good. Since we seek an interior solution to the decision problem, we can collapse the budget constraints to obtain

$$c_{2t} = (1 + r)(w - c_{1t}) - [p_t(1 + r) - (1 - \delta)p_{t+1}]D_t - [q(1 + r) - p_{t+1}]m_t.$$

From this constraint we can define effective "prices" for D_t and m_t according to

$$Q_{Dt} = p_t(1 + r) - (1 - \delta)p_{t+1} \tag{9.12a}$$

and

$$Q_{mt} = q(1 + r) - p_{t+1}. \tag{9.12b}$$

In each effective "price", the first term is the direct opportunity cost of the respective "good" while the second term is the benefit of selling the improved durable good.

Using (9.11) and the definitions in (9.12), the first-order conditions can be written as

$$U_{c1}/U_{c2} = 1 + r, \tag{9.13a}$$

$$[s_1 U_{S1} + s_2(1 - \delta)U_{S2}]/U_{c2} = Q_{Dt}, \tag{9.13b}$$

$$s_2 U_{S2}/U_{c2} = Q_{mt}, \tag{9.13c}$$

where $U_{c1} = \partial U/\partial c_1$ and so on. As before, (9.13a) governs the intertemporal consumption decision, (9.13b) governs the durable good decision, and (9.13c) governs the maintenance decision. We can solve these conditions to obtain the following demand functions:

$$c_{1t} = C(w, r, Q_{Dt}, Q_{mt}),$$

$$D_t = D(w, r, Q_{Dt}, Q_{mt}),$$

$$m_t = M(w, r, Q_{Dt}, Q_{mt}).$$

Unfortunately, the comparative statics of the consumer's decision problem are ambiguous. However, it seems reasonable to assume that $C_w = \partial c_1/\partial w > 0$, $C_r = \partial c_1/\partial r < 0$, $D_w = \partial D/\partial w > 0$, $D_D = \partial D/\partial Q_D < 0$, $M_w = \partial m/\partial w > 0$, and $M_m = \partial m/\partial Q_m < 0$. One can easily imagine that maintenance and the durable good itself are substitutes; one can buy a better quality durable requiring less maintenance or a lower quality durable requiring more maintenance. Therefore, it seems reasonable to suppose that the cross price effects are positive, $D_m = \partial D/\partial Q_m > 0$ and $M_D = \partial m/\partial Q_D > 0$.

We can close the model in the following way. In a stationary equilibrium the value of the durable good will settle down to a constant. Hence

$$p_t D_t = p_{t+1} D_{t+1}.$$

Using the law of motion for the durable good and rearranging, we have

$$p_t D_t = p_{t+1}(1 - \delta)D_t + p_{t+1}m_t.$$

Finally, substituting for D and m from the solution to the representative consumer's decision problem, we have the equilibrium condition governing the evolution of the price of the durable good at time t,

$$[p_t - p_{t+1}(1 - \delta)]D(w, r, p_t(1 + r) - (1 - \delta)p_{t+1}, q(1 + r) - p_{t+1})$$
$$= p_{t+1}M(w, r, p_t(1 + r) - (1 - \delta)p_{t+1}, q(1 + r) - p_{t+1}). \quad (9.14)$$

It will be useful for the purpose of undertaking comparative statics to define the term

$$\Omega = p(\delta D_m - M_m) - p(r + \delta)(\delta D_D - M_D). \quad (9.15)$$

If the own price effects are negative, then they will work in the direction of making this term positive; that is, D_D, $M_D < 0$ work in the direction of making $\Omega > 0$. The cross price effects also work in the direction of making $\Omega > 0$ if D and m are substitutes.

In equilibrium when the price of the durable is constant, the equilibrium condition is given by

$$\delta D(w, r, (r + \delta)p, q(1 + r) - p) = M(w, r, (r + \delta)p, q(1 + r) - p). \quad (9.16)$$

Whether or not a change in a parameter increases the equilibrium price depends on the relative responses of the demand for the durable good and the demand for maintenance. An increase in demand for the durable will increase the price. However, an increase in maintenance will increase the effective supply of the durable in the future and this will tend to lower the price. For example, a permanent increase in the first-period endowment leads to the following long run response:

$$dp/dw = (\delta D_w - M_w)/\Omega.$$

If both the demand for the durable and the demand for maintenance increase with the first-period endowment as they would if they were both normal goods, the response of the price of the durable is ambiguous. However, there is a bias toward the response of maintenance since the response of the durable itself is weighted by $\delta < 1$.

The model of this section encompasses several possibilities and thus is very general in its application. For example, if $s_1 = s_2 = 0$, and there is no depreciation and no maintenance required, then the durable good can be considered a pure asset, and instead of (9.14) we have the usual arbitrage condition,[3]

$$(1 + r) = p_{t+1}/p_t.$$

If the durable good can depreciate and maintenance can be undertaken but $s_1 = s_2 = 0$, then from the first-order conditions we have

$$p_t(1 + r) = (1 - \delta)p_{t+1},$$

and

$$q(1 + r) = p_{t+1}.$$

The latter condition implies that $p_t = p$, a constant, namely $p_t = q(1 + r)$. Thus, $1 + r = 1 - \delta > 0$. Of course, if r is constant this latter condition may not hold. However, if m, $D > 0$, it must hold. Since the marginal product of capital is bounded below by zero, the agent would eventually be driven to a corner solution in m. At the corner, $p_{t+1}(1 - \delta) = p_t(1 + r)$ and $p_{t+1} < q(1 + r)$. This last statement simply says that, at a corner where $m = 0$, the opportunity cost of improving the durable, $q(1 + r)$, is greater than the price of selling the durable, p_{t+1}, at the margin. Thus, maintaining the durable does not make economic sense in this case. Finally, and more generally, the durable may provide services from which the consumer derives utility, the most general version of the model of this section. As we will see in the next section, this feature can significantly alter the impact of the consumption tax.

9.3.2. Taxation and durable goods

First, consider the interest income tax. The first-order conditions in the presence of the interest income tax become

$$U_{c1}/U_{c2} = 1 + r(1 - t_r),$$
$$[s_1 U_{S1} + (1 - \delta)s_2 U_{S2}]/U_{c2} = [1 + r(1 - t_r)]p_t - (1 - \delta)p_{t+1},$$
$$(1 - \delta)_{s2} U_{S2}/U_{c2} = q(1 + r(1 - t_r)) - p_{t+1}.$$

The tax has the usual effect on the intertemporal consumption decision. Second, the tax reduces the opportunity cost of buying the durable or maintaining it. Notice that the direct opportunity cost of the durable is $(1 + r)p_t$ while the monetary benefit of the durable is $(1 - \delta)p_{t+1}$. The tax lowers the net opportunity cost of the durable good by reducing the advantage in acquiring physical capital. The same point is true about the maintenance decision. The direct opportunity cost of maintaining the stock of the durable is $q(1 + r)$ while the monetary benefit of doing so is p_{t+1}. The interest income tax lowers the net opportunity cost of maintaining the durable. The tax thus provides the consumer with an incentive to acquire more of the durable and to maintain it better than would otherwise have been the case.

To obtain the response of the price of the durable, replace Q_D with $(r(1 - t_r) + \delta)p$ and replace Q_m with $q(1 + r(1 - t_r)) - p$ in (9.16) and differentiate to obtain

$$dp/dt_r = -[rp(\delta D_{Du} - M_{Du}) + rq(\delta D_{mu} - M_{mu})]/\Omega, \qquad (9.17)$$

assuming a lumpsum rebate of the revenue, where the subscript u denotes a compensated derivative. The interest income tax lowers the net opportunity cost of buying the durable and maintaining it. The first term, $rp(\delta D_{Du} - M_{Du})$, captures the effect of the tax on the price of the durable. Since $D_{Du} < 0$ and $M_{Du} > 0$, the first term is negative. The second term, $r_q(\delta D_{mu} - M_{mu})$, captures the effect of the tax on the cost of maintaining the durable. Since $M_{mu} < 0$ and $D_{Mu} > 0$, this term is positive and works in the opposite direction of the first term. If the former (latter) effect dominates, the price will rise (fall).

How is the equilibrium affected by the consumption tax? The wealth constraint becomes

$$c_{2t} = [(1 + r)[w - (1 + \theta)c_{1t}] - [p_t(1 + r)(1 + \theta_D) - (1 - \delta)p_{t+1}]D_t$$
$$- [q(1 + r)(1 + \theta_m) - p_{t+1}]m_t]/(1 + \theta),$$

where θ_m is the consumption tax rate imposed on maintenance expenditures and θ_D is the consumption tax rate imposed on the purchase of the durable. It follows from this that the first-order conditions of the consumer's problem are given by

$$U_{c1}/U_{c2} = 1 + r,$$
$$[s_1 U_{S1} + (1 - \delta)s_2 U_{S2}]/U_{c2} = [(1 + r)p_t(1 + \theta_D) - (1 - \delta)p_{t+1}]/(1 + \theta)$$
$$(1 - \delta)s_2 U_{S2}/U_{c2} = [q(1 + r)(1 + \theta_m) - p_{t+1}]/(1 + \theta).$$

The intertemporal consumption decision remains undistorted as long as the tax rate is constant over the life cycle. However, the durable good and maintenance decisions will both be distorted by the tax even if neither is directly taxed. The impact of the tax depends critically on the treatment of the durable when purchased and on the tax treatment of maintenance expenditures under the tax.

Consider the case where neither the purchase of the durable or the maintenance expenditures is taxed, $\theta_D = \theta_m = 0$. This yields

$$Q_D = [(1 + r)p_t - (1 - \delta)p_{t+1}]/(1 + \theta)$$

and

$$Q_m = q(1 + r) - p_{t+1}/(1 + \theta).$$

Both of these prices fall with the consumption tax and we would expect both D and m to increase. The intuition is simple enough; the durable and the maintenance of it become favored forms of consumption under the simple version of the consumption tax. Of course, the net effect of this on the equilibrium price of the durable will be ambiguous for the reasons already stated.

Second, suppose m and c_1 are difficult to distinguish for tax purposes. For example, suppose the durable good is a house and maintenance involves buying a hammer to repair the house. However, a hammer can also be used for projects unrelated to repairing the house such as building a bird feeder, fixing a piece of furniture, or constructing a tree house for the neighborhood children. This would come under general consumption and would be difficult to distinguish from maintenance of the durable good.

In this case $\theta_m = \theta$ and $\theta_D = 0$. The effective prices of D and m become

$$Q_D = [(1+r)p_t - (1-\delta)p_{t+1}]/(1+\theta),$$

and

$$Q_m = q(1+r) - p_{t+1}/(1+\theta).$$

The durable is still unambiguously favored over general consumption and Q_D falls as a result. However, the consumption tax now raises the effective net price of maintenance. Why? Because maintenance and first-period consumption are now treated in the same manner, and this raises the price of maintenance relative to the durable good. We might expect demand for the durable to increase and maintenance to fall. In this case, the price of the durable will rise unambiguously. To see this, note that the equilibrium condition is given by

$$\delta D[(w, r, (r+\delta)p)/(1+\theta), [q(1+r) - p/(1+\theta)]]$$
$$= M[(w, r, (r+\delta)p)/(1+\theta), [q(1+r) - p/(1+\theta)].$$

Differentiate this condition to obtain

$$dp/d\theta = -[(r+\delta)p(\delta D_D - M_D) - p(\delta D_m - M_m)]/\Omega$$

under a lumpsum rebate of the revenue. Since $\Omega > 0$, $\delta D_D - M_D < 0$, $\delta D_m - M_m > 0$ under our assumptions, $d_p/d\theta > 0$.

If the purchase of the durable and maintenance expenditures are both taxed at the consumption tax rate, $\theta_D = \theta_m = 0$, and the effective prices of these two activities become

$$Q_D = (1+r)p_t - (1-\delta)p_{t+1}/(1+\theta)$$

and

$$Q_m = q(1+r) - p_{t+1}/(1+\theta).$$

Both prices increase with the tax rate, and we would expect demand for both the durable good and maintenance to fall. Once again this will lead to an ambiguous response in the price of the durable. However, these two decisions will be distorted none the less.

We can also consider taxing services from the durable as part of the consumption tax. If $s_1 D_t$ and $s_2 D_{t+1}$ are taxed in the first and second periods, respectively, the budget constraints become

$$w - (1+\theta)c_{1t} - k_t - p_t D_t - qm_t - \theta_s s_1 D_t = 0,$$
$$(1+r)k_t + p_{t+1}D_{t+1} - (1+\theta)c_{2t} - \theta_s s_2 D_{t+1} = 0.$$

It is a straightforward matter to show that the first-order condition for D_t becomes

$$[s_1 U_{S1} + s_2(1-\delta)U_{S2}]/U_{c2} = [(1+r)p_t + \theta_s s_1 + \theta_s s_2(1-\delta) - (1-\delta)p_{t+1}]/(1+\theta).$$

The new terms are $\theta_s s_1$ and $\theta_s s_2 (1 - \delta)$. If $\theta_s = \theta$, the decision to buy the durable good will be distorted by the consumption based tax. The condition for maintenance under the extended consumption tax is given by

$$s_2 (1 - \delta) U_{S2} / U_{c2} = [(1 + r)q + \theta_s s_2 - p_{t+1}] / (1 + \theta).$$

Moreover, the decision to maintain the durable good will be distorted by the consumption tax if $\theta_s = \theta$.

We should point out that the reason we were able to derive any general comparative statics results with respect to the price of the durable good was because the return to storage was fixed. One justification for this might be that the economy is open to capital flows. If capital is perfectly mobile and labor and land or the durable good are not, it follows that the interest rate will be exogenous while the price of the durable and the wage rate will be determined by local conditions.

9.4. The land model with maintenance

We can extend the land model studied in Section 9.2 by including a maintenance expenditure. We can simultaneously extend the model of Section 9.3 to allow resale of the durable good, in this case land. If resale of the durable occurs, then it is also an asset in addition to generating utility from its services. To be specific, we will focus on land as the durable good. Land constantly used in production without any effort to maintain its quality will eventually be incapable of producing. Therefore, maintenance of the land may be necessary in order for it to be productive. The model of this section also generalizes the model of Section 9.3 by allowing the durable good to be productive at the margin.

Suppose the law of motion for land is given by

$$A_{t+1} = (1 - \delta)A_t + m_t, \tag{9.18}$$

where m is a maintenance expenditure as before. The consumer buys A_t at time t after it has been used in production. He can then decide how much to spend on maintaining the land. Next period A_{t+1} becomes available for production and can be sold after production takes place. The budget constraints become

$$w_t - (1 + \theta)c_{1t} - k_{t+1} - (1 + \theta_m)qm_t - (1 + \theta_A)p_t A_t = 0,$$
$$[1 + r_{t+1}(1 - t_r)]k_{t+1} + (p_{t+1} + v_{t+1})A_{t+1} - (1 + \theta)c_{2t} = 0,$$

where θ_m is the consumption tax rate imposed on maintenance and θ_A is the consumption tax rate imposed on the purchase of the land. It is straightforward to show that the "prices" are given by

$$Q_A = \{p_t[1 + r(1 - t_r)](1 + \theta_A) - (1 - \delta)(p_{t+1} + v_{t+1})\} / (1 + \theta) \tag{9.19a}$$

and

$$Q_m = \{q[1 + r(1 - t_r)](1 + \theta_m) - (p_{t+1} + v_{t+1})\} / (1 + \theta), \tag{9.19b}$$

where the variables are as defined in Section 9.2. When land is simply an asset, $Q_A = 0$ and $Q_m = 0$. It follows that

$$p_t[1 + r(1 - t_r)](1 + \theta_A) = (1 - \delta)(p_{t+1} + v_{t+1}), \tag{9.20a}$$

and

$$q[1 + r(1 - t_r)](1 + \theta_m) = (p_{t+1} + v_{t+1}). \tag{9.20b}$$

However, the two conditions (9.20) in turn imply that

$$p_t = (1 - \delta)q(1 + \theta_m)/(1 + \theta_A). \tag{9.21}$$

This condition has several implications. First, if $m, A > 0$, it follows that the price of land is fixed by (9.21) as long as q is fixed, since m and A are perfect substitutes in (9.18). The price of land will jump to its new level immediately if the equilibrium is perturbed by a change in tax policy as long as the tax parameter enters equation (9.21). An increase in θ_m will raise the price of land as agents shift from maintenance to land, and vice versa if θ_A increases. Second, the interest income tax rate does not affect the price of land in this version of the model. It will however affect the inputs into the production of the consumption good. Third, if $\theta_m = \theta_A = \theta$ under the consumption tax, or if $\theta_m = \theta_A = 0$, then the price of land will be unaffected by the consumption tax. If $\theta_m = \theta > 0$ and $\theta_A = 0$, then the price of land will jump to a higher level when the consumption tax is imposed. The intuition is that, if maintenance is taxed, the supply of effective land will fall and this will raise the price. Finally, if $\theta_m = 0$ and $\theta_A = \theta > 0$, then the price of land will fall when the consumption tax is imposed. If land is taxed when purchased but maintenance is not, the demand for land will fall relative to the supply and the price will fall as a result.

Next, suppose the agent obtains utility from land, as before, and obtains utility from maintenance as well. In that case the utility function is given by

$$U(c_{1t}, c_{2t}, A_{t+1}, m_t).$$

The law of motion for land is (9.18) and the budget constraints are the same as before. Equations (9.19) define the "prices" for land and maintenance. The first-order conditions are given by

$$U_1 - (1 + r_n)U_2 = 0,$$
$$(1 - \delta)U_A - Q_A U_2 = 0,$$
$$U_m + U_A - Q_m U_2 = 0.$$

Now land and maintenance are imperfect substitutes. We can solve these conditions for a first-period consumption function, a demand for land, and a maintenance function,

$$C(w, r_n, Q_A, Q_m), \quad A(w, r_n, Q_A, Q_m), \quad \text{and} \quad M(w, r_n, Q_A, Q_m).$$

From the first-order conditions, we can see that the interest income tax will distort all three decisions since the interest income tax rate enters the marginal rate of transformation (MRT) in all three equations. Indeed, the interest income tax lowers the MRT in each case. This provides the consumer with an incentive to lower the marginal rate of substitution (MRS) in each case. It follows that the consumer has an incentive to increase first-period consumption, purchases of land, and maintenance of the land relative to second-period consumption.

The flat rate consumption tax will also distort the decisions to purchase land and maintain it. The consumption tax imposed on the consumption good serves to lower the MRT in the second and third conditions, providing the consumer with an incentive to increase land purchases and maintenance. Second, the consumption tax imposed on purchases of land serves to raise the MRT Q_A. This provides the consumer with an incentive to reduce her purchase of land relative to second-period consumption. Finally, the consumption tax imposed on maintenance expenditures also serves to raise the MRT Q_m. This provides the consumer with an incentive to reduce maintenance of the land.

To our knowledge, researchers have not as yet included maintenance expenditures in the land model. Yet, this seems a natural extension of the model and it does seem to have important implications for tax policy.

9.5. The Ramsey growth model with durable goods

9.5.1. *The basic model*

In this section we will extend the Ramsey growth model to include a durable good without resale value. As we will see, the model's predictions are somewhat sharper than the OG model's predictions. It should be pointed out that resale markets in some durables like cars and houses exist in many countries. However, there are countries where secondary resale markets for durables operate haphazardly at best because the transactions costs are so high. Examples include a broad variety of consumer durables like wristwatches, coffee makers, microwave ovens, stereos, television sets, VCRs, shoes, and so on.

Time is discrete and the economy lasts for ever; $t = 0, 1, 2, \ldots$ Population is constant and normalized to one. There is one consumption good denoted C that is produced via a neoclassical constant-returns-to-scale technology as in previous chapters. Thus, output of the consumption good is determined by $Y_t = f(K_t)$ which is assumed to have the usual properties, where Y is output per worker and K is capital per worker. There is a second commodity, a durable good, denoted D. The durable good is produced according to a simple linear technology. The consumer can transform the consumption good into the durable good at a constant rate q. The durable good depreciates at the same rate as physical capital, δ. Let X denote investment in the durable good. The durable good thus evolves according to

$$D_{t+1} = (1 - \delta)D_t + X_t. \tag{9.22}$$

The law of motion for physical capital is

$$K_{t+1} = f(K_t) + (1 - \delta)K_t - C_t - qX_t. \qquad (9.23)$$

Under profit maximization, $f_K(K) = r - \delta$ and $w = f - rK$.

The consumer's period utility function is given by $U(C_t, S_t)$, where S represents the service flow from the durable good. The utility function is twice continuously differentiable, quasi-concave, and monotone increasing. For simplicity, we will assume that the service flow is linear in the stock of the durable, $S_t = sD_t$, as before, where $s > 0$ is a constant. Intertemporal preferences are represented by

$$\sum_{t=0}^{\infty} \beta^t U(C_t, sD_t), \qquad (9.24)$$

where $\beta = 1/(1 + \rho)$ is the discount factor and ρ is the rate of time preference.

Finally, the agent is endowed with one unit of labor each period which is supplied in a perfectly inelastic fashion. The consumer's budget constraint is

$$w_t + (1 + r_t - \delta)K_t - K_{t+1} - C_t - qX_t = 0. \qquad (9.25)$$

The consumer's decision problem is to choose a sequence $\{C_t, K_{t+1}, X_t, D_{t+1}\}$ to maximize (9.24) subject to (9.23) and (9.25) taking K_0 and D_0 as given. The first-order conditions are given by

$$U_{Ct} = \lambda_t,$$
$$\beta s U_{St+1} = \alpha_t - \beta(1 - \delta)\alpha_{t+1},$$
$$\alpha_t = q\lambda_t,$$

and

$$\lambda_t = \beta(1 + r_{t+1} - \delta)\lambda_{t+1},$$

where λ is the multiplier for (9.23) and α is the multiplier for (9.25), and where $U_{Ct} = \partial U/\partial C_t$, and so on. These conditions imply that

$$f_K(K) = \delta + \rho, \qquad (9.26a)$$
$$sU_S/U_C = rq = f_K(K)q, \qquad (9.26b)$$
$$f(K) = \delta K + C + qX, \qquad (9.26c)$$
$$X = \delta D. \qquad (9.26d)$$

These conditions also characterize the social optimum. Equation (9.26a) characterizes the optimal expansion path for capital; the modified golden rule is optimal; (9.26b) governs the optimal decision between the durable good and nondurable consumption; (9.26c) is the equilibrium resource constraint; and (9.26d) is the long-run relationship between investment in the durable and the durable stock; new investment is undertaken to replace the depreciated durable capital in the long run.

The capital per worker is fixed at K^* by (9.26a). Collapsing (9.26b)–(9.26d), we obtain

$$sU_S(f(K^*) - \delta K^* - q\delta D, sD) - rqU_C(f(K^*) - \delta K^* - q\delta D, sD) = 0. \quad (9.27)$$

The comparative statics are ambiguous for the most part because of conflicting income and substitution effects. However, it can be shown that the steady state stock of the durable good decreases with its cost at the margin, q. In addition, the steady state stock of the durable good is decreasing in the depreciation rate.[4]

9.5.2. Taxation and durable goods in the Ramsey growth model

Under the interest income tax, the budget constraint becomes

$$w_t + [1 + r_t(1 - t_r) - \delta]K_t - K_{t+1} - C_t - qX_t + T_t = 0, \quad (9.28)$$

where T is a lumpsum rebate of the revenue. Only the last condition of the first-order conditions presented in the last section is affected; it becomes $\lambda_t = \beta(1 + r_{t+1}(1 - t_r) - \delta)\lambda_{t+1}$. As a result, (9.26a) becomes

$$f_K(K)(1 - t_r) = \delta + \rho.$$

It is immediate that our earlier result derived in previous chapters still holds; K is decreasing in the interest income tax rate, which is to say that $dK/dt_r = 1/f_{KK} < 0$. This will permanently lower welfare since the economy will move away from the golden rule expansion path as a result of the tax. We can write K as a function of the tax rate, $K(t_r)$, where $dK/dt_r = K_{tr} < 0$, as mentioned.

We can also collapse the rest of the system down to the following two equations under a lumpsum rebate of the tax revenue:

$$sU_S(C, sD) - q(\delta + \rho)U_C(C, sD) = 0,$$
$$C + qD - f(K(t_r)) - \delta K(t_r) = 0.$$

Differentiate and solve to obtain

$$dC/dt_r = (r - \delta)K_{tr}(sq\beta rU_{CS} - s^2\beta U_{SS})/H$$
$$dD/dt_r = (r - \delta)K_{tr}(s\beta U_{SC} - q\beta rU_{CC})/H,$$

where $H = qs\beta U_{SC} + sq\beta(\delta + \rho)U_{SC} - q^2\rho rU_{CC} - s^2\beta U_{SS} > 0$ if $U_{SC} \geq 0$. Both consumption and the durable good fall with the tax rate if $U_{SC} \geq 0$. The interest income tax lowers the return to accumulating capital and thus reduces the demand for general consumption and the durable good.

As mentioned, the consumption tax will not affect the equilibrium at the margin as long as both general consumption and investment in the durable good are taxed at the same rate; the tax will only cause income effects. Suppose instead that the investment in durable goods is not taxed at the consumption tax rate but that general consumption C is. The first-order conditions of the consumer's decision problem become

$$U_{Ct} = (1 + \theta)\lambda_t$$
$$\beta s U_{St+1} = \alpha_t - \beta(1 - \delta)\alpha_{t+1},$$
$$\alpha_t = q\lambda_t,$$
$$\lambda_t = \beta(1 + r - \delta)\lambda_{t+1}.$$

These conditions imply (9.7a), (9.7c), and (9.7d) once again. However, (9.7b) becomes

$$sU_S - [qr/(1 + \theta)]U_C = 0,$$

where the MRT is given by $qr/(1 + \theta)$. The consumption tax rate reduces the MRT between services and consumption. This provides the consumer with an incentive to lower consumption and raise the demand for the durable at the margin.

To see this, we can collapse the system down to the same two equations as before. The difference is that the physical capital stock is unaffected by the consumption tax. However, in this case the allocation between the consumption good and the durable is affected by the tax. It is straightforward to show that consumption falls and the durable rises with the tax rate.[5]

This is a realistic case to consider, since we can interpret the durable good as housing. Traditionally, in many countries including the United States and Japan, housing is heavily tax favored, and in some countries it is actually subsidized; for example, in the United States mortgage interest can be deducted from taxable income. Indeed, many observers do not believe that the income tax system in the United States can be reformed without maintaining the existing subsidy to homeowners. As another example, in Japan capital gains on the sale of one's residence are treated very generously. In addition, the imputed rents from housing are almost never taxed. This gives housing a tremendous advantage relative to other assets. One way of maintaining the subsidy is to tax general consumption but not the purchase of a home under the consumption tax.

Finally, consider the case where there is a consumption tax imposed on the service from the durable good. The budget constraint becomes

$$w_t + (1 + r_t - \delta)K_t - K_{t+1} - (1 + \theta)C_t - \theta_s s D_t - q X_t + T_t = 0,$$

where θ_s is the consumption tax rate imposed on the service from the durable. The first-order condition for the durable good becomes

$$s\beta U_S - (1 + \theta_s)\beta\lambda_{t+1} + \beta\lambda_{t+1}(1 - \delta)q - q\lambda_t = 0,$$

and the other conditions are the same as before. This implies that

$$sU_S/U_c = \theta_s/(1 + \theta) + qr/(1 + \theta).$$

There are several cases to consider. If services are taxed at the same rate as general consumption, the MRT is $(\theta + rq)/(1 + \theta)$ and the durable goods decision is distorted. If $\theta_s = 0$, then we obtain our earlier result; the consumption tax lowers the MRT between the durable good and consumption. Finally, it is straightforward to show that, when $\theta_s = 0$ and investment in the durable is taxed at the same rate as consumption, the MRT is qr and the consumption based tax is nondistorting.

9.6. Tax prepayment

Under tax prepayment, an asset is ignored when calculating the consumption tax base. Consider the model of the Section 9.4. If prepayment is applied to the durable good, land, the consumption tax base is $w - k$ in the first period, which is equal to $c_1 - p_t A_t + q m_t$. In the second period the base is $(1 + r)k$, which is equal to $c_2 - (p_{t+1} + v_{t+1})[(1 - \delta)A_t + m_t]$, where we have used the law of motion for land. The budget constraints after applying the tax to the definition of the base are

$$w - k - (1 + \theta_1)(c_1 + qm + p_t A_t) = 0$$
$$(1 + r)k - (1 + \theta_2)\{c_{2t} - (p_{t+1} + v_{t+1})[(1 - \delta)A_t + m]\} = 0,$$

where the tax rate may differ over time if the consumer finds herself in a different tax bracket.

It is straightforward to show that none of the consumer's decisions will be distorted by the consumption under this method of calculating the base if the tax maintains a flat rate. However, if the tax is progressive we obtain

$$U_1/U_2 = (1 + r)(1 + \theta_1)/(1 + \theta_2),$$
$$(1 - \delta)U_A/U_2 = p_t(1 + \theta_1)(1 + r)/(1 + \theta_2) - (p_{t+1} + v_{t+1}),$$
$$(U_m + U_A)/U_2 = (1 + r)(1 + \theta_1)/(1 + \theta_2) - (p_{t+1} + v_{t+1}).$$

Table 9.1.   Summary of results[a]

Section	Model	Interest income tax	Consumption tax
9.2	OG model with productive land	L and s are distorted	L is distorted if land is taxed, s is not
	Amenity value model	L and s are distorted	L is distorted even when it is exempt, s is not
	Two-class model	s is distorted, L is not	L is distorted only when taxed, s is not
9.3	Durable good with service	s, D, and m are distorted	D and m are distorted, s is not
9.4	Land model with maintenance	s, L, and m are distorted	L and m are distorted, s is not
9.5	Ramsey model of a durable good providing services	s and D are distorted	D is distorted if D is exempt, s is not distorted

[a] $s = $ *saving* (intertemporal consumption), $L = $ land, $m = $ maintenance, $D = $ durable good.

If the tax is constant over the life cycle, either because the tax is flat rate or because the agent finds herself in the same tax bracket, the tax will not distort any economic decisions in this model. However, all three decisions will be distorted if the tax is progressive and the consumer finds herself in different tax brackets across the life cycle. If income is higher when working than when retired, then $(1 + \theta_1)/(1 + \theta_2) > 1$ and the tax raises the MRTs in all three decisions. The agent then has an incentive to raise the MRSs by increasing first-period consumption, land purchases, and maintenance relative to second-period consumption.

9.7. Conclusion

We have studied several models of durable goods, including the land model, the land model with an amenity value, a two-class model of land, a model with a durable good and maintenance expenditures of the durable good, the land model where the land must be maintained in order to produce, and a pure durable goods model. The structure of the different models differs slightly. However, the implications for the income and consumption taxes are relatively constant across models in the pattern of distortions created by each tax.

If the durable good is merely an asset, then taxation of the interest income of other assets causes the durable good to be favored. The consumption tax will have no impact on the durable good in this case. If the durable also has an amenity value which is not taxed, then the consumption tax will generally distort the durable good decision. Finally, if the durable good can depreciate over time but can be maintained, the implications of the consumption tax become more complex. The consumption tax will generally distort either the decision to buy the durable good or the decision to maintain it or both, depending on how the tax is imposed.

We also considered the important case where the service flow from the durable was taxed under the extended consumption tax. If the services of the durable are taxed at the consumption tax rate, the consumption tax will generally distort the decision to buy the durable good and the maintenance decision as well; the consumption tax will not be neutral with respect to the decision to invest in the durable good relative to general consumption, nor will it be neutral with regard to the decision to maintain the durable if the services from the durable are taxed at the consumption tax rate. There will be less of an incentive to invest in durable goods as a result of the consumption tax on the services of the durable, and we would expect the demand for the durable good to fall as a result.

Finally, we considered the tax prepayment method of calculating the consumption tax base. Under this method, an asset is ignored when actually calculating the base; the asset is not included in the base as consumption when the initial purchase is made, and the income from the asset later on is also not included. It was shown that the flat rate consumption tax is nondistorting under this method. However, if the tax is progressive, then it will generally distort the intertemporal consumption decision, the decision to purchase the asset, and the decision to maintain the asset relative to future consumption.

NOTES TO CHAPTER 9

1. See Rosen (1985) for a broad survey of the literature. A popular model of the demand for housing posits that demand depends on income, the effective price of housing, and demographic characteristics. The effective price of housing includes the tax advantages to owning the house rather than renting it. A popular model of housing supply deduces the properties of the supply of housing from a production function for housing. It is typically assumed that competition prevails in the market for housing. The main difficulty for empirical researchers lies in constructing the price and income variables used in the estimation since they are not directly observable. Data from England and Wales and the USA indicate that the subsidy for owner occupied housing had a substantial effect on the demand for housing. See sections 3.3 and 3.4 in Rosen (1985).

2. Previous static estimates place the welfare cost associated with the housing subsidy at 0.1–0.4 per cent of GNP. Skinner (1996) calculates a dynamic welfare cost of 2.2 per cent.

3. From this one can easily see that there is a logical error contained in Skinner (1996). He assumes the consumer obtains a utility benefit from the durable good housing in the second period of life but then he also assumes that the pure arbitrage condition between housing and other financial assets holds with equality. The latter condition is inconsistent with the former assumption. To see this, notice from (9.13b) that if $s_1 = 0$, as assumed by Skinner, we have

$$s_2(1 - \delta)U_{S2}/U_{c2} = Q_{Dt}$$

in our notation. It follows that $Q_{Dt} > 0$ as long as the service from the durable good provides positive marginal utility. This implies that the arbitrage condition for pure assets does not hold. Skinner assumes that arbitrage holds, however, $Q_D = 0$ in our notation, at the same time that $s_2(1 - \delta)U_{S2}U_{c2} > 0$, a contradiction. Intuitively, if the durable good provides utility, there is a "consumption return" that must be added to the financial return of the durable in equilibrium. The pure form of the arbitrage condition $Q_D = 0$ will not hold with equality if there is a consumption benefit attached to the durable good.

4. More formally, if $U_{SC} \geq 0$, then

$$dD/dq = rU_C/E + \delta D(sU_{SC} - rqU_{CC})/E < 0,$$

$$dD/d\delta = (K + qD)(sU_{SC} - rqU_{CC})/E < 0,$$

where $E = s^2 U_{SS} - (sq\delta + rsq)U_{CS} + r\delta q^2 U_{CC} < 0$.

5. $dC/d\theta = -q^2\beta(r - \delta)/H < 0$ and $dD/d\theta = q\beta(r - \delta)/H > 0$.

10

Income and Consumption Taxation in a Monetary Economy

10.1. Introduction

In this chapter we will explore the effect of the interest income and consumption taxes on the demand for money and the government's ability to collect seigniorage. Unbacked fiat money plays several roles in an economy. It is a durable good that can be exchanged for other goods, and people are willing to accept it as such. It provides a form of liquidity services. It provides a common unit of account. And it serves as an important store of value. In addition to this, people may also hold fiat money because of legal restrictions on the private sector's ability to intermediate assets.

The demand for money will generally be affected by the imposition of a tax system and may respond differently depending on which tax system is introduced. In addition to this, there are different models of a monetary economy currently in use, and, unfortunately, different models may make different predictions about the effect of taxation on the demand for money and the ultimate impact of the tax on the economy.

We will study several models of money and compare the results across the different models. First, we will study different versions of the Ramsey model. The first version assumes that money provides a liquidity service and hence real money balances enter the utility function as a separate argument. This is the so-called money in the utility function (MUF) model which was initially studied by Sidrauski (1967) and Brock (1974). Then we will study a version of the Lucas and Stokey (1983) cash and credit goods (CCG) model which includes two kinds of commodities, cash and credit goods; money must be used to purchase the cash good and so there is a so-called "cash in advance (CIA) constraint." Lucas and Stokey show that the two models are closely related to one another. However, we will provide examples where some of the implications of the two models relative to tax policy may differ.

Next, we will study the MUF and CCG versions of the overlapping generations (OG) model. As it turns out, the implications of the OG model may differ from those of the Ramsey growth model. For example, in the Ramsey model the long run capital per worker ratio is fixed by the discount factor in a monetary economy. It follows that many tax policies like the consumption tax may not affect the long run capital intensity of production. This is no longer true in the OG model where agents have a finite horizon.

A third type of model, based on legal restrictions, has generated some interest as well. This type of model is based on the notion that governments impose laws that restrict the private sector's ability to intermediate assets in order to give the government a monopoly in issuing currency. This monopoly power allows the government to collect seigniorage by providing fiat money with greater value than would otherwise have been the case. This class of models has been studied by Wallace (1983, 1984, 1998), Bryant and Wallace (1984), Sargent and Wallace (1982), and, more recently, Freeman and Huffman (1991), and Espinosa-Vega and Russell (1998). See also the discussion in Azariadis (1993).

In one version of the legal restrictions (LR) model we will study the effect of imposing a reserve requirement in both the Ramsey growth model and a pure exchange version of the OG model. We will also study a model of a borrowing restriction and another model involving fixed costs coupled with other restrictions on private intermediation. As it turns out, the effect of a tax policy may differ in these models relative to the earlier models studied (e.g. MUF) and may differ depending on the legal restriction imposed.

We also study the effects of tax policy on the government's ability to collect seigniorage, that is its ability to command resources through the use of its issuance of fiat money. While seigniorage accounts for only a small fraction of the government's budget in large countries like the United States, Japan, and Western Europe, it is much more important in smaller economies such as in Latin America and Russia. In some cases it can account for 20 per cent of the government's revenue. Cukierman, Edwards, and Tabellini (1992) report that in the period 1971–82 Bolivia, the Central African Republic, Ghana, Jordan, Mexico, Peru, and Uganda collected more than 20 per cent of government expenditures from seigniorage. In addition, 27 countries out of 79 in their sample collected more than 10 per cent of their expenditures from printing money. See also Haslag (1998) for evidence on the prevalence of seigniorage across countries.

The chapter is organized in the following manner. In the next section we present two versions of the Ramsey model with money, the MUF and the CCG. The two models make very similar predictions about the impact of tax policy. However, there are some differences. In Section 10.3 we study the implications of the MUF and CCG versions of the OG model. Models involving legal restrictions are presented in Section 10.4. We compare results across models in Section 10.5. Section 10.6 studies the tax prepayment methodology of calculating the tax base relative to money. Under prepayment money is completely ignored when calculating the tax base. We show that the consumption tax will be neutral in such a case. However, this will no longer be true if there is a legal restriction like a reserve requirement. Section 10.7 concludes the chapter.

There are some issues we will not be concerned with. For example, many governments tax nominal income, in which case inflation can interact with the tax system so as to create greater distortions than would otherwise have been the case. Ihori (1996a) discusses this issue in great detail. Nor will we be concerned with the optimal inflation rate issue; again, see the summary and discussion in Ihori (1996a) and the literature cited.

10.2. Money in the Ramsey growth model

10.2.1. *The money in the utility function (MUF) in the Ramsey growth model*

There is one consumption good produced via a neoclassical, constant returns technology using labor and capital. Output per worker is given by $y_t = f(k_t)$, where k_t is capital per worker at time t, and $df/dk = f_k$ is the marginal product of capital per worker. We will make the usual assumptions regarding the technology. The aggregate resource constraint confronting the economy is given by

$$y_t = c_t + k_{t+1} - k_t + g_{mt}, \tag{10.1}$$

where c_t is consumption, $k_{t+1} - k_t$ is investment, and g_{mt} is government seigniorage. The firms that produce the consumption good act as perfect competitors and maximize profit. Thus, $r = f_k$ and $y = w + rk$ since profit is zero, where r is the real interest rate and w is the real wage.

There are a large number of consumers who experience an infinite horizon and each behaves competitively. We will normalize on the population by assuming there is one representative consumer. In the MUF version of the model, the consumer receives utility not only by consuming the consumption good, but also by using cash to purchase it. Cash thus provides liquidity services for the agent that produces utility. The period utility function is $U(c_t, m_t)$, where m is real per capita money balances. The utility function satisfies the usual assumptions. We will also assume for simplicity that $\partial U/\partial m = U_m > 0$ throughout our analysis. The utility function for the infinite planning horizon is given by $\Sigma_t \beta^t U(c_t, m_t)$, where $\beta = 1/(1+\rho)$ is the discount factor and $\rho > 0$ is the rate of time preference.

The consumer is endowed with one unit of labor each period and supplies it completely to the labor market in exchange for a wage. Her budget constraint is

$$T_t + w_t + [1 + r_t(1 - t_{rt})]k_t + (1 + r_{mt})m_{t-1} - k_{t+1}$$
$$-(1 + \theta_m)m_t - (1 + \theta_t)c_t = 0. \tag{10.2}$$

T is a lumpsum rebate of the tax revenue in the same period the revenue was collected, t_r is the capital income tax rate, m_{t-1} is beginning-of-the-period cash balances, m_t is end-of-the-period cash balances, r_m is the return to holding money balances, θ is the consumption tax rate, and θ_m is the consumption tax rate imposed on money balances. Note that $1 + r_{mt} = p_{t-1}/p_t$, where p_t is the price level at time t.

The representative consumer's decision problem is to choose an infinite sequence of consumption, capital, and money to maximize her utility function subject to her budget constraint, taking the initial capital stock and the initial stock of money as given. Following the method developed in Chapters 3 and 4 for studying the Ramsey growth model, it is straightforward to show that in a steady state the first-order conditions imply; that is, $1 + r(1 - t_r) = 1/\beta$, or

$$r_n = r(1 - t_r) = \rho. \tag{10.3}$$

Thus, (10.3) implies that the steady state level of capital per worker in the Ramsey growth model is fixed by the interest income tax rate and the rate of time preference. We also have the following condition:

$$U_m(c, m)/U_c(c, m) = [1 + \theta_m - \beta(1 + r_m)]/(1 + \theta). \tag{10.4}$$

This states that the marginal rate of substitution between liquidity and consumption is equal to the opportunity cost of holding money.

The last element of the model is the government's budget constraint. We will assume throughout this chapter that the government collects taxes that are rebated back to the consumer in a nondistorting fashion in the same period the revenue is collected. In addition, the government issues money in order collect seigniorage. The money supply grows at the rate μ according to

$$M_t = (1 + \mu)M_{t-1}, \tag{10.5}$$

where M_t is the total nominal stock of money at time t. The government's budget constraint net of any taxes is

$$g_{mt} = (M_t - M_{t-1})/p_t, \tag{10.6}$$

where p_t is the price level at time t. This is the amount of seigniorage the government can collect at time t. The government is constrained by the amount of money private agents are willing to hold.

In a steady state with money or *stationary monetary equilibrium* (SME), the real per capita value of money is constant, $m_t = m_{t-1}$. It follows that $1 + r_m = 1/(1 + \mu)$. To see this, note that in an SME, $M_t/p_t = M_{t+1}/p_{t+1}$ since $M/p = m$ in a representative agent economy. Thus, after rearranging, $p_t/p_{t+1} = M_t/M_{t+1} = 1/(1 + \mu)$. But $1 + r_m = p_t/p_{t+1}$ and the conclusion follows that $1 + r_m = 1/(1 + \mu)$, where μ is also the rate of inflation. In equilibrium, we can rewrite (10.6) using (10.5) as

$$g_{mt} = \mu M_t/p_t(1 + \mu) = \mu m_t/(1 + \mu). \tag{10.7}$$

First, consider the interest income tax. Let $t_r > 0$, $\theta = \theta_m = 0$, and $T = rt_r k$. It is immediate from (10.3) that capital per worker is decreasing in the interest income tax rate. We can equation (10.3) to obtain $K(t_r)$ with $dk/dt_r = K' < 0$. Thus, the real interest rate is increasing in the interest income tax rate, $dr/dt_r > 0$.

Next, notice that (10.2) matches up with the resource constraint in a steady state since $w + rk = y$ and $T = rt_r k$. Thus, we have the two-equation system in (c, m),

$$c + \mu m/(1 + \mu) = f(K(t_r)),$$
$$U_m(c, m) = [1 - \beta(1 + r_m)]U_c(c, m).$$

It is straightforward to show by differentiating this system that both consumption and real cash balances fall in response to the interest income tax rate if the marginal utility of cash balances is nondecreasing in consumption, $U_{mc} \geq 0$. It follows that seigniorage decreases with the interest income tax, from (10.7). Therefore, a government that attempts to rely more heavily on the taxation of capital may lose some of its ability to collect seigniorage.

The intuition is that the tax on capital reduces capital accumulation and this reduces income. The reduction in income causes both consumption and liquidity to fall. The drop in demand for money reduces the ability of the government to collect seigniorage.

Next, consider the consumption tax. First, suppose money is included in the tax base, $\theta_m = \theta > 0$ and $T = \theta c + \theta_m m$. Equation (10.3) will continue to hold. It is immediate from (10.3) that the consumption tax has no effect on capital accumulation and hence none on the real interest rate in the steady state. In addition, the system is given by

$$c + \mu m/(1 + \mu) = y^*,$$
$$U_m(c, m)/U_c(c, m) = 1 - \beta(1 + r_m)/(1 + \theta),$$

where $y^* = f(k^*)$ is fixed. The consumption tax rate enters the MRT. Indeed, it serves to raise it and thus provide the agent with an incentive to raise the MRS by reducing the ratio of liquidity to consumption. It is straightforward to show by differentiating the last two equations that the demand for money falls with the consumption tax, while consumption paradoxically increases with the consumption tax rate. In addition, seigniorage falls as the demand for money falls.

The reason for this result is that capital accumulation is a favored means of saving for the future relative to liquidity when cash balances are taxed at the consumption tax rate. However, in this model capital accumulation in an SME is fixed relative to the consumption tax. Therefore, if the consumer wishes to reduce her holdings of money, she must increase her consumption since her steady state income is fixed relative to the tax. Thus, if money is taxed at the consumption tax rate, the consumer has an incentive to shift from liquidity toward consumption, given her fixed income level.

Finally, consider the case where money is not included in the consumption tax base, $\theta_m = 0$ and $T = \theta c$. Once again, capital accumulation and the real interest rate are not affected by the tax. Second, the system is given by

$$c + \mu m/(1 + \mu) = y^*,$$
$$U_m(c, m)/U_c(c, m) = [1 - \beta(1 + r_m)]/(1 + \theta).$$

Now liquidity is favored relative to consumption, and it can be shown that the demand for money increases with the tax while consumption falls. In addition, seigniorage increases as a result.

10.2.2. *Cash and credit goods in the Ramsey growth model*

There is one consumption good, which can be purchased in two different ways, using cash or credit. Cash goods, as the name suggests, can be purchased only with real cash balances, while credit goods can be financed. Let c_{1t} represent the cash good at time t and c_{2t} represent the credit good, where $c_t = c_{1t} + c_{2t}$ is consumption. The one consumption good available is produced via a neoclassical, constant-returns-to-scale technology, as before. Firms producing the consumption good maximize profit and profit is zero in equilibrium. The resource constraint at time t is (10.1) again, where $c_t = c_{1t} + c_{2t}$ for all $t \geq 0$.

The agent's period utility is given by $U(c_{1t}, c_{2t})$, which satisfies the usual assumptions, and her lifetime utility function is $\Sigma_t \beta^t U(c_{1t}, c_{2t})$. The representative consumer's budget constraint is (10.2) with $c_t = c_{1t} + c_{2t}$. In addition to this, the so-called cash in advance (CIA) constraint is

$$(1 + r_{mt})m_{t-1} \geq (1 + \theta)c_{1t}; \qquad (10.8)$$

the consumer must have enough cash at the beginning of the period to buy the cash good each period. Notice that when the consumption tax is imposed the agent must have at least enough cash to buy the cash good and pay the tax imposed on it. We will assume that this constraint is binding in equilibrium.

Equation (10.5) governs the supply of money so the stock of nominal money grows at rate μ as before. The government continues to collect seigniorage according to (10.6) and lumpsum rebates tax revenue back to the consumer in the period the revenue is collected. Markets are competitive and per capita real cash balances settle down to a constant in an SME. It follows from this that $1 + r_m = 1/(1 + \mu)$ in an SME.

The consumer's decision problem is to choose infinite sequences of the cash good, the credit good, cash balances, and capital to maximize lifetime utility subject to the budget constraint each period, the CIA constraint each period, and the initial stocks of capital and money. The first-order conditions of this decision problem can once again be used to inform us about the effects of tax policy.[1]

First, consider the interest income tax in an SME. It can be shown that we obtain (10.3) once again from the first-order conditions of the consumer's problem. From this, it is immediate that the interest income tax has the same impact on capital accumulation in this model as in the MUF version of the model studied in the last section; capital accumulation falls, and the real interest rate rises in response to the tax.

To close the model, solve (10.3) for k once again to obtain $K(t_r)$, and use the definition of the lumpsum rebate, $T = rt_r k$, the CIA constraint, and $y = w + rk$, in the consumer's budget constraint in a steady state to get[2]

$$f(K(t_r)) = m + c_2.$$

We also obtain the following first-order condition:

$$\beta U_1[m/(1+\mu), c_2] - (1+\mu)U_2[m/(1+\mu), c_2] = 0.$$

By differentiating these last two equations, it is straightforward to see that the demand for money will decrease in equilibrium in response to the capital income tax. The amount of seigniorage the government can collect will also fall with the tax rate.

The intuition is that the tax will induce a decline in capital accumulation. This lowers income and reduces the demand for both the cash and credit goods. Since less of the cash good is being consumed, the consumer needs to hold less cash and so the demand for cash falls and seigniorage falls as a result.

Next, consider the consumption tax when money is taxed at the consumption tax rate. Set $\theta_m = \theta > 0$ and $T = \theta_c + \theta_m m$. As in the last section, we obtain $r = f_k(k) = \rho$ and it follows that capital accumulation is unaffected by the consumption tax. The system can be collapsed to the following:

$$[\mu + 1/(1+\theta)]m + c_2 = f(k^*),$$
$$\beta U_1[m/(1+\mu)(1+\theta), c_2] - (1+\mu)(1+\theta)U_2[m/(1+\mu)(1+\theta), c_2] = 0.$$

There are now two effects to consider because the tax rate enters the MRT and it enters the CIA constraint. To see this, rewrite the last equation to obtain $\beta U_1/U_2 = (1+\mu)(1+\theta)$. Clearly, the tax rate increases the MRT. This provides the consumer with an incentive to reduce her consumption of the cash good and increase her consumption of the credit good because of a substitution effect. However, the tax rate also enters the CIA constraint, forcing the consumer to obtain more cash in order to pay the consumption tax imposed on the cash good. The consumer thus has an incentive to obtain more cash and less credit because of this. We can label this a "cash constraint" effect.

The response of the demand for money and the credit good is ambiguous because the two effects work in opposite directions (see Appendix 10A). And, since the response of money is ambiguous, the effect of the tax on seigniorage will also be ambiguous. It is also shown in Appendix 10A that total consumption may rise or fall in response to the tax.

Suppose cash balances are not taxed, $\theta_m = 0$. In that case we obtain (10.3) once again, so capital accumulation is still unaffected by the tax, and the system becomes

$$[\mu + 1/(1+\theta)]m + c_2 = f(k^*),$$
$$\beta U_1[m/(1+\mu)(1+\theta), c_2] - (1+\mu)U_2[m/(1+\mu)(1+\theta), c_2] = 0.$$

Now there is only a "cash constraint" effect. The demand for money increases while the demand for credit falls with the tax. Total consumption also falls with the tax. In addition, since the demand for money increases, seigniorage will increase with the tax.

Table 10.1. Results from the Ramsey growth model[a]

Model	Interest income tax	Consumption tax
Money in the utility function (MUF) model	$dr/dt_r > 0$, $dg_m/dt_r < 0$.	$\theta_m = \theta$: $dr/d\theta = 0$, $dg_m/d\theta < 0$. $\theta_m = 0$: $dr/d\theta = 0$, $dg_m/d\theta > 0$.
Cash and credit goods (CCG) Model	$dr/dt_r > 0$, $dg_m/dt_r < 0$.	$\theta_m = \theta$: $dr/d\theta = 0$, $dg_m/d\theta(\lessgtr)0$. $\theta_m = 0$: $dr/d\theta = 0$, $dg_m/d\theta(>)0$.

a   The tax experiment entails a lumpsum rebate of the revenue in the period it is taken and the results are evaluated at the initial no-tax equilibrium.

10.2.3. Summary

Our results from the Ramsey growth model are depicted in Table 10.1. Clearly, the two versions of the model deliver the same qualitative implications with regard to the interest income tax. One surprising difference between the models is that consumption actually *increases* under the consumption tax when money is taxed at the consumption tax rate in the MUF model but may fall in the CCG model. In addition, their implications also differ slightly with respect to the consumption tax when money is taxed.

The reason for the difference in results is that real money balances enter the utility function directly in the MUF version of the model but indirectly by substituting the CIA constraint when it is binding into the utility function in the CCG version of the model. We have $U(c, m)$ in the MUF model and $U(m/(1 + \mu)(1 + \theta), c_2)$ in the cash and credit goods model. Thus, the consumption tax rate inadvertently enters the utility function through the CIA constraint in the CCG version of the model, and this can cause the results to differ. Indeed, this is the source of the "cash constraint" effect.

10.3. The overlapping generations model

10.3.1. The money in the utility function (MUF) in the OG model

The economy lasts for ever and time is discrete. The population is stationary. At time t, N_t identical agents are born and each lives for two periods, working in the first and retired in the second. We will normalize by assuming $N_t = 1$ for all t. The initial old generation owns K_1/N_0 units of physical capital and M_1/N_0 units of fiat currency, where K_1 is the total capital stock in the first period of the economy and M_1 is the total stock of money in the first period.

There is one consumption good available which is produced via a well behaved neoclassical CRS technology. The preferences of the representative agent born at time t depend on consumption in each period and real cash balances according to $U(c_{1t}, c_{2t}, m_t)$, where c_{jt} is the consumption of the representative agent in the jth period of life, and m_t is real cash balances. The agent's decision problem is to choose consumption, capital, and money to maximize utility subject to the following constraints:

$$T_{1t} + w_t - (1 + \theta)c_{1t} - s_t - (1 + \theta_m)m_t = 0,$$
$$T_{2t} + [1 + r_{t+1}(1 - t_{rt+1})]s_t + (1 + r_{mt+1})m_t - (1 + \theta)c_{2t} = 0,$$

where s is capital accumulation and T_{jt} is a lumpsum rebate of revenue collected in period of life j. Since we seek an equilibrium where capital is strictly positive, we can collapse the budget constraints to obtain the wealth constraint,

$$T_{1t} + w_t - (1 + \theta)c_{1t} + R_{nt+1}[T_{2t} - (1 + \theta)(c_{2t} - q_n m_t)] = 0,$$

where $R_{nt+1} = 1/[1 + r_{t+1}(1 - t_{rt+1})]$ and $q_n = [(1 + \theta_m)(1 + r_n) - (1 + r_m)]/(1 + \theta)$ is the net opportunity cost of liquidity. Solve for c_2 and substitute the resulting equation into the utility function in order to derive the first-order conditions for c_1 and m,

$$U_1/U_2 = 1 + r_n \quad \text{and} \quad U_m/U_2 = q_{nt+1}.$$

The first condition governs the intertemporal consumption decision while the second condition governs the liquidity decision.

We can generally solve the first-order conditions to obtain the demand functions $c(w, 1 + r_n, q_n, T_1, T_2)$ and $m(w, 1 + r_n, q_n, T_1, T_2)$. The supply of capital can be defined as

$$s(w, 1 + r_n, q_n) = w + T_1 - (1 + \theta)c(w, 1 + r_n, q_n) - (1 + \theta_m)m(w, 1 + r_n, q_n),$$

where we have abstracted from the revenue rebates as arguments in the functions.

Firms maximize profit and hence $r = f_k(k)$. Solving, $k(r)$ determines the amount of capital per worker that firms in the aggregate are willing to hire. The gross wage is determined by $w = f(k(r)) - rk(r) = w(r)$, with $w_r = -k$. In an SME equilibrium, $1 + r_m = 1/(1 + \mu)$, as before. In addition, to close the model we have the equilibrium condition that characterizes the capital market,

$$s(w, 1 + r_n, q_n) = (1 + n)k(r). \tag{10.9}$$

This is a major difference between the OG model and the Ramsey growth model. Capital is not fixed in a steady state in the OG model.

First, consider the interest income tax. Set $T_{1t} = 0$, $\theta_m = \theta = 0$, and $T_{2t} = rt_r s$. The experiment involves $dT_2 = rsdt_r$ evaluated in the initial equilibrium. Both decisions will be distorted by the tax since the tax rate enters both r_n and q_n. It is shown in Appendix 10B that we can write the response to the tax in the following way:

$$c_{tr} = dc_1/dt_r = -r(c_{ru} + c_{qu}), \tag{10.10a}$$
$$m_{tr} = dm/dt_r = -r(m_{ru} + m_{qu}), \tag{10.10b}$$

where X_{ru} is the compensated effect of r on X and X_{qu} is the compensated effect of q on X, for $X = c, \mu$. The response of the supply of capital is given by

$$s_{tr} = ds/dt_r = -r(s_{ru} + s_{qu}) = r(c_{ru} + m_{ru} + c_{qu} + m_{qu}). \qquad (10.10c)$$

The first term in each derivative in (10.10a) and (10.10b) captures the effect of the tax on the net interest rate, while the second term captures the effect of the tax on the net opportunity cost of liquidity. Similarly, in the response of capital, $c_{ru} + m_{ru}$ captures the effect of the tax rate working through the after tax interest rate while $c_{qu} + m_{qu}$ captures the effect of the tax rate working through the opportunity cost of liquidity.

Several remarks are in order. The comparative statics for this model are derived in Appendix 10B. If first-period consumption and money demand are both decreasing in the real interest rate when compensated, then capital accumulation will be increasing in the real interest rate. If, in addition, first-period consumption and money demand are both decreasing in the opportunity cost of holding money when compensated, then capital accumulation will also be increasing in the opportunity cost of holding money. In that case, the supply of capital decreases with the tax on income.

Second, the tax affects the net cost of liquidity, and this causes a new effect on consumption and hence on saving in physical capital. This is captured by the second term in (10.10a), c_{qu}, which also enters (10.10c) through s_{qu}. This is what makes the comparative statics somewhat ambiguous. It is possible for consumption to fall and the supply of capital to rise in response to the tax, the opposite of our earlier results in Chapters 2 and 3, although this possibility is somewhat unlikely.

Third, there is an additional effect in (10.10c) that works through the demand for money directly. If the effect involving m_{tr} is ignored, one may incorrectly estimate the response of capital accumulation to the imposition of the tax.

It is an easy exercise to show that the compensated demand for money is decreasing in the opportunity cost of holding money and that first-period consumption is also decreasing in the interest rate when compensated. If the compensated demand for money is also decreasing in the interest rate, then first-period consumption must also be decreasing in the opportunity cost of holding money. This follows by symmetry of the Slutsky matrix. If this is true, it then follows that the supply of capital is increasing in the interest rate and in the opportunity cost of holding and thus is decreasing in the interest income tax rate.[3]

Essentially, the interest income tax has three effects on saving behavior. First, total saving, $s + m$, will be affected by the tax, since the tax will generally affect the agent's intertemporal consumption plan. It is most likely that a dramatic increase in the taxation of capital would induce agents to shift their consumption from the future to the present and thus would reduce their total saving. This is a *savings effect* and is mentioned by Feldstein, among others, as a reason for eliminating the tax on capital. (See our discussion in Chapter 2.) Second, the composition of saving between physical capital and money will also be affected by the tax. We would most likely expect a decrease in the return to physical capital and a decline in the opportunity cost of holding money to induce a shift from capital to money, holding the level of total saving fixed. This is a *portfolio composition effect*. Finally, labor earnings is also reduced by the income tax, although we have abstracted from this effect in this chapter. In general, we would expect this effect to reduce total saving and hence the supply of capital as well.

To obtain the response of capital per worker to the tax, differentiate the capital market equilibrium condition,

$$dr/dt_r = -s_{tr}/D = r(s_{ru} + s_{qu})/D, \qquad (10.11)$$

where $D = s_r + s_q - ks_w - (1+n)k_r > 0$ implies that the initial equilibrium in the capital market is stable. The result in (10.11) extends the classic result of the literature on the incidence of the interest income tax, e.g. Diamond's (1970) result, discussed in Chapter 2.

The most likely case to consider is where capital accumulation is increasing in the return on capital and increasing in the opportunity cost of money. Therefore, it is most likely that the real interest rate will increase with the tax rate as total savings falls with the tax, as agents shift their portfolios from capital to money, and as they respond to the tax on labor earnings. It is the second effect that extends Diamond's result and serves to reinforce it, under our assumptions. However, it is theoretically possible for capital accumulation to increase with the tax since the comparative statics are formally ambiguous, although this is somewhat unlikely.

It is also straightforward to show that the effect of the income tax on seigniorage is ambiguous:

$$dg_m/dt_r = -[r\mu/(1+\mu)](m_r + m_q)[1 + (1 - 1/t_r)\varepsilon], \qquad (10.12)$$

where $\varepsilon = (t_r/r)(dr/dt_r)$ is the elasticity of the interest rate with respect to the tax rate. The term $(m_r + m_q)$ captures the direct effect of the tax on the demand for money and is most likely negative. For small values of the tax rate and the elasticity, it is possible for the term $(1 - 1/t_r)\varepsilon$ to be negative; for example, if $\varepsilon = 0.1$ and $t_r = 0.05$, $(1 - 1/t_r)\varepsilon = -0.9$. However, for more realistic values it will be positive; for example, if $\varepsilon = 0.1$ and $t_r = 0.2$, then $(1 - 1/t_r)\varepsilon = 0.60$. So for realistic values for the tax rate, seigniorage increases with the tax.

The response of lifetime consumption to the tax is ambiguous. In this model consumption will respond directly to the tax and indirectly to the change in the real interest rate. An increase in the tax rate may shift consumption from the second period to the first period. However, whether the individual's total consumption will rise or fall cannot be determined.

To analyze the consumption tax when money is included in the base, set $t_r = 0$, $T_1 = \theta_m m + \theta_{c_1}$, $\theta = \theta_m$, and $T_2 = \theta_{c_2}$, and once again adjust the lumpsum rebates to eliminate any income effects. The representative agent's budget constraint is

$$w_t + T_{1t} - (1 + \theta_{1t})c_{1t} - R_{t+1}[(1 + \theta_{2t})c_{2t} + q_{nt+1}m_t - T_{2t}] = 0,$$

where $q_n = 1 + r - (1 + r_m)/(1 + \theta)$. Now only the liquidity decision will be distorted by the tax since the consumption tax rate enters the opportunity cost of liquidity:

$$U_m/U_2 = 1 + r - (1 + r_m)/(1 + \theta).$$

We can solve the first-order conditions to obtain the decision functions

$$c(w, r, q_n), \quad m(w, r, q_n), \quad \text{and} \quad s(w, r, q_n),$$

where the supply of capital is defined as $s_t = w_t + T_{1t} - (1 + \theta_{1t})(c_{1t} + m_t)$. The representative agent's response to the consumption tax, assuming lumpsum redistribution of the tax revenue, is

$$dc_1/d\theta = [1/(1 + \mu)]c_{qu}, \tag{10.13a}$$

$$dm/d\theta = [1/(1 + \mu)]m_{qu} < 0, \tag{10.13b}$$

$$ds/d\theta = -(1 + \theta)(dc_t/d\theta + dm/d\theta). \tag{10.13c}$$

It follows immediately that the demand for money falls with the tax, which should follow intuitively. If the supply of capital decreases with the tax, capital accumulation will also fall. This response will serve to increase the real interest rate. However, if first-period consumption falls with the tax, capital accumulation may increase, and as a result the real interest rate may fall. In addition, the drop in the demand for money will serve to reduce the amount of seigniorage the government can collect. To see this, notice that

$$dg_m/d\theta = [\mu/(1 + \mu)]\{[1/(1 + \mu)]m_{qu} + (m_r + m_q - km_w)(dr/d\theta)\}.$$

The first term, $[1/(1 + \mu)]m_{qu}$, captures the direct effect of the tax. The second term, $(m_r + m_q - km_w)(dr/d\theta)$, is negative if the demand for money is decreasing in r and q and increasing in w, and if the real interest rate rises or if the direct effect dominates.

When cash balances are not included in the consumption tax base the opportunity cost of holding cash is $q_n = (r - r_m)/(1 + \theta)$. Once again, the liquidity decision will be distorted by the tax. The response to the tax is

$$dc_1/d\theta = -qc_{qu}, \tag{10.14a}$$

$$dm/d\theta = -qm_{qu} > 0, \tag{10.14b}$$

$$ds/d\theta = -(1 + \theta)dc_t/d\theta - dm/d\theta. \tag{10.14c}$$

This is very different from the earlier response when cash balances were taxed. The demand for money increases unambiguously in response to the tax.

The intuition is that the tax reduces the opportunity cost of holding cash relative to consumption and the agent responds by increasing her demand for money. If first-period consumption and money are compensated complements, which follows by symmetry if money demand is decreasing in the interest rate when compensated, consumption will also increase in response to the tax. This is somewhat paradoxical; one would think that consumption would decrease in response to the imposition of the consumption based tax. The supply of capital will fall if both money and first-period consumption increase. This will serve to raise the real interest rate. However, formally the response is ambiguous.

The response of seigniorage is ambiguous. Differentiate the government's budget constraint to obtain

$$dg_m/d\theta = -[\mu/(1+\mu)][qm_{qu} - (m_r + m_q - km_w)(dr/d\theta)].$$

The first term is negative and this serves to increase seigniorage. This is the direct effect of the tax. However, the second term is positive if the real interest rate increases with the tax. Therefore, the net result is ambiguous—seigniorage could rise or fall with the tax. If the direct effect dominates, then seigniorage increases with the tax.

10.3.2. *Cash and credit goods in the OG model*

In this section we will specialize the OG model to include cash and credit goods. Population is constant, production is neoclassical, and the government supplies money to obtain seigniorage as before. Agents live for two periods. However, we will assume that utility depends only on second-period consumption. Let c_1 represent the cash good and c_2 represent the credit good.

The representative consumer's utility is $U(c_{1t}, c_{2t})$, which satisfies the usual properties. The budget constraints are

$$w_t + T_{1t} = s_t + (1 + \theta_m)m_t,$$
$$[1 + r_{t+1}(1 - t_{rt+1})]s_t + T_{2t} + (1 + r_{mt+1})m_t - (1 + \theta)(c_{1t} + c_{2t}) = 0.$$

The cash in advance constraint is

$$(1 + r_{mt+1})m_t \geq (1 + \theta)c_{1t}.$$

This will hold with equality in equilibrium. Collapse the two budget constraints, eliminating s, substitute the resulting constraint and the CIA constraint into the utility function, and differentiate with respect to cash balances to obtain

$$L_m = (1 + r_m)U_1 - (1 + r_n)(1 + \theta_m)U_2 = 0. \qquad (10.15)$$

First, consider the interest income tax. Set $T_1 = 0$, $\theta = \theta_m = 0$, $T_2 = rt_r s$. Since $1 + r_m = 1/(1 + \mu)$, the first-order condition becomes $U_1/U_2 = (1 + \mu)$ $[1 + r(1 - t_r)]$ and the allocation decision between the cash and credit goods will be distorted by the tax.

A convenient way of developing the model is to notice that from profit maximization we know that capital per worker will be a function of the real interest rate, $k(r)$ with $dk/dr = k_r < 0$. We also know that the real wage rate too will be a function of the real interest rate, $w(r)$ with $dw/dr = w_r = -k$. In addition, we have $k = s$, and $y = w + rk$. Add the budget constraints of the consumer, use the CIA, the definition of the lumpsum rebate, and the information just mentioned, $k(r)$ and $w(r)$, to simplify the resulting equation:

$$f(k(r)) = m + c_2. \qquad (10.16)$$

We also have the first-period budget constraint,

$$w(r) = k(r) + m. \qquad (10.17)$$

Equations (10.15)–(10.17) are three equations in (r, c_2, m) as a function of the tax rate, t_r. Differentiating,

$$dr/dt_r = rU_2/H, \qquad (10.18)$$
$$dm/dt_r = -rU_2(k + k_r)/H, \qquad (10.19)$$
$$dc_2/dt_r = rU_2(rk_r + k + k_r)/H, \qquad (10.20)$$

where $H = U_2 + (k + k_r)[(1 + r_m)^2 U_{11} - (2 + r_n)(1 + r_m)U_{12} + (1 + r_n)U_{22}]$. $H > 0$ if $k + k_r < 0$ and $U_{12} \geq 0.$[4]

It is immediate that the real interest rate increases in response to the tax rate. This coincides with our earlier results. However, it appears that the demand for money increases with the tax. Furthermore, demand for the credit good also falls with the tax. The tax induces agents to shift from the credit good to the cash good. Seigniorage increases as a result. However, by combining results and using the CIA, it can be shown that total consumption falls with the tax.

Next, consider the consumption tax and suppose cash balances are taxed at the consumption tax rate. Set $t_r = 0$ and $T = \theta_m m + \theta(c_1 + c_2)$. The first-order condition from the representative consumer's decision problem is

$$(1 + r_m)U_1 - (1 + r)(1 + \theta_m)U_2 = 0.$$

The tax rate enters the MRT and thus distorts the allocation decision between the cash and credit goods.

To close the model (10.16) and (10.17) will still apply. Differentiate the three-equation system composed of the first-order condition, (10.16) and (10.17) to obtain

$$dr/d\theta = -\{(1 + r)U_2 + c_1[(1 + r_m)U_{11} - (1 + r)U_{21}]\}/H, \qquad (10.21)$$
$$dm/d\theta = \{(1 + r)U_2 + c_1[(1 + r_m)U_{11} - (1 + r)U_{21}](k + k_r)\}/H, \qquad (10.22)$$
$$dc_2/d\theta = \{(1 + r)U_2 + c_1[(1 + r_m)U_{11} - (1 + r)U_{21}](k + k_r - rk_r)\}/H. \qquad (10.23)$$

In general, these results are ambiguous. For example, the response of the real interest rate has two terms that work in the opposite direction: $(1 + r)U_2$ and $c_1[(1 + r_m)U_{11} - (1 + r)U_{21}]$.

The intuition for this is that the tax causes two effects in the CCG version of the model. First, the tax rate enters the MRT and causes the usual substitution effects. This is captured by the first term in the derivatives. Second, the tax rate enters the CIA constraint and this accounts for the second term: a higher consumption tax rate forces the consumer to hold more cash to satisfy the CIA, as in the Ramsey growth model. The substitution effect causes the consumer to switch from cash balances to real capital. This induces both the interest rate and the demand for money to fall. On the other hand, the "cash constraint" effect serves to cause the opposite to occur. And the response of seigniorage is ambiguous as a result.

If cash balances are not taxed, then there is only a "cash constraint" effect. In that case, the consumption tax induces a shift from real capital to money. This causes an increase in both the real interest rate and the demand for money, and seigniorage increases as a result.

10.3.3. Summary

Our results from the OG model are depicted in Table 10.2. The results with regard to the interest income tax match up exactly between the two versions of the model. The interest income tax in both versions of the model will cause a shift away from capital toward money. The real interest rate rises as a result. In addition, seigniorage will also increase in both versions of the model. This is an added benefit of imposing the interest income tax. However, the results with respect to the consumption tax are somewhat ambiguous and also differ between the two versions of the model.

The reason for the disparity in results across versions of the model rests with the separate CIA constraint imposed in the CCG version of the model. As in the Ramsey growth model, the consumption tax enters this constraint regardless of whether or not cash balances are taxed. However, there is no direct analogy in the MUF version of the model.

Table 10.2. Results from the OG model[a]

Model	Interest income tax	Consumption tax
Money in the utility function (MUF) model	$dr/dt_r > 0$, $dg_m/dt_r > 0$.	$\theta_m = \theta$: $dr/d\theta(\lessgtr)0$, $dg_m/d\theta < 0$. $\theta_m = 0$: $dr/d\theta(\lessgtr)0$, $dg_m/d\theta > 0$.
Cash and credit goods (CCG) model	$dr/dt_r > 0$, $dg_m/dt_r > 0$.	$\theta_m = \theta$: $dr/d\theta(\lessgtr)0$, $dg_m/d\theta \lessgtr 0$. $\theta_m = 0$: $dr/d\theta > 0$, $dg_m/d\theta > 0$.

[a] The tax experiment entails a lumpsum rebate of the revenue in the period it is taken and the results are evaluated at the initial no-tax equilibrium. The results depicted assume the direct effects dominate.

10.4. Models of legal restrictions

In this section we will study the incidence of the different tax systems within several different models and with different legal restrictions. In the next two subsections we will focus our attention on a legal restriction involving a reserve requirement. Many countries require domestic banks to hold a minimum amount of cash on reserve and so it seems reasonable to impose this sort of restriction and study its effects.[5]

In Section 10.4.3 we will study a legal restriction on issuing private debt and intermediating private debt. Many countries also restrict the ability of the private sector to intermediate private debt. Both sorts of restrictions create a demand for the government's currency which allows the government to collect seigniorage.

10.4.1. Reserve requirement in the Ramsey growth model

Consider the Ramsey growth model. Output is produced via a neoclassical technology, population is stationary and normalized to one, the money supply grows at rate μ, and the government collects seigniorage as before. We will assume that the agent must hold at least as much cash as a fraction of her capital investment, $m_t \geq \phi k_{t+1}$, where $0 < \phi < 1$. There will be two types of equilibrium, an "excess reserves" equilibrium where the reserve requirement is not binding, and a "constrained reserves" equilibrium where the constraint is binding. We will focus on the latter case, since money will be dominated in its rate of return in a "constrained reserves" equilibrium, an empirically plausible prediction.

The representative agent's lifetime utility function is $\sum_t \beta^t U(c_t)$ and her budget constraint is

$$T_t + w_t + [1 + r_t(1 - t_{rt})]k_t - k_{t+1} + (1 + r_m)m_{t-1}$$
$$- (1 + \theta_m)m_t - (1 + \theta)c_t = 0.$$

Assuming the reserve requirement is binding, we can write the budget constraint as

$$T_t + w_t + [1 + r_t(1 - t_{rt}) + \phi(1 + r_m)]k_t - [1 + \phi(1 + \theta_m)]k_{t+1}$$
$$- (1 + \theta)c_t = 0.$$

The main implication of the first-order conditions of the consumer's decision problem is the following, a version of (10.3):

$$1 + \phi(1 + \theta_m) = \beta[1 + r(1 - t_r) + \phi(1 + r_m)]. \tag{10.24}$$

Second, using the lumpsum rebate and $y = w + rk$, the budget constraint becomes

$$f(k) + \phi r_m k = c. \tag{10.25}$$

(Note that $r_m = -\mu/(1 + \mu)$, the term $\phi r_m k = -\phi \mu k/(1 + \mu) = -g_m$.) Equations (10.24) and (10.25) determine (k, c) as functions of the tax rates. Seigniorage is determined by

$$g_m = [\mu/(1 + \mu)]\phi k. \tag{10.26}$$

First, consider the interest income tax. Equation (10.24) implies that capital is decreasing in the interest income tax rate, $dk/dt_r < 0$, as before. Equation (10.25) implies that consumption is also decreasing in the tax rate. Essentially, the tax reduces capital accumulation and hence income. The decline in income in turn reduces consumption. Finally, since the agent is not investing as much after the tax as before, less cash must be held in reserve and so the derived demand for money decreases and seigniorage decreases as a result, from (10.26).

Next, consider the consumption tax when cash balances are taxed at the consumption tax rate. In that case it follows immediately from (10.24) that capital accumulation is decreasing in the consumption tax rate. An increase in the tax rate imposed on the cash balances the agent is obliged to hold is similar in spirit to an increase in the reserve requirement, and capital falls as a result of the tax. It follows from (10.26) that seigniorage falls as well.

Finally, if cash balances are not taxed, the consumption tax rate does not affect capital. The derived demand for money will also be unaffected at the margin by the tax. It follows from (10.25) and (10.26) that consumption and seigniorage will also be unaffected by the tax in this case.

10.4.2. *Reserve requirement in a borrowing–lending OG model*

Consider a pure exchange overlapping generations model where there are N_t identical lenders and N_t identical borrowers born at time t, each of whom lives for two periods. The population of both groups is stationary and normalized to one lender and one borrower. Lenders are endowed with α units of the one good available in the first period of life and none in the second period. Borrowers are endowed with β units of the good in the second period but none in the first. Preferences are the same between the two groups, $U(c_{1t}, c_{2t})$, for an agent who consumes (c_{1t}, c_{2t}) over her lifetime; that is, c_{jt} is consumption of the one consumption good available in the jth period of life. We will assume $U()$ satisfies the usual assumptions. In what follows we will not need to distinguish between the consumption of borrowers and lenders.

There are two assets that lenders can accumulate, private bonds or credit, and fiat currency issued by the government. The money supply grows at rate μ and the government collects seigniorage as before. The reserve requirement takes the form $m \geq \phi L$, where $0 < \phi < 1$ and L is the lender's total volume of loans.

There are two equilibria in this sort of model: an "excess reserves" equilibrium, where $m > \phi L$ and $r = r_m$, and a "constrained reserves" equilibrium, where $r > r_m$ and $m = \phi L$. We will focus our attention on the "constrained reserves" case as before.

The representative lender's constraints are given by

$$T_{1t} + \alpha - (1 + \theta)c_{1t} - L_t - (1 + \theta_m)m_t = 0,$$
$$T_{2t} + [1 + r_{t+1}(1 - t_{rt+1})]L_t + (1 + r_{mt+1})m_t - (1 + \theta)c_{2t} = 0,$$
$$m_t = \phi L_t.$$

We can use the last constraint to rewrite the first two in the following way:

$$T_{1t} + \alpha - (1+\theta)c_{1t} - [1 + (1+\theta_m)\phi]L_t = 0,$$
$$T_{2t} + [1 + r_{t+1}(1 - t_{rt+1}) + (1+r_m)\phi]L_t - (1+\theta)c_{2t} = 0.$$

Substitute the two constraints into the utility function for consumption and differentiate with respect to loans to obtain

$$q_2 U_2[(T_1 + \alpha - q_1 L)/(1+\theta), (T_2 + q_2 L)/(1+\theta)]$$
$$- q_1 U_1[(T_1 + \alpha - q_1 L)/(1+\theta), (T_2 + q_2 L)/(1+\theta)] = 0,$$

where $q_1 = 1 + \phi(1+\theta_m)$ and $q_2 = 1 + r_n + \phi(1+r_m)$. We can interpret q_1 as the net cost of making a loan and q_2 as the net return to making a loan.

We can solve the first-order condition for the loan function. Loans will be a function of the endowment, the net cost q_1, the net return q_2, and the lumpsum rebates. Abstracting from the rebates, we have the loan supply function $L(w, q_1, q_2)$. If consumption is a normal good, loans will be increasing in the endowment. If the substitution effects dominate, the loan will be an increasing function of the net return and a decreasing function of the net cost: $\partial L/\partial \alpha = L_\alpha > 0$, $\partial L/\partial q_1 = L_1 < 0$, and $\partial L/\partial q_2 = L_2 > 0$. Let L_I be an income effect. If $U_{12} \geq 0$, $L_I < 0$; a receipt of income in the second period reduces loans. The Slutsky equation is $L_2 = L_{2u} + LL_I$, where $L_{2u} > 0$ is a compensated effect.

The taxes will cause only income effects for the borrower, so for simplicity we will assume that the borrower pays no tax. The representative borrower chooses consumption and borrowing to maximize utility subject to the budget constraints

$$B_t = c_{1t} \quad \text{and} \quad \beta - (1+r_{t+1})B_t = c_{2t}.$$

The solution to the problem is a borrowing function, $B(\beta, 1+r)$. Borrowing will be an increasing function of the endowment if consumption is a normal good. In addition, the income and substitution effects work in the same direction to imply that borrowing is decreasing in the real interest rate. Thus, $B_r < 0$.

The "constrained reserves" equilibrium (CRE) is characterized by

$$L(\alpha, q_1, q_2) = B(\beta, 1+r). \tag{10.27}$$

Once again, lumpsum rebates will eliminate any income effects from the different tax policies. So we have not included them as arguments in the loan function.

First, consider the interest income tax and set $\theta_m = \theta = 0$, $T_1 = 0$, $T_2 = rt_r L$. It follows that $q_1 = 1 + \phi$ and $q_2 = 1 + r(1 - t_r) + \phi/(1+\mu)$. The equilibrium condition becomes

$$L(\alpha, 1 + \phi, 1 + r(1 - t_r) + \phi/(1+\mu)) = B(\beta, 1+r).$$

Differentiate to obtain

$$dr/dt_r = rL_{2u}/[(1 - t_r)L_2 - B_r] > 0.$$

It is immediate that the interest rate is increasing in the interest income tax rate.
    Seigniorage is given by

$$g_m = \mu\phi L[\alpha, 1 + \phi, 1 + r(1 - t_r) + \phi/(1 + \mu)]/(1 + \mu)$$

The response of seigniorage will depend on the response of loans, and hence on
the derived demand for money, to the after tax interest rate r_n. Unfortunately, this
is ambiguous:

$$dg_m/dt_r = \phi\mu L_2(rB_r - r_n LL_1)/(1 + \mu)[(1 - t_r)L_2 - B_r]. \qquad (10.28)$$

The denominator is positive. However, the numerator is ambiguous. If B_r
dominates, the after tax interest rate increases, loans increase, and lenders must
raise the amount of cash they hold in reserve. Seigniorage increases as a result.
The opposite occurs if L_1 dominates.
    Next, consider the consumption tax and suppose that cash balances are taxed
at the consumption tax rate. Set $t_r = 0$, $\theta_m = \theta$, $T_1 = \theta_m \phi L + \theta c_1$, and $T_2 = \theta c_2$.
It follows that $q_1 = 1 + \phi(1 + \theta)$ and $q_2 = 1 + r + \phi/(1 + \mu)$. The CRE con-
dition becomes

$$L[\alpha, 1 + \phi(1 + \theta), 1 + r + \phi/(1 + \mu)] = B(\beta, 1 + r).$$

Differentiate this condition to obtain

$$dr/d\theta = -\phi L_{1u}/(L_2 - B_r) > 0, \qquad (10.29)$$
$$dg_m/d\theta = -\mu\phi^2(LL_2 L_\alpha + L_1 B_r)/(1 + \mu)(L_2 - B_r) < 0. \qquad (10.30)$$

The tax on cash balances increases the net cost of holding money and hence of
making loans. The lender responds by reducing loan volume, since this will also
reduce the amount of cash reserves she is required to hold. In turn, the reduction
in loans causes the real interest rate to increase. In addition, seigniorage falls as
the derived demand for money falls.
    On the other hand, if cash balances are not taxed, then the consumption tax is
completely nondistorting. Under our definition of the tax experiment, the tax will
have no impact on the real interest rate or seigniorage.

10.4.3. *Borrowing restrictions with limited heterogeneity*

Consider extending the model of the last subsection to include heterogeneity
among the lenders. Suppose there are rich lenders and poor lenders. A rich lender
is endowed with α_1 units of the consumption good in the first period and a poor
lender is endowed with α_2 units of the consumption good in the first period. For
simplicity, there is one of each.
    Instead of a reserve requirement, we will assume that the government passes a
law stating that there is a minimum denomination restriction on issuing bonds. A
borrower cannot issue a bond with a real value less than x, where $\alpha_1 > x > \alpha_2$. In
addition, it is illegal for small lenders to get together to intermediate a private
bond among themselves.

The restrictions will imply that only the rich lenders will be able to make loans to the borrowers. The poor lenders will hold money. The borrower solves the same decision problem as in the last subsection. This again yields the borrowing function, $B(\beta, 1 + r)$. The rich lender's decisions will be distorted only by the interest income tax, while the poor lender's decision will be distorted only by the consumption tax which includes cash balances in the tax base.

First, consider the interest income tax. From our earlier analysis, the rich lender's loan supply function is given by $L[\alpha_1, 1 + r(1 - t_r)]$. In equilibrium, this will be equal to the borrowing function. It is straightforward to show that the real interest rate will be increasing in the tax rate. However, seigniorage will not be affected because the poor lender does not pay the interest income tax.

Next, consider the consumption tax that includes cash balances in the base. The poor lender's loan function is $L(\alpha_2, 1 + r_m, \theta_m)$. Seigniorage is given by

$$g_m = [\mu/(1 + \mu)]L(\alpha_2, 1 + r_m, \theta_m),$$

where $1 + r_m = 1/(1 + \mu)$. Seigniorage is decreasing in the consumption tax rate. The tax causes the poor lender to reduce his demand for money and this in turn reduces the amount of seigniorage the government can collect. Since the poor lender is the only agent paying the tax, the real interest rate, which is determined by the interaction between rich lenders and borrowers, is unaffected by the tax. Of course, if cash balances are not taxed, the consumption tax is not distorting.

10.4.4. *Borrowing restrictions with a continuum of agents*

Next consider a simple pure exchange OG model with a stationary population where agents are endowed only in the first period but differ in their first-period endowment. Let α be the endowment and assume there is a continuum of agents. Let $f(\alpha)$ be the density function of α on the set $[\alpha_2, \alpha_1]$, where $0 < \alpha_2 < \alpha_1 < +\infty$, and assume $f()$ is uniform; $f(\alpha) = 1$ for $\alpha \in [\alpha_2, \alpha_1]$. Everyone has the same well behaved utility function $U(c_{1t}, c_{2t})$.

There are two assets available, fiat money and savings at a bank. Fiat money pays a return equal to $1 + r_m = p_t/p_{t+1}$, as before, where p_t is the price level. A deposit at the bank pays $1 + r$. However, there is a fixed cost, F, of identifying oneself to the bank in the second period in order to receive the deposit. It follows that $r > r_m$. The legal restriction is that the poorer agents cannot pool their resources in order to overcome the fixed cost of depositing the good at the bank to earn the higher rate of return. Furthermore, we will assume that $r = A(D)$ where D is the total amount deposited at the bank and $A' = dr/dD < 0$.

The budget constraints for an agent holding money are

$$T_{1t} + \alpha - (1 + \theta_m)m - (1 + \theta)c_{1t} = 0,$$
$$T_{2t} + (1 + r_m)m - (1 + \theta)c_{2t} = 0.$$

The solution to the decision problem is a savings function $s(\alpha, 1 + r_m; \theta_m)$. As in previous sections, the consumption tax will distort the money demand decision only when cash balances are taxed. The budget constraints for an agent who deposits at a bank are

$$T_{1t} + \alpha - k - (1 + \theta)c_{1t} = 0,$$
$$T_{2t} + (1 + r_n)k - F - (1 + \theta)c_{2t} = 0,$$

where k is the amount deposited and F is the fixed cost of identifying oneself to the bank correctly. The interest income tax will distort the deposit decision and the consumption tax will be neutral. The solution to this agent's decision problem is a savings function of the form $s(\alpha, 1 + r_n, F)$.

There is a cutoff endowment, α^*, such that the α^*-agent is indifferent between holding money or depositing at the bank. Agents with an endowment less than the cutoff level save by holding money, while agents with an endowment greater save by depositing at the bank. Thus total deposits are given by

$$D = \int_{\alpha^*}^{\alpha_1} s(\alpha, 1 + r_n, F)d\alpha \tag{10.31}$$

while seigniorage is given by

$$g_m = [\mu/(1 + \mu)] \int_{\alpha_2}^{\alpha^*} s(\alpha, 1 + r_m; \theta_m)d\alpha. \tag{10.32}$$

The cutoff endowment satisfies

$$U(\alpha^* - k, (1 + r)k - F) = U(\alpha^* - m, (1 + r_m)m),$$

after the tax revenue is rebated back to the consumer. The cutoff endowment is an increasing function of the interest rate on deposits and a decreasing function of the fixed cost and the return on money.[6]

We can now study the impact of taxation on the equilibrium. First, consider the interest income tax. From (10.29), the tax will affect the savings function. Differentiate using Leibnitz's rule for differentiating under an integral to obtain

$$dr/dt_r = -rA' \int s_r d\alpha / [1 - (1 - t_r)A' \int s_r d\alpha + s^* A'(d\alpha^*/dr)],$$

where $s^* = s(\alpha^*, 1 + r_n)$. Both the numerator and denominator are positive if $ds/dr = s_r > 0$. This result coincides with our earlier results. Differentiate (10.30) to obtain the response of seigniorage,

$$dg_m/dt_r = [\mu/(1 + \mu)]s^+(d\alpha^*/dr)(dr/dt_r) < 0,$$

where $s^+ = s(\alpha^*, 1 + r_m)$. The demand for money falls with the tax rate and seigniorage declines as a result.

The intuition is that when the tax is rebated income is unaffected by the tax. As the tax rate rises saving falls, and this raises the real interest rate. As the real interest rate rises, more people are attracted into the capital market from the money market and the aggregate demand for money falls as a result.

When the consumption tax is imposed and money is taxed at the consumption tax rate, the marginal rate of transformation, $(1 + r_m)/(1 + \theta_m)$, falls with the tax. The agent, therefore, has an incentive to reduce the marginal rate of substitution, U_1/U_2, by increasing first-period consumption and reducing second-period consumption. If the substitution effects dominate, saving, and hence the demand for money, falls. Seigniorage falls as a result. However, the cutoff endowment α^* is unaffected after the rebate of the revenue. It follows immediately that the real rate of interest is unaffected by the tax. Of course, when money is not taxed, the consumption tax is nondistorting in this model.

10.4.4. Summary

For the most part, the models involving legal restrictions make the same predictions. The interest income tax reduces capital accumulation or deposits at the bank and also lowers seigniorage in some but not all cases. The consumption tax that includes cash balances in the base invariably reduces the demand for money, and hence seigniorage falls as a result. The results of the legal restriction models are depicted in Table 10.3.

Table 10.3. Results from the legal restrictions models[a]

Model	Interest income tax	Consumption tax
Ramsey model with reserve requirement	$dr/dt_r > 0$, $dg_m/dt_r < 0$	$\theta_m = \theta$: $dr/d\theta > 0$, $dg_m/d\theta < 0$. $\theta_m = 0$: tax is not distorting
Borrowing–lending model with reserve requirement	$dr/dt_r > 0$, $dg_m/dt_r(\lessgtr)0$	$\theta_m = \theta$: $dr/d\theta > 0$, $dg_m/d\theta < 0$. $\theta_m = 0$: tax is not distorting
Borrowing–lending model with restrictions on intermediation	$dr/dt_r > 0$, $dg_m/dt_r = 0$	$\theta_m = \theta$: $dr/d\theta = 0$, $dg_m/d\theta < 0$. $\theta_m = 0$: tax is not distorting
Fixed cost model with a continuum of agents and restrictions on intermediation	$dr/dt_r > 0$, $dg_m/dt_r < 0$.	$\theta_m = 0$: $dr/d\theta = 0$, $dg_m/d\theta < 0$ $\theta_m = 0$: tax is not distorting

[a]   The tax experiment entails a lumpsum rebate of the revenue in the period it is collected and the results are evaluated at the initial no-tax equilibrium.

10.5. Discussion

The results of the different models contain some similarities but also some differences. Most of the models predict that the substitution effects of the interest income tax serve to reduce capital accumulation and thus raise the real interest rate. However, the models make different predictions regarding the response of seigniorage. The Ramsey model predicts that the tax will reduce capital accumulation and this reduces income in turn. The decrease in income induces the agent to lower her consumption so less cash is needed in both the MUF and CCG versions of the model. Seigniorage falls as a result. The OG model makes the opposite prediction owing to a portfolio effect. The interest income tax reduces the return to acquiring capital so the agent shifts to holding other assets like money. This increases the demand for cash and hence increases seigniorage. The models based on legal restrictions tend to predict that the demand for money will fall as agents either invest less or make fewer loans and thus need to hold less cash to meet a reserve requirement. Seigniorage falls as a result, although there is some ambiguity in this set of models.

In terms of the consumption tax when money is included in the base, the Ramsey model predicts that capital accumulation is not affected in a steady state. Both versions of the OG model predict that capital accumulation may be adversely affected. Taxing money under the consumption tax may cause agents to save less although capital accumulation may increase because of a portfolio effect. However, the CCG version of the model makes an ambiguous prediction because of a conflict between the portfolio effect and a "cash constraint" effect. The legal restrictions models mainly predict that capital accumulation may be adversely affected. In addition, all of the legal restrictions models predict that the demand for money will be adversely affected in this case and seigniorage will fall as a result.

Finally, the predictions of the models also differ significantly when money is not included in the consumption tax base. The Ramsey model predicts that the tax will not affect capital but may induce an increase in the demand for money, hence seigniorage will increase. The MUF version of the OG model makes an ambiguous prediction regarding the demand for money and capital, while the CCG version predicts that the demand for money will increase but capital will decrease. The tax in this case is nondistorting in the legal restrictions models.

The main difference between the Ramsey and OG models stems from the effect of taxes on capital accumulation. The Ramsey model makes an extreme prediction in this regard, namely, that capital accumulation in the long run will be affected only by taxes that directly affect the steady-state condition $1 = \beta(1 + r)$. This condition stems from the first-order condition

$$U_c(c_t)/U_c(c_{t+1}) = \beta(1 + r_{t+1}).$$

In a steady state, the consumption profile is flat. Therefore, $1 = \beta(1 + r)$. If the model is extended to include real cash balances as an argument in the utility function or separate utilty from cash and credit goods, the same result applies.

In the life cycle framework of the OG model, consumption may differ over the life cycle. It does not follow that

$$U_1(c_1, c_2)/U_2(c_1, c_2) = 1.$$

Therefore, the real interest rate need not be fixed in a steady state. This is also true when the basic model is extended to allow for liquidity or cash and credit goods.

The models involving legal restrictions create a demand for money by imposing a law that inhibits the ability of the private sector to intermediate private assets. In some cases we obtain the same incidence results as in the earlier models. However, in other cases the predictions differ, especially with regard to seigniorage. For example, in the last model we examined it appeared that seigniorage decreased with the interest income tax. This is the opposite prediction to that of the OG model.

10.6. Tax prepayment

Under the prepayment method of calculating the consumption tax base relative to cash, the base is $w + (1 + r)k_t - k_{t+1}$, which equals $m_t + c_{1t} + c_{2t} - (1 + r_{mt})m_{t-1}$. Thus, the agent's budget constraint in the cash and credit goods Ramsey growth model, for example, is given by

$$w_t + (1 + r_t)k_t - k_{t+1} - (1 + \theta_t)[m_t + c_{1t} + c_{2t} - (1 + r_{mt})m_{t-1}] = 0,$$

where we have applied the tax rate to $m_t + c_{1t} + c_{2t} - (1 + r_{mt})m_{t-1}$. The first-order conditions from the consumer's decision problem imply that

$$U_1/U_2 = (1 + \theta)[1 - \beta(1 + \mu)].$$

The decision between the cash and credit goods will still be distorted by the tax since the tax rate still enters the CIA constraint, even if the consumption tax is flat rate. So in this case prepayment will not suffice to eliminate the distortions of the consumption tax.

Next, consider the simplest case of the Ramsey growth model where there is a reserve requirement. Under prepayment the consumption tax base is $w_t + (1 + r_t)k_t - k_{t+1}$. This is equal to $(1 + r_m)m_{t-1} - m_t - c_t$. But with a reserve requirement, $m_{t-1} = \phi k_t$, and the base is equal to

$$w_t + (1 + r_t)k_t - k_{t+1} = (1 + r_m)m_{t-1} - m_t - c_t = (1 + r_m)\phi k_t - \phi k_{t+1} - c_t.$$

So the budget constraint is

$$w_t + (1 + r_t)k_t - k_{t+1} + (1 + \theta)[(1 + r_m)\phi k_t - \phi k_{t+1} - c_t] = 0$$

or

$$w_t + [1 + r_t + (1 + \theta)(1 + r_m)\phi]k_t - [1 + \phi(1 + \theta)]k_{t+1} - (1 + \theta)c_t = 0.$$

With this last equation as the budget constraint, the first-order conditions imply that in a steady state

$$r - \rho = (\rho - r_m)\phi(1 + \theta).$$

Now, the consumption tax will have an effect on capital accumulation. Indeed,

$$dr/d\theta = \phi(\rho - r_m).$$

In general, this is not equal to zero. It follows that the tax affects capital accumulation at the margin. Prepayment does not necessarily lead to the consumption tax being neutral. Indeed, if $r > \rho$ it follows that $\rho > r_m$ and thus $r > r_m$ so that money is dominated in its rate of return, which is observed empirically. Therefore, capital accumulation falls and the real interest rate rises with the consumption tax rate under prepayment.

The intuition is that under a binding reserve requirement the agent's asset holding is distorted; the consumer must hold assets in a certain ratio. Tax prepayment shifts the tax burden from one period to another but does nothing to ease the constraint when the constraint is binding. Therefore, the consumer's decisions will still be distorted under prepayment when the reserve requirement is binding.

10.7. Conclusion

In this chapter we have studied the tax incidence problem in the context of a monetary economy. A broad variety of models were used including the money in the utility function and the cash and credit goods versions of the Ramsey growth model and the OG model. We also studied incidence analysis within the context of models, which assumes a demand for money on the basis of a legal restriction imposed on the private sector's ability to intermediate assets.

There is a great deal of conformity in the results obtained from the different models. However, there are also some important differences. Most of the models predict that the interest income tax will reduce capital accumulation and raise the real interest rate. However, differences exist in the prediction about the effect of the tax on seigniorage. Most of the models predict that the consumption tax will distort the decision to hold money when cash balances are included in the consumption tax base. However, the consumption tax may be neutral in certain circumstances. For example, the consumption tax that exempts money will be neutral in the legal restrictions models.

We also examined the issue of tax prepayment. If money is completely ignored in calculating the tax base under the consumption tax, the tax may be neutral with respect to the decision to hold money in certain models. In other models, for example the CCG model, this will not be true. In addition, this will not be true if there is a reserve requirement. In that case, the tax will reduce the incentive to undertake investment or make deposits that are subject to the requirement. This may have a detrimental effect on capital accumulation as well. Thus, prepayment does not necessarily lead to neutrality of the consumption tax.

APPENDIX 10A: THE CASH AND CREDIT GOODS (CCG) MODEL

The representative agent chooses sequences of the cash good, the credit good, money, and capital to maximize utility subject to the budget constraint each period and the cash in advance constraint each period. The first-order conditions are

$$U_2 = \lambda_t(1+\theta), \quad \beta U_1/(1+\mu) = \lambda_t(1+\theta_m), \quad \lambda_t = \lambda_{t+1}\beta[1 + r(1 - t_r)].$$

In a steady state the multiplier is constant. Hence

$$1 = \beta[1 + r(1 - t_r)], \tag{A1}$$

or $r(1 - t_r) = f_k(k)(1 - t_r) = \rho$. Combining the first two conditions, we obtain

$$\beta U_1[m/(1+\theta)(1+\mu), c_2] - (1+\theta_m)(1+\mu)U_2[m/(1+\theta)(1+\mu), c_2] = 0. \tag{A2}$$

In a steady state the budget constraint is

$$T + y - r_t rk + [1 + r_m - (1+\theta_m)]m - (1+\theta)(c_1 + c_2) = 0, \tag{A3}$$

since $y = w + rk$. Next, use the CIA constraint to obtain

$$T + y - rt_r k - (1+\theta_m)m - (1+\theta)c_2 = 0.$$

Finally, we can use the lumpsum rebate to eliminate some of the tax parameters in the budget constraint depending on which tax policy we are studying. For the interest income tax we obtain $T = rt_r k$, and hence

$$f(k) - m - c_2 = 0. \tag{A4}$$

Therefore, we can use (A1, A2, A4) to analyze the interest income tax. The system is recursive. Solve (A1) for k as a function of t_r and substitute the resulting function into (A4) to obtain

$$f(k(t_r)) - m - c_2 = 0. \tag{A4'}$$

Also, notice that (A2) in this case becomes,

$$\beta U_1[m/(1+\mu), c_2] - (1+\mu)U_2[m/(1+\mu), c_2] = 0. \tag{A2'}$$

Thus, $(A2', A4')$ is a two-equation system in (m, c_2) and the tax rate t_r since μ is fixed. Differentiate $(A2')$ and $(A4')$ to obtain,

$$\{[\beta U_{11} - (1+\mu)U_{21}]/(1+\mu)\}dm + [\beta U_{12} - (1+\mu)U_{22}]dc_2 = 0,$$

$$dm + dc_2 = f_k k' dt_r.$$

Solving yields the comparative statics results discussed in the text when $U_{12} \geq 0$, evaluated at the initial no-tax equilibrium.

Next, consider the consumption tax. Use $t_r = 0$ and $T = \theta_m m + \theta(c_1 + c_2)$ in (A3) to obtain

$$y + r_m m - (c_1 + c_2) = 0.$$

Notice that $r_m = -\mu/(1 + \mu)$ since $1 + r_m = 1/(1 + \mu)$. From the CIA, $m = (1 + \mu)$
$(1 + \theta)c_1$. Thus, $r_m m = -\mu(1 + \theta)c_1$ and $r_m m - c_1 = -[1 + \mu(1 + \theta)]c_1 = -[1/(1 + \theta)$
$+ \mu]m/(1 + \mu)$. This yields

$$y - [\mu + 1/(1 + \theta)]m/(1 + \mu) - c_2 = 0. \tag{A4''}$$

Differentiate (A2) and (*A4''*) to obtain, when $\theta_m = \theta$,

$$dm/d\theta = (1 + \mu)U_2/J + c_1[\beta U_{11} - (1 + \mu)U_{12} - \beta U_{21} + (1 + \mu)U_{22}]/J, \tag{A5}$$

$$dc_2/d\theta = -(1 + \mu)U_2/J - [\mu c_1/(1 + \mu)][\beta U_{11} - (1 + \mu)U_{21}]/J, \tag{A6}$$

where $J = (\beta U_{11} - (1 + \mu)U_{21}/(1 + \mu) - \beta U_{12} + (1 + \mu)U_{22} < 0$ if $U_{12} \geq 0$. The
first term in (A5) captures the substitution effect and is negative; the consumption tax
imposed on cash balances raises the cost of holding cash. The second term captures the
"cash constraint" effect and is positive; a higher tax rate imposed on consumption induces
the agent to hold more cash to pay the consumption tax imposed on the cash good.
Also notice that

$$dc_1/d\theta = -c_1 + [1/(1 + \mu)](dm/d\theta) = U_2/J + [\mu c_1/(1 + \mu)U_{22}]/J.$$

It follows that

$$dc/d\theta = dc_1/d\theta + dc_2/d\theta = -\mu U_2/J + [\mu c_1/(1 + \mu)][\beta U_{12}$$
$$- (1 + \mu)U_{22} - \beta U_{11} + (1 + \mu)U_{21}]/J.$$

Finally, consider the case where cash is not taxed under the consumption tax. The first
terms drop out of (A5) and (A6), thus $dm/d\theta > 0$, $dc_2/d\theta < 0$, and $dc/d\theta < 0$.

APPENDIX 10B: MONEY IN THE UTILITY FUNCTION IN THE OG MODEL

In the MUF model under the income tax, define the first-order conditions in the
following way:

$$L_1(c_1, m; w, r_n, q_n, t_r) = U_1 - (1 + r_n)U_2,$$

$$Lm(c_1, m; w, r_n, q_n, t_r) = U_m - qnU_2,$$

where $r_n = r_{t+1}(1 - t_{rt+1})$ and $q_n = [1 + r_{t+1}(1 - t_{rt+1})] - (1 + n)/(1 + \mu)$. At the constrained optimum, $L_1 = 0$ and $L_m = 0$. Each condition can be rearranged as

$$U_1/U_2 = 1 + r(1 - t_r) \quad \text{and} \quad Um/U_2 = [1 + r_{t+1}(1 - t_r)] - (1 + n)/(1 + \mu).$$

A change in r, t_r, or q as it enters the MRT on the righthand side of each condition causes
substitution effects. The nondistorting transfer adjusts so as to eliminate the income
effects of the tax. The effect of the tax can be written in terms of the gross compensated
price effect according to

$$dc_1/d\tau = -r(dc_1/dr)_u - r(dc_1/dq)_u = -rc_{ru} - rc_{qu},$$

where $c_{ru} = (dc_1/dr)_u$ and $c_{qu} = (dc_1/dq)_u$ are compensated price effects. The first effect
captures the tax rate as it affects $(1 + r_n)$, while the second term captures its effect on q_n.
Totally differentiate the first-order conditions and solve to obtain the following
compensated price effects:

$$c_{ru} = (dc_1/dr)_u = U_2 L_{11}/J < 0,$$

$$c_{qu} = (dc_1/dq)_u = -U_2 L_{1m}/J$$

$$m_{ru} = (dm/dr)_u = -U_2 L_{m1}/J,$$

$$m_{qu} = (dm/dq)_u = U_2 L_{11}/J < 0,$$

where $L_{11} = \partial L_1/\partial c_1 = U_{11} - 2(1+r)U_{12} + (1+r)^2 U_{22} < 0, L_{mm} = \partial L_m/\partial m = U_{mm} - 2qU_{2m} + q^2 U_{22} < 0, J = L_{11}L_{mm} - L_{1m}L_{m1} > 0$, and so on. It is immediate that $c_{ru} < 0$ and $m_{qu} < 0$. If utility is separable in m and $U_{12} \geq 0$, then $L_{1m} = L_{m1} < 0$ and $c_{qu} > 0$ and $m_{ru} > 0$. More generally, if $U_{1m} = \partial U_1/\partial m > 0$ and is large in magnitude, then $L_{1m} > 0$ is possible and in that case $c_{qu} < 0$ and $m_{ru} < 0$. Intuitively, an increase in r, given q, might cause the individual to shift toward holding more capital in his portfolio and less money when compensated. If liquidity is required for most transactions, then consumption would also tend to fall with an increase in the opportunity cost of money when compensated.

Capital accumulation can be defined as $s = w - c - m$. Thus, the compensated responses are given by

$$s_{ru} = -(c_{ru} + m_{ru}),$$
$$s_{qu} = -(c_{qu} + m_{qu}).$$

It follows from this that capital accumulation increases with the real interest rate and the opportunity cost of holding money if first-period consumption and the demand for money are both decreasing in the two variables. The methodology for the case involving the consumption tax is very similar and is left to the reader.

NOTES TO CHAPTER 10

1. The Lagrangean for the consumer is

$$\Sigma_t \beta^t \{U[(1 + r_{mt-1})m_{t-1}/(1+\theta), c_{2t}] + \lambda_t[T_t + w_t + (1+r_n)k_t - k_{t+1} - m_t - (1+\theta)c_{2t}]\},$$

   where we have used the CIA for c_{1t}.
2. After using $T = rt_r k$ and $k_t = k_{t+1}$ in a steady state, we obtain

$$w + rk + (1 + r_m)m - c_1 - c_2 - m = 0.$$

   Since $y = w + rk$ and $(1 + r_m)m = c_1$, we have,

$$y - (1+\mu)c_1 - c_2 = 0,$$

   where $(1 + r_m) = 1/(1+\mu)$ as before.
3. Unfortunately, we know of no empirical work on the consumption function, for example, that includes the opportunity cost of holding money in the estimation. This model would suggest that this is an oversight which might lead to an "omitted variables" bias in the existing literature. In other words, the estimated interest elasticity of saving might be confounding two effects: the direct interest rate effect and an indirect effect involving the opportunity cost of holding money, if the opportunity cost of holding money is not included in the estimation as a separate variable.
4. Suppose production is Cobb–Douglas, $y = k^\alpha$. Then $r = \alpha k^{\alpha-1}$ so $k(r) = (r/\alpha)^{1/(\alpha-1)}$ and $k_r = (1/\alpha)[1/(\alpha - 1)](r/\alpha)^{(2-\alpha)/(\alpha-1)} = (1/\alpha)[1/(\alpha - 1)]k^{2-\alpha}$. Thus, $k + k_r = k\{1 + (1/\alpha)[1/(\alpha - 1)]k^{1-\alpha}\}$. Suppose $\alpha = 1/3$. Then $k + k_r = k[1 - (9/2)k^{2/3}]$. It follows that if $k > [\alpha(1 - \alpha)]^{1/(1-\alpha)}$, then $k + k_r < 0$. For example, if $\alpha = 1/3$, then the condition is: $k > 0.1047$.

5. In what follows we will abstract from the banking system and impose the reserve requirement directly on the individual agents holding the money for the sake of simplicity. We could include a competitive banking sector in the model without altering our results at all. See Fama (1980).

6. Let (c_{1k}, c_{2k}) be consumption if the α^*-agent holds k and (c_{1m}, c_{2m}) be consumption if the α^*-agent holds money instead. Take a Taylor's series expansion to obtain

$$U_1(c_{1k}, c_{2k}) \cong U_1(c_{1m}, c_{2m}) + (c_{1k} - c_{1m})U_{11}(c_{1m}, c_{2m}) + (c_{2k} - c_{2m})U_{12}(c_{1m}, c_{2m}).$$

Clearly, $c_{1k} < c_{1m}$ and $c_{2k} > c_{2m}$. Therefore, if $U_{12} \geq 0$, then $U_1(c_{1k}, c_{2k}) > U_1(c_{1m}, c_{2m})$. This is sufficient to sign the comparative statics obtained by differentiating the condition defining α^*.

11

Consumption Taxation in the Presence of Bequests

11.1. Introduction

The models we have considered so far treat the individual as the basic decision-maker for the most part. However, in reality people are connected to one another in a variety of ways. One such way is the manner in which people interact within the family. The salient feature of this interaction for our purpose is the fact that many people within families are connected by transfers.

The purpose of this chapter is to study the neutrality of the consumption tax and the impact a non-neutral tax may have in the presence of cash transfers across generations within the family when there are different motives for bequeathing. Several models of bequests will be studied. The two main models we will study are the altruism model, where the parent cares about the consumption or welfare of the offspring, and the bequest as consumption model, where the parent cares about the actual size of the bequest itself. We will also briefly study the strategic bequest model, where the parent uses the bequest to strategically induce the offspring to take an action the parent cares about. However, the implications of this model with regard to the consumption tax are very similar to the altruism model. The assumptions that are common across models are that the parent has perfect access to the capital market, the consumption tax is constant across generations, and labor supply is exogenous. These assumptions, if taken alone, would imply that the consumption tax would be neutral with regard to economic behavior at the margin in the absence of bequests. Of course, the consumption tax will distort the labor–leisure decision regardless of the treatment of bequests.

The main issue when bequests exist is whether or not they should be taxed under the consumption tax. There are equity as well as efficiency arguments that must be considered. Obviously, one could easily justify a tax on bequests, especially a tax on large bequests, on equity grounds.[1] Indeed, many countries tax estates at very high rates. However, in this chapter we will focus on the efficiency properties of the tax treatment of bequests. In terms of the efficiency properties of the tax, we will show that the altruism model and the bequest as consumption model make the exact opposite predictions about the neutrality of the consumption tax and about what happens when neutrality fails in each model.

This difference in the implications for neutrality of the different models is quite significant, because the rest of our assumptions in this chapter would imply that the consumption tax is completely neutral. Extending the simple two-period model by incorporating heterogeneous agents, who differ only in their motive for making a bequest to the next generation, would imply that it would be virtually impossible for the government to introduce a neutral consumption tax. The reason is that it would be very difficult, if not impossible, for the government to tell which parents make a bequest to their children out of altruism and which make a bequest out of other motives. For example, parents who behave strategically should not be taxed to maintain neutrality, while parents who care only about the size of the bequest itself should be taxed to maintain neutrality. Of course, knowing this, parents would try to mask their behavior, frustrating the government's effort to impose a neutral consumption tax. Therefore, the conclusion of this chapter is that the consumption tax will not be neutral in the presence of bequests when there are different motives for bequeathing, the most realistic case to consider.

The Meade Commission (Meade 1978) and Mieszkowski (1980) raised the issue of the appropriate tax treatment of bequests under the consumption tax and advocated that bequests be taxed for equity reasons. In particular, Mieszkowski also noted that this might reduce the incentive to save for a bequest and thus could lead to a decrease in capital accumulation. In that case, the consumption tax would not be neutral with respect to capital accumulation if the bequest were taxed. Therefore, if bequests are taxed for equity reasons, one might usefully question whether or not the consumption tax would promote capital formation, since it would appear there is a conflict between equity and efficiency in this context.

Interestingly enough, Menchik and David (1982) reached the exact opposite conclusion, namely, that the consumption tax would be neutral when labor supply was exogenous only if the bequest were taxed at the consumption tax rate. In that case, one need not worry about the ability of the tax to promote capital accumulation, even if bequests are taxed for equity reasons, since equity and efficiency are not in conflict.

Batina (1987, 1995) showed how the different results could be reconciled. Under the altruism model the parent cares about either the welfare or the consumption of the offspring and thus takes into account the possibility that the offspring might pay the consumption tax when he consumes the bequest. In the bequest as consumption model, the parent cares about the actual bequest itself and thus ignores the possibility that the offspring might pay the consumption tax later if he consumes the bequest. Under altruism the bequest plays the same role as the parent's life cycle savings. Taxing the bequest treats it asymmetrically relative to life cycle savings. On the other hand, in the bequest as consumption model, the bequest enters the model in exactly the same way as parental consumption, that is, once in the utility function and once in the budget constraint. Taxing the bequest treats it in exactly the same fashion as parental consumption. The altruism model tends to support the conclusions suggested by Mieszkowski (1980), while the bequest as consumption model supports the conclusion reached by Menchik and David (1982).

A third model has gained some empirical support in recent years, and that is the strategic bequest model. In this model the parent makes a bequest to her offspring in exchange for some action taken by the offspring, such as running errands for the parent, visiting the parent, doing chores around the house for the parent. The parent uses the bequest as an incentive for the offspring to take the desired action; a larger bequest elicits greater action. The parent chooses the bequest as a Stackelberg leader, taking into account the incentive compatibility constraint that delivers the appropriate level for the action. The parent thus takes into account the economic circumstances of the offspring in choosing the optimal bequest. More specifically, the parent will take into account the possibility that the offspring will pay the consumption tax when he consumes the bequest. Therefore, this model makes a prediction about the neutrality of the consumption tax with respect to capital accumulation that is similar in spirit to the altruism model.

In the next section we introduce the subject by studying two versions of the one-period model considered briefly in Section 3.4, the altruism model and the bequest as consumption model. In Section 11.3 we discuss some of the early work on bequests as background. In Section 11.4 we extend the one-period model to two periods and include life cycle saving as well as saving for a bequest. Section 11.5 studies the differential incidence of the tax when the neutrality of the tax fails in each model. In Section 11.6 the potential international spillover effects are discussed. Section 11.7 studies several extensions including strategic bequests, decisions involving the quantity of offspring as well as the bequest per child, and the case where there is heterogeneity in the population based on the motive for bequeathing. Section 11.8 concludes.

11.2. One-period models of bequests

First, consider the model of Section 3.4, where the representative agent lives for one period and cares about her offspring's welfare. The parent produces one offspring. The parent's utility function is $U^t = u(c_t) + \beta^+ u(c_{t+1})$, where β^+ is the generational discount factor. This difference equation can be solved to obtain equation (3.23) as in Chapter 3:

$$U^t = \sum_{j=0} \beta^{+j} u(c_{t+j}).$$

The agent supplies her one unit of labor in exchange for a wage and saves to make a bequest. Her budget constraint is given by

$$w_t + (1 + r_t)b_t - (1 + \theta_t)c_t - (1 + \theta_{bt})qb_{t+1} + T_t = 0,$$

where q is the cost of making a bequest, b_t is the inheritance she received from her parent, b_{t+1} is the bequest she makes to her offspring, θ is the consumption tax rate, θ_b is a tax imposed on the bequest, and T is a lumpsum rebate of the tax revenue.

It is straightforward to show that the bequest decision will be distorted if the bequest is taxed when given. The first-order condition of the parent's decision problem is

$$(1 + \theta_{bt})qU_1(c_t)/(1 + \theta_t) = \beta^+(1 + r_{t+1})U_1(c_{t+1})/(1 + \theta_{t+1}),$$

where $dU/dc = U_1$. In a steady state where consumption across generations is constant, this becomes

$$1 + \theta_{bt} = \beta^+(1 + r).$$

It follows under profit maximization that $r = f_k(k)$. It is immediate that capital investment decreases with the tax on bequests since $dk/d\theta_b = 1/\beta^+ f_{kk} < 0$. The parent in this model takes into account the fact that the bequest is being taxed twice, once when it is given and once when it is consumed by the offspring. We will label this model, the "altruism" model.

Alternatively, we could assume the parent cares about the level of the bequest itself according to $U(c_t, b_{t+1})$ rather than about the utility of the offspring. The first-order condition of the parent's decision problem in this case is

$$[(1 + \theta_{bt})/(1 + \theta_t)]U_c(c_t, b_{t+1}) = U_b(c_t, b_{t+1}).$$

Now the consumption tax is not distorting if the bequest is taxed at the same rate as consumption. This is because the parent ignores the offspring's use of the bequest and the fact that the offspring will pay the consumption tax when the bequest is consumed. In a steady state where the bequest is not taxed, we have $(1 + \theta)U_b = qU_c$. If the lumpsum tax adjusts so as to maintain disposable income, it is straightforward to show that

$$db/d\theta = -q(db/dq)_u > 0,$$

where $(db/dq)_u$ is a substitution effect. Since $b = k$ in this simple model, capital accumulation increases when the consumption tax distorts the bequest decision. We will label this model the "bequest as consumption" model.

The predictions of the one-period model are rather sharp. Unfortunately, they do not necessarily carry over to the two-period version of each model. In the next section we will examine the empirical work on bequeathing behavior to provide some background on modeling bequest behavior. Later we will study a two-period version of each model.

11.3. Empirical evidence on bequeathing

The idea that members of a family are connected in a variety of ways is certainly not a new one. However, the work of Garry Becker and his coauthors has certainly popularized the notion. In a series of papers, e.g. Becker and Lewis (1973), Becker (1974), Becker and Tomes (1979), culminating in his 1981 book, *A Treatise on the Family*, Becker studied the interaction between family members. One critical idea in this work is that the people within a family may alter their behavior in response to public policy so as to frustrate the intentions of the policy.[2] He also pointed out that policy may have adverse and unintended side effects in the context of optimizing behavior on the part of the family members.

Becker and Lewis (1973) studied a simple model with rather dramatic implications. Parents are assumed to choose the number of children to produce and the amount of resources to devote to each child. Parents thus invest in the quantity and quality of their children. The interesting implication of this is that the shadow price of the quantity of children depends positively on the quality expenditure per child and the shadow price of quality depends positively on the number of children produced. If there is a change in the economic environment that causes parents to increase expenditures on children, quality will increase, the cost of raising a child will increase, and parents will respond by producing fewer children albeit of higher quality. This interaction between quantity and quality is used by Becker and Lewis to explain the demographic transition from high fertility rates coupled with low investments in education to low fertility rates with high investments in education. There are also some dramatic implications with respect to the consumption tax, as we will see in Section 11.6.

The idea that family members are connected by cash transfers is an extension of this basic idea and was used by Barro (1974) in a paper that set off a tremendous controversy involving the impact of government debt on the economy and the equivalence of debt and taxation. Keynesian economists had argued that a tax cut financed by the issuance of debt would stimulate consumption and thus boost the economy out of a recession. On the other hand, a tax increase could be used to reduce consumption and cool off the economy if inflation started to become a problem.

Prior to Barro's work, Bailey (1962) and Thompson (1967) pointed out that taxpayers are forward looking and might perceive a government deficit today as requiring the government to raise taxes at some time in the future in order to balance its budget in a long run sense. If the taxpayer experiences a tax cut today and believes that it will be followed by a tax increase in the future, she might not alter her intertemporal consumption path in response to the tax cut. She might simply save the tax cut instead in order to pay her increased tax liability in the future. If she confronts the same interest rates in the capital market as the government does, there will be no net increase in wealth; new government obligations in the form of bonds are perfectly offset by the increase in saving.

The interest rate and the real consumption allocation of the economy will be unaffected by the tax cut. However, it was acknowledged that, if the taxpayer believes the future tax increase will not occur in her lifetime, she may increase her current consumption in response to the tax cut.[3] The proposition that debt and taxes have the same effect on the economy and are thus equivalent is originally due to David Ricardo and has become known as the Ricardian Neutrality Proposition.

Barro (1974) extended this argument by connecting family members by cash transfers. Imagine that the parent cares about the consumption or wellbeing of his offspring and makes a bequest to the offspring on the basis of altruism. If the government cuts taxes today and the parent expects the government to raise taxes imposed on the offspring in the future, then he may save the tax cut in the form of a larger bequest. If the entire tax cut is passed along to the offspring, then the family will be able to completely offset the government's attempt to alter the real consumption allocation across generations. Therefore, it is possible that the equivalence of debt and taxation, first noted by Ricardo and resurrected by Bailey and Thompson, may extend beyond an individual's own lifetime.[4]

This set off a firestorm of controversy and generated much useful research on the linkages within the family, models of the interaction among family members, and empirical investigation of the economic behavior within the family. For example, Bernheim, Shleifer, and Summers (1985) put forth a competing model of family behavior whereby the parent makes a bequest strategically with the express intention of altering the offspring's behavior. The parent might, for example, desire visits from the offspring and hold out the promise of a large bequest in exchange for the visits. In that case, an increase in government debt that alters the relative cost of the bequest–visit transaction occurring between the parent and the offspring would alter behavior at the margin and thus produce real effects.[5]

Bernheim and Bagwell (1988) argue that people are linked in much more complicated ways through intermarriage across families and they set up a very general model with an extraordinary amount of interlinkage between agents. They then show that any change in relative prices can be neutralized if the interlinkages are significant enough. The idea is to extend Barro's model in a logically cogent fashion to all private agents and show that such interlinkages would completely rob the price mechanism of its ability to allocate resources. A change in relative prices sets off a complicated sequence of responses in transfers throughout the network of interlinkages that neutralize the impact of the initial change in relative prices. Since no one believes this to be so, there must be something wrong with the idea that agents are interlinked via pure altruism. There may be other motives for making bequests, for example the strategic bequest motive, where neutrality will fail. Therefore, which model of bequests is most appropriate becomes an empirical issue.[6] Empirical work on the nature of transfers within the family is quite extensive. Some of the important studies are summarized in Table 11.1.

Tomes (1981) found strong support for the altruism model. One hypothesis implied by this model is that parents will invest more in the human capital of their more able children, inducing earned income inequality, but will compensate their less able children by leaving them a larger estate thereby contributing to equality in the distribution of wealth. This is not necessarily true however if bequests are strategic or if parents care about the bequest itself. Tomes found that parents tended to give larger cash bequests to children of lesser ability and to make greater human capital investments in their more able children.

This was disputed by Menchik (1980). He found evidence of equal sharing of estates in his data refuting Tomes' finding; an equal division of an estate among offspring who experience different earnings contradicts the altruism model. This would also contradict the strategic bequest model as well; equal sharing would only be implied by the strategic bequest model if all children provide the same amount of the desired action for the parent, an unlikely outcome if children experience different earnings. On the other hand, equal sharing of an estate could be taken as evidence supporting the bequest as consumption model if the bequest given to each offspring itself enters the parent's utility function as a separate argument.

Table 11.1. Empirical work on bequests

Author	Data[a]	Main result
Tomes (1981)	panel/estate	Parents made unequal investments in children
Menchick (1980)	estate	Estates were shared equally
Cox (1987)	inter vivos gifts	Parental gifts increased with offspring income
Bernheim, Shleifer, and Summers (1985)	panel	Children increased contact when there was more bequeathable wealth available
Cox and Jakubson (1995)	US (PCPP)	Income and consumption within the family are correlated rejecting pure altruism
Altonji, Hayashi, and Kotlikoff (1992)	PSID (Food expenditures)	Cannot reject the life cycle model
Wilhelm (1996)	Income tax/estate	Significant equal sharing
Bernheim (1991)	LRHS	Found evidence against the life cycle model
Cox, Hansen, and Jimenez (1996)	panel—Phillipines	Significant support for the altruism model
Laitner and Juster (1996)	TIAA–CREF	Significant support for the altruism model

[a] *LRHS* = Longitudinal Retirement History Survey; *PSID* = Panel Study of Income Dynamics (US); *PCPP* = President's Commission on Pension Policy; *NSFH* = National Survey of Families and Households; TIAA–CREF= Teacher's Insurance and Annuity–College Retirement Fund.

Cox (1987) noted that most transfers within the family occur inter vivos (a lower bound is about 60 per cent of all private transfers in the United States) and used a unique data set containing information on such transfers to test the different models of bequeathing. He found that inter vivos gifts to the offspring tended to increase with the offspring's income, a contradiction of the Altruism model, although this would tend to support the strategic bequest model. Under Altruism parents can share in the good fortune of their offspring by reducing the bequest or gift to the offspring if the offspring is expected to experience an increase in her earned income. However, in the strategic bequest model, an increase in the offspring's earned income might induce her to take more of the action desired by the parent thus eliciting a larger bequest as a result. In addition to this, Bernheim, Schleifer, and Summers (1985), using data from the Long-itudinal Retirement History Survey, discovered that children increased contact with their parents by visiting or phoning them when there was more bequeath-able wealth available. This also tends to support the strategic bequest model.

Cox (1990) studied similar data but focused attention on liquidity constrained households. Cash transfers within the family that are targeted at members who are liquidity constrained may be a non-market way of overcoming the constraint imposed by the credit market. Cox found strong evidence for this hypothesis. This is interesting, because typically transfers within the family are thought to increase capital formation; however, in this instance it would mean that a transfer is going for increased consumption rather than capital accumulation.

Cox and Rank (1992) found evidence more consistent with the Strategic Bequest model than with the altruism model. The cross-sectional National Survey of Families and Households contains information on inter vivos transfers, measures of inkind services, and parental characteristics that can be used to estimate permanent income. They found that offspring contact with the parent was positively related to the amount of the transfer, evidence in favor of the exchange motive rather than altruism. Also, altruism predicts that a dollar increase in the offspring's income coupled with a dollar decline in parental income should reduce transfers from the parent to the offspring by one dollar: this hypothesis was strongly rejected.

Cox and Jakubson (1995) argued that another implication of the altruism model is that, if family members are connected by altruistic transfers, the con-sumption and income of an individual within the family should be independent of the income distribution within the family. If one family member loses a job, for example, other members of the family will help the individual out until he or she finds another job. In addition to this, public transfers should be offset by changes in private transfers. They found some evidence against this hypothesis using US data from the President's Commission on Pension Policy (PCPP).

Altonji, Hayashi, and Kotlikoff (1992) argue that the timing of bequests is somewhat arbitrary and that tests of the different models of bequeathing are difficult to construct. However, if the altruism model is correct, then the distribution of consumption across family members should be independent of the distribution of income across family members, as noted by Cox and Jakubson (1995). They focus their attention on this particular implication and use micro panel data to estimate a fixed effects model. Their results indicate that dynasty resources have only a limited effect on an individual's own consumption. Indeed, they cannot reject the life cycle model after controlling for the possibility that the extended family's resources help predict the individual's own permanent income. Unfortunately, given the paucity of data on families over time, Altonji, Hayashi, and Kotlikoff were forced to use food expenditures as a proxy for consumption. It is certainly possible that decisionmaking on food expenditures could be independent of transfers and hence of the extended family's resources. Indeed, car payments and home mortgages far outweigh food in a household's budget, and parents may be more altruistically inclined to help their children in buying a car or their first home than in helping pay their grocery bill. And Altonji, Hayashi, and Kotlikoff admit that transfers arising from altruism probably exist, "particularly among the wealthy, who are underrepresented in the PSID."

Using matched estate and income tax records for a sample of wealthy taxpayers in the United States, Wilhelm (1996) found evidence against the altruism model. Estate and income tax records for a sample of decedents and their offspring were combined for 1982. Wilhelm found that there was significant equal sharing of estates in his data, and even though an increase in the offspring's earnings were offset somewhat by a smaller bequest in his estimated inheritance equation, it was not offset on a one-for-one basis, contradicting the altruism model. Unfortunately, inter vivos gifts were included only for the three years prior to the time the data were collected (1982) and not earlier in the life cycle. This may be a significant omission, given Cox's (1987) argument that most transfers within the family occur inter vivos. In addition to this, assets transferred to children through trusts were also not discernible from the data used by Wilhelm. This is an important omission that also tends to reduce the importance of Wilhelm's results since 25 per cent of the decedents in his sample left some of their assets to their offspring in the form of a trust.

On the other side of the debate, Barro (1989) argued that interest rates should not be affected by government policies like social security and government debt if the Ricardian Neutrality Proposition is correct. Essentially, a government transfer from the young to the old can be offset by a larger bequest within the family from the old to the young. He cites empirical support for this proposition in Paul Evans (1987), who found that budget deficits had no discernible effect on interest rates, a proposition supported by the altruism model—although it is somewhat difficult to explain the shift in the flow of international capital investment into the United States and the rise of the dollar during the early part of the 1980s if the real interest rate did not increase in the USA during that period.

Bernheim (1991) estimated a reduced form model that could support either the altruism model or the strategic bequest model using the Longitudinal Retirement

History Survey. He tested his model against the life cycle model and found significant evidence against the latter model. Cox, Hansen, and Jimenez (1996) find significant evidence that transfers are widespread in the Philippines and seem to conform to the predictions of the altruism model using micro data. This suggests that public transfers in developed countries like the United States may have already crowded out most private transfers that may be due to altruism. It also has certain policy implications. For example, if most private transfers have been crowded out, certain policies will have real effects that they might not have had when private transfers were significant, such as government debt policy. Finally, Laitner and Juster (1996) found significant evidence in support of altruism using survey data on retirees in TIAA–CREF, the main pension plan for college teachers in the United States. However, in their data saving for altruistic reasons was dominated by life cycle saving.

Given this mixed bag of evidence, it would appear that bequests are an important phenomenon, that life cycle savings motives may explain only a small albeit significant fraction of saving behavior, and that there may be a variety of motives for bequeathing. From this evidence it would appear that altruism, caring about the bequest itself, and strategic interaction are important reasons for bequeathing resources to the next generation. In what follows we will focus our attention on the altruism model and the consumption as bequest model and study the neutrality properties of the consumption tax. Later in Section 11.6 it will be shown that the implications of the strategic bequest model for the neutrality of the consumption tax are similar to those of the altruism model.

11.4. Two-period models of bequeathing in the presence of the consumption tax

11.4.1. The altruism model

The first two-period model we will study is the altruism model, where the parent (donor) cares about either the welfare or the consumption of her offspring (recipient). We will assume the parent lives for two periods and the offspring lives for only one period, so the two agents overlap for one period. This can easily be extended to an overlapping generations model where the economy lasts for ever, or to a framework in which the agents overlap for an arbitrary number of periods without affecting the comparison between models (see Appendix 11B). Labor supply is exogenous and the parent has perfect access to the capital market. There is no population growth, for simplicity. Furthermore, we will assume that it is impossible for the parent to leave the offspring a negative bequest.

The models in this chapter differ only on the basis of the motive for bequeathing. In the version of the altruism model we will study in this chapter, the parent cares about her own consumption and the consumption of her offspring according to

$$u_p = U^p\big(c_{p1}, c_{p2}, c_o\big), \tag{11.1}$$

where c_{pj} is parental consumption in period j, c_o is the offspring's consumption. We will assume that the utility function is twice continuously differentiable, quasi-concave, and monotone increasing in all of its arguments.

The parent's budget constraints are given by

$$w_p - (1 + \theta_p)c_{p1} - s - p(1 + \theta_p)b - T_{p1} = 0, \tag{11.2}$$

$$(1 + r)s - (1 + \theta_p)c_{p2} - T_{p2} = 0, \tag{11.3}$$

where w_p is the parent's labor earnings in the first period, r is the interest rate, s is the parent's life cycle savings, b is the bequest, θ_p is the consumption tax rate paid by the parent, α_p is an estate tax imposed on the bequest, p is the price of making a bequest evaluated at $p = 1$, and T_{p1} and T_{p2} are lumpsum taxes. The inclusion of a price of bequeathing in (11.2) will give us a useful way of interpreting the parent's response to tax policy experiments and comparative statics results in the next section. The offspring's budget constraint is given by

$$w_o - (1 + \theta_o)c_o + (1 + r)b - T_o = 0, \tag{11.4}$$

where w_o is the offspring's labor earnings, θ_o is the consumption tax rate confronting the offspring, and T_o is a lumpsum tax. We have distinguished the tax rate across agents merely for convenience in interpreting the distortions caused by the tax.

The parent's decision problem is to choose (c_{p1}, c_{p2}, s, b) to maximize (11.1) subject to (11.2)–(11.4). The first-order conditions can be arranged to yield

$$(1 + r)U_2^p - U_1^p = 0, \tag{11.5a}$$

$$(1 + r)U_o^p/(1 + \theta_o) - p(1 + \alpha_p)U_1^p/(1 + \theta_p) \leq 0, \tag{11.5b}$$

where subscripts denote partial derivatives; for example, $\partial U^p/\partial c_o = U_o^p$. Equation (11.5a) governs the intertemporal consumption decision of the parent, while (11.5b) governs the bequest decision. Essentially, the parent saves for her own retirement and to make a bequest to her offspring.

The first point to notice about (11.5b) is that the parent takes into account any variable confronting the offspring, including policy parameters, when choosing the optimal bequest; that is, θ_o enters into the parent's bequest decision. Second, from (11.5b) it follows intuitively that the bequest is more likely to be positive the higher the interest rate, the lower the estate tax imposed on the bequest, the lower the consumption tax rate imposed on the offspring, and the higher the consumption tax rate imposed on the parent. Third, for an interior solution we can write (11.5b) as an equality:

$$(1 + r)U_o^p/(1 + \theta_o) - p(1 + \alpha_p)U_1^p/(1 + \theta_p) = 0. \tag{11.6}$$

It is immediate that the consumption tax will be neutral only if $(1 + \theta_p)/(1 + \alpha_p)(1 + \theta_o) = 1$.

Several remarks are in order. There are two ways in which the bequest decision will not be distorted: if the tax rates are zero, or if they offset one another in some way. Only the latter possibility is of interest in the current context. So, if $1 + \alpha_p = (1 + \theta_p)/(1 + \theta_o)$, then the tax parameters will not enter the MRT on the righthand side of (11.6) and the bequest decision will not be distorted by the tax. If, for example, $\theta_p > \theta_o$, then $\alpha_p > 0$. This might occur if the tax is progressive and the parent is in a higher tax bracket than the offspring. On the other hand, under a flat rate consumption tax, $\theta_p = \theta_o$ and the tax will not distort the bequest decision only if the bequest is untaxed, $\alpha_p = 0$. Since the agents overlap for one period, it follows that the tax rate in that period may have to be the same to avoid possible tax evasion; that is, $\theta_p = \theta_o$.[7] It follows immediately from (11.6) that to maintain neutrality the government should *not tax bequests under the altruism model* of bequests; that is, $\alpha_p = 0$, to maintain neutrality with respect to capital accumulation.[8] If the bequest is taxed, it follows from (11.6) that the consumption tax will fail to be neutral and will distort the bequest decision as a result.

An interior solution to the parent's decision problem can be written as

$$b = B^A(w_p, w_o, r, p, \theta_p, \theta_o, \alpha_p, T_{p1}, T_{p2}, T_o), \tag{11.7a}$$

$$s = S^A(w_p, w_o, r, p, \theta_p, \theta_o, \alpha_p, T_{p1}, T_{p2}, T_o). \tag{11.7b}$$

There is some evidence from the empirical literature that bequests are a normal good, $db/dw_p > 0$. If the substitution effects dominate, then the bequest will be increasing in the interest rate and decreasing in the cost of making a bequest, $db/dr > 0$ and $db/dp < 0$. We would also expect the bequest to be decreasing in the child's wealth, $db/dw_o < 0$. The purpose of making a bequest is to make the offspring better off. If there is some change in the economic environment that makes the offspring better off anyway, such as economic growth, the parent can share in that good fortune by lowering the bequest and can still see the offspring achieve a favorable level of utility.[9] The comparative statics of this model are discussed in Appendix 11A.

In terms of the policy parameters, notice that α_p and θ_o enter the MRT in (11.6) in the same way as the price of making a bequest. Therefore, the model would predict that the parent's response to the compensated, utility-constant price effect with respect to the tax rate confronting the child and the tax on bequests will be of the same sign as the compensated price of bequeathing effect. The parent's compensated response to the consumption tax rate confronting her directly will be of the opposite sign, since that tax rate enters the numerator in (11.6) while the price of bequeathing enters the denominator.

What is the parent's response to a non-neutral consumption tax? Suppose the parent and offspring pay the same consumption tax rate and that the bequest is taxed, $\theta_p = \theta_o = \theta$ and $\alpha_p > 0$. In that case the MRT in (11.6) becomes $(1 + r)/p(1 + \alpha_p)$, and the tax on the bequest serves to lower the MRT, shifting the parent's expenditures away from the bequest toward her own consumption, holding utility constant. Indeed, it is straightforward to show that

$$(db/d\alpha_p)_u = (1 + \alpha_p)(db/dp)_u < 0.$$

where $(db/d_p)_u$ is a compensated price effect. The intuition behind this result is that in this particular model the bequest serves the same purpose as life cycle savings, transferring resources into the future. Taxing the bequest but not the parent's own life cycle savings treats the bequest in an asymmetric fashion relative to life cycle savings and provides a disincentive to save for the purpose of making a bequest.

11.4.2. *The bequest as consumption model*

We will now present an alternative model where the parent cares about the size of the bequest itself according to

$$u_p = U^p(c_{p1}, c_{p2}, b). \tag{11.8}$$

We will assume that this function is twice continuously differentiable, increasing in each argument, and quasi-concave.

The parent's decision problem in this model is to choose (c_{p1}, c_{p2}, s, b) to maximize (11.8) subject to (11.2) and (11.3). The first-order conditions are

$$(1 + r)U_2^p - U_1^p = 0, \tag{11.9a}$$

$$U_b^p - p(1 + \alpha_p)U_1^p/(1 + \theta_p) = 0. \tag{11.9b}$$

Equation (11.9a) governs the parent's intertemporal consumption decision and (11.9b) governs the optimal choice of the bequest. Notice that the parent ignores the variables confronting the offspring. In particular, she will ignore the possibility that the offspring will have to pay the consumption tax when he consumes the bequest. This is in marked contrast to the altruism model.

Rearranging (11.9b), the MRT of parental consumption for the bequest is given by

$$(1 + \theta_p)/p(1 + \alpha_p) \tag{11.10}$$

Neutrality will prevail in this model only if the *bequest is taxed* at the parent's consumption tax rate.[10] This is the exact opposite conclusion reached by the altruism model. The intuition is that the bequest enters this model in virtually the same way as the parent's own consumption: once in the utility function and once in the parent's budget constraint. Therefore, taxing the bequest at the same rate as parental consumption is taxed treats the bequest in the same manner as the parent's own consumption.

We can solve the first-order conditions (11.9) to obtain the following solution for the bequest as consumption model:

$$b = B^C(w_p, r, p, \alpha_p, \theta_p, T_{p1}, T_{p2}), \tag{11.11a}$$

$$s = S^C(w_p, r, p, \alpha_p, \theta_p, T_{p1}, T_{p2}). \tag{11.11b}$$

The price variables (r, p) will cause the usual substitution and income effects. If the substitution effects dominate, then $db/dp < 0$, and ds/dr, $db/dr > 0$. If the bequest is a normal good, as the empirical evidence seems to suggest, then $db/dw_p > 0$. The main difference between the two models, as embodied in (11.7) and (11.11), is that the parameters confronting the offspring do not enter (11.11) and hence do not affect the parent's decisionmaking. This will have a profound impact on the effects of the consumption tax policy experiments we will study in the next section.

Notice the parent's response when neutrality fails. If $\alpha_p = 0$ so that neutrality fails in the bequest as consumption model, an increase in the consumption tax rate at the margin raises the MRT of parental consumption for the bequest. Therefore the consumption tax would tend to raise the price of consumption relative to the bequest and thus cause an increase in the bequest, $(db/d\theta)_u > 0$. Indeed, it is easy to show that we can write the compensated response under a lumpsum rebate of the tax revenue to the non-neutral consumption tax in the bequest as consumption model as a price effect according to $(db/d\theta)_u = -[p/(1 + \theta)](db/dp)_u > 0$. Again, this is the exact opposite conclusion reached by the altruism model when neutrality fails in that model.

The results of the two models are summarized in Table 11.2. It is of some interest that the two models make the exact opposite predictions, since neither model is unambiguously supported by the empirical work.

Table 11.2.   The effect of an increase in the consumption tax rate on the bequest

	Altruism model	Bequest as consumption model
$\alpha_p = 0$	Neutral	+
$\alpha_p = \theta > 0$	−	Neutral

One final remark is in order. A general income tax that includes a tax on interest income will also distort the bequest decision. A higher tax rate on interest income raises the cost of making a bequest and would provide a disincentive for making a bequest; see Ihori (1994), who studies bequest taxation.

11.5. The differential incidence of a non-neutral consumption tax

To close the model, imagine there is one good available, the consumption good. In the first period the parent is endowed with w_p units of the consumption good. In the second period, the parent is retired and consumes the proceeds of her life cycle savings plus interest. The offspring is endowed with one unit of labor which is supplied exogenously to the labor market in exchange for a wage, w_o. Competitive firms combine labor and capital in the second period in order to produce the consumption good according to a neoclassical constant returns technology, $Y = F(K, L)$, where Y is output, K is capital, and L is labor. We will assume that the production function is twice continuously differentiable, increasing in each argument, and concave, as in Chapter 2. Profit maximization will imply the usual conditions determining the wage and the interest rate:

$$r = f_k(k) \quad \text{and} \quad w_o = f(k) - kf_k(k), \tag{11.12}$$

where $f(k) = F(K/L, 1)$ and $f_k(k) = df/dk$ is the marginal product of capital. Solving the first condition yields the demand for capital per unit of labor, $k = k(r)$, where $dk/dr = k_r(r) = 1/f_{kk} < 0$. Substituting the demand for capital into the equation for the wage yields $w_o = f(k(r)) - k(r)f_k(k(r)) = w(r)$, where $dw_o/dr = w_r(r) = -k < 0$. In equilibrium in both models,

$$k = s + b. \tag{11.13}$$

Finally, we must introduce the government's tax policy experiment. In order to focus on the specific distortions caused by the consumption tax, we will assume that the government rebates the revenue to the taxpayer it was taken from in the period it was taken so as to maintain each taxpayer's disposable income on a period-by-period basis. This will eliminate any income effects associated with the tax policy and any possible timing effects that might exist because of a shifting of the taxpayer's tax liability through time. This will provide us with a pure experiment allowing us to study the substitution effects created by the tax policy.[11] If the main conclusion of our analysis is that the consumption tax is generally not neutral, then perhaps the main benefit of a switch to the consumption tax stems not from switching to the consumption tax per se but from switching away from the income tax. In that case, there might be another income tax system with different features, say, exclusions and deductions, more favorable in an efficiency sense than the consumption tax.

The government's budget constraints in the first and second period are given by, respectively,

$$\theta_p c_{p1} + \phi \alpha_p b + T_{p1} = 0, \tag{11.14a}$$

$$\theta_p c_{p2} + \theta_o c_o + T_{p2} + T_o = 0, \tag{11.14b}$$

where $\phi = 1$ when the bequest is taxed and $\phi = 0$ when the bequest is not taxed. The policy experiments we will study are defined by the following conditions:

$$d\theta_p = d\alpha_p = d\theta_o = d\theta, \tag{11.15a}$$

$$d\theta_p = d\theta_o = d\theta, \text{and } d\alpha_p = 0, \tag{11.15a'}$$

$$dT_{p1} + c_{p1} d\theta_p = 0, \tag{11.15b}$$

$$dT_{p2} + c_{p2} d\theta_p = 0, \tag{11.15c}$$

$$dT_o + c_o d\theta_o = 0, \tag{11.15d}$$

evaluated at the initial equilibrium. Equation (11.15a) governs the tax policy experiment when the bequest is taxed while (11.15a') governs the experiment when the bequest is not taxed. Equations (11.15b)–(11.15d) are our assumptions that maintain disposable income. It is a straightforward matter to show that (11.15) will eliminate the income and timing effects of the tax policy experiments we study in this chapter. This will allow us to focus attention on the substitution effects and hence on the distortions caused by the different consumption tax policies.

The parent's budget constraints in the presence of our tax policy experiment are given by

$$w_p - (1 + \theta_p)c_{p1} - T_{p1} - s - (1 + \phi\alpha_p)b = 0,$$
$$(1 + r)s - (1 + \theta_p)c_{p2} - T_{p2} = 0.$$

The offspring's constraint is

$$w_o - (1 + \theta_o)c_o - T_o + (1 + r)b = 0,$$

where $\phi = 1$ when the bequest is taxed and $\phi = 0$ when the bequest is exempt from taxation.

Formally, the solution to the parent's decision problem in each model will depend on all of the parameters confronting the parent, including variables like T_{p1}, T_{p2}, and so on. However, under our policy experiment only the utility compensated price responses will be relevant. Therefore, we can abstract from the additional variables that enter the model only in order to maintain the taxpayer's disposable income, such as T_{p1}, T_{p2}, and so on. This allows us to write the bequest and saving functions under altruism as

$$b = B^A(w_p, w_o, r, p, \theta) \qquad (11.16a)$$
$$s = S^A(w_p, w_o, r, p, \theta) \qquad (11.16b)$$

and under the bequest as consumption model as

$$b = B^C(w_p, r, p, \theta) \qquad (11.17a)$$
$$s = S^C(w_p, r, p, \theta). \qquad (11.17b)$$

The response to the consumption tax in each model can be written as a compensated price effect under our experiment, and this will differ between the two models as discussed in the last two sections. This can be shown by differentiating the first-order conditions of the parent's decision problem in each model and then making use of the assumptions in (11.15).

To obtain the response to the tax policy experiment in the altruism model, substitute the demand for capital, the wage function, and the bequest and savings functions in (11.16) into (11.13) to obtain

$$k(r) = S^A(w_{p1}, w(r), r, \theta) + B^A(w_{p1}, w(r), r, \theta).$$

Differentiate this equation to obtain

$$dr/d\theta = -[(ds/d\theta)_u + (db/d\theta)_u]/D, \qquad (11.18)$$

where $D = S_r^A + B_r^A - k(S_o^A + B_o^A) - k_r(r)$, and where $S_r^A = ds/dr$, $S_o^A = ds/dw_o$, and so on. If $D > 0$, the equilibrium will be stable.

From our earlier results, we know that the consumption tax will be neutral in the altruism model only when the bequest is not taxed. In that case there would be no response to our tax policy experiment, and hence $dr/d\theta = 0$. On the other hand, if the bequest is taxed, neutrality will fail in this model and the bequest will decrease with the consumption tax rate under the assumptions of our experiment; that is, $db/d\theta = (1 + \alpha_p)(db/dp)_u < 0$. Substituting this information into (11.18), we obtain the following response when neutrality fails:

$$dr/d\theta = -(1 + \theta)[(ds/dp)_u + (db/dp)_u]/D. \qquad (11.19)$$

The second term is unambiguously negative and contributes to a decrease in capital formation and an increase in the interest rate. Unfortunately, we do not know of any evidence that would allow us to sign the first term in (11.19). If the two forms of saving are compensated complements, that is if $(ds/dp)_u < 0$, then, clearly, capital accumulation will *fall* when the tax is introduced and the bequest is taxed in the altruism model.[12] This is contrary to the express intention of introducing a consumption based tax, which is to foster greater capital accumulation. If capital accumulation does fall with the introduction of the tax, the offspring's wage will fall since $dw/d\theta = -kf_{kk}(dk/d\theta)$.

On the other hand, just the opposite conclusion is reached in the bequest as consumption model. Neutrality requires taxing the bequest when given. In that case there will be no response to our experiment. However, if the bequest is not taxed, neutrality will fail in this model. To obtain the response when neutrality fails, substitute (11.12) and (11.17) into the equilibrium condition (11.13) to obtain

$$k(r) = S^C(w_{p1}, r, \theta) + B^C(w_{p1}, r, \theta).$$

Differentiating this last equation and using the information from the last section, we obtain the following response under the bequest as consumption model:

$$dr/d\theta = [p/(1 + \theta)][(ds/dp)_u + (db/dp)_u]/E, \qquad (11.20)$$

where $E = S_r^A + B_r^A - k_r(r)$. If $E > 0$, the equilibrium will be stable. This response is of the opposite sign relative to the response under altruism to the same policy experiment. Once again, the models make the exact opposite prediction.

The consumption tax raises the price of consumption relative to the bequest in this model and parents shift toward the bequest, thus increasing capital formation,

Table 11.3. The effect of an increase in the consumption tax rate on the interest rate

	Altruism model	Bequest as consumption model
$\alpha_p = 0$	0	$-(?)$
$\alpha_p = \theta > 0$	$+(?)$	0

which in turn causes the interest rate to fall and the wage to rise. The response of the parent's life cycle savings makes the response to the tax policy experiment somewhat ambiguous. It will tend to magnify (reverse) the response of the bequest to the tax if the two forms of saving are complementary (substitutable). We can summarize the results of this section in Table 11.3. The question marks denote that the response is formally ambiguous. However, a strong case can be made for the signs depicted.

11.6. International spillover effects from consumption taxation

Next, we consider the possible spillover effects of the tax on the world economy when neutrality fails in each model. The two models will once again make the exact opposite prediction about the potential spillover effects of the tax when it distorts the bequest decision.

Imagine there are two countries: the home country introducing the consumption tax and a foreign country. The home country is as previously described. Let an asterisk denote the appropriate variable for the foreign country. For simplicity, we will assume there is only one consumer in the foreign country who lives for two periods. He is endowed with e^* units of the consumption good in the first period. He consumes c_1^* in the first period and saves the rest of his endowment, s^*. In the second period he is endowed with one unit of labor, which is supplied to the labor market in a perfectly exogenous manner in exchange for a wage rate w^*. He consumes the proceeds of his savings plus interest and his labor earnings, c_2^* in the second period.

Firms use capital and labor to produce the consumption good in the second period according to a neoclassical, constant returns technology, $f^*(k^*)$, where $k^* = K^*/L^*$ is the amount of capital per worker, and $L^* = 1$. Profit maximization ensures that $r^* = f_{k^*}^*(k^*)$ and $w^* = f^*(k^*) - k^* f_{k^*}^*(k^*)$. The demand for capital per unit of labor is $k^* = k^*(r^*)$, where $dk^*/dr^* = k_{r^*}^* = 1/f_{k^*k^*}^* < 0$, and the wage is given by $w^* = w^*(r^*)$, where $w_{r^*}^* = dw^*/dr^* = -k^* < 0$, just as in the home country.

The foreign consumer's decision problem is to choose a consumption path (c_1^*, c_2^*) to maximize $U^*(c_1^*, c_2^*)$ subject to a lifetime budget constraint $e^* - c_1^* = (w^* - c_2^*)/(1 + r^*)$, where the utility function satisfies the usual assumptions. The solution for first-period consumption is $c_1^* = C^*(e^*, w^*, r^*)$. This allows us to define a savings function for the foreign country according to

$$S^*(e^*, w^*, r^*) = e^* - C^*(e^*, w^*, r^*).$$

If the agent in the foreign country can invest in the home country, then $s^* = k^* + x^*$, where x^* is foreign direct investment if positive. Arbitrage will imply that $r^* = r$. This will not necessarily imply that capital per worker will be the same across countries unless the technology is the same.

In the home country, the parent's decision problem is basically the same as before except that the parent is allowed to invest in the foreign country, so that $s + b = k + x$, where $x > 0$ is the foreign direct investment of the home country in the foreign country.

Equilibrium in the international capital market requires,

$$s + b + s^* = k + k^* \tag{11.21}$$

since $x + x^* = 0$ must hold in equilibrium; that is, capital imports must equal capital exports. More specifically, equilibrium in the altruism model requires

$$S^A\left(w_{p1}, w(r), r, \theta\right) + B^A\left(w_{p1}, w(r), r, \theta\right) + S^*(e^*, w^*(r), r) = k(r) + k^*(r). \tag{11.22}$$

Under the bequest as consumption model, we obtain instead

$$S^C\left(w_{p1}, r, \theta\right) + B^C\left(w_{p1}, r, \theta\right) + S^*(e^*, w^*(r), r) = k(r) + k^*(r). \tag{11.23}$$

Let

$$G = S_r^A + B_r^A + S_r^* - k(S_o^A + B_o^A) - k^* S_{w*}^* - k_r(r) - k_r^*(r)$$

and

$$H = S_r^C + B_r^C + S_r^* - k^* S_{w*}^* - k_r(r) - k_r^*(r).$$

If $G > 0$ the equilibrium is stable under altruism, and if $H > 0$ the equilibrium is stable in the bequest as consumption model.

It is straightforward to show that the response of the world interest rate depends on the same factors as in the last section; that is, (11.19) and (11.20) still hold with the denominator replaced by G and H, respectively. If the two types of saving are compensated complements, then world capital accumulation will fall in the altruism model if the bequest is taxed and will rise under the bequest as consumption model if the bequest is not taxed. The response is somewhat ambiguous in both models if the two types of saving are compensated substitutes.

Finally, we can calculate the spillover effect of the tax policy on the foreign country's welfare. Welfare in the foreign country is given by

$$U^* = U^*(e^* - s^*, w^* + (1 + r)s^*). \tag{11.24}$$

Differentiate (11.24) and simplify to obtain the spillover effects of the tax policy pursued in the home country,

$$dU^* = U_2^*(dw^* + s^* dr) = U_2^*(s^* dr - k^* dr) = x^* U_2^* dr. \tag{11.25}$$

Therefore, $dU^*/d\theta = x^* U_2^* dr/d\theta$. The response of welfare in the foreign country to a distorting tax policy imposed in the home country will depend on the flow of capital between the two countries and on the response of the interest rate to the tax policy in the home country. The foreign country will be better (worse) off if x^* and $dr/d\theta$ are of the same (opposite) sign. For example, in the altruism model, the foreign country will be worse off if $x^* < 0$ and the bequest is taxed since the interest rate will increase in that case. On the other hand, welfare in the foreign country will fall in the bequest as consumption model if $x^* < 0$ since the interest rate will rise in that case if the bequest is not taxed.

11.7. Extensions

11.7.1. Strategic bequests

First, we will present a model of strategic bequests. Suppose the parent cares about some action the offspring might take and denote the action by a. Further, assume that the action produces positive utility for the parent but negative utility for the child. The parent's utility in the strategic bequest model is given by

$$U^p(c_{p1}, c_{p2}, a),$$

while the child's utility is given by

$$U^o(c_o, -a).$$

Both utility functions are twice continuously differentiable, quasi-concave, and montone increasing in all of their arguments; that is, U^o is increasing in $-a$ or decreasing in a. The budget constraints are the same as in Section 11.3.

The parent chooses the bequest in order to manipulate the action the offspring takes in favor of the parent. Following the literature, the parent acts like a Stackelberg leader in the game played with the offspring while the offspring acts as a Stackelberg follower. Presumably, the action the offspring takes is increasing in the bequest in the sense that a larger bequest will induce the offspring to undertake more of the action. However, the action might be onerous enough that the offspring refuses to take it. In that case, the parent responds by refusing to make a bequest to the recalcitrant child. If this occurs, the offspring's utility becomes

$$U^+ = U^o(w_o/(1 + \theta_o), 0), \tag{11.26}$$

and the offspring is essentially cut off completely. On the other hand, if the action is taken and a positive bequest is made, then the offspring receives utility of

$$U^o((w_o + b)/(1 + \theta_o), -a) \tag{11.27}$$

instead. Thus, the incentive compatibility constraint confronting the parent when choosing the optimal bequest to make to the offspring is determined by the combination of (11.26) and (11.27) according to

$$U^o((w_o + b)/(1 + \theta_o), -a) \geq U^+ = U^o(w_o/(1 + \theta_o), 0). \tag{11.28}$$

In equilibrium the additional constraint (11.28) will be binding, since we seek an equilibrium where the parent and offspring are not estranged but interact with one another. At equality, we can solve this constraint to obtain the action the offspring will take as a function of the bequest, the offspring's wage, and the consumption tax rate confronting the offspring according to

$$a = A(b, w_o, \theta_o). \tag{11.29}$$

This "action" function determines the action the offspring will take once the bequest is chosen by the parent. In game theory terminology, (11.29) is the reaction function of the offspring.

By differentiating the constraint (11.28), we can obtain the derivative properties of the action function,

$$A_b = da/db = U_1^o/U_2^o(1 + \theta_o),$$
$$A_w = da/dw_o = (U_1^o - U_1^+)/U_2^o(1 + \theta_o) < 0,$$
$$A_\theta = da/d\theta_o = [w_o(U_1^o - U_1^+) + bU_1^o]/U_2^o(1 + \theta_o) < 0,$$

where $\partial U^o/\partial c = U_1^o > 0$ and $\partial U^o/\partial a = -U_2^o < 0$. It follows immediately that the action is increasing in the bequest. Second, since the marginal utility of consumption is decreasing in consumption, $U_c^o < U_c^+$ follows because $c_o = (w_o + b)/(1 + \theta_o) > w_o/(1 + \theta_o) = c_o^+$, where c_o^+ is the offspring's consumption in the absence of the bequest. In addition, the marginal utility of consumption is decreasing in the action taken by assumption, so again $U_c^o < U_c^+$. It follows from this that $A_w < 0$. When the offspring becomes wealthier, he feels less need to earn a large bequest from his parents by undertaking a large amount of the action and so he will reduce the amount of the action he undertakes as a result of the increase in his own income. Finally, there are essentially two terms in the last response, $w_o(U_c^o - U_c^+)$ and bU_c^o. The first term is negative while the second term is positive.

The parent's decision problem is to maximize utility $U^p(c_{p1}, c_{p2}, a)$ subject to (11.2), (11.3), and the compatibility constraint (11.28), which can also be fully captured by using the action function from (11.29). Using (11.29), we can write the parent's decision problem in the following manner:

$$\max U^p((w_p - s/(1 + \theta_p), ((1 + r)s - (1 + \alpha_p)pb)/(1 + \theta_p), A(b, w_o, \theta_o)).$$

The first-order condition governing the bequest is given by

$$-U_2^p(1 + \alpha_p)p/(1 + \theta_p) + U_a^p A_b = 0, \tag{11.30}$$

where $U_a^p = \partial U^p/\partial a > 0$. Since $A_b = U_1^o/U_2^o(1 + \theta_o)$, we can write (11.30) as

$$pU_2^p(1 + \alpha_p)/(1 + \theta_p) = U_a^p U_1^o/U_2^o(1 + \theta_o).$$

If the parent and offspring pay the same consumption tax rate in the period they overlap and the bequest is taxed at the consumption tax rate, then $\theta_p = \theta_o = \alpha_p = \theta$, and (11.30) becomes

$$pU_2^p(1 + \alpha_p) = U_a^p U_1^o/U_2^o.$$

The taxation of the bequest will distort the bequest decision as in the altruism model. And the bequest will fall with the consumption tax rate; that is, $db/d\theta = p(db/dp)_u < 0$, as in the altruism model under our previous policy experiment. On the other hand, if the bequest is not taxed, then we obtain instead

$$pU_2^p = U_a^p U_1^o/U_2^o.$$

In this case the tax experiment involving a lumpsum rebate of the revenue will have no effect on the bequest.

It follows from this analysis that the action taken by the offspring will decrease in response to a distorting consumption tax that includes a tax on bequests. This follows since the distorting tax lowers the bequest and the action is increasing in the bequest. On the other hand, if the bequest is not taxed, the bequest will not respond and neither will the action undertaken by the offspring. These results coincide with those of the altruism model studied earlier in Sections 11.3 and 11.4.

11.7.2. The quantity and quality of children

Next, we will study the potential impact of the tax on the interaction between the quantity and quality of children. Following Becker (1981), suppose parents can choose the number of offspring to produce as well as the bequest per child. Assume the parent cares about the number of offspring produced, in addition to her own consumption and the consumption of the representative offspring, according to

$$U^p\left(c_{p1}, c_{p2}, c_o, n\right),$$

where n is the number of offspring produced. The parent's budget constraints become

$$w_p - \left(1 + \theta_p\right)c_{p1} - s - \left(1 + \theta_n\right)qn - p(1 + \theta_b)bn = 0,$$
$$(1 + r)s - \left(1 + \theta_p\right)c_{p2} = 0,$$

where q is the cost of producing one child, the parent pays a consumption tax of θ_n per child under the consumption tax, p is the cost of making a bequest per child, θ_b is the consumption tax rate imposed on bequests, and such a bequest is made to each of the n children; and (11.4) still represents the budget constraint of the representative offspring.

The first-order conditions governing the parent's optimal decisionmaking for the bequest and the number of children are

$$U_o^p(1 + r)/(1 + \theta_o) - [p(1 + \theta_b)/\left(1 + \theta_p\right)]nU_1^p = 0, \tag{11.31}$$

$$U_n^p - [q(1 + \theta_n)/\left(1 + \theta_p\right) + p\left(1 + \theta_b\right)b/\left(1 + \theta_p\right)]U_1^p = 0, \tag{11.32}$$

where $U_o^p = \partial U^p/\partial c_o$ and $U_n^p = \partial U^p/\partial n$. As before, if the consumption tax rate is constant across generations at a point in time, $\theta_p = \theta_o$. In addition, if expenditures on children are taxed at the same rate as other expenditures, $\theta_n = \theta_p$. The first-order conditions become

$$U_o^p(1+r) - p(1+\theta_b)nU_1^p = 0,$$
$$U_n^p - [q + p(1+\theta_b)b/(1+\theta_p)]U_1^p = 0.$$

The key extension in this case involves the marginal rate of transforming resources from the parent's first-period consumption into children,

$$q + p(1+\theta_b)b/(1+\theta_p).$$

This is related to the "shadow price" of the quantity decision mentioned by Becker (1981). There are two components to this shadow price. First, there is the direct cost of producing the child, for example, consumption per child, captured by q. If these expenditures on children are taxed at the same rate as parental consumption, this part of the shadow price will not be distorted by the consumption tax policy. The second term in the shadow price involves the "quality" decision per child, that is, the effective bequest given to each child,

$$p(1+\theta_b)b/(1+\theta_p).$$

If the bequest is taxed at the consumption tax rate, this second term becomes pb, and this part of the quantity shadow price will not be distorted by the tax. On the other hand, if the bequest is not taxed, this second term is given by $pb/(1+\theta_p)$, and the consumption tax will distort the parent's quantity decision.

In the altruism model, where parental utility is given by $U^p(c_{p1}, c_{p2}, c_0, n)$, our previous result in Section 11.2 indicated that the tax would be neutral if and only if the bequest were not taxed. However, as we have just seen, if the bequest is not taxed, then the shadow price of the parent's quantity decision is given by

$$q + pb/(1+\theta_p),$$

and the quantity decision will be distorted. Interestingly enough, a higher consumption tax rate in this case serves to lower the net price of the bequest relative to the parent's own consumption because the bequest is not being taxed. This will, in turn, lower the shadow price per child, because the relative cost of making a bequest has gone down, and will increase the incentive to produce children at the margin.

In the bequest as consumption model, where parental utility is given by $U^p(c_{p1}, c_{p2}, b, n)$, we saw earlier that neutrality would prevail only if the bequest is taxed at the consumption tax rate. In this model, neither the quantity decision nor the bequest decision will be distorted if the bequest is taxed at the consumption tax rate. If the bequest is not taxed, then both of these decisions will be distorted. The bequest will be less expensive to make relative to the parent's own consumption, and we would expect bequests to increase with the tax. In addition, since the shadow price of the quantity dimension is also lower relative to the parent's own consumption, we would also expect this version of the tax to provide a greater incentive to produce children.

11.7.3. Parental investments in the human capital of the children

We can extend the analysis further by including parental investments in the offspring's human capital.[13] It is imagined the parent produces n identical children at a cost of p per child, invests b as a cash bequest per child at a cost of p per unit, and invests e in each child's human capital at a cost of q per unit. Next period the child becomes a young adult with a human capital endowment of $h(e)$ and receives his cash bequest plus interest. We will assume that $h(0) = 1, h(e) > 1$ for $e > 0$, $dh/de = h_e > 0$, and $h_{ee} < 0$.

As before, the key to understanding the incentive effects associated with the government's tax policy is the impact of the policy on the shadow prices confronting the parent. This will depend on the motive for investing in children. First, consider the altruism model where the parent cares about the consumption of the representative offspring according to $U^p(c_{p1}, c_{p2}, n, c_0)$. The representative offspring's consumption is given by

$$(1 + \theta_o)c_o = w_o h(e) + (1 + r)b,$$

where $h(e)$ is his stock of human capital and w_o is the offspring's wage per unit of human capital. It is easy to show that the shadow prices for the quantity of children, the bequest per child, and the human capital investment in each child in the presence of the consumption tax are given by

$$[p(1 + \theta_n) + qe(1 + \theta_e) + b(1 + \theta_b)]/(1 + \theta_p),$$
$$n(1 + \theta_b)(1 + \theta_0)/(1 + r)(1 + \theta_p),$$

and

$$nq(1 + \theta_e)(1 + \theta_0)/w_o h_e(e)(1 + \theta_p),$$

where θ_e is the consumption tax rate imposed on human capital expenditures, θ_b is the consumption tax rate imposed on bequests, and θ_n is the consumption tax rate imposed on producing children.

If the parent and offspring pay the same tax rate on their general consumption, these shadow prices become

$$[p(1 + \theta_n) + qe(1 + \theta_e) + b(1 + \theta_b)]/(1 + \theta_p),$$
$$n(1 + \theta_b)/(1 + r),$$

and

$$nq(1 + \theta_e)/w_o h_e(e).$$

It is impossible to impose the tax in a manner that is fully neutral. If $\theta_n = \theta_b = \theta_e = 0$, the cash bequest and educational investment decisions are not distorted. However, the quantity of children decision is. If $\theta_n = \theta_b = \theta_e = \theta_p$, the quantity of children decision is not distorted but the cash bequest and educational investment decisions are.

Notice that the last two equations imply

$$w_o b_e(e)(1 + \theta_b) = (1 + r)q(1 + \theta_e).$$

This acts as an arbitrage condition between the two investments. It describes e as a function of the other parameters in the equation. If $b(\ )$ is a concave function, it is straightforward to show that e is decreasing in q, r, and θ_e and increasing in w_o and θ_b.

In the bequest as consumption model extended to include human capital investments, the parent's utility function is $U^p(c_{p1}, c_{p2}, b, n, e)$. Neutrality will prevail only if the cash bequest and the educational investment are taxed at the parent's consumption tax rate, the exact opposite conclusion of the altruism model.

Finally, we can extend the previous analysis by incorporating different types of agent into the model simultaneously based on their motive for bequeathing. The empirical work suggests that the population contains numerous people who are not connected to other family members, others who care altruistically about their offspring, a third group who view the bequest strategically, a fourth group who care about the size of the bequest itself, and another group who die unexpectedly and thus leave behind an unintended or accidental bequest.

A consumption tax with a tax on bequests will generally distort the bequest decisions of the second and third types but not those of the first group, since they are unconnected and do not make a bequest, nor of the last group, since their bequest is not intentional. And as we have seen, such a tax will also not distort the bequest decision of the fourth group, since they treat the bequest as if it were parental consumption. We would, therefore, expect the consumption tax to exert some downward pressure on bequests if bequests are taxed.

In addition to this, it also becomes difficult, if not impossible, for the government to impose the consumption tax in a way that does not distort some bequest decisions. One possible way out is for the government to try to figure out which group a donor belongs to and to tax those whose sole motive is to make a bequest because they care about the size of the bequest itself and not those who choose the bequest strategically. However, it would probably be too difficult for the government to differentiate between the different groups. And donors who believe they might be subject to the tax if they revealed themselves to be of a certain type will obviously mask their behavior accordingly so as to reduce their tax burden.

Individuals may have multiple motives for bequeathing as well. It is certainly conceivable that an altruist might also care about the size of her bequest. In that case, her bequest decision will be distorted regardless of the tax treatment of bequests. Or a strategic donor might also care about the size of the bequest itself.

While this confers an advantage to the offspring in the game played between the parent and the offspring in the strategic bequest model, it also means that the strategic bequest decision will be distorted regardless of the tax treatment of bequests.

Our main conclusion would be that it is virtually impossible to impose a neutral consumption tax in the presence of bequests. Heterogeneity and multiple motives for bequeathing will serve to upset the neutrality of the tax even when labor supply is fixed. If the government wishes to impose the tax so as to induce greater capital accumulation, it should not impose the tax on bequests. The bequest decisions of altruists and strategic donors will not be affected at the margin, and donors who care about the bequest itself will shift more resources into the bequest since consumption is taxed but the bequest is not. This will tend to have a beneficial effect on capital accumulation, presumably the reason for shifting toward the consumption tax in the first place. Of course, this would tend to clash with a concern for equity, which suggests that large estates should be taxed when passed on to the next generation.

11.8. Conclusion

In this chapter we studied three models of bequeathing: the altruism model, where the parent cares about the consumption or welfare of her offspring; the bequest as consumption model, where the parent cares about the actual size of the bequest itself; and the strategic bequest model, where the parent uses the bequest to induce the offspring to take certain actions favorable to the parent. The altruism model and the strategic bequest model make similar predictions in terms of the neutrality of the consumption tax with respect to capital accumulation. However, it was shown that the bequest as consumption model makes the exact opposite predictions as to when the consumption tax is neutral with regard to the parent's intertemporal decisionmaking, what the parent's response is when neutrality fails, what the economy's response is when neutrality fails, and what the international spillover effects are when neutrality fails.

In the altruism model the bequest enters much like the parent's own life cycle savings, as a means of transferring resources into the future. On the other hand, if instead the parent cares about the bequest itself, the bequest enters the model much like the parent's own consumption, once in the parent's utility function and once in the parent's budget constraints. Thus, in the altruism model the bequest should not be taxed to maintain neutrality with respect to capital formation, while under the bequest as consumption model the bequest should be taxed to maintain neutrality. The other results mentioned follow from this quite naturally. For example, when neutrality fails in the altruism model it is because the bequest is being taxed. In that case, the compensated response to the consumption tax is for the parent to reduce the bequest when the consumption tax is imposed. This leads to a drop in capital accumulation and an increase in the interest rate, which may spill over to other countries. Just the opposite occurs in the bequest as consumption model.

The basic problem is that it is of some importance for the government to introduce a tax system that distorts economic decisionmaking as little as possible. Therefore, the issue that we have posed is not just of academic interest. The practical difficulty lies in implementing the consumption tax in an environment where it might be difficult, if not impossible, to discriminate between altruism and strategic donations on the one hand, and donors who care about the bequest itself on the other hand. Most likely there is significant heterogeneity in the population and multiple motives for bequeathing may exist. It would, therefore, be impossible to introduce a consumption tax that was completely neutral with respect to capital accumulation. This makes the prima facie case in support of the consumption tax on efficiency grounds somewhat weaker. However, if the government wishes to promote capital accumulation, bequests should not be taxed. It would be somewhat ironic for the government to introduce a consumption tax to promote capital formation and then to reduce the incentive to acquire capital under such a tax by taxing bequests.

APPENDIX 11A: COMPARATIVE STATICS UNDER ALTRUISM

In the absence of taxation, the wealth constraint of the parent in the altruism model is $c_{p2} = (1 + r)(w_p - pb - c_{p1})$. The offspring's budget constraint is $c_o = w_o + (1 + r)b$. Substituting these equations into the objective function yields

$$U^p\left(c_{p1}, (1 + r)\left(w_p - pb - c_{p1}, \right), w_o + (1 + r)b\right).$$

The first-order conditions are

$$L_1 = U_1^p - (1 + r)U_2^p = 0,$$
$$L_b = (1 + r)U_o^p - pU_2^p = 0,$$

where $\partial U/\partial c_o$ is the parent's marginal utility derived from her offspring's consumption. Totally, differentiate

$$L_{11}dc_{p1} + L_{1b}db = U_2^p dr - [U_{1o}^p - (1 + r)U_{2o}^p]dw_o - [U_{1o} - (1 + r)U_{2o}]bdr$$
$$- [U_{12}^p - (1 + r)U_{22}^p][(1 + r)\left(dw_p - bdp\right) - c_2 Rdr]$$

$$L_{b1}dc_{p1} + L_{bb}db = -U_o^p dr + U_2^p dp - [(1 + r)U_{oo} - U_{2o}]dw_o - [(1 + r)U_{oo} - U_{2o}]bdr$$
$$- [(1 + r)U_{o2}^p - (1 + r)U_{22}^p][(1 + r)\left(dw_p - bdp\right) - c_2 Rdr],$$

where $L_{11} = \partial L_1/c_{p1} = U_{11}^p - 2(1 + r)U_{12}^p + (1 + r)^2 U_{22}^p < 0$, $L_{1b} = (1 + r) [(U_{1o}^p - (1 + r)U_{2o}^p) - p(U_{12}^p - (1 + r)U_{22}^p)]$, and so on, and where $J = L_{11}L_{bb} - 2L_{1b} > 0$.

Solving, we obtain the response of the parent to various parameters. For example, the compensated response to the price of bequeathing is

$$(dc_1/dp)_u = -U_2^p L_{1b}/J,$$
$$(db/dp)_u = U_2^p L_{11}/J < 0,$$

and the response of saving is

$$(ds/dp)_u = -[(dc_1/dp)_u + p(db/dp)_u]$$

or, after simplifying,

$$(ds/dp)_u = U_2^p \{(1+r)[U_{1o}^p - (1+r)U_{2o}^p] - p[U_{11}^p - (1+r)U_{12}^p]\}/J.$$

It follows that

$$(ds/dp)_u < (>) 0 \quad \text{if and only if} \quad [U_{1o}^p - (1+r)U_{2o}^p] < (>) p[U_{11}^p - (1+r)U_{12}^p]R,$$

where $(1+r) = 1/R$.

The other comparative statics are generally ambiguous. Suppose utility is separable in the offspring's consumption. Then the system becomes

$$L_{11}dc_{p1} + L_{1b}db = U_2^p dr - [U_{1o} - (1+r)U_{2o}]bdr - [U_{12}^p - (1+r)U_{22}^p]$$

$$[(1+r)(dw_p - bdp - c_2 Rdr)]$$

$$L_{b1}dc_{p1} + L_{bb}db = -U_o^p dr + U_2^p dp - (1+r)U_{oo}dw_o$$

$$- (1+r)U_{oo}bdr - (1+r)U_{22}^p[(1+r)(dw_p - bdp) - c_2 Rdr].$$

It follows that

$$dc_{p1}/dw_o = -(1+r)^2 pU_{oo}[U_{12}^p - (1+r)U_{22}^p]/J,$$

$$db/dw_o = -(1+r)U_{oo}[U_{11}^p - 2(1+r)U_{12}^p + (1+r)^2 U_{22}^p]/J < 0.$$

Furthermore, if $U_{12}^p \geq 0$, then $dc_{p1}/dw_o > 0$. The parent increases her own consumption and reduces the bequest if she expects her offspring to be wealthier than would otherwise have been the case. The response of saving is

$$ds/dw_o = p(1+r)U_{oo}[U_{11}^p - (1+r)U_{12}^p]/J > 0.$$

APPENDIX 11B: BEQUESTS IN THE OG MODEL

In this appendix we will present a version of the overlapping generations model of bequests in the presence of the consumption tax. Time is discrete, there is one good available produced via a constant-returns-to-scale technology using capital and labor, and the population is stationary. Each period $N_t = 1$ agents are born and each agent lives for three periods, first as a helpless child in need of a parent to make its decisions, second as a young economic decisionmaker, and finally as an old age retiree. The agent works in the second period and saves some of his earnings which are invested in the capital market. There are two motives for saving: retirement and bequests. Labor supply in the second period of life is exogenous. In the second period of life, the agent costlessly produces an offspring who becomes a young adult in the next period.

Under altruism the parent's utility is given by $U^t = U(c_{1t}, c_{2t}, U^{t+1})$, where c_{jt} is consumption in period j and U^{t+1} is the offspring's welfare. It is simplest to assume that preferences are separable according to $U^t = u(c_{1t}, c_{2t}) + \delta U^{t+1}$. We can solve the resulting difference equation to obtain $U^t = \sum \delta^j u(c_{1t+j}, c_{2t+j})$, where the sum runs from zero to infinity. The function $u(c_{1t+j}, c_{2j+1})$ satisfies the usual properties; for example, it is a member of the C^2 class of functions, and so on. In the bequest as consumption model the parent's preferences are represented by $U^t = u(c_{1t}, c_{2t}, b_{t+1})$, where b_{t+1} is the bequest made to the next generation.

The budget constraints in both models are given by

$$w_t + b_t - s_t - (1 + \theta_t)c_{1t} = 0$$
$$(1 + r_{t+1})s_t - (1 + \alpha_t)b_{t+1} - (1 + \theta_{t+1})c_{2t} = 0,$$

where the variables are as defined in the text with the appropriate time subscript. The first-order conditions are easily derived and similar to those presented in the text. Similarly, the policy experiments discussed in the text holding disposable income constant on a period-by-period basis will also go through in the same manner as described in the text.

The model can be closed in the same manner as in Diamond (1965), extended to include bequests and the consumption tax. See Barro (1974), Carmichael (1982), and Batina (1987).

NOTES TO CHAPTER 11

1. In particular, the Meade Commission strongly urged adoption of a consumption based tax coupled with a tax on wealth distributions for equity concerns. In certain circumstances the tax on wealth distributions may distort the bequest decision, as we will see in this chapter.

2. For example, the intention of a government sponsored school lunch program may be to increase the nutritional intake of children living in poverty. However, the goal of the program may be frustrated if parents respond to the program by not giving the child breakfast. This is an example of a neutrality theorem whereby economic agents alter their behavior in response to a public policy in a way that frustrates the goal of the policy.

3. There is a subtle issue involved in trying to test this proposition which involves the dynamics associated with the life cycle hypothesis. Simply observing a higher level of consumption after a tax cut is announced is not sufficient to provide evidence in favor of the Keynesian hypothesis. This is so because an individual agent's consumption over her lifetime may have increased anyway in response to the individual's perception of her lifetime labor earnings prior to the tax cut. The distinction involves the difference between her lifetime consumption path being upward sloping *vis-à-vis* age and the entire path shifting upwards in response to the tax cut.

4. In addition, see Carmichael's (1982) extension and correction of Barro's argument. See also a recent paper by Sutherland (1997), who presents a model where debt has Keynesian effects at low levels of debt but can have a contractionary effect at higher levels of debt. This is because the higher level of debt signals to consumers that the probability of a tax increase has gone up.

5. A tax cut saved by the parent increases the size of the eventual bequest and might tend to increase the parent's leverage over the offspring in their transaction. The parent might be able to elicit more visits of higher quality as a result. This would tend to alter the consumption trajectory of both the parent and the offspring, in general.

6. See Ihori (1996a, page 208) for a summary of reasons why the Ricardian neutrality hypothesis fails.

7. If $\theta_p > \theta_o$, only young people will shop and then make private transactions at home in exchange for a larger bequest, and vice versa if $\theta_p < \theta_o$. It would be very difficult indeed, if not impossible, to enforce a law prohibiting private resales among family members.

8. Mieszkowski (1980) alludes to this result heuristically but did not derive it analytically. See Batina (1987) for the original derivation of the result.

9. There is some evidence that parents may tend to invest more in their more able children's human capital development while compensating their less able children with greater cash bequests. This supports the idea that the parent takes the economic circumstances of the offspring into account in choosing the cash bequest. See the exchange between Tomes (1981) and Menchik (1980).

10. This result was first derived by Menchik and David (1982).

11. Any tax will inevitably create an income effect. However, taxes also affect the timing of transactions by altering disposable income in different periods. As discussed in Chapter 1, a switch from an income tax that includes a tax on interest income to the consumption tax will shift the timing of the taxpayer's tax liability even though her lifetime liability may be unaltered. Our experiment holds this effect constant.

12. In Appendix 11A we derive the following condition under which saving decreases with the cost of bequeathing: $(ds/dp)_u < 0$ if $(U_{1o}^p - (1+r)U_{2o}^p) < p(U_{11}^p - (1+r)U_{12}^p)R$.

13. This is discussed at length by Batina (1987).

12

Conclusion

We have surveyed an enormous body of literature. At this point readers may feel somewhat overwhelmed by the various models considered in the book. This chapter is intended not as a comprehensive survey of the results, but rather as a summary some of the key points and conclusions for policy.

12.1. Economic effects of consumption taxes

When one considers the tremendous complexity of modern economic behavior, it would not be surprising to discover that the consumption tax will generally distort a broad variety of that behavior. Consumers may have special circumstances, such as large medical bills, that may call for special treatment under the tax code. There is a broad variety of assets and resources that agents can own as stores of value, some of which may have amenity value. Durable goods exist and maintenance expenditures may help the durable in providing services. Agents provide contributions to privately produced public goods under a variety of motives. Consumers use money as a store of value and as a medium of exchange. Many agents within the context of the family are connected by transfers with multiple motives or with motives that differ across the population. Even in the simplest model that incorporates labor supply, the consumption tax will distort the labor supply decision. We have shown that it is very important to investigate the economic effects of consumption taxation in a dynamic setting such as the overlapping generations model, the Ramsey growth model, or the endogenous growth model.

Governments also severely restrict a variety of these behaviors. Many governments restrict financial intermediation by limiting the types of financial instruments the private sector can issue and restricting the denomination of those assets. Many governments also impose exchange controls, restrictions on the ownership of foreign assets, restrictions on foreign ownership of domestic assets, and price controls. In this sort of environment it would not be surprising to discover that the consumption tax was not better in its pattern of distortions and subsequent welfare loss than the income tax. In addition, the government itself will have a strong incentive to exploit the capital levy by maintaining high taxes on capital income and thus will have a strong incentive to cooperate with other countries in so doing, although it may also have an incentive not to cooperate because of tax competition.

12.2. Optimality of taxing consumption and capital

We have basically assumed throughout the book that the government's spending is exogenous. This allowed us to focus on the effects of taxation. What this means is that the government's tax revenue must be at least as large as the level of spending. If the government has access to the capital market, then the present value of its tax stream must be at least as great as the present value of its spending stream plus the initial value of its outstanding debt. In terms of the optimal tax problem, this leaves us with two questions. First, how should the government levy taxes over time? Second, what is the optimal mix of taxes, for example consumption, general income, or differentiated income taxes?

In a strong sense the two questions are difficult to separate. The set of policy parameters available to the government can affect the optimal choice of tax policy. As discussed in Chapter 3, it is best if the government keeps the competitive economy on the optimal growth path through use of its debt policy. If this is accomplished, then under certain conditions it is suboptimal to tax capital income. (See the discussion of Atkinson and Sandmo's results derived in an OG model in Chapter 3.) In that case the government should rely on labor taxes alone, which is equivalent to the consumption tax in the pattern of distortions caused by the tax.

If debt policy is not available, it is unlikely the competitive economy will evolve along the optimal growth path. Under the same conditions on behavior that implied it was suboptimal to tax capital income when debt policy was chosen optimally, there is a very simple condition which governs the optimal tax on capital: the optimal tax rate on capital is positive (negative) if the competitive economy is undercapitalized (overcapitalized) relative to the optimal growth path. This is somewhat paradoxical but is due to the tax timing effect. A tax imposed on capital income will mainly be paid near the end of the consumer's finite planning horizon when she receives the bulk of her capital income. A higher tax rate on capital income will induce the consumer to save more when young. A lower tax will induce the consumer to save less. So, for example, it is optimal to subsidize capital accumulation if the economy is overcapitalized relative to the optimal growth path, because this will induce consumers to save less and the economy will move closer to the optimal growth path as a result. However, many observers believe that large economies like that of the United States are undercapitalized. Thus, a tax on capital may be optimal in this sort of planning environment.

On the other hand, Judd (1985) and Chamley (1986) argued that it is not optimal to tax capital income in the long run in the context of the Ramsey growth model where the consumer has an infinite planning horizon. In the long run in such a model the equilibrium is optimal and debt policy is not needed to maintain the economy on the optimal growth path. The marginal productivity of capital will be equal to the sum of the depreciation rate of capital and the discount rate in the steady state equilibrium. It is inefficient to impose a tax that distorts this condition. Therefore, the consumption tax appears to be optimal in this model in the long run.

This result can be extended to include human capital. Indeed, Lucas (1990) extended this result to a growing economy with human capital where the growth rate of the economy is endogenous. He showed that it is suboptimal to tax capital income since it may reduce the long run growth rate of the economy. Judd (1999) later showed that a consumption tax was preferred to an income tax that includes a tax on capital, when coupled with a subsidy for the accumulation of human capital.

We extended this analysis of the Ramsey growth model by showing that, if production and consumption cause a pollution externality and hence a deterioration in the environment, a tax on capital may be justified. We also showed that, if public spending is given by a fixed portion of output, a tax on capital will be justified in the long run. In addition, if there is "clean" consumption and "dirty" consumption and the latter is taxed under a differential consumption tax, the optimum allocation can be supported by the competitive economy. However, if it is difficult to distinguish between the two types of consumption, a general consumption tax will not support the optimum. If the government cannot employ the optimal debt policy, additional policy tools will be necessary, and hence taxing capital income may well be justified.

12.3. International considerations and monitoring problem

A further complication arises when the economy is open to international trade flows. Some analysts, notably Razin and Sadka (1991a, b) and Gordon (1992), have argued that it is suboptimal to tax capital if it is mobile internationally. If the government in a small, open economy attempts to tax domestically generated capital income, investors will simply avoid the tax by investing abroad. If the government attempts to tax capital income flows from abroad, it may not collect much revenue because taxpayers can easily evade their tax liability since it is difficult for the government to monitor such flows. Source based taxes are ruled out on efficiency grounds. If the government attempts to tax capital at its source, mobile capital will leave and immobile labor will ultimately bear the burden of the tax. It is best to tax labor directly since this will avoid distorting capital allocation decisions.

Much of this argument is based on the production efficiency result due to Diamond and Mirrlees (1971) and extended by Mirrlees (1972). They showed that it was optimal to maintain production efficiency when introducing the optimal tax system as long as there was one good consumed by everyone and pure profits could be taxed. However, Mirrlees provided an example in which inefficiency was optimal if the government's policy parameters were restricted. In addition, it is not clear if the production efficiency result is applicable in the context of a world economy if transfers between countries do not exist. In that case, taxing capital flows across countries may substitute for transfers between countries and thus source based taxes on capital may be part of an optimal tax package.

Interestingly enough, capital does not appear to be as mobile as one would think. Feldstein and Horioka (1980) first argued against the case of perfect capital mobility, and more recent empirical work has tended to confirm a lack of mobility, a lack of international portfolio diversification, and the existence of interest rate differentials across countries, even after adjusting for risk. A number of explanations have been provided and more recent evidence suggests that capital is becoming more mobile. However, a strong case can be made that capital is not perfectly mobile and that we are a long way from it being so. This suggests that perhaps the closed-economy results are not as far fetched as they seem.

Some have argued that as capital markets become more sophisticated it will become increasingly difficult to tax capital income because of the monitoring problem. However, as technology evolves it may actually become easier to track capital investments, just as it is easier now than it was thirty years ago to exclude people from television programming by using cable boxes that scramble the signal. As suggested in Chapter 5, the government could set up a central electronic clearing house that withholds tax liability and tracks investments internationally. Random electronic auditing would play the same role that auditing plays today. In addition, we would expect governments to respond to greater investor sophistication by signing more tax treaties and cooperating more on catching tax cheaters. The point is that arguments that rely on sophisticated investors hoodwinking lame-brained tax officials may be misplaced. Tax officials will have an incentive to become more sophisticated as well, just as law enforcement officials in Scotland Yard, Interpol, and the FBI have generally become more sophisticated in catching high-tech criminals and international terrorists.

12.4. Taxing consumption in complicated environments

Unfortunately, much of the economic behavior studied in Chapters 7–11 has not found its way into the modeling of the optimal tax problem. This is due to the mathematical complexity involved. Even simple models can generate complicated results. Complicating the structure of these models further can easily make them intractable. Progress is being made, but we still have a long way to go.

In addition to this, there is the pure politics of tax policy to consider, which we have not touched on. Much of the dissatisfaction with the income tax stems from the imperfect way in which it is imposed, with its myriad of deductions, exclusions, exemptions, and special treatment of different types of taxpayer. Much of this special treatment is difficult to justify. For example, blind people receive an additional exemption in the US tax code but deaf people do not. In many countries home ownership is subsidized through the tax code, while renting is not. The problem is that, even if the consumption tax is introduced in some country, it will be subject to the same political pressures that produced the imperfect income tax. We would not expect, therefore, a country to introduce the sort of consumption tax that the theoretical literature has focused its attention on.

For example, if home ownership is subsidized under the income tax for purely political reasons, too much of the nation's capital will be invested in the housing stock. This can have a detrimental effect on the country's growth rate. The same problem will arise if home ownership is subsidized under the consumption tax. Indeed, it is conceivable that the consumption tax so imposed may not have its intended effect of stimulating non-residential capital accumulation or the growth rate.

If the consumption tax is to be imposed, the government may wish to consider the following ramifications.

First, the consumption tax will generally distort the labor supply decision. Second, the argument made by Judd for subsidizing human capital investment and training is compelling. Third, if the tax is progressive, as suggested by most advocates, then it will still generally distort the intertemporal consumption decision.

Taxing charitable donations may be inappropriate. If the tax is imposed and donations are exempt, more will be donated and this will presumably serve a useful social purpose.

A general consumption tax that does not distinguish between "clean" consumption, which is not polluting, and "dirty" consumption, which is, will not generally be optimal. However, a general consumption tax will typically reduce demand for both "clean" and "dirty" consumption and may help to partially reduce pollution externalities.

Taxing the purchase of durable goods may be inappropriate if such goods serve as a store of value since this may induce less accumulation of all assets. Taxing maintenance expenditures may induce a shift toward purchasing higher quality durable goods while shifting away from maintenance and may induce an increase in capital accumulation.

Taxing cash balances under a consumption tax may inhibit the general accumulation of assets. Tax prepayment will not necessarily avoid this if there is a binding reserve requirement imposed by the central bank or other restrictions on financial intermediation.

Taxing bequests may be a good idea for equity reasons since wealthy people tend to leave larger bequests than poor people. However, it may very well distort bequest decisions, and this could lead to a fall in capital accumulation.

For further research we would suggest the following.

First, consumption tax is often considered an effective means of raising government revenue. It should be noted however that the tax system is chosen by politicians, who respond to pressure from the public. Krussell, Quadrini, and Rios-Rull (1996) and Becker and Mulligan (1998) both have suggested that democracies may choose a higher degree of spending under a consumption tax than under an income tax if the consumption tax is less distorting. Indeed, some opponents of consumption taxation fear that the consumption tax will become a "money machine" for the federal government. It would be useful to investigate the impact of consumption and income taxes on the spending side of government from the viewpoint of political considerations.

Second, equity concerns could usefully be studied. We have basically investigated a variety of efficiency issues and positive questions associated with consumption and capital income taxation. Some regard consumption taxes as indirect taxes since sales taxes and the VAT dominate the taxation of consumption. The income tax is usually regarded as a direct tax and thus can be tailored to the individual taxpayer. However, the cashflow consumption tax can also be tailored to the individual taxpayer and can be made progressive as well. It would be useful to investigate the equity issues associated with consumption and capital income taxes by incorporating heterogeneous individuals into the model explicitly in future research.

The worldwide introduction of the VAT could be considered the most important event in the development of tax structures in the last half of the twentieth century. Yet, questions relating to the efficiency and equity of taxing consumption and capital will remain prevalent in public policy discussions for many years. We hope we have convinced readers that these issues are amenable to rigorous analysis in a dynamic setting. We feel that the analysis contained in this book is a useful attempt to bring tax reforms in the real world under the purview of the theories of modern public economics.

References

Aiyagari, S. Rao, 1995, Optimal Capital Income Taxation with Incomplete Markets, Borrowing Constraints, and Constant Discounting, *Journal of Political Economy*, vol. 103, no. 6, 1158–1175.

Alesina, Alberto, and Allan Drazen, 1991, Why Are Stabilizations Delayed? *American Economic Review*, vol. 81, no. 5, 1170–1188.

Allingham, Michael, and Agnar Sandmo, 1972, Income Tax Evasion: A Theoretical Analysis, *Journal of Public Economics*, vol. 1, no. 4, 323–338.

Altonji, Joseph, Fumio Hayashi, and Laurence J. Kotlikoff, 1992, Is the Extended Family Altruistically Linked? Direct Tests Using Micro Data, *American Economic Review*, vol. 82, no. 5, 1177–1198.

Andreoni, James, 1988, Privately Provided Goods in a Large Economy: The Limits of Altruism, *Journal of Public Economics*, vol. 35, no. 1, 57–73.

Andreoni, James, 1990, Impure Altruism and Donations to Public Goods: A Theory of Warm-Glow Giving, *Economic Journal*, vol. 100, no. 401, 464–477.

Andrews, William D., 1974, A Consumption-Type Cash Flow Personal Income Tax, *Harvard Law Review*, vol. 87, no. 6, 1113–1188.

Arrow, Kenneth, and Mordecai Kurz, 1970, *Public Investment, The Rate of Return, and Optimal Fiscal Policy*, Baltimore: Johns Hopkins University Press.

Atkeson, Andrew, V. V. Chari, and Patrick Kehoe, 1999, Taxing Capital Income: A Bad Idea, *Federal Reserve Bank of Minneapolis Quarterly Review*, Summer, 3–18.

Atkinson, Anthony, 1973, How Progressive Should Income Tax Be? in *Essays in Modern Economics*, ed. M. Parkin and A. R. Nobay, London: Longman.

Atkinson, Anthony, and Agnar Sandmo, 1980, Welfare Implications of the Taxation of Savings, *Economic Journal*, vol. 90, 529–549.

Atkinson, Anthony, and Joseph Stiglitz, 1972, The Structure of Indirect Taxation and Economic Efficiency, *Journal of Public Economics*, vol. 1, no. 1, 97–119.

Atkinson, Anthony and Joseph Stiglitz, 1980, *Lectures on Public Economics*, New York: McGraw-Hill.

Auerbach, Alan, and Laurence Kotlikoff, 1987, *Dynamic Fiscal Policy*, New York: Cambridge University Press.

Azariadis, Costas, 1993, *Intertemporal Macroeconomics*, Cambridge, Mass.: Basil Blackwell.

Babu, P., K. S. Guruswamy, Kavi Kumar, and N. S. Murthy, 1997, An Overlapping Generations Model with Exhaustible Resources and Stock Pollution, *Ecological Economics*, vol. 21, no. 1, 35–43.

Bailey, Martin J., 1962, *National Income and the Price Level: A Study in Macroeconomic Theory*, New York: McGraw Hill.

Barro, Robert, 1974, Are Government Bonds Net Wealth? *Journal of Political Economy*, vol. 82, no. 6, 1095–1117.

Barro, Robert, 1989, The Ricardian Approach to Budget Deficits, *Journal of Economic Perspectives*, vol. 3, no. 2, 37–54.

Batina, Raymond G., 1987, The Consumption Tax in the Presence of Altruistic Cash and Human Capital Bequests with Endogenous Fertility Decisions, *Journal of Public Economics*, vol. 34, no. 6, 329–354.

Batina, Raymond G., 1990a, Public Goods and Dynamic Efficiency: The Modified Samuelson Rule, *Journal of Public Economics*, vol. 41, no. 3, 389–400.

Batina, Raymond G., 1990b, Tax Evasion and the Time Consistency of the Government's Income Tax Policy, discussion paper, Washington State University.

Batina, Raymond G., 1991, Equity and the Time Consistent Taxation of Income, *Scandinavian Journal of Economics*, vol. 93, no. 3, 407–419.

Batina, Raymond G., 1992, Time Consistent Income Taxation, *Quarterly Review of Economics and Finance*, vol. 32, no. 3, 68–81.

Batina, Raymond G., 1995, On the Consumption Tax and the Tax Treatment of Bequests in Different Models of Bequeathing Behavior, *Japanese Economic Review*, vol. 46, no. 4, 398–412.

Batina, Raymond G., and Jeffrey Krautkraemer, 1996, Renewable Resources and Conservation: Pigovian Subsidies and Monetary Policy, discussion paper, Department of Economics, Washington State University.

Becker, Gary, 1974, A Theory of Social Interactions, *Journal of Political Economy*, vol. 82, no. 6, 1063–1093.

Becker, Gary, 1981, *A Treatise on the Family*, Cambridge, Mass.: Harvard University Press.

Becker, Gary, and H. Gregg Lewis, 1973, On the Interaction between the Quantity and Quality of Children, *Journal of Political Economy*, vol. 81, no. 2, part 2, S279–S288.

Becker, G. S., and C. B. Mulligan, 1998, Deadweight Costs and the Size of Government, NBER working paper 6789.

Becker, Gary, and Nigel Tomes, 1979, An Equilibrium Theory on the Distribution of Income and Intergenerational Mobility, *Journal of Political Economy*, vol. 87, no. 6, 1153–1189.

Bergstrom, Theodore C., Larry Blume, and H. R. Varian, 1986, On the Private Provision of Public Goods, *Journal of Public Economics*, vol. 29, no. 1, 25–49.

Bernheim, B. Douglas, 1986, On the Voluntary and Involuntary Provision of Public Goods, *American Economic Review*, vol. 76, no. 4, 789–793.

Bernheim, B. Douglas, 1991, How Strong are Bequest Motives? Evidence Based on Estimates of the Demand for Life Insurance, *Journal of Political Economy*, vol. 99, no. 5, 899–927.

Bernheim, B. Douglas, and Kyle Bagwell, 1988, Is Everything Neutral? *Journal of Political Economy*, vol. 96, no. 2, 308–338.

Bernheim, B. Douglas, Andrei Shleifer, and Lawrence Summers, 1985, The Strategic Bequest Motive, *Journal of Political Economy*, vol. 93, no. 1, 1045–1076.

Blinder, Alan, 1975, Distributional Effects and the Aggregate Consumption Function, *Journal of Political Economy*, vol. 83, no. 3, 447–475.

Boadway, Robin, and Michael Keen, 1998, Evasion and Time Consistency in the Taxation of Capital Income, *International Economic Review*, vol. 39, no. 2, 461–476.

Boadway, Robin, Pierre M. Pestieau, and David Wildasin, 1989, Tax-Transfer Policies and the Voluntary Provision of Public Goods, *Journal of Public Economics*, vol. 39, no. 2, 157–176.

Bond, Eric, and Larry Samuelson, 1989, Strategic Behavior and the Rules for International Taxation of Capital, *Economic Journal*, vol. 99, no. 398, 1099–1111.

Boskin, Michael, 1978, Taxation, Saving and the Rate of Interest, *Journal of Political Economy*, vol. 86, no. 2, part 2, S3–S27.

Bovenberg, A. Lans, 1986, Capital Income Taxation in Growing Open Economies, *Journal of Public Economics*, vol. 31, 347–377.

Bovenberg, A. Lans, 1989, The Effects of Capital Income Taxation of International Competitiveness and Trade Flows, *American Economic Review*, vol. 79, no. 5, 1045–1064.

Bovenberg, A. Lans, and Ruud A. de Mooij, 1994, Environmental Levies and Distortionary Taxation, *American Economic Review*, vol. 94, no. 4, 1085–1089.

Bovenberg, A. Lans, and F. van der Ploeg, 1994, Environmental Policy, Public Finance and the Labour Market in a Second-Best World, *Journal of Public Economics*, vol. 55, no. 3, 349–390.

Bovenberg, A. Lans, and Sjak Smulders, 1995, Environmental Quality and Pollution-Augmenting Technological Change in a Two-Sector Endogenous Growth Model, *Journal of Public Economics*, vol. 57, no. 3, 369–391.

Bradford, David, 1980a, The Economics of Tax Policy toward Saving, in *The Government and Capital Formation*, ed. George von Furstenburg, Cambridge, Mass.: Ballinger.

Bradford, David, 1980b, The Case for a Personal Consumption Tax, in *What Should Be Taxed: Income or Expenditure?* ed. Joseph A. Pechman, Washington D.C.: Brookings Institution.

Bradford, David, 1986, *Untangling the Income Tax*, Cambridge, Mass.: Harvard University Press.

Brainard, William, 1986, Comment on Liquidity Constraints, Fiscal Policy, and Consumption, *Brookings Papers on Economic Activity*, no. 1, 53–57.

Brock, William A., 1974, Money and Growth: The Case of Long Run Perfect Foresight, *International Economic Review*, vol. 15, no. 3, 750–777.

Browning, Martin, and John Burbidge, 1990, Consumption and Income Taxation, *Oxford Economic Papers*, vol. 42, no. 2, 281–292.

Bryant, John, and Neil Wallace, 1984, A Price Discrimination Analysis of Monetary Policy, *Review of Economic Studies*, vol. 51, no. 2, 279–288.

Buchholz, W., 1993, A Further Perspective on Neutrality in a Public Goods Economy with Conjectural Variations, *Public Finance Quarterly*, vol. 21, no. 1, 115–118.

Buchholz, W., and Kai Konrad, 1993, Strategic International Transfers and Private Provision of Public Goods, discussion paper, Free University of Berlin.

Calvo, Guillermo, Laurence Kotlikoff, and Carlos A. Rodriguez, 1979, The Incidence of a Tax on Pure Rent: A New (?) Reason for an Old Answer, *Journal of Political Economy*, vol. 87, no. 4, 869–874.

Carmichael, Jeffrey, 1982, On Barro's Theorem of Debt Neutrality: The Irrelevance of Net Wealth, *American Economic Review*, vol. 72, no. 1, 202–213.

Chamley, Christophe, 1981, The Welfare Cost of Capital Income Taxation in a Growing Economy, *Journal of Political Economy*, vol. 89, no. 3, 468–496.

Chamley, Christophe, 1985a, Efficient Tax Reform in a Dynamic Model of General Equilibrium, *Quarterly Journal of Economics*, vol. 100, no. 2, 335–356.

Chamley, Christophe, 1985b, Efficient Taxation in a Stylized Model of Intertemporal General Equilibrium, *International Economic Review*, vol. 26, no. 2, 451–468.

Chamley, Christophe, 1986, Optimal Taxation of Capital Income in General Equilibrium with Infinite Lives, *Econometrica*, vol. 54, no. 3, 607–622.

Chamley, Christophe, 1998, Capital Income Taxation, Wealth Distribution and Borrowing Constraints, discussion paper, EHESS and CREST.

Chamley, Christophe, and Brian Wright, 1987, Fiscal Incidence in an Overlapping Generations Model with a Fixed Asset, *Journal of Public Economics*, vol. 32, no. 1, 3–24.

Chari, V. V., and Patrick Kehoe, 1990, Sustainable Plans, *Journal of Political Economy*, vol. 98, no. 4, 783–802.

Chari, V. V., Patrick Kehoe, and Edward Prescott, 1989, Time Consistency and Policy, in *Modern Business Cycle Theory*, ed. Robert Barro, Cambridge, Mass.: Harvard University Press.

Clark, C. (1976), *Mathematical Bioeconomics: The Optimal Management of Renewable Resources*, New York: John Wiley.

Clotfelter, Charles, 1983, Tax Evasion and Tax Rates: An Analysis of Individual Returns, *Review of Economics and Statistics*, vol. 65, no. 3, 363–373.

Clotfelter, Charles, 1984, *Federal Tax Policy and Charitable Giving*, Chicago: University of Chicago Press.

Coakley, J., and F. Kulasi, 1997, Cointegration of Long Span Saving and Investment, *Economics Letters*, vol. 54, 1–6.

Correia, Isabel, 1996, Should Capital Income be Taxed in the Steady State? *Journal of Public Economics*, vol. 60, no. 1, 147–151.

Cowell, Frank, 1990, *Cheating the Government*, Cambridge, Mass.: MIT Press.

Cox, Donald, 1987, Motives for Private Transfers, *Journal of Political Economy*, vol. 95, no. 3, 508–546.

Cox, Donald, 1990, Intergenerational Transfers and Liquidity Constraints, *Quarterly Journal of Economics*, vol. 105, no. 1, 187–217.

Cox, Donald, Bruce E. Hansen, and Emmanuel Jimenez, 1996, Are Households Altruistic? Private Transfers in a Laissez-Faire Economy, discussion paper, Boston College.

Cox, Donald, and George Jakubson, 1995, The Connection between Public Transfers and Private Interfamily Transfers, *Journal of Public Economics*, vol. 57, no. 1, 129–167.

Cox, Donald, and Mark Rank, 1992, Inter Vivos Transfers and Intergenerational Exchange, *Review of Economics and Statistics*, vol. 74, no. 2, 305–314.

Cukierman, A., S. Edwards, and G. Tabellini, 1992, Seigniorage and Political Instability, *American Economic Review*, vol. 82, no. 3, 537–555.

Deaton, Angus, 1987, Life Cycle Models of Consumption: Is the Evidence Consistent with the Theory? in *Advances in Econometrics, Fifth World Congress*, ed. Truman Bewley, Cambridge: Cambridge University Press.

Deaton, Angus, 1992, *Understanding Consumption*, Oxford: Clarendon Press.

DeJuan, Joseph P., and John J. Seater, 1999, The Permanent Income Hypothesis: Evidence from the Consumer Expenditure Survey, *Journal of Monetary Economics*, vol. 43, no. 2, 351–376.

Department of Treasury, 1992, *Income Tax Compliance Research: Gross Tax Gap Estimates and Projections for 1973–1992*, Washington D.C.: Department of Treasury.

Diamond, Peter, 1965, National Debt in a Neoclassical Growth Model, *American Economic Review*, vol. 55, no. 5, 1026–1050.

Diamond, Peter, 1970, Incidence of an Interest Income Tax, *Journal of Economic Theory*, vol. 2, no. 3, 211–224.

Diamond, Peter, 1975, A Many-Person Ramsey Tax Rule, *Journal of Public Economics*, vol. 4, no. 4, 335–342.

Diamond, Peter, and James Mirrlees, 1971a, Optimal Taxation and Public Production I: Production Efficiency, *American Economic Review*, vol. 61, no. 1, 8–27.

Diamond, Peter, and James Mirrlees, 1971b, Optimal Taxation and Public Production II: Tax Rules, *American Economic Review*, vol. 61, no. 3, 261–278.

Dixit, Avinash, and Agnar Sandmo, 1977, Some Simplified Formulae for Optimal Income Taxation, *Scandinavian Journal of Economics*, vol. 79, no. 4, 417–423.

Dooley, D., J. Frankel, and D. Mathieson, 1987, International Capital Mobility: What Do Saving–Investment Correlations Tell Us? *IMF Staff Papers*, vol. 34, 503–530.

Eaton, Jonathan, 1988, Foreign-Owned Land, *American Economic Review*, vol. 78, 76–88.

Engen, Eric M., William G. Gale, and John Karl Scholz, 1996, The Illusory Effects of Saving Incentives on Saving, *Journal of Economic Perspectives*, vol. 10, no. 4, 113–138.

Espinosa-Vega, Marco, and Steven Russell, 1998, A Public Finance Analysis of Multiple Reserve Requirements, discussion paper, Federal Reserve Bank of Atlanta.

Evans, Owen J., 1983, Tax Policy, the Interest Elasticity of Saving, and Capital Accumulation: Numerical Analysis of Theoretical Models, *American Economic Review*, vol. 73, no. 3, 398–410.

Evans, Paul, 1987, Do Budget Deficits Raise Nominal Interest Rates? Evidence from Six Industrial Countries, *Journal of Monetary Economics*, vol. 20, no. 2, 281–300.

Fama, Eugene, 1980, Banking in the Theory of Finance, *Journal of Monetary Economics*, vol. 6, no. 1, 35–58.

Farzin, Y. H., 1996, Optimal Pricing of Environmental and Natural Resource Use with Stock Externalities, *Journal of Public Economics*, vol. 62, no. 1, 31–57.

Feenstra, Robert, 1986, Functional Equivalence between Liquidity Costs and the Utility of Money, *Journal of Monetary Economics*, vol. 17, no. 2, 271–291.

Feldstein, Martin, 1974a, Tax Incidence in a Growing Economy with Variable Factor Supply, *Quarterly Journal of Economics*, vol. 88, no. 4, 551–573.

Feldstein, Martin, 1974b, Incidence of a Capital Income Tax in a Growing Economy with Variable Saving Rates, *Review of Economic Studies*, vol. 41, no. 4, 505–513.

Feldstein, Martin, 1976, On the Theory of Tax Reform, *Journal of Public Economics*, vol. 6, no. 1, 77–104.

Feldstein, Martin, 1977, The Surprising Incidence of a Tax on Pure Rent: A New Answer to an Old Question, *Journal of Political Economy*, vol. 85, no. 2, 348–360.

Feldstein, Martin, 1978a, The Welfare Cost of Capital Income Taxation, *Journal of Political Economy*, vol. 86, no. 2, part 2, S29–S51.

Feldstein, Martin, 1978b, The Rate of Return, Taxation and Saving, *Economic Journal*, vol. 88, no. 351, 482–487.

Feldstein, Martin, 1983, Domestic Saving and International Capital Movements in the Long Run and in the Short Run, *European Economic Review*, vol. 21, no. 1, 139–151.

Feldstein, Martin, 1986, Supply Side Economics: Old Truths and New Claims, *American Economic Review Papers and Proceedings*, vol. 76, no. 2, 26–30.

Feldstein, Martin, 1989, Tax Policy for the 1990s: Personal Saving, Business Investment, and Corporate Debt, *American Economic Review Papers and Proceedings*, vol. 79, no. 2, 108–112.

Feldstein, Martin, and David Hartman, 1979, The Optimal Taxation of Foreign Source Income, *Quarterly Journal of Economics*, vol. 93, no. 4, 613–629.

Feldstein, Martin, and Charles Horioka, 1980, Domestic Saving and International Capital Flows, *Economic Journal*, vol. 90, no. 358, 314–329.

Findlay, Christopher, 1986, Optimal Taxation of International Income Flows, *Economic Record*, vol. 62, 208–214.

Finn, Mary, 1990, On Savings and Investment Dynamics in a Small Open Economy, *Journal of International Economics*, vol. 29, no. 1, 1–21.

Fischer, Stanley, 1980, Dynamic Consistency, Cooperation and the Benevolent Dissembling Government, *Journal of Economic Dynamics and Control*, vol. 2, no. 1, 93–107.

Fisher, Irving, 1937, Income in Theory and Income Taxation in Practice, *Econometrica*, vol. 5, no. 1, 1–55.

Fisher, Irving, 1939, The Double Taxation of Savings, *American Economic Review*, vol. 29, no. 1, 16–33.

Fisher, Irving, and Herbert Fisher, 1942, *Constructive Income Taxation: A Proposal for Reform*, New York: Harper.

Freeman, Scott, and Greg Huffman, 1991, Inside Money, Output, and Causality, *International Economic Review*, vol. 32, no. 3, 645–667.

Frenkel, Jakob, and Assaf Razin, 1986a, Fiscal Policies in the World Economy, *Journal of Political Economy*, vol. 94, no. 3, part 1, 564–594.

Frenkel, Jakob, and Assaf Razin, 1986b, The International Transmission and Effects of Fiscal Policies, *American Economic Review*, vol. 76, no. 3, 330–335.

Frenkel, Jakob, and Assaf Razin, 1989, International Effects of Tax Reforms, *Economic Journal*, vol. 99, no. 394, 38–59.

Frenkel, Jakob, Assaf Razin, and Efraim Sadka, 1991, *International Taxation in an Integrated World*, Cambridge, Mass.: MIT Press.

Frenkel, Jakob, Assaf Razin, and Steve Symansky, 1990, International Spillovers of Taxation, in *Taxation in the Global Economy*, ed. Assaf Razin and Joel Slemrod, Chicago: University of Chicago Press, ch. 6.

Frenkel, Jakob, Assaf Razin, with Chi-Wa Yuen, 1996, *Fiscal Policies and Growth in the World Economy*, Cambridge Mass.: MIT Press.

Fried, Joel, and Peter Howitt, 1988, Fiscal Deficits, International Trade and Welfare, *Journal of International Economics*, vol. 24, no. 2, 1–22.

Fudenberg, Drew, and Jean Tirole, 1991, *Game Theory*, Cambridge, Mass.: MIT Press.

Futagami, Koichi, 1989, A Game Theoretic Approach to Reconstruction of Public Finance, *Journal of Public Economics*, vol. 40, no. 1, 135–150.

Giovannini, Alberto, 1989, National Tax Systems versus the European Capital Market, *Economic Policy*, vol. 9, 346–386.

Golub, S., 1990, International Capital Mobility: Net versus Gross Stocks and Flows, *Journal of International Money and Finance*, vol. 9, no. 4, 424–439.

Goode, Richard, 1969, *The Individual Income Tax*, Washington: Brookings Institution.

Goode, Richard, 1980, The Superiority of the Income Tax, in *What Should Be Taxed: Income or Expenditure?* ed. Joseph A. Pechman, Washington: Brookings Institution.

Gordon, Roger, 1986, Taxation of Investment and Savings in a World Economy, *American Economic Review*, vol. 76, no. 5, 1086–1102.

Gordon, Roger, 1992, Can Capital Income Taxes Survive in Open Economies? *Journal of Finance*, vol. 47, no. 3, 1159–1180.

Gordon, Roger, and A. Lans Bovenberg, 1996, Why is Capital so Immobile Internationally? Possible Explanations and Implications for Capital Income Taxation, *American Economic Review*, vol. 86, no. 5, 1057–1075.

Gordon, Roger, and Hal R. Varian, 1989, Taxation of Asset Income in the Presence of a World Securities Market, *Journal of International Economics*, vol. 26, no. 3, 205–226.

Guo, Jang-Ting, and Kevin J. Lansing, 1999, Optimal Taxation of Capital Income with Imperfectly Competitive Product Markets, *Journal of Economic Dynamics and Control*, vol. 23, no. 7, 967–995.

Hall, Robert, 1978, Stochastic Implications of the Life Cycle–Permanent Income Hypothesis: Theory and Evidence, *Journal of Political Economy*, vol. 86, no. 6, 971–987.

Hall, Robert, 1986, Comment on "Liquidity Constraints, Fiscal Policy, and Consumption," *Brookings Papers on Economic Activity*, no. 1, 51–53.

Hall, Robert, 1989, Consumption, in *Modern Business Cycle Theory*, ed. Robert Barro, Cambridge, Mass.: Harvard University Press.

Hamada, Koichi, 1966, Strategic Aspects of Taxation on Foreign Investment Income, *Quarterly Journal of Economics*, vol. 80, no. 3, 362–375.

Hamilton, James, 1994, *Time Series*, Princeton: Princeton University Press.

Harberger, Arnold, 1964, The Measurement of Waste, *American Economic Review*, vol. 54, no. 3, 58–76.

Haslag, Joseph H., 1998, Seigniorage Revenue and Monetary Policy: Some Preliminary Evidence, Federal Reserve Bank of Dallas *Economic Review*, Q3, 10–20.

Hendricks, Lutz, 1999, Taxation and Long-Run Growth, *Journal of Monetary Economics*, vol. 43, no. 2, 411–434.

Hobbes, Thomas, 1985, *Leviathan*, New York: Penguin Books.

Horst, Thomas, 1980, A Note on the Optimal Taxation of International Investment Income, *Quarterly Journal of Economics*, vol. 94, no. 4, 793–798.

Howry, E. Philip, and Saul H. Hymans, 1978, The Measurement and Determination of Loanable-Funds Saving, *Brookings Papers on Economic Activity*, no. 3, 655–685.

Hubbard, R. Glenn, and Kenneth Judd, 1986, Liquidity Constraints, Fiscal Policy and Consumption, *Brookings Papers on Economic Activity*, no. 1, 1–50.

Hubbard, R. Glenn, and Jonathan S. Skinner, 1996, Assessing the Effectiveness of Saving Incentives, *Journal of Economic Perspectives*, vol. 10, no. 4, 73–90.

Hussein Khaled A., 1998, International Capital Mobility in OECD Countries: The Feldstein–Horioka Puzzle Revisited, *Economics Letters*, vol. 59, no. 2, 237–242.

Ihori, Toshihiro, 1984, Partial Welfare Improvements and Capital Income Taxation, *Journal of Public Economics*, vol. 24, no. 1, 101–109.

Ihori, Toshihiro, 1987, Tax Reform and Intergenerational Incidence, *Journal of Public Economics*, vol. 33, no. 3, 377–387.

Ihori, Toshihiro, 1990, Economics Effects of Land Taxes in an Inflationary Economy, *Journal of Public Economics*, vol. 42, no. 2, 195–211.

Ihori, Toshihiro, 1991, Capital Income Taxation in a World Economy: A Territorial System versus a Residence System, *Economic Journal*, vol. 101, no. 407, 958–965.

Ihori, Toshihiro, 1992, Impure Public Goods and Transfers in a Three Agent Model, *Journal of Public Economics*, vol. 46, no. 3, 379–390.

Ihori, Toshihiro, 1994, Bequest, Fiscal Policy, and Social Security, in *Savings and Bequests*, ed. T. Tachibanaki, Ann Arbor: University of Michigan Press.

Ihori, Toshihiro, 1996a, *Public Finance in an Overlapping Generations Economy*, London: Macmillan.

Ihori, Toshihiro, 1996b, A Dynamic Model of Fiscal Reconstruction, discussion paper, Department of Economics, University of Tokyo.

Ihori, Toshihiro, 1999a, Environmental Externalities and Growth, in *Global Competition and Integration*, ed. R. Sato, R. V. Ramachandran, and K. Mino, Amsterdam: Kluwer.

Ihori, Toshihiro, 1999b, Environmental Externalities, Abatement Behavior, and Consumption Taxes, discussion paper, Department of Economics, University of Tokyo.

Ihori, Toshihiro, and Jun-ichi Itaya, 1998, Fiscal Reconstruction Policy and Free Riding Behavior of Interest Groups, discussion paper, Department of Economics, University of Tokyo.

Ishi, Hiromitsu, 1993, *The Japanese Tax System*, Oxford: Clarendon Press.

John, A., R. Pecchenino, D. Schimmelpfennig, and S. Shreft, 1995, Short-Lived Agents and Long-Lived Environment, *Journal of Public Economics*, vol. 58, no. 1, 127–141.

Jones, Larry E., Rodolfo E. Manuelli, and Peter E. Rossi, 1993, Optimal Taxation in Models of Endogenous Growth, *Journal of Political Economy*, vol. 101, no. 3, 485–517.

Judd, Kenneth, 1985, Redistributive Taxation in a Simple Perfect Foresight Model, *Journal of Public Economics*, vol. 28, no. 1, 59–83.

Judd, Kenneth, 1987, The Welfare Cost of Factor Taxation in a Perfect Foresight Model, *Journal of Political Economy*, vol. 95, no. 4, 675–709.

Judd, Kenneth, 1997, The Optimal Tax Rate for Capital Income is Negative, NBER working paper 6004.

Judd, Kenneth, 1999, Optimal Taxation and Spending in a General Competitive Growth Model, *Journal of Public Economics*, vol. 71, no. 1, 1–26.

Kaldor, Nicholas, 1955, *An Expenditure Tax*, London: Allen and Unwin.

Kay, John A., and Mervyn King, 1986, *The British Tax System*, Oxford: Oxford University Press.

Keen, Michael, and Hannu Piekkola, 1997, Simple Rules for the Optimal Taxation of International Capital Income, *Scandinavian Journal of Economics*, vol. 93, no. 3, 447–461.

Kehoe, Patrick, 1989, Policy Coordination among Benevolent Governments May Be Undesirable, *Review of Economic Studies*, vol. 56, no. 2, 289–296.

Kemp, Murray C., Ngo Van Long, and Koji Shimomura, 1993, Cyclical and Noncyclical Redistributive Taxation, *International Economic Review*, vol. 34, no. 2, 415–429.

Kennedy, Peter, 1994, Rethinking Sustainability, discussion paper, Department of Economics, University of Victoria.

Killingsworth, Mark, and James Heckman, 1986, Female Labor Supply: A Survey, *Handbook of Labor Economics*, ed. Orley Ashenfelter and Richard Layard, Amsterdam: North-Holland.

Kim, Se-Jik, 1998, Growth Effects of Taxes in an Endogenous Growth Model: To What Extent Do Taxes Affect Economic Growth? *Journal of Economic Dynamics and Control*, vol. 23, no. 1, 125–158.

King, Mervyn, 1980, Savings and Taxation, in *Public Policy and the Tax System*, ed. G. A. Hughes and G. M. Heal, London: Allen and Unwin.

Kingma, Bruce, 1989, The Private Provision of Public Goods: Altruism and Voluntary Giving, *Journal of Political Economy*, vol. 97, no. 6, 1197–1207.

Kneller, Richard, Michael F. Bleaney, and Norman Gemmell, 1999, Fiscal Policy and Growth: Evidence from OECD Countries, *Journal Of Public Economics*, vol. 74, no. 2, 171–190.

Kotlikoff, Laurence, and Lawrence Summers, 1981, The Role of Intergenerational Transfers in Aggregate Capital Accumulation, *Journal of Political Economy*, vol. 89, no. 4, 706–732.

Krusell, Per, Vincenzo Quadrini, and Jose-Victor Rios-Rull, 1996, Are Consumption Taxes Really Better than Income Taxes? *Journal of Public Economics*, vol. 37, no. 5, 475–503.

Kydland, Finn, and Edward Prescott, 1977, Rules rather than Discretion: The Inconsistency of Optimal Plans, *Journal of Political Economy*, vol. 85, no. 3, 473–491.

Kydland, Finn, and Edward Prescott, 1980, Dynamic Optimal Taxation, Rational Expectations and Optimal Control, *Journal of Economic Dynamics and Control*, vol. 2, no. 1, 79–91.

Laitner, John, and F. Thomas Juster, 1996, New Evidence on Altruism: A Study of TIAA–CREF Retirees, *American Economic Review*, vol. 86, no. 4, 893–909.

Lewis, Karen K., 1995, Puzzles in International Financial Markets, in *Handbook of International Economics*, ed. Gene Grossman and Kenneth Rogoff, Amsterdam: North-Holland.

Lord, William, and Peter Rangazas, 1992, Tax Reform with Altruistic Bequests, *Public Finance*, vol. 47, no. 1, 61–81.

Lucas, Robert, 1988, On the Mechanics of Development, *Journal of Monetary Economics*, vol. 22, no. 1, 3–42.

Lucas, Robert, 1990, Supply-Side Economics: An Analytical Review, *Oxford Economic Papers*, vol. 42, no. 2, 293–316.

Lucas, Robert, and Nancy L. Stokey, 1983, Optimal Fiscal and Monetary Policy in an Economy without Capital, *Journal of Monetary Economics*, vol. 12, no. 1, 55–93.

MaCurdy, Thomas, 1981, An Empirical Model of Labor Supply in a Life Cycle Setting, *Journal of Political Economy*, vol. 89, no. 6, 1059–1085.

Malinvaud, Edmund, 1972, *Lectures on Microeconomic Theory*, Amsterdam: North-Holland.

Marshall, Alfred, 1925, The Equitable Distribution of Taxation, in *Memorials of Alfred Marshall*, ed. A. C. Pigou, London: Macmillan.

Meade, James E., 1978, *The Structure and Reform of Direct Taxation*, London: Allen and Unwin.

Menand, Louis, 1999, Billion-Dollar Baby, *New York Review of Books*, vol. 46, no. 11, 8–11.

Menchik, Paul, 1980, Primogeniture, Equal Sharing, and the US Distribution of Wealth, *Quarterly Journal of Economics*, vol. 94, no. 2, 299–316.

Menchik, Paul, and Martin David, 1982, The Incidence of a Lifetime Consumption Tax, *National Tax Journal*, vol. 35, no. 2, 189–204.

Mieszkowski, Peter, 1980, The Advisability and Feasibility of an Expenditure Tax System, in *What Should Be Taxed: Income or Expenditure?* ed. Joseph A. Pechman, Washington: Brookings Institution.

Milesi-Feretti, Gian, and Nouriel Roubini, 1998, On the Taxation of Human and Physical Capital in Models of Endogenous Growth, *Journal of Public Economics*, vol. 70, no. 2, 237–254.

Mill, John Stuart, 1888, *Principles of Political Economy*, New York: Appleton.

Mill, John Stuart, 1967, *Collected Works of John Stuart Mill: Essays on Economics and Society*, vol. 5, Toronto: University of Toronto Press.

Mintz, Jack, and Henry Tulkens, 1986, Commodity Tax Competition between Member States of a Federation: Equilibrium and Efficiency, *Journal of Public Economics*, vol. 29, no. 2, 133–172.

Mintz, Jack, and Henry Tulkens, 1996, Optimality Properties of Alternative Systems of Taxation of Foreign Capital Income, *Journal of Public Economics*, vol. 60, no. 3, 373–399.

Mirrlees, James, 1971, An Exploration in the Theory of Optimum Income Taxation, *Review of Economic Studies*, vol. 38, no. 2, 175–208.

Mirrlees, James, 1972, On Producer Taxation, *Review of Economics Studies*, vol. 39, no. 1, 105–111.

Mohtadi, Hamid, 1996, Environment, Growth, and Optimal Policy Design, *Journal of Public Economics*, vol. 63, no. 1, 119–140.

Mourmouras, Alexander, 1993, Conservationist Government Policies and Intergenerational Equity in an Overlapping Generations Model with Renewable Resources, *Journal of Public Economics*, vol. 51, no. 2, 249–268.

Mroz, Thomas, 1987, The Sensitivity of an Empirical Model of Female Married Women's Hours of Work to Economic and Statistical Assumptions, *Econometrica*, vol. 55, no. 4, 765–799.

Muellbauer, John, and Ralph Lattimore, 1995, The Consumption Function: An Empirical and Theoretical Overview, in *Handbook of Applied Econometrics*, ed. M. Hashem Pesaran and M. R. Wickens, Oxford: Blackwell.

Murphy, Robert, G., 1984, Capital Mobility and the Relationship between Saving and Investment Rates in OECD Countries, *Journal of International Money and Finance*, vol. 3, no. 3, 327–342.

Musgrave, Peggy, 1969, *United States Taxation of Foreign Investment Income: Issues and Arguments*, Cambridge, Mass.: International Tax Program, Harvard Law School.

Musgrave, Richard, 1976, ET, OT, and SBT, *Journal of Public Economics*, vol. 6, no. 1, 3–16.

OECD, 1995, Revenue Statistics of OECD Members, Paris: OECD.

Ordover, J. A., 1976, Distributive Justice and Optimal Taxation of Wages and Interest in a Growing Economy, *Journal of Public Economics*, vol. 5, no. 2, 139–160.

Ordover, J. A., and Edmund Phelps, 1979, The Concept of Optimal Taxation in an Overlapping Generations Model of Capital and Wealth, *Journal of Public Economics*, vol. 12, no. 1, 1–26.

Park, No-Ho, 1992, Steady State Solutions of Optimal Tax Mixes in an Overlapping Generations Model, *Journal of Public Economics*, vol. 46, no. 3, 227–246.

Pecorino, Paul, 1993, Tax Structure and Growth in a Model with Human Capital, *Journal of Public Economics*, vol. 52, no. 2, 251–271.

Pencavel, John, 1986, Labor Supply of Men: A Survey, *Handbook of Labor Economics*, ed. Orley Ashenfelter and Richard Layard, Amsterdam: North-Holland.

Perrson, Torsten, and Guido Tabellini, 1990, *Macroeconomic Policy, Credibility and Politics*, Chur, Switzerland: Harwood Academic Publishers.

Pigou, Arthur C., 1947, *A Study in Public Finance*, London: Macmillan.

Pollack, Robert A., 1968, Consistent Planning, *Review of Economic Studies*, vol. 35, no. 2, 201–208.

Poterba, James M., 1987, Tax Evasion and Capital Gains Taxation, *American Economic Review*, vol. 77, no. 2, 234–239.

Poterba, James M., Steven F. Venti, and David A. Wise, 1996, How Retirement Saving Programs Increase Saving, *Journal of Economic Perspectives*, vol. 10, no. 4, 91–112.

Ramsey, Frank, 1927, A Contribution to the Theory of Taxation, *Economic Journal*, vol. 37, no. 145, 47–61.

Razin, Assaf, and Efraim Sadka, 1991a, International Tax Competition and Gains from Tax Harmonization, *Economics Letters*, vol. 37, no. 1, 69–76.

Razin, Assaf, and Efraim Sadka, 1991b, Efficient Investment Incentives in the Presence of Capital Flight, *Journal of International Economics*, vol. 31, 171–181.

Razin, Assaf, and Joel Slemrod, 1990, Taxation in the Global Economy, Chicago: University of Chicago Press.

Razin, Assaf, and Chi-Wa Yuen, 1996, Capital Income Taxation and Long-Run Growth: New Perspectives, *Journal of Public Economics*, vol. 59, no. 2, 239–263.

Renstrom, Thomas, I., 1998, Tax Evasion as a Disciplinary Mechanism for Fiscal Policy, in *The Welfare State, Public Investment, and Growth*, ed. H. Shibata and T. Ihori, Tokyo: Springer-Verlag.

Roberts, Russell, 1984, A Positive Model of Private Charity and Public Transfers, *Journal of Political Economy*, vol. 92, no. 1, 136–148.

Roberts, Russell, 1987, Financing Public Goods, *Journal of Political Economy*, vol. 95, no. 1, 420–437.

Rogers, Carol Ann, 1986, The Effect of Distributive Goals on the Time Inconsistency of Optimal Taxes, *Journal of Monetary Economics*, vol. 17, no. 2, 251–269.

Romer, Paul, 1986, Increasing Returns and Long Run Growth, *Journal of Political Economy*, vol. 94, no. 5, 1002–1037.

Rosen, Harvey, 1985, Housing Subsidies: Effects on Housing Decisions, Efficiency, and Equity, in *Handbook of Public Economics*, ed. A. J. Auerbach and M. S. Feldstein, Amsterdam: North-Holland.

Sadka, Efraim, 1976, On Income Distribution, Incentive Effects, and Optimum Income Taxation, *Review of Economic Studies*, vol. 43, no. 2, 261–268.

Samuelson, Paul, 1958, An Exact Consumption-Loan Model of Interest with or without the Social Contrivance of Money, *Journal of Political Economy*, vol. 66, 467–482.

Samuelson, Paul, 1986, Theory of Optimal Taxation, *Journal of Public Economics*, vol. 30, no. 2, 137–143.

Sandmo, Agnar, 1976, Optimal Taxation: An Introduction to the Literature, *Journal of Public Economics*, vol. 6, no. 1, 37–54.

Sargent, Thomas, and Neil Wallace, 1982, The Real-Bills Doctrine versus the Quantity Theory: A Reconsideration, *Journal of Political Economy*, vol. 90, no. 6, 1212–1236.

Schelling, Thomas, 1980, *The Strategy of Conflict*, Cambridge, Mass.: Harvard University Press.

Seidman, Laurence, 1983, Taxes in a Life Cycle Growth Model with Bequests and Inheritances, *American Economic Review*, vol. 73, no. 3, 437–441.

Seidman, Laurence, 1984, Conversion to a Consumption Tax: The Transition in a Life-Cycle Growth Model, *Journal of Political Economy*, vol. 92, no. 2, 247–267.

Shibata, Hirofumi, 1971, A Bargaining Model of the Pure Theory of Public Expenditures, *Journal of Political Economy*, vol. 79, no. 1, 1–29.

Sibert, Anne, 1985, Capital Accumulation and Foreign Investment Taxation, *Review of Economic Studies*, vol. 52, no. 2, 331–345.

Sibert, Anne, 1990, Taxing Capital in a Large, Open Economy, *Journal of Public Economics*, vol. 41, no. 3, 297–317.

Sidrauski, Miguel, 1967, Rational Choice and Patterns of Growth in a Monetary Economy, *American Economic Review: Proceedings*, vol. 57, no. 2, 534–544.

Sillamaa, M. A., 1999, How Work Effort Responds to Wage Taxation: An Experimental Test of a Zero Top Marginal Tax Rate, *Journal of Public Economics*, vol. 73, no. 2, 125–134.

Simons, Henry, 1938, *Personal Income Taxation*, Chicago: University of Chicago Press.

Skinner, Jonathan, 1996, The Dynamic Efficiency Cost of Not Taxing Housing, *Journal of Public Economics*, vol. 59, no. 3, 397–417.

Slemrod, Joel, 1992, *Do Taxes Matter? The Impact of the Tax Reform Act of 1986*, Cambridge, Mass.: MIT Press.

Smith, Vincent H., Michael R. Kehoe, and Mary E. Cremer, 1995, The Private Provision of Public Goods: Altruism and Voluntary Giving, *Journal of Public Economics*, vol. 58, no. 1, 107–126.

Strotz, Robert, 1956, Myopia and Inconsistency in Dynamic Utility Maximization, *Review of Economic Studies*, vol. 23, no. 3, 165–180.

Summers, Lawrence, H., 1981, Capital Taxation and Accumulation in a Life Cycle Growth Model, *American Economic Review*, vol. 71, no. 4, 533–544.

Summers, Lawrence H., 1986, Comment on Liquidity Constraints, Fiscal Policy, and Consumption, *Brookings Papers on Economic Activity*, no. 1, 53–57.

Sutherland, Alan, 1997, Fiscal Crises and Aggregate Demand: Can High Public Debt Reverse the Effects of Fiscal Policy? *Journal of Public Economics*, vol. 65, no. 2, 147–162.

Svennson, L. G., and J. W. Weibull, 1987, Constrained Pareto-Optimal Taxation of Labor and Capital Income, *Journal of Public Economics*, vol. 34, no. 3, 355–366.

Tachibanaki, Toshiaki, 1996, *Public Policies and the Japanese Economy*, London: Macmillan.

Tesar, Linda, 1991, Savings, Investment and International Capital Flows, *Journal of International Economics*, vol. 31, no. 1–2, 55–78.

Thompson, Earl, 1967, Debt Instruments in Macroeconomic and Capital Theory, *American Economic Review*, vol. 57, no. 5, 1196–1210.

Toder, Eric, 1996, Issues in Evaluating Consumption Tax Proposals, *National Tax Journal*, Proceedings of the 88th Annual Conference of the National Tax Association, 34–39.

Tomes, Nigel, 1981, The Family, Inheritance, and the Intergenerational Transmission of Inequality, *Journal of Political Economy*, vol. 89, no. 5, 928–958.

van Wijnbergen, Sweder, 1986, On Fiscal Deficits, the Real Exchange Rate, and the World Rate of Interest, *European Economic Review*, vol. 30, no. 5, 1013–1024.

Wallace, Neil, 1983, A Legal Restrictions Theory of the Demand for "Money" and the Role of Monetary Policy, *Federal Reserve Bank of Minneapolis Quarterly Review*, Winter, 1–7.

Wallace, Neil, 1984, Some of the Choices for Monetary Policy, *Federal Reserve Bank of Minneapolis Quarterly Review*, Winter, 15–24.

Wallace, Neil, 1998, A Dictum for Monetary Theory, *Federal Reserve Bank of Minneapolis Quarterly Review*, Winter, 1–9.

Warr, Peter, 1982, Pareto Optimal Redistribution and Private Charity, *Journal of Public Economics*, vol. 19, no. 1, 131–138.

Warr, Peter, 1983, The Private Provision of a Public Good is Independent of the Distribution of Income, *Economic Letters*, vol. 13, 207–211.

Westphal, U., 1983, Comments on "Domestic Saving and International Capital Movements in the Long Run and in the Short Run," *European Economic Review*, vol. 21, no. 1/2, 157–159.

Wildasin, David E., 1977, Production Efficiency in Tax-Distorted Economies with Multiple Revenue Constraints, Discussion Paper, University of Illinois at Chicago Circle.

Wildasin, David E., 1988, Nash Equilibria in Models of Fiscal Competition, *Journal of Public Economics*, vol. 35, no. 2, 229–240.

Wilhelm, Mark O., 1996, Bequest Behavior and the Effect of Heirs Earnings: Testing the Altruistic Model of Bequests, *American Economic Review*, vol. 86, no. 4, 874–892.

Zhu, Xiaodong, 1992, Optimal Fiscal Policy in a Stochastic Growth Model, *Journal of Economic Theory*, vol. 58, no. 2, 250–289.

Author Index

Subject Index